BUSINESS RESEARCH METHODS

GRID SERIES IN MANAGEMENT

Consulting Editor
STEVEN KERR, University of Southern California

Adams & Ponthieu, *Administrative Policy and Strategy: A Casebook*,
    Second Edition
Anthony & Nicholson, *Management of Human Resources: A Systems Ap-*
    proach to Personnel Management
Chung, *Motivational Theories and Practices*
Deitzer & Shilliff, *Contemporary Management Incidents*
Knapper, *Cases in Personnel Management*
Lewis, *Organizational Communications: The Essence of Effective Man-*
    agement
Lundgren, Engel & Cecil, *Supervision*
Murdick, Eckhouse, Moor, & Zimmerer, *Business Policy: A Framework*
    for Analysis, Second Edition
Ritti & Funkhouser, *The Ropes to Skip and The Ropes to Know: Studies*
    in Organizational Behavior

OTHER BOOKS IN THE GRID SERIES IN MANAGEMENT

Balsley, *Basic Statistics*
Klatt & Urban, *Kubsim: A Simulation in Collective Bargaining*
Morris, *Decision Analysis*
Nykodym & Simonetti, *Business and Organizational Communication: An*
    Experiential Skill Building Approach
Rosen, *Supervision: A Behavioral View*

BUSINESS RESEARCH METHODS

Second Edition

by

Vernon T. Clover
Department of Economics
Texas Tech University

and

Howard L. Balsley
Department of Economics and Finance
University of Arkansas at Little Rock

Grid Publishing, Inc., Columbus, Ohio

© GRID, INC. 1979
4666 Indianola Avenue
Columbus, Ohio 43214

I.S.B.N. NO. 0-88244-164-7

Library of Congress Catalog Card Number 78-50046

1   2   3   4   5   6 ☒ 4   3   2   1   0   9

Contents

Preface

The use of research has been expanding in recent years. The "growth" firm is often characterized as one with 10 percent or greater growth in earnings annually; most of these earnings are plowed back into research and development of the firm and its products. Not only large-growth companies, but medium- and small-size companies find greater and greater use of research on products and packaging, operations of the company, its personnel policies, its recordkeeping, its communications, its sales and promotion.

Many colleges, schools, and departments of business administration have a required course in business research because of the increasing importance of research to the firm, to the industry, and to the economy. All curricula of business administration require statistics as an undergraduate subject, and statistics itself provides a fundamental set of devices and techniques for business research.

The purpose of this book is to serve as a textbook for undergraduate courses in business research. It is designed as a one-semester course. Although the book has been planned for business research at the undergraduate level, it has been used in graduate programs both as a textbook and as a supplement to more advanced textbooks. It has also been used by firms and by individual business persons as a reference work. It requires only a minimum of knowledge of statistics and algebra. The statistics involved in this book include chi-square analysis, trend analysis, and correlation-regression analysis. The tests of significance between means and percentages and the analysis of variance are presented in applications to business problems. Besides being used in business research courses, this text has also been used in research courses in marketing, in journalism, and in the social sciences.

The coverage of topics in this edition has been expanded over that of the first edition. Both descriptive techniques and quantitative analyses are used in the presentation of research methods. Thus, the design of questionnaires, the definition and formulation of problems, the scientific method of investigation are given attention, as well as the aforementioned statistical techniques. Careful attention is given to the adequacy of samples: the size of sample required to attain reliability in the results of a research project.

In this edition, a summary has been added at the end of each chapter. These summaries serve as a review for both the student and the instructor. The summary constitutes a learning technique: After the material in the chapter has been studied, the summary serves to draw together in a succinct statement the topics that have been covered in the chapter.

The selected references at the ends of chapters have been revised and brought up to date. Some chapter titles have been changed to reflect more accurately the chapter content. Exhibits, illustrations, charts and graphs, have been revised and brought up to date. Statistical symbols and formulas have been standardized in accordance with current practice. References with a "sexist" connotation have been deleted; for example, "businesspersons" has been substituted for "businessmen." Numerous editorial changes have been made.

In chapter 3, "Problems, Hypotheses, and Data," a discussion of the levels of data measurement—nominal, ordinal, interval, ratio—has been added to relate the techniques of analysis to the limitations of the data. The "Appendix on Information Acquirement" has been revised and made an integral part of the chapter, headed "Sources of Data," to put more emphasis on secondary data.

Former chapter 7, "Observation and Experimentation," has been relocated to chapter 4. The section "Experimental Design" has been rewritten and expanded. In chapter 5, "Survey Techniques," a description of the National Longitudinal Survey of the U.S. Department of Labor has been added.

Chapter 13, "Preparing Business Reports," has been revised and expanded. A discussion of the differences in findings and conclusions, with an example, has been added. Examples of outlines have been added. A comprehensive example of a business research report has been reproduced and accompanied with discussions of the problem, hypothesis, and data; the findings and conclusions; and the eleven steps followed in the procedures of scientific method, the steps originally outlined in chapter 2, "Reason and the Scientific Method."

The subject matter included in this book has been tested in both the classroom and in the business community on actual research projects. Much of the material selected for examples has been taken from consulting practice, and represents successful results in the application of proper research techniques.

The plan of the book follows generally the plan of a research project, beginning with the inception of an idea, definition, hypotheses, gathering evidence, testing the evidence, drawing conclusions, and presenting results. Thus, chapters 1 and 2 introduce the subject matter of business research and explain its approach to problem solving. Chapter 3 describes the formulation of a problem and the planning of the research project.

Chapters 4 through 7 are concerned chiefly with the methods of gathering evidence and in some measure weighing such evidence when nonquantitative research analysis is indicated. Chapters 8 through 11 present the methods of quantitative analysis of data, requiring the usual business school undergraduate understanding of statistical methods. Chapter 12 describes tables, charts and graphs, so widely used in presenting findings of studies. Finally, chapter 13 explains the preparation of business reports.

We are indebted to the Literary Executor of the late Sir Ronald A. Fisher, F.R.S., to Dr. Frank Yates, F.R.S., and to Longman Group Ltd., London, for permission to reprint tables III and IV from their book *Statistical Tables for Biological, Agricultural and Medical Research*.

The Iowa State University Press kindly granted permission to reproduce the table in Appendix D, "Values of the F-Distribution," from *Statistical Methods*, 5th edition, by George W. Snedecor, © 1956 by the Iowa State University Press.

Acknowledgment of the kind permission to reprint is due to the following organizations and persons:
Arizona Business Bulletin, Arizona State University, Tempe, Arizona
Commercial Credit Company, Baltimore
Georgia Business, University of Georgia, Athens, Georgia
Prentice-Hall, Inc., Englewood Cliffs, New Jersey
Prof. John A. Ryan, Dean, College of Business Administration, Lamar University, formerly Professor of Marketing, Texas Tech University.

Vernon T. Clover
Howard L. Balsley

Introduction to Business Research

Few businesspersons are completely satisfied with all the conditions that exist in their firms. Most managers would like to cut costs, increase sales, improve gross revenues, or take steps to increase net profits. In order to accomplish such goals, the majority of enterprisers continually strive to improve their efficiency. The more successful of them are usually those who face facts and make their decisions in accordance with the realities of the situation.

Research is to a large extent the process of obtaining and correctly interpreting the information required to reach a decision in regard to what should be done about a condition that is considered unsatisfactory. One of the important roadblocks to effective decision making is the difficulty of obtaining accurate, significant, and pertinent information. Many persons in responsible positions have experienced the frustration of facing a problem without the data essential to a wise choice of action. All too often these persons believe that, although the data are of great importance, the data, nevertheless, are not available or cannot be obtained at a reasonable cost in money or time. Smaller organizations are thought to be especially unable to obtain the desired facts. That these beliefs are not true will become evident. Fact-finding methods are feasible for use by smaller establishments as well as for larger ones.

DEFINITION OF RESEARCH

A useful definition of research is as follows: Research is the process of systematically obtaining accurate answers to significant and pertinent questions by the use of the scientific method of gathering and interpreting information. The researcher is *systematic* because a systematic approach is most likely to lead through all the steps, areas, and phases necessary to make certain that he will not overlook any facts or processes essential to arriving at a correct conclusion. *Accurate* answers, of course, are the only kind that are acceptable. *Significant* and *pertinent questions* must be asked in the process of analyzing a problem and in deciding what information shall be sought when fact finding is started. A basic characteristic of a good researcher is the ability to determine what questions are most important and closely related to the situation being studied. The *scientific method* is a term that refers to the procedures followed by careful investigators and thinkers in arriving at conclusions.

BASIC AND APPLIED RESEARCH

Basic research seeks essentially an extension of knowledge. It is not necessarily problem oriented, though it may be. Basic research is sometimes called *pure* research or *fundamental* research. Since it is carried on for the purpose of extending the frontiers of man's knowledge and thus may have no known immediate application, it normally requires underwriting by foundations or universities or government. The findings of basic research, of course, compose a valuable storehouse of knowledge that can be drawn upon in the future to help practical researchers solve their problems.

While basic research may, to some degree, be carried on within major business firms, business research itself is usually classified as applied research. Applied research is problem oriented in that the research is carried on to solve a specific problem about which a decision must be reached. For example, production research is very often carried on with a view to increasing immediately the efficiency of a production line or for solving a production-line problem. Financial research may be carried on for the purpose of making a decision among alternative investment opportunities or among alternative sources of capital funds. Marketing research normally is carried on to resolve questions concerning the extent of a market, the possible acceptance of a new product, the possible acceptance of a packaging design, or the purchasing power available in a given region.

EXPERIMENTAL, HISTORICAL, AND STATISTICAL METHODS

The experimental, historical, and statistical methods are the three general methods followed in research investigation. They are also followed in business research. *Experimentation* may be defined as a closely controlled procedure for testing hypotheses. It often involves *sampling* because in many projects it would be too time consuming and costly to obtain data from every unit in the universe concerned. For example, a production experiment might be conducted to test the hypothesis that the average number of defects in products arising from two kinds of processes were identical. A small number of the products turned out by the two processes would be examined. Such a study would be a sampling study. An example in marketing might test the acceptance of an experimental product with a specialized packaging design against a control product with the standard packaging design in an attempt to discover if the average percentage of purchases was the same for the two packages. Such experiments can be closely controlled, and they serve to test a hypothesis chiefly using sampling procedures.

The *historical method* involves the study of records of the past to reach conclusions about possible future conditions. Sometimes one of the most helpful ways to obtain a reasonably useful picture of what is ahead is to look backward. In these situations, research into the past may be rewarding. The historical method sometimes involves gathering both primary and secondary data, that is, data originally gathered and recorded for the first time as well as data coming from published sources. Sometimes interviewing is required in gathering information about the past. Sometimes library research is necessary. At times, the study of the records of an individual firm is required. As an example, consider a firm that is about to make a decision concerning the establishment of a new personnel policy. The gathering of information, both past and present, about the personnel policies and practices of other employers in the area would be useful; this information would be primary in nature. A study of the firm's past personnel experiences would require study; an investigation into the records of the past and current employee performance would be required. Further, some study into the experiences of other firms, possibly through examining publications of trade associations in the library, may also be required. The net result of such a historical study might be a far superior decision as to the establishment of a new personnel policy than could have been made without consulting these three sources of information.

The *statistical method* is a system of procedures and techniques of analysis applied to quantitative data. The *system*, or *structure*, consists of a body of mathematical methods and models, and is applicable, of course, only to data in numerical form. The statistical method is, therefore, particularly useful to research in business and other fields in which quantities of numerical data are generated. All quality-control procedures in manufacturing are statistical in nature, for example. The financial statements of a firm are statistical in nature. A statistical experiment may consist of comparing the average sales of two similar products. Another may compare the fraction defectives among several manufacturing processes. Another may attempt to learn if there is an association between two economic factors so that one may be predicted from the other.

RESEARCH AND MANAGEMENT

Fact finding and research are, of course, only part of the complex process of managing an organization. Managers must draw together the various agents of production, painstakingly mold them into a coordinated going concern, and keep the organization functioning properly. Decisions will need to be made continually, and most of them will be made on the basis of past experience and facts available without the amount of searching that would classify the activity as research. Even in a large business, the research department is not a decision-making or managing agency. Instead, its function is to supply information in a usable form. Nevertheless, the researcher has an important place in business today. Specifically, the job of the researcher is to collect, organize, and report the information that top management believes necessary to the process of decision making.

It is apparent from the foregoing statements that one of the most important characteristics of business research is that the results are to be decision oriented. Business research chiefly arises because a problem must be faced by a firm. This problem requires a decision to be made. The decision maker desires to have at his hand the facts, that is, all of the pertinent facts possible, as well as an elimination of extraneous facts so that he can focus his attention on the important parts of the problem and at the same time have alternatives to choose among. Business research, therefore, arises in response to the need for solving problems; and the facts presented, the alternatives opened up, will be used in decision making. The problem will, therefore, be faced and solved by an executive or a group of executives arriving at a decision.

SMALL BUSINESS RESEARCH

It may be contended that research is more essential for large businesses than for small ones because mistakes can be costly when made in a large-scale enterprise. It is undoubtedly true that responsible officials in a huge corporation must have facts upon which to base their decisions because millions of dollars may be involved, as well as thousands of security holders, employees, and customers. It should be pointed out, however, that mistakes in a smaller concern, although not involving so much money or so many people, may be even more serious from the point of view of the life of the firm. Large, well-established companies usually have some resources on which they can call to tide them over a crisis caused by problems faced by management. Smaller firms are less likely to have the funds or widespread reputation to carry them through such a crisis. Making reasonable use of research as a guide in decision making is, therefore, as essential for smaller concerns as it is for larger ones.

Elaborate projects in smaller firms will usually not be practicable to the degree that they would be in large companies; but, for the solution of most of the problems in which research would be needed, complex, costly procedures are not necessary. Often all that is required is a rather brief, systematic search through available records or the reading of articles or sections of books dealing with the problem. Perhaps telephone calls to several qualified persons or personal interviews planned to elicit the required information will bring forth the facts needed. In other cases, a somewhat more lengthy investigation will be necessary.

For example, suppose a retail store manager would like to know what percentage of his customers subscribe to a neighborhood weekly newspaper to determine whether it would be worth-while to advertise in the paper. He may decide that if at least 25 percent of his customers read the paper, it would be a good medium in which to place advertisements. How could he obtain this information? One relatively inexpensive method might be to look through his customer records to obtain a list of names of a representative sample of his customers. This sample might not have to contain more than fifty names. He could then phone these people and ask them if they read the neighborhood newspaper. The actual calling could be spread over a week or so and could be done during slack periods of the day. To be sure, a larger sample and the use of personal interviews would obtain somewhat more accurate data; but a simple, inexpensive survey can often obtain results that are accurate enough to serve as a basis for a particular decision. In most instances, an inexpensive research project, if done according to recognized research procedures, can at least produce findings that can make it possible to reach considerably better managerial decisions than would have been possible without the research.

RESEARCH VERSUS EXPERIENCE

Research is a method of gaining experience that can greatly speed up the process of learning. The researcher may not deny that experience is the best teacher; he merely concentrates and accelerates the acquisition of knowledge obtained through controlled and intensified experience. If the research methods used by the investigator in telescoping experience are sound, scientific methods, research can often have several advantages over ordinary experience.

Advantages of Research over Experience

Research can be conducted on a smaller, less expensive scale than ordinary experience. For example, instead of installing new machines of a certain type in all plants of a large corporation, the new machines might first be placed in one typical plant to determine whether a complete change-over in all plants should be made.

Carefully conducted investigations can frequently secure facts within a few hours, days, or weeks that ordinary experience would turn up only in the course of months or years. An illustration would be research into the best possible location for a new gasoline filling station before it is built. Investigation could in a few weeks' time accumulate various facts, such as, volume and types of traffic moving by several potential sites. To build and then to observe the operating results of stations on one or all possible sites to learn which one is best would require months or years, not to mention a large expenditure of money.

Research can bring to light information that might never be discovered fully during the course of the ordinary operations of a business. For example, a well-planned study of possible new uses for an old product could result in discovery of uses that would never have shown up if the specific research had not been undertaken.

Information gained by soundly conducted research can be more accurate than information accumulated by relatively haphazard, unplanned, inaccurately remembered and incompletely recorded information gained in the course of ordinary experience. The facts collected during regular day-by-day activities in the business are also based on the occurrences in that one business only, and the conditions faced by this particular firm may not have been typical of other organizations of this kind. These facts, therefore, cannot be used in making decisions in connection with other firms in the industry. It sometimes happens that even the facts observed and remembered in a given firm are not representative of the conditions in this one firm. Most persons have a tendency to remember the more unique or pleasant events and to forget others.

Research can ascertain current conditions, while ordinary experience must be based chiefly on past activities, many of which are no longer representative of the present situation.

Research can uncover needed facts on which sound decisions can be based. These facts can be made available before, not after, action is taken and time, money, and effort expended. What is learned by ordinary experience may be valuable but too late to benefit a bankrupt firm.

Research is peculiarly important when a potentially harmful or dangerous new product is being developed and certain margins of safety in usage are desired. For instance, the safe dosages of a medicine or protection against failures in materials in a product can be provided by prior research more satisfactorily than by ordinary experience.

Advantages of Experience over Research

The preceding discussion of the advantages of research over experience as a method of learning is not meant to imply that experience is useless or an inferior process. Actually, learning by the experiences met in the course of the operation of a firm most certainly always will be effective and necessary in obtaining knowledge and managerial know-how. Before leaving this subject, therefore, some of the possible advantages of experience over research in the process of obtaining facts should be described.

Only the experience gained in the operation of a firm can provide the actual and complete conditions of the real life situation. Research cannot fully duplicate in laboratories or in the process of field research all of the actual conditions that do or can exist in the real world. Herein lies the most important advantage of experience over research.

Experiences have greater impact on the mind of the observer than research results. Experiences are more realistic and striking. They are often more believable because they actually happened in the day-to-day operation of the business. Some persons find it difficult to learn thoroughly by such abstract methods as those represented by the study of results of simulated conditions set up in a research project.

Learning is sometimes made more complete by repetition and by the passage of sufficient time to enable the absorption of information. Research may not provide for sufficient repetition or for sufficient time for many persons to learn as thoroughly as they could by the slower process of day-by-day experience.

Experience may often be more widely accepted as a process of learning. Traditionally, experience carries great weight as being a safer, surer method of learning. Many businesspersons who will rely on experience in making decisions will be reluctant to act on the basis of research findings. For such managers, experience, rather than research, will often continue to be their guide in decision making.

In conclusion, it should be remembered that even when learning is being accomplished by experience rather than by research, the learning will be more effective if the manager is a careful, systematic, and accurate observer. The very qualities which make for a good researcher also make for a good learner from experience. If the decision maker uses the decision-reaching methods of the scientific researcher, more can be learned from whatever experiences occur during the time spent in any type of firm or organization.

THE SCOPE OF BUSINESS RESEARCH

It is apparent from the preceding discussion that business research is a function of management. The management of a business enterprise will originally determine if problems exist, it will determine the problems that need solution, and it will order the research done. Finally, upon completion of the research, management will make decisions and take appropriate action.

PECULIARITIES OF BUSINESS RESEARCH

Certain peculiarities of business research distinguish it from research in other fields of knowledge. First and foremost, it is generally applied research in that it is problem oriented and decision oriented. Since business research normally comes about because a problem exists and a need, therefore, develops for seeking information by which the problem can be resolved, the research itself usually is applied rather than basic. Its decision orientation is apparent in that since the research is ordered by management, its usefulness will be found in offering information and alternative possibilities among which management can choose in making a decision in the course of resolving the problem situation.

Another peculiarity of business research is the almost universal quality of time limitation placed on the research. In nearly all cases, the research must be accomplished within a given space of time. For example, a study of style requirements for the inventory of a retail establishment for the following fall would have no usefulness if the research took place too late. A study to correct the immediate mistakes being made on a production line in response to a customer's complaint would have no usefulness if completed after the order had been shipped. Very often, the need for information comes in response to telephone calls, and results or decisions must be made within matters of hours or days.

Another peculiarity of business research lies in the dynamic nature of the environment in which the research takes place. Business conditions change rapidly, as do the habit patterns of customers. The styles, the demands, and the supplies and materials available are constantly changing so that the research takes place within a dynamically changing environment. These changes, it may be noted, are sometimes of a rather permanent nature. Thus, products drop out of a product line, new products enter, customers are lost, new customers are gained, market areas shrink, new ones expand, and others are discovered. This very dynamic nature of the environment in which business research takes place puts a further premium on the limitations of the time factor.

Another characteristic of business research lies in the cost limitations usually imposed upon the research project. Generally, management will consider engaging in a research project only after considering the cost of the project. The matter of efficiency, which is always with management, is, thus, important in considering research projects as well as with other decisions. The economic calculus of choosing among alternatives to satisfy competing needs is present with the research project, as well as in other areas of business decision making.

A CLASSIFICATION OF SOME FIELDS OF BUSINESS RESEARCH

A listing of some of the fields into which business research may be classified for the individual firm or for an industry is presented in exhibit 1-1.

EXHIBIT 1-1
A General Classification of Fields of Business Research

I. Production Facilities and Methods

  A. Physical Plant (or Store Facilities)

    1. Layout: arrangement of machinery, store fixtures, display cases, etc.
    2. Location: proximity to markets or raw material or power, etc.; downtown or outlying area, corner or inside lot, etc.

  B. Production Methods

    1. Types of equipment: most efficient machines for job, etc.
    2. Raw materials: best materials for job, sources of supply, etc.
    3. Personnel management: types of employees needed; personnel training required; etc.
    4. Quality-control methods: mechanical, human, etc.

  C. Financial Requirements

    1. Fixed capital needed — present and future
    2. Operating capital needed — present and future
    3. Sources of funds — inside and outside of firm

  D. Other conditions important in the type of firm under study

II. Product or Service Produced

  A. Nature of Product

    1. Uses, potential uses, durability; comparison with product of competitors; trends in quality of output of firm; correctness of size, shape, color, package, etc.

  B. Nature of Service

    1. Luxury or necessity; used for entertainment or in work; fluctuation with seasons and business cycles; etc.

EXHIBIT 1-1 (*continued*)

C. Other aspects of the product or service under consideration

III. Methods of Distributing Product or Service

A. Channels Used

1. Wholesaler, jobbers, or directly to retailers or final consumer, etc.
2. Salesmen and/or advertising; door to door, mail order; etc.
3. Advertising media: newspaper, magazine, radio or television, etc.

B. Pricing Policies

1. Cash, credit
2. Discounts
3. Sales and special seasonal promotions; etc.

C. Services Provided

1. Freight absorption
2. Accepting returned items
3. Responsibility for repairing or replacing faulty items
4. Field service men
5. Providing selling aids or funds to dealers

D. Other phases pertinent to the type of firm under study

IV. The Nature of the Market

A. Characteristics of Customers

1. Present customers: size, number, commercial, industrial or consumer; age, sex, occupation, income, other socio-economic characteristics; urban or rural; marital status; size of family; long-time users of product or new users; reading and entertainment interests; etc.
2. Potential customers: (Same as 1.)
3. Opinions of customers about the product or service
4. Actual customer uses of product or service
5. Potential uses of product or service

B. Characteristics of other producers in the market area

1. Number, size
2. Relative efficiency
3. Methods of production and distribution
4. Characteristics of products or services

C. Other characteristics of market area itself

1. General economic characteristics
2. Geographical characteristics: climate, topography, etc.
3. Political conditions: type of government, kinds and levels of taxes, laws, city ordinances, prevailing attitudes
4. Social characteristics of the area

D. Other possibly pertinent aspects of the market area under study

10

EXHIBIT 1-1 (*continued*)

V. Policies in Regard to Items I, II, III, and IV

  A. Intended policies

  B. Comparison of intended policies with actual practices

  C. Degree of correctness of intended policies and actual practices

Such an outline as appears in exhibit 1-1 can be of use in research in two ways: (1) as a checklist indicating the various types and aspects of the activities of a business organization that may benefit from research; and (2) as a guide for a preliminary investigation in a firm leading to the selection of the final specific problem(s) to be researched. It is important in the early analysis and planning of a research project to avoid overlooking any aspect of the business that may hold the most promising possibilities for solving a problem or for taking advantage of an opportunity for improvement. A reasonably complete and systematically conducted preliminary general survey of this kind can usually increase the efficiency of research.

SUMMARY

Research is the process of systematically obtaining accurate answers to significant and pertinent questions by the use of the scientific method of gathering and interpreting information.

Research may be *basic* or *applied*. Basic research is essentially an effort to extend knowledge. Sometimes it is called *pure* research or *fundamental* research. It is research for the sake of increasing knowledge. Applied research, on the other hand, is chiefly problem oriented. Applied research arises from a need to solve a problem and, therefore, seeks an immediate and practical result.

The three methods used in research, whether basic or applied, may be classified as (1) experimental, (2) historical, and (3) statistical. Experimentation may be defined as a closely controlled procedure for testing hypotheses. It is often of the nature of *sampling studies*, in that samples are taken, kept under close control, the procedures closely controlled, and finally, inferences made about the universe from which the sample came.

The historical method involves a study of the records of the past to reach conclusions. These records may be written, they may be numerical data, they may be the conditions existing currently that need study. The result of the historical method of research usually is a narrative explanation.

The statistical method is a system of procedures and techniques of analysis applied to quantitative data. The statistical method has a body of mathematical methods and models, and applies only to numerical data. It is used, however, in experimentation and historical studies in order to have a system of statistical testing of hypotheses.

The large business firm will normally carry on research in the various activities of this large-scale enterprise. However, small business can usefully apply research to problems. Costly procedures such as are used by large business firms are not always necessary. The problems of the small businessperson are generally of smaller dimensions, and, therefore, cn be handled by telephone conversations, by the use of hand calculators, and by studies of immediate records, such as, accounting records of the firm.

A controversy often exists as to whether research or experience is the most valuable method of gaining knowledge. Research has certain advantages over experience: (1) It can be conducted on a small scale, for example, by a model, (2) It can also achieve results in a shorter time, (3) It may bring to light information that would never be discovered during the course of regular operations, (4) The information from research may be more accurate because of the carefully conducted and controlled procedures.

Experience, however, has some advantages over research: (1) The impact of an experience is a powerful teacher, (2) It is a most effective method of learning; it provides the actual and complete conditions of the real life situation, (3) Experience is widely accepted as a basis of decisions, (4) It carries great weight with businesspersons.

There are certain peculiarities of business research: (1) Usually it is applied research rather than basic; thus, it is problem oriented and directed toward making decisions, (2) The time factor is a limitation—there is often a time limit to do the study for the results to be useful, (3) The dynamic nature of the environment—rapidly changing economic, political, and social conditions—affects the research, (4) Cost limitations affect the research—the project must be *cost effective*.

The fields in which business research occurs may be classified in the following categories: (1) physical facilities and methods; (2) product or service produced; (3) methods of distributing the product or service; (4) the nature of the market; (5) policies in regard to each of the foregoing fields.

EXERCISES

1. Define research in your own words, including the elements of the definition that make it meaningful. Does your definition apply only to business, or is it a general one?
2. Is business research exclusively applied, as contrasted to basic research? Explain. Try to give some examples from your personal knowledge.
3. Define experimentation. Then, contrast your definition with the historical method of research.
4. Why is the statistical method a broader method of research investigation than the experimental or the historical method?
5. What is the role of business research in respect to the executive decision maker?
6. Is business research activity confined to large firms? Explain.
7. Describe the advantages and disadvantages of research in respect to experience for problem solving in the business firm.
8. How valuable is experience to the decision maker? Can experience displace research for making decisions? Explain.
9. Four distinct peculiarities of business research are described in the text. List them, and explain them briefly.
10. Make an outline similar to exhibit 1-1 of the text of one of the following: food supermarket; small men's clothing store; women's shoe store; private hamburger stand.

11. Devise three examples of operations that part I, production facilities and methods, of exhibit 1-1 of the text would apply.
12. What is the usefulness of classifying the fields of research for a firm as is done in exhibit 1-1 of the text?

SELECTED REFERENCES

Balsley, Howard L. *Quantitative Research Methods for Business and Economics*. New York: Random House, 1970.

Emory, William. *Business Research Methods*. Homewood, Ill.: Irwin, 1976.

Murdick, Robert G. *Business Research: Concept and Practice*. Scranton, Pa.: International Textbook, 1969.

Rigby, Paul H. *Conceptual Foundations of Business Research*. New York: Wiley, 1965.

2

Reason and the Scientific Method

The mental processes through which decisions are reached determine to a large extent the accuracy of conclusions. Facts, of course, are essential materials in thinking, and without facts there can be little thought. But facts must be handled correctly in the mind, or they may lead to inaccurate conclusions. Wrong decisions may be reached even though the facts are right.

The scientific method is a systematic step-by-step procedure following the logical processes of reasoning. Therefore, the scientific method is closely related to the reasoning process.

THE REASONING PROCESS

Books have been written on the subject of logic and the processes of reasoning. This discussion, however, will be confined to the basic aspects of the logical methods of induction and deduction and the process of reasoning from cause to effect.

INDUCTION AND DEDUCTION

The *inductive method* of reasoning consists of studying many individual instances or cases in order to formulate a generalized conclusion. This procedure is, of course, followed in most research projects. It would seem apparent, then, that inductive reasoning is the process followed when new facts are being studied, new truths are being uncovered, and new generalizations are being formulated on the basis of information forthcoming from a research project. For example, if the wages of laundry workers in two adjacent communities were to be compared, a sample of the wages paid in the establishments in each would be taken; the average of each would be computed; and then the hypothesis would be tested. The hypothesis may be of this order: that the difference between the means is zero. Such a study involves collecting the individual cases, organizing the individual cases, stating a hypothesis, and testing the hypothesis. The inductive method of reasoning is the chief procedure of thought used in the analysis.

Consider another example. For several days, the persons who patronized a certain drive-in movie theater were observed. The number of persons in 1,000 of the 5,000 cars which drove into the theater during the period was recorded, and it was found that three-fourths of the cars contained two persons. The following conclusion could emerge: Seventy-five percent of the cars that entered this drive-in theater contained two persons. Such a conclusion is a general one with no qualifications given concerning the possibility that a different conclusion could have been reached if the observations had occurred during a different period of time. Sound procedure often requires that the researcher offer an explanatory or qualifying statement along with his conclusion. In the statement concerning the conclusion of the theater study, the researcher should mention the conditions under which the observations took place. The potential user of the findings would then be in a better position to determine the possible applications and limitations of the conclusion. For instance, the generalized conclusion might be followed by such a qualifying statement as this: The personal observations on which this conclusion is based were made by trained observers on the nights of July 21–27, 1977, at the Starlight Theater in Old Town, Indiana.

Four conditions essential to satisfactory induction are:

1. Observations must be correctly performed and recorded; data studied must be accurate and must be collected from the universe in which the researcher is interested.
2. Observations must cover representative cases.
3. Observations must cover a sufficient number of cases.
4. Conclusions must be confined to statements that are fully substantiated by the findings and are not too general or too inclusive.

A brief explanation of these four rules follows:

(1) Mistakes in conducting experiments or interviews and faulty recording of the information obtained can destroy the value of any conclusions reached regardless of the quantity of data collected and the soundness of the analysis of these data. The records from which information is taken must be accurate, the meaning clear, and the correctness verifiable. In some survey projects, the universe is composed of individual items that are scattered widely and are highly similar to items not in the universe. In such projects, field workers will have to be well trained in locating and identifying the items to be studied. For example, in a survey of drivers' opinions about disk brakes on automobiles, it would be necessary to find such cars and their drivers and to determine that the brakes on their cars were actually the disk type. Cars with drum-type brakes are not in the universe being studied.

(2) If only a part of all the persons or items of the kind being investigated are to be studied, observations must cover a representative sample of the universe involved. For instance, in the drive-in movie survey to determine the average number of patrons per car, the cars to be observed should have been selected in such a manner that all kinds of cars and patrons were included. The observations should have occurred throughout all the hours of the days that the theater was open, on all the days of the week, during the various types of movies, and during the major kinds of typical weather conditions.

(3) In order for a sample to be representative, the number of cases studied must be large enough to provide for the inclusion of the various types of cases that exist in the universe. In addition, the size of the sample must be large enough to reduce the probability of error to an acceptable amount. Sampling procedures are discussed in detail in chapter 10.

(4) Conclusions reached after analysis of information based on the study of a number of cases must be confined to statements that are adequately supported by the available data. For example, in the research on disk brakes mentioned earlier, if only large cars driven during a period of dry weather on smooth roadbeds were included in the survey, the conclusions should be confined to large cars operated under such conditions. The conclusions should not be generalized to apply to all cars driven under every kind of weather and road condition.

The *deductive method* consists of reasoning from a general rule or principle regarded as an accepted fact to a specific case which properly falls under the general rule. It sometimes is represented as reasoning from the general to the particular or as applying a general principle to a certain individual situation.

A simple example of deduction follows. Suppose that the following general rule has been accepted. "College graduates make the most successful salespersons in company A." The company manager is attempting to decide which of several prospective new salespersons to employ. The qualifications of the prospects are the same with the exception that one has a college degree while the others do not. The general rule is applied to the situation, and the decision is reached that the individual with the college degree should be employed. The general rule or principle has been applied to a particular case in arriving at a logical decision.

Two conditions necessary to satisfactory deduction are:

1. The general rule or principle must be correct.
2. The general rule must be applied only to those cases which properly fall under that general rule.

A brief discussion of these two rules follows:

(1) A common error in reasoning is the acceptance of an original rule or assumption that is faulty. In the preceding example of company A, the general rule or premise that college graduates make superior salespersons in the company must be correct if the reasoning by deduction is to lead to a correct conclusion and decision. If the general rule has not been arrived at by careful study, it may be an oversimplification; or, it may be partly the result of personal preferences or a hope on the part of the manager who wants to assume that this general rule is correct and should be followed.

It should be recognized, in addition, that a premise or rule may be correct at the time it is established or substantiated by research, but may cease to be correct at a later date after conditions have changed. This possibility makes it necessary for managers to reconsider carefully rather frequently the basic assumptions or principles upon which they rely in the deductive process of reaching decisions.

(2) The general rule must be applied only to those cases which properly fall under the rule. This second condition necessary to satisfactory deduction is also often violated. Suppose, in the example used here, that the manager decided to apply the general rule for salespersons to the hiring of a truck driver. It is highly doubtful that the rule can be correctly used to cover truck drivers. The principle or rule may be correct for salespersons but not for other types of personnel.

It can be seen now that in actual practice, a businessperson needs to use both induction and deduction. *Induction* is the process by which dependable, general rules or principles are established. *Deduction* is the process by which the general rules are put to work to help the manager know what to do in regard to specific cases. Sometimes, the general rules can be accepted as valid because they are printed in textbooks or professional journals, or they are stated by professional persons who are authorities in their fields. Always, however, the user of these principles will need to decide whether they are valid in the particular case under consideration. Sometimes, new general rules will need to be scientifically developed for the specific firm in which the problem has arisen. This situation will probably require that a research project be undertaken to discover the exact nature of the principle as it applies to the particular firm involved.

CAUSE AND EFFECT

The process of solving a problem requires that its cause or causes be determined. Rules of logic are sometimes violated in a peculiarly dangerous manner by mistakenly believing that a certain condition is a cause instead of a result of a second condition. The true cause and effect relationship may be reversed completely in the thinking of the researcher.

Suppose that the proprietor of a beauty parlor knew two facts: (1) fewer customers had been visiting the shop than formerly, and (2) the beauty operators in the shop are glum and irritable. An offhand guess as to the cause and effect relationship in this situation might be that patronage was down because the operators were unpleasant and gloomy. The true cause and effect relationship might be just the opposite—the decline in patronage was the cause of the glumness and irritability of the beauty operators. The manager may experience disappointing results if she tries to increase patronage by replacing her present operators.

When two or more events or conditions occur or exist at the same time, it is often difficult to determine what cause and effect relationships, if any, exist. It is altogether possible that two known conditions are the effect of a third condition. For example, suppose that these two conditions are known to exist:

1. Attendance is down at the baseball games in a town.
2. A local radio station is broadcasting all home games.

It might be assumed that the decrease in attendance at games was caused by the radio broadcasts. The actual relatoinship between these two facts may be that they are an effect of a third condition which is the true cause of both of them. The third condition could be the fact that television is holding more persons in their homes than formerly stayed at home for recreation. The baseball fans among the stay-at-home persons like to listen to radiobroadcasts of the games in between the more popular television programs or at least to listen to periodic radio reports to keep them posted on the progress of the game.

A somewhat more difficult case in logical thinking arises in a situation in which two known conditions are the effect of a third unknown condition. This possibility should always be kept in mind. Assume for purposes of illustration that these two facts are known:

1. Meat is spoiling in the refrigerator in a restaurant.
2. Deliveries of the meat from the packing house are now being made by new trucks which have different cooling systems than the old trucks.

The third unknown fact is:

3. The refrigerator in the restaurant has developed a mechanical condition that causes the temperature to rise periodically above the level necessary to preserve fresh meat.

Now, if (3) is the actual cause of the effect listed in (1), it must be discovered before a correct conclusion can be reached as to the cause of the spoilage of the meat. This case points up the importance of not overlooking any possible hypothesis as to causes of a problem.

Basic and Secondary Causes

A distinction between causes that can be helpful to clear thinking is made evident by the classification of causes into two groups: basic and secondary. *Basic* causes are the deeper, more fundamental reasons for a condition. Basic causes might be called "original" causes of conditions which in turn may be considered the causes of other conditions or effects. A *secondary* cause is one that is the result of a basic cause.

For example, suppose that the following four conditions are known:

1. There has been an increase in the sales of a store in a certain part of town.
2. There has been an increase in the amount of traffic on the street in front of this store.
3. There has been an increase in the population living in the part of town in which the store is located.
4. Two large factories employing a total of 5,000 workers who live nearby have recently opened on the outskirts of the part of town in which the store is located.

The manager of the store is interested in determining the cause of the increase in sales, that is, condition (1). Now, which of the other conditions, (2), (3), and (4), are secondary causes and which one is the most fundamental or basic cause of condition (1)? Suppose that after careful investigation, it can be established that point (4) is the cause of the other three conditions. Therefore, (4) can be said to be the basic cause of (1), while (2) and (3) are secondary causes.

The importance of recognizing the differences between basic and secondary causes arises from the necessity of learning the actual cause of a condition before attempting to change it or perhaps merely to understand it. In the example given here, the manager of the store needs to know that he must watch the actual and expected employment levels in the two new factories to be able to predict what will happen to his sales. The increased traffic and the growth of the population in his trade area are actually effects of the basic condition (cause), that is, the establishment of the two new factories. Of course, the increase in traffic and population can be called causes of the gain in sales; but, still they must be recognized as secondary, not basic causes.

Actually, nearly all conditions that are causes can to a certain degree be called secondary due to the fact that ultimate, final, or basic causes may be very deep-seated and considerably less numerous than the great number of resulting conditions that appear to be and often are themselves causes of further effects. These secondary conditions that do cause added effects are often so important, definite, measurable, and predictable that they may be acceptable as *basic* causes themselves for all practical purposes.

For example, in the case cited, the manager of the store probably can satisfactorily assume that the location of the two new factories can be taken as the basic cause of the increase in his sales. Actually, the cause (whatever it might be) for the locating of the factories in this particular town could be given as the true or basic cause. But pushing the search for causes this far might not be feasible or necessary. The investigation usually need not be carried beyond the research required to establish a cause basic enough to form a reasonably firm foundation for sound decision making.

A summary of conditions necessary for establishing correct cause and effect relationships follows:

1. Be certain that the assumed conditions, that is, the cause and effect, actually exist. Much wasted time and effort can often be saved if this rule is heeded.
2. Consider carefully whether one known condition is a cause or an effect of a second known condition. Do not move too quickly from an hypothesis to a conclusion.
3. Consider carefully whether one known condition is a cause or an effect of some unknown condition instead of a second known condition.
4. Consider carefully whether two known conditions have any cause and effect relationship or are actually a result of a third known or possibly unknown condition.
5. Distinguish correctly between basic and secondary causes.

Pitfalls to Be Avoided in Reasoning

Before concluding this discussion of the reasoning process, three pitfalls that should be avoided in reasoning and in formulating the conclusion should be mentioned:

1. Reaching an insufficiently substantiated conclusion because of the fear of admitting that a correct, exact conclusion has not been found. Most persons are reluctant to admit that they "don't know." Many businesspersons also want definite conclusions which do not contain qualifications or limitations. The writer of a research report may, therefore, be tempted to state all of the conclusions in strong, definite statements, some of which are not warranted by the available evidence.
2. Assuming that a proposition is true if it cannot be shown to be false, and the converse. For example, it is erroneous reasoning to believe that it would be wise to follow a certain practice because no disadvantages of the practice were substantiated in the findings of a research project. The reverse would be faulty reasoning, too; that is, the assumption that a practice is definitely unsound because it has not been shown to be sound.
3. Assuming that quantity of evidence determines its value. Quality as well as quantity of data must be considered in reaching a conclusion. Condition A should not be held to be the cause of condition B merely because ten items of evidence support that contention, while only five items of evidence contradict it.

THE SCIENTIFIC METHOD

The scientific method is usually defined to consist of the systematic procedures of formulating a problem, measuring or observing occurrences, and testing the hypotheses concerning those occurrences. It involves the procedures of collecting the data. It may furnish results which contribute to the formulation of theories. The procedures themselves in the scientific method are considered to be relatively closely controlled and follow the logical processes of reason.

In the natural sciences, research is often closely controlled and often consists of experimentation. Research in the physical sciences, such as, biology, or botany, may often be pure or basic research as contrasted to applied research. Since close control over the subjects of the experiments may usually be exercised as well as careful control over the procedures of the research, the results are often exact and possible of relatively precise determination and interpretation.

In the humanities, consisting of history and languages, experimentation is not often feasible. The historical method is most often followed; and, therefore, experimentation with hypotheses to be substantiated or rejected is often precluded. Control over the objects of the research is usually not possible; but, close control over the procedures is, of course, usually practiced.

In the social sciences, as for example, sociology and psychology, the behavior of man is the chief object of study. Since the behavior of man is not subject to close control, experimentation is often precluded; and, therefore, the scientific method in its purest sense is not followed. However, the scientific method, insofar as it is defined to include careful consideration and control of procedures rather than objects of experimentation, is indeed followed rigorously. Since the field of business activity is usually classified as a social science, a more detailed discussion of the social sciences related to the scientific method follows.

THE SOCIAL SCIENCES AND THE SCIENTIFIC METHOD

The scientific method of investigation and analysis is used by all scientists. The subject matter being studied does not determine whether the process is called scientific. It makes no difference whether the investigation is in the fields traditionally held to be sciences, such as, chemistry and physics, or is in the various areas of human relations, including business and the other social sciences. The activity of an investigator is scientific if he correctly uses the scientific method.

It is true that much of the research in the social sciences covering various areas of human relations results in answers that are often less tangible or exact than are the findings of researchers in the physical sciences. The reasons for this fact are to be found in the greater complexity often encountered in the social sciences, in the difficulty of carrying on experiments under controlled conditions, and in the long periods of time that often must elapse before the final results can be known.

A striking illustration of the relatively great complexity of problems in the social sciences is the case of atomic energy. The chemical and physical research required and the applied industrial engineering involved in the development and production of the atomic bomb are almost beyond human comprehension. But the process of converting the results of the basic theoretical research into the practical product was accomplished in a comparatively short period of four or five years. In contrast, the research into the problems in human relatons arising from the use of atomic energy as manifested in the areas of military affairs and in social and economic fields will undoubtedly prove to be several times more complex; and the final decisions and results will take decades to work themselves out.

Another example of this contrast between the physical and social sciences can be taken from a rather common type of problem in the world of business. Suppose a retailer of women's shoes decides to have tests run to determine which of several types of shoes will be most durable. Laboratory tests of the physical-science type can be designed to obtain reasonably accurate results in a few days or perhaps hours. On the other hand, the determination of whether women will actually buy the type of shoe that is shown to be most durable will require several weeks or months. Even then the findings may be rendered of little use if fashions change, a competitor does a better job of selling, or the customers experience a sudden decline in their purchasing power. None of these three conditions just named is subject to appreciable control or is exactly predictable by the shoe manufacturer or the retail merchant.

It should be emphasized that these illustrations are offered merely to show the relative complexity of research in the fields of human affairs. They are not intended to imply that such investigations are valueless. In fact, the findings of careful research into the human and economic aspects of business problems will go a long way toward reducing the complexity and uncertainty involved in managerial decision making.

THE PROCEDURES OF THE SCIENTIFIC METHOD

An outline of the steps involved in the use of the scientific method of investigation and analysis can contain as few as three or four main headings, or up to several times that number. The eleven-step outline presented later is one that has proved appropriate in the cases of several hundred research projects dealing with the problems of various types of businesses. Different names can be given these steps; and in some projects certain of the steps can be covered rather quickly, while in other cases a longer, more intense process might be required. Also, in actual practice, more than one step may be under way at the same time. The steps may be taken in somewhat different order by different researchers and for various types of projects. Often certain steps may have to be retraced.

Before starting the listing and detailed discussion of the eleven steps of the scientific method, it should be pointed out again that in the solution of many business problems, no elaborate field work or detailed study of records will be necessary. Instead, for instance in simple situations, perhaps all that will be required will be careful thinking about the problem, correct recall and interpretation of facts already known, and the application of this information in arriving at a conclusion. In fact, this is the way that most decisions are reached by managers. The type of activity involved in such decision making obviously would not be elaborate enough to be called full-fledged research.

Many somewhat more complex problems can be solved by the process sometimes referred to as *preliminary or informal investigation*. For example, the manager looking for the facts on which to base his decision may find them by searching through readily available records. His own employees, perhaps his chief accountant or sales manager, may be able to supply him with the necessary data and to furnish him with their opinions on the matter. Or he may decide to talk over the situation with some of his friends or business acquaintances. A few well-placed telephone calls to other businesspersons or persons with the desired information may bring the data required. Letters to trade association offices, governmental agencies, schools, colleges, and such organizations as local chambers of commerce may obtain the desired answers. A visit or telephone call to the nearest public library may turn up some publications that contain much of the needed material. The librarian can usually point out various sources of information. These activities certainly do not constitute a complex research program incorporating long, involved procedures.

It is probably true, nevertheless, that most capable executives are systematic in their thinking and acting; and even in reaching many of their daily decisions, they actually go through each of the eleven steps discussed in this chapter. The steps, of course, in simple cases can be covered in a short period of time.

The eleven steps into which the procedures of the scientific method of research may be divided for discussion are:

1. Become aware that a problem exists.
2. Define the problem and purpose(s) of the research.
3. Set forth hypotheses as to cause(s) and/or solutions of the problem.
4. Determine what information will be required.
5. Decide which methods to use in collecting information.
6. Collect information or evidence.
7. Compile findings in systematic form.
8. Analyze findings to determine whether they substantiate or eliminate hypotheses.
9. Write final research report to bring out full significance of findings and any indicated conclusions.
10. Make specific recommendations as to feasible actions.
11. Remember the follow-up, which may aid in the application of recommendations or help determine the results of the application of recommendations.

⊾**Step 1: Become aware that a problem exists.** The accomplishment of this step is not so automatic and so unimportant as might be thought at first glance. The step involves the highly significant point that a manager first must become aware of a problem and must be willing to admit that a difficulty exists. Without this conscious recognition of a problem, research will not occur. It should be mentioned, in addition, that the problem need not necessarily be in the form of a breakdown of some function or of an obviously unsatisfactory condition. Many of the "problems" that efficient managers recognize as such are really in the form of questions about whether a given activity may be improved or new opportunities developed for increasing the net income of the business.

One earmark of an efficient businessperson is awareness of the conditions, good and bad, in the firm. The businessperson is constantly on the lookout for "problems," that is, conditions that can be improved or avoided. He usually is aware of such problems and will be found to be continually doing some research.

⊾**Step 2: Define the problem and purpose(s) of the research project.** What exactly is the difficulty? What is the nature of the problem? What is the location of the unsatisfactory condition? How many parts of the firm are involved? Is the problem serious, of long standing, or of recent origin? These are some of the questions which it may be necessary to answer to arrive at an accurate definition of the problem.

The definition of the problem should also include a detailed consideration of the possible uses to which the results are to be put, to establish the precise nature of the problem, and to set forth and clarify the purposes of the research. An essential part of this step, then, is to determine why the study is to be conducted and what value the findings may possess. Research can bring practical results only if the research director knows why the investigation is being undertaken and knows something about the possible ways in which the findings can be helpful in making wiser decisions in the future.

To persons eager to remedy a difficulty, the process of carefully defining the problem may seem to be so much wheel spinning. It is not. It is an essential step that will show the direction to take, the possible routes that must be followed, the amount of money, effort, and time that will be required, and the data that must be found if the research is to be successful.

Step 3: Set up hypotheses as to cause(s) and/or solutions of the problem. This step requires that careful guesses be made as to the possible causes or solutions of the problem. In this process, experience in and knowledge about the business under study will usually be quite helpful, assuming that the researcher does not allow his close connections with a firm to bias or blind him in his thinking.

Some persons are more imaginative than others; they are more adept at seeing possible causes and solutions of problems. A fertile mind that can be thorough in recalling information and recognizing possible cause-and-effect relationships will be highly useful at this stage in the scientific method of investigation. But a brilliant mind with an unusually good memory, although desirable, is not essential. A careful person who is willing to do some hard, reflective thinking can ordinarily come up with the most likely hypotheses needed to point out the paths to be followed and the further steps required in the fact-finding procedures necessary to carry out the research to successful completion.

If it is practical to do so, talking about the problem with other qualified persons may prove worth-while. Another experienced person may be able to provide added ideas that may lead to fruitful hypotheses. The manager of a store, for example, may be so closely associated with the firm that he may not be able to see some of the possible causes of a difficulty as easily or readily as someone who is an "outsider."

The successful completion of this step may require the advice and services of persons who are specialists in the major fields of the business under study. An accountant may be needed for advice on accounting aspects of the problem; a marketing specialist for selling problems; and so forth. It is also likely that, in research about many business problems, the advice and services of specialists in various fields other than strictly business may be needed. For example, due to the almost unlimited number of fields of activity covered by various types of firms, it may be necessary to use the services of such professionals as chemists, engineers, mathematicians, lawyers, physicians, psychologists, sociologists, public relations experts, and artists.

In some business concerns, specialists who are staff members of the firm can be consulted. In other cases, special consultants may have to be retained for brief periods. These consultants and, perhaps, also specialists in research methods may be needed in some instances in one or more steps in the research process.

Step 4: Determine what information will be required. The definition of the problem and the possible uses to which the results are to be put, as well as the hypotheses that are set forth, all help to determine the exact nature of the information which must be obtained. In turn, the fact-finding procedures to be used, the data-collecting techniques necessary, and the personnel, time, and money required to accomplish the research are all things that can be decided upon only after the researcher has determined what information and data he must obtain to complete his research successfully.

Step 5: Decide which methods to use in collecting information. The required information should be obtained with the use of the most efficient methods available. *Efficient* as used here means those methods that will obtain the necessary information with the minimum of expenditures in time, money, and manpower consistent with the standards of accuracy and completeness desired.

A general classification of data-collecting methods or techniques, based partially on types of sources of information, follows:

1. published material—in libraries and elsewhere
2. unpublished material—records of the firm under study; official records in governmental agencies; available records from private organizations or persons
3. survey techniques—personal interviews; questionnaires; telephone inquiries; panels
4. observation
5. experimentation

These methods will be discussed in detail in later chapters.

Step 6: Collect information or evidence. The process of obtaining the required information, which in step 5 was determined to be essential, should be planned and set up before the data collecting begins. Pretesting of procedures, questionnaires, schedules, or other forms to be used, as well as training and instructing of personnel, should be completed before the final process of gathering information starts. Careful management and control of research personnel, materials, and devices used will bring more accurate results, as well as save time, money, and effort. Even though the preceding five steps in the research project have been well done, the chances of completing the project successfully will be destroyed if a slipshod, inaccurate job of data collecting is done.

Sometimes a false economy is attempted by undue skimping on the time allowed and expenditures necessary to provide satisfactory personnel and techniques for collecting information. Sufficient time and money must be provided to obtain accurate findings; or the results may be even worse than useless—they may be dangerously misleading.

Step 7: Compile findings in systematic form. An accurately compiled statistical and informational report should be prepared to show the data found in the research. The "truth, the whole truth, and nothing but the truth" well describes the nature of the material called for in this step. The factual findings must be prepared in a clear, concise form that will enable the researcher to consider carefully these findings as to meaning and significance in regard to the project under study. The report mentioned here, however, is not the final research report. Instead, it is merely an important step toward the completion of the project and the subsequent final research report, which is described later.

Step 8: Analyze findings to determine whether they substantiate or eliminate hypotheses. This step involves detailed, careful consideration of the accumulated evidence to discover whether it sufficiently supports the original assumptions as to the causes or solutions of the problem. It may involve testing the hypotheses by statistical techniques. The exact significance of the findings must be determined; too much or too little should not be claimed. The researcher must constantly keep in mind the imperativeness of determining whether the difficulty being studied was actually caused by the assumed cause(s) set forth in step 3. Wishful thinking must not be allowed to lead to an erroneous conclusion about whether an hypothesis has been substantiated or eliminated by the data collected.

A possible disappointing outcome of this step is that sometimes all the careful guesses as to causes or possible solutions of the problem are discovered to be without adequate foundation in fact; and, therefore, the whole research process, has to revert to step 3 in which new hypotheses must be set up. This eventuality rather painfully underlines the importance of doing as good a job as possible in step 3.

Step 9: Write the final research report to bring out full significance of findings and any indicated conclusions. At this stage in the research process, a formal, final written report will be required. It should be carefully prepared. Enough discussion about each of the other steps will be included in this report to provide the necessary knowledge for full understanding of the procedures followed in the project and of the findings. The report often will not need to be long and elaborate. The length and complexity will depend on the nature of the research project and the detail desired by users of the report.

This step carries the analysis of findings to the final stages of making decisions to direct the actions of management. The results are studied carefully to determine what they mean. Each fact must be analyzed by itself and as to its meaning when related to all the other data collected. The researcher will usually find it is helpful to look at each piece of information obtained and ask the following questions: What is the exact meaning and importance of this fact? What does this fact mean when it is considered in the light of all the other facts? What is the meaning of all the facts when considered together as a whole?

The nature of the problem and the purposes of the project must always be kept in mind in this step. The business manager needs an evaluation that deals with the pertinent and significant data directly related to the problem being investigated. Specifically, management must have the information essential to accurate decision making in regard to the particular problem under study.

Step 10: Make specific recommendations as to feasible actions. This step in research is, of course, a most important one because the need for recommendations as to sound actions is the reason why the investigation was undertaken. The researcher, however, may have been requested to cover the first nine steps only. If so, the manager will then have to go through step 10 alone. Even if the research proper does include this tenth step, the manager will still need to review it himself to be certain that the recommendations are definitely practical. When the actual research is being done by a manager, he will naturally carry it through all ten of these steps.

In no other step in the research project will the importance of the correct use of the scientific method of investigation be more emphatically apparent to the user of research results. A decision must now be made which, if wrong, may cost considerable money or even failure of the enterprise or, if right, can mean appreciable financial gain. The researcher is now faced with having to accept the consequences of any errors of omission or commission in his research. This is one of the reasons why research organizations may charge clients considerably more for a project including this tenth step. A client may well find the extra cost worth-while, however, if the research company is staffed with experienced experts who can make sound recommendations.

It should be pointed out that sometimes in actual practice the recommendations are for no action; that is, present policies and actions are found to be the best to follow. No superior alternatives are discovered. This situation should not necessarily be taken as evidence that the research was useless. Sometimes it is worth-while to find out whether current policies and practices are the best of the several possible ones that could be followed. Changes should not be made unless improvements will be realized.

In some projects, the purpose of the research is not merely to make recommendations as to actions, but also to attempt to foresee future developments, such as, trends or changes in markets, production, cost, or other conditions. Learning about probable future changes will enable managers to make sound plans to meet the changes.

The final written research report will contain detailed substantiation of all points in the form of careful citation of the supporting data given throughout the report. Every recommendation will be based on the facts obtained in the research process. The reasoning followed must lead to logical, unquestionable conclusions, fully documented by material contained in the findings of the project.

Step 11: Follow-up. The follow-up is important for three major reasons: (1) Unless research results are carefully considered and acted upon, if it is found wise to do so, the project will have been useless. The follow-up, therefore, has as its purpose the carrying through of the research process to its final goal. (2) As part of the follow-up, the researcher will be available to the users of the research findings to aid in any explanations needed. (3) The results of the application of the research findings in actual practice can be studied. This study will aid in establishing the feasibility of such research projects and in improving research techniques.

Researchers are persons who might well consider themselves members of a profession who feel responsible for their clients in somewhat the same manner as physicians who usually attempt to see that their patients follow the doctor's orders. In the case of the researcher, the client may need some explanations and advice as to the exact meaning and uses to which the findings should be put. For a reasonable period, therefore, after a research project has been completed, the researcher should be available for consultation, as well as to lend his "moral support" by perhaps paying a visit or two to his client to see how he is getting along with the prescribed "medicines." The formal, final research report, to be sure, will contain complete information and explanations. The report alone, however, may not be sufficient because it cannot render all the functions mentioned here.

It is true, of course, that in some situations the researcher may be instructed and expected to merely collect, organize, and present his findings. No further action may be desired by the client or the user of the research results. In such a case, naturally, the researcher would not impose himself on the client. In any case, the researcher should remember that he serves in an advisory, not an administrative, capacity.

SUMMARY

The reasoning process may involve induction and/or deduction. The inductive method consists of studying many individual instances and results in a generalization. This is the procedure followed in most research. The result of inductive reasoning is a conclusion or generalization which may be used as a principle in future investigations. Reasoning from a principle to individual instances is the process of deductive reasoning. Thus, deduction requires that a generalization exist which has been established and is then applied to inferring the occurrence of individual cases.

Four conditions may be listed as essential to satisfactory inductive reasoning: (1) The observations must be accurate and collected from the proper universe. (2) The observations must be representative of the universe. (3) The observations must cover a sufficient number of cases. (4) The conclusions must be confined to the findings of the inductive process.

Deductive reasoning—reasoning from a principle to a specific case—requires at least two conditions: (1) The principle itself must be correct. (2) The principle must be applied to those cases which properly fall under that principle.

The cause and effect associations in a research project require careful analysis and limitation. Correct cause and effect relationships can be assured if the following conditions are met: (1) Establish that the cause and effect actually exist. (2) Determine whether one known condition is a cause or an effect of a second known condition. (3) Establish whether one known condition is a cause or an effect of some unknown condition instead of a second known condition. (4) Establish whether two known conditions have a cause or effect relationship or actually result from a third, possibly unknown condition. (5) Distinguish carefully between basic and secondary causes.

In this process of reasoning with cause and effect, three pitfalls may be mentioned: (1) Reaching an insufficiently substantiated conclusion. (2) Assuming a proposition to be true if it cannot be shown to be false, and vice versa. (3) Assuming that quantity of evidence determines its value, without considering also its quality.

It is often considered that the scientific method applies only to experimentation, in that only with controlled experiments can conditions be made static so that the pertinent variable may be studied. This narrow definition of scientific method, however, is not used in this book. The scientific method is a procedure as well as a statement of conditions. A study may be scientific even though it is not experimentation if the procedures of the scientific method are followed. These procedures may be listed as follows:

1. Become aware of the problem.
2. Define the problem.
3. Establish hypotheses.
4. Determine the information required.
5. Decide on methods of collecting the data.
6. Collect the data.
7. Compile the findings in a systematic form.
8. Analyze the findings to determine fi they substantiate or eliminate the hypotheses.
9. Write a final research report.
10. Make specific recommendations.
11. Conduct a follow-up, if necessary.

EXERCISES

1. Compare and contrast induction and deduction, giving examples of each.
2. Describe the four conditions necessary to satisfactory induction.
3. Explain the two conditions of satisfactory deduction, using examples.
4. How can both induction and deduction be used in the same research project? Give an example.
5. How may cause and effect be confounded or misunderstood? Give an example.
6. How do basic and secondary causes differ? Using an example, explain how secondary causes may be mistaken for basic causes.
7. Explain the conditions necessary for establishing correct cause and effect relationships.
8. Explain how a researcher may avoid the three chief pitfalls in reasoning.
9. Does the term *scientific method* refer to a set of procedures or to *science* as a subject? Explain.
10. Can the scientific method be applied in the humanities and the social sciences as well as to the natural sciences? How can you justify your answer?
11. Desribe how the social sciences may employ the scientific method. Give an example.
12. How does *preliminary or informal investigation* aid in solving complex research problems?
13. Explain the importance of the first three steps of the procedures of the scientific method to the remainder of the procedures.
14. What role does information planning and acquirement play in the procedures of the scientific method?
15. Describe in your own words each of the eleven steps in the procedures of the scientific method.

16. Devise an example of a business research problem and outline your procedures in applying the scientific method to its solution.
17. What is the usefulness of *follow-up* procedures? Why may follow-up not be required?

SELECTED REFERENCES

Balsley, Howard L. *Quantitative Research Methods for Business and Economics*. New York:
Random House, 1970.
Murdick, Robert G. *Business Research: Concept and Practice*. Scranton, Pa.: International
Textbook, 1969.
Wilson, E. Bright, Jr. *An Introduction to Scientific Research*. New York: McGraw-Hill,
1952.

3

Problems, Hypotheses, and Data

In the first two chapters, the nature of business research and scientific research as applied to business were described, and a general orientation to scientific procedures in research was given. Research was defined generally; then, research in its relationship to management was described and the scope of business research was explained with some attention given to the specific characteristics of business research. The relationship between the reasoning process and the scientific method was given attention, and the difficulties involved in the social sciences in which business is classified were explained. Finally, the step-by-step procedures of the scientific method applied in business were presented in some detail.

Formulation of problems involves locating a problem within a firm or industry, and specifically defining the problem. It includes setting up hypotheses to be tested. Following the locating and defining of a problem and the forming of hypotheses, the planning of the project in respect to the collection of data and the analysis of the data are required.

LOCATING AND DEFINING PROBLEMS

How can a businessperson go about setting up effective procedures for discovering how well his firm is getting along and whether changes are needed? This is, of course, a question that is as general as the whole area of management. All the managerial techniques of control and direction that are appropriate for the operation of the firm under consideration would constitute an important part of the devices and sources of information upon which the manager would rely in his search for possible problems in his establishment that might call for research.

These devices and techniques of managerial control, when used as agencies of information, can become effective ways of finding problems:

1. study of records and reports of the firm
2. careful observation of conditions in the firm
3. purposeful conversation with other qualified persons in the firm
4. careful observation and study of the procedures and techniques of the most efficient and successful firms in the industry
5. reading pertinent published materials
6. use of checklists in evaluating the operations of a firm
7. *brain storming*—intensified discussion within a group of interested persons.

(1) The records and reports of the firm coming to the manager or available to him should be accurate, on time, and up-to-date. From study of these reports, the manager will be able to learn many of the facts he needs to know how well the firm is getting along and whether a difficulty or problem exists or is developing. The kinds of records available will depend on the type and size of the establishment, which in turn will determine the kind and amount of records needed by management officials. A manager who is prone to ignore or read too hastily these indicators of the conditions in his organization may cut himself off from the knowledge required to become aware of a problem or to foresee a developing trouble spot.

An executive should also realize that, ordinarily, written reports and records are superior to oral reports as a means of keeping informed about the operations of an organization. The superiority of written reports over oral reports is due to these characteristics of written reports:

a. can be read more quickly than oral reports can be heard
b. will be more carefully and accurately prepared
c. can be reread and studied for significance and relationship of different items
d. reliance on memory is reduced to a minimum
e. can be filed for future reference

(2) Careful observation of conditions in a firm will sometimes bring to light unsatisfactory situations. For instance, the manager of a bus company in his rides on the various routes may notice that on windy, cold days fewer patrons are waiting at each bus stop, and many of the passengers seem to come running from various nearby buildings in order to catch the bus. These observations can result in the recognition that this an unsatisfactory situation. Again, the manager has become aware of a possible problem.

The efficient executive will not rely entirely on chance, haphazard observations to bring possible problems to his attention. He will provide for the use of systematic observation techniques. Periods of observation may be set for certain times of the year or may be decided on whenever conditions seem to call for some sort of survey. Some managers are continually on the lookout for possible problems.

(3) Purposeful conversation with qualified persons in the firm can uncover the existence of situations that may constitute a problem. A manager

is fortunate if his employees can and will talk freely and frankly with their superiors. An important channel of information is thereby opened to the manager. He can know more accurately and completely what is going on. Any conditions that have developed or might develop into problems can be recognized sooner and more easily.

An executive who also encourages his fellow executives of equal or higher rank to express themselves freely in their conversations will find that another important avenue of information has been created. There is little doubt that most persons can usually learn more by asking intelligent questions and then attentively listening to the answers than they can learn by talking themselves.

It should be pointed out that the term *purposeful conversation* is the key to the value of conversation as a means of becoming aware of a problem. To be most successful in bringing out useful facts and ideas, the purpose must be definitely known and kept in mind throughout the discussion. Happily, such informative conversation usually pleases both parties—the person who is after the information, as well as the one whose ideas are considered so important as to hold the attention of the listener. Whenever a businessperson meets other informed persons in his field, whether in business conferences or at conventions, purposeful conversation can often prove productive of many ideas.

(4) Careful observation and study of the procedures and techniques of the most efficient and successful firms in the industry will sometimes provide yardsticks to aid in measuring the adequacy of operations in a given plant. Where such comparative studies are feasible, reasonable use should be made of them. Conditions will vary from plant to plant, and so it must be recognized that techniques applicable in one firm may not be entirely practicable in another. Even so, useful ideas may be picked up which, when adapted to the special conditions of a given company, may result in valuable improvements.

Awareness that an efficient firm is conducting an operation in a certain way can well pose for another firm the worth-while problem of determining whether this second firm should adjust its method of operation to take advantage of the techniques used by the admittedly more efficient establishment. One of the advantages of belonging to the trade association which covers a given industry stems from the situation just mentioned. This is also a valid reason for attendance at conventions of members of the industry.

(5) Reading pertinent published material in the field in which a business operates is an increasingly fruitful way to become aware of new procedures and trends that will affect the firms in an industry. An innovation can create a serious problem for the manager who is unaware of the possible impact of the innovation. A businessperson cannot hope to keep fully abreast of the changes in his field by conversations with customers, other businesspersons, and from his own experiences in his business activities. He needs the additional knowledge that can be gained by reading a carefully selected group of informative printed materials.

(6) The use of checklists in evaluating the operations of a firm may be especially effective in bringing about the awareness of a problem in a busi-

ness. A checklist, as the term is used here, contains an array of items covering the various activities of a given type of firm. The list may be composed of numerous questions about how the different functions of the business are conducted. The questions may cover all the kinds of activities that are or may be carried on.

When the checklists are carefully studied and answers are made to the numerous questions, it may become apparent that some of the answers show that unsatisfactory conditions exist in certain parts of the firm under study. At least, uncertainty may arise as to the degree of efficiency with which the firm is operating. Later in this chapter, there will be a detailed discussion of the use of checklists in the research work required in the analysis and definition of a situation or problem.

(7) Brain storming—intensified discussion within a group of interested persons—may often be a means of encouraging thinking and of developing new ideas about a problem. When several persons get into a concentrated conversation, the expressed ideas of each one are likely to lead to added ideas among others in the group. One mind stimulates other minds to the degree that usually the total output of ideas will be greater in a group of thinkers than if each person were to do his thinking alone.

The main purpose of brain storming may be to increase the quantity of ideas. But, it may also be used to increase the output of sound ideas. It is altogether possible that group consideration may lead to improvement in the quality (feasibility, usability, practicality) of the ideas brought out, because the ideas expressed before a group of other persons will be more carefully considered before they are stated, and the following discussion may refine and improve the original ideas. Most successful brain-storming techniques require, however, that participants be encouraged to express their ideas freely. Therefore, they should be told not to hold back a thought merely because of the fear that it may, after further consideration, be found to possess weaknesses.

These idea-stimulating sessions may be held among the officers and certain employees of a firm, or outsiders may be brought in. A discussion group composed of customers or patrons may bring out ideas about how to improve products and services from the consumer's viewpoint. The persons brought into the group can be selected either to be representative of all customers, or they may be chosen because they are prolific thinkers with pertinent ideas about the needs and reactions of typical consumers or customers.

A list of some of the possible purposes of brain storming would include attempts to discover:

a. hypotheses as to probable causes of a given problem
b. new uses for old products
c. possibilities for developing new products or services to meet old or new needs
d. ways to cut costs, increase production, increase sales, improve public relations, and so forth, ranging over the entire field of all of the activities of an organization.

DEFINITION OF THE PROBLEM

A problem clearly and accurately stated is a problem that is often well on its way to being solved. Before research or fact finding can successfully start, the investigator must know what the problem is that he is attempting to solve. He must also know why he wants a solution. The *what* of a problem is answered by an accurate definition of the situation. The *why* can be established by the determination of the uses to which the findings will be or can be put. A complete definition of a problem must include both the *what* and the *why* aspects.

The researcher is likely to find this step one of the most difficult to get through successfully. He may feel uncertain about where and how to begin the search that will pinpoint the problem. Much of the work in this step is concerned with thinking about and reflecting upon various possibilities instead of going forth overtly with yardstick or other tangible measuring or counting devices for the collection of visible, material information. The researcher, especially if he is relatively inexperienced in research, may feel that nothing is being accomplished. But just the opposite will be or should be the case. No researcher should begrudge the time and effort spent in this step in which he defines the problem and decides on the specific purposes of the investigation.

It is well to keep in mind that there are usually two kinds of purposes in a research project—the immediate and the ultimate. The immediate purpose will be to obtain the particular types of information needed to accomplish the final, overall objective of the project, that is, the ultimate purpose. For example, the manager of a downtown parking lot may desire to increase his net profits. This is the ultimate purpose of his research. He will need to secure information about the shopping habits and parking preferences of his customers to accomplish his ultimate purpose. Acquiring data about shopping habits and parking preferences, therefore, will be the immediate purposes in his research project.

CHECKLISTS

In attempting to locate problems and define problems, making up a checklist can often prove a valuable step. A checklist consists of a detailed listing of all of the pertinent areas of the operations of a business firm to consider concerning a problem situation, with a listing of all the significant questions that should be asked.

A summary of the reasons why checklists may prove valuable aids in planning research projects is given as follows:

1. The process of constructing a checklist stimulates thinking and results in more clear and logical consideration of the problem.
2. Use of a checklist results in a more complete consideration of all aspects of the problem and reduces the chances that important aspects will be overlooked.
3. Use of a checklist results in more complete, exact identification and definition of the problem.

4. A checklist assists in setting up hypotheses as to causes of the problem.
5. A checklist aids in determining the information and data that will be required in the solution of the problem(s).

The task of preparing a checklist may seem quite large, especially to busy managers of smaller firms. First, it should be said that a checklist should not be excessively long or complex. It should be only as detailed and complex as the problem demands. In smaller businesses or for simpler problems, the general list may be considerably less detailed than the example given in exhibit 3-1. In some simple cases, the checklist may not need to go beyond a sheet or two or longhand notes that the manager has written down as he has carefully thought about the situation. If these conditions are satisfied, the notes can constitute a sufficient checklist.

Secondly, the task of constructing a checklist may prove much less difficult and time consuming than the inexperienced person may realize. Once the writing process begins, ideas will usually start to come to mind and call for expression in the written notes. The immediate purpose of this writing session is to get all the pertinent, possible ideas on paper. Sometimes the ideas may come to the prospective researcher as he is going about his business. New ideas and helpful evaluations of the checklist being compiled can often be obtained by showing it to other qualified persons.

The actual process of preparing a checklist can be summarized in the following steps:

1. Write out a list of ideas, points, questions, or comments pertaining to the problem as it is carefully turned over in the mind.
2. Go through what seem to be the most pertinent records of the firm to obtain ideas and possible leads to further items to be placed in the checklist.
3. Talk to other persons in the firm and outside if it seems advisable.
4. Do some browsing through pertinent publications.
5. Evaluate the items included in the written notes that have been made so far in the process of preparing the checklist. Compile a logically arranged checklist which contains the apparently pertinent problems or conditions that should be investigated in the proposed research project.
6. If feasible, show this revised checklist to several qualified persons to get their opinions about its completeness and pertinency in regard to the proposed project.
7. Make any revisions that seem necessary and compile the final checklist.

FORMING HYPOTHESES

After the problem has been precisely defined, the next step is to begin the process of setting up possible reasons for the difficulty. These hypotheses or guesses as to the causes or solutions must be carefully made because they will determine what facts will be sought and what research procedures

EXHIBIT 3-1
Suggested Checklist of Some Items to Be Considered in Locating and Defining a Problem for a Manufacturer of Consumer Goods

A.   *Historical Background of Company*

Possible items: Age; when and where founded and by whom; amount of experience and demonstrated ability of management; changes in financial status; growth record; changes, if any, in the type of product produced; etc.

Possible significance of items: Is firm an old established business or a new one which has not yet shown that it has survival powers? Has the firm had a steady or irregular growth? Has its financial position always been satisfactory? Has it changed recently to a new, untried product?

B.   *Production Characteristics and Conditions*

Possible items: Sources of raw materials, power, labor; degree of mechanization and kinds of equipment; nature of labor force; types of raw materials; storage facilities; status of costs of production; etc.

Possible significance of items: Are adequate amounts of raw materials, power, and labor available at costs that will enable the firm to compete satisfactorily? Is firm equipped with a satisfactory amount of efficient, up-to-date machinery? Does firm have adequate storage space? Are management-labor relations satisfactory? Are costs per unit at lowest feasible level? Would cost rise, fall, or remain unchanged if output were to be changed?

C.   *Characteristics of Product(s)*

Possible items: Exactly what are the characteristics of the product(s) — size, shape, weight, color, possible uses, durability, type of package, price, sale unit, etc.

Possible significance of items: Does the product have the best combination of characteristics for the market for which it is intended? Is the product the right size, shape, weight, color? Is the product as durable as other brands? Is the price right? Is the sales unit too large or too small? Are there potential new uses to which the product might be put?

D.   *Characteristics of the Market*

Possible items: (a) Present and/or potential customers — age, sex, occupation, income, marital status, size of families, social interests, recreational habits, reading habits, radio and television programs enjoyed, etc. (b) Characteristics of other manufacturers of the same or similar products — number, size, output, quality and price of product, relative efficiency; etc. (c) Characteristics of the market area itself — climate and topography; general economic characteristics; political conditions and attitudes of people, social characteristics of people, etc. (d) Nature of demand for product(s) of the firm: relative elasticity, etc.

Possible significance of items: (a) Is the manufacturer producing the type of product that will appeal to the kinds of persons who are his present and potential customers? In what magazines should he advertise, and what types of radio and television programs should he sponsor if he wishes to reach prospective customers? (b) How many other manufacturers of this or similar products are selling in this trade territory? What are the characteristics of

EXHIBIT 3-1 (*continued*)

their products? What percentage of the market do they have? Is the share of market of the firm under study increasing or decreasing? How do its prices compare with those of the other producers? How does it compare in efficiency with the other producers in the area? (c) What kinds of weather and seasons are experienced in the trade territory? How can these climatic data help a manufacturer to plan his production and shipment schedules to take advantage of seasonal changes and peaks or to determine the characteristics which his products should possess in order to best meet the needs of customers in the area? Is the area dominated by certain economic activities such as farming or manufacturing or trade? What are the political conditions of the area in regard to tax rates, efficiency of government, governmental regulations, attitudes of public toward role of government? What are the general philosophies of the people in regard to religious and other social matters? (d) What influence would price changes have on the volume of sales of the product(s) of the firm?

E.   *Marketing or Selling Channels and Techniques*

Possible items: (a) Type of sales organization within the firm — personnel, methods of compensation, number of salesmen, methods of control and supervision, relative degree of importance ascribed to selling by the management of the firm, etc. (b) Outside channels used — wholesalers, jobbers, retailers, direct-to-consumer, etc. (c) Advertising methods — degree of use of different media, expenditures for advertising, methods used for determining effectiveness, etc.

Possible significance of items: (a) Does the firm have a recognized sales division or person whose primary duty is to promote sales? Is the sales function adequately staffed with effective sales personnel? Are the salesmen satisfactorily trained? Is the method of compensation the best possible? Are efficient techniques used in supervising and promoting salesmen? (b) Are the most effective outside channels used? Are there any methods used to determine the relative performances of different available channels? (c) What are the advertising techniques and media used by the firm? Are the most effective media used? Is it possible that better results could be obtained by changing the media used? Does the firm have any way of finding out the relative effectiveness of the different media and methods used? Is the firm spending too much or too little on advertising or more or less on any medium than it should?

F.   *Financial Structure and Condition*

Possible items: Information shown on balance sheets and income statements; conditions indicated by various significant financial ratios, etc.

Possible significance of items: Is the firm in sound financial condition? Is it relying too heavily on borrowed funds? Is it using the best available sources of funds? Does it have adequate funds to carry out present and planned operations? What are its major items of revenue and costs? Are the pertinent financial ratios satisfactory?

G.   *Policies of Company*

Possible items: (a) Intended policies; (b) comparison of intended policies with actual practices; (c) degree of correctness of intended policies and actual practices.

EXHIBIT 3-1 (*continued*)

Possible significance of items: Does the firm have established policies in regard to the various matters under study? Exactly what are those policies? Do the responsible employees and executives know what the policies are? Do they agree that the policies are sound? Are actual operations in the firm in conformity with the intended policies? Are the policies the correct ones for the company to follow?

will be used. Intelligent insight and sound judgment are of importance in all the steps of research, but in none are they of more importance than in the establishment of reasonable hypotheses. If poor, illogical guesses as to causes or solutions are made, much useless investigation may take place, with the result that the data collected cannot answer the basic questions that should have been answered.

The more the researcher knows about the situation, the more likely it is that the hypotheses will be correct. Not only is wide knowledge about the particular situation under study of importance, but knowledge in various other fields often will also be of great value in the process of seeking possible causes or solutions for a problem.

To illustrate, consider the case of the bakery in a Southwestern city which found that its bread was not selling well in the Latin-American section of the city. In a research project that was undertaken, one of the hypotheses was based on knowledge of the fact that Latin-Americans are fond of lively colors. This hypothesis led through research to a satisfactory solution of the problem. The wrapper on the bread was changed, and the number of loaves sold increased 25 percent.

The process of setting up hypotheses is facilitated by writing down a list of possible causes or solutions. The least likely ones can then be marked out after a little reflection. Those remaining should be considered further. It will usually be worth-while to look back through the earlier checklists compiled and used in the process of analyzing the situation and defining the problem. Discussing the tentative hypotheses with other qualified persons may result in the elimination of some of the remaining items on the original list and possibly the addition of some new hypotheses. The continuation of the process of setting up and considering hypotheses should go on until sufficient consideration has occurred to assure the completion of a list of logical, intelligent hypotheses which constitute reasonable possibilities.

EXAMPLE OF ESTABLISHMENT OF HYPOTHESES

Suppose that Mr. Jones, the owner of a manufacturing firm, has been experiencing a steady increase in the percentage of his products which his customers are returning as unsatisfactory. He has carried his research through the first two steps discussed in this chapter. That is, he has become fully aware of the problem and has analyzed the situation. The result was that his problem has been accurately defined and the purpose of the research determined.

He is now ready to start to collect data to solve the difficulty. But first he must decide what facts are needed. He will find that before he can do this, it will be necessary to establish hypotheses as to possible causes and solutions of the condition. These hypotheses will determine the specific data needed. Without these carefully selected hypotheses, the search for data will be without the clear-cut direction necessary to the acquisition of pertinent information.

Mr. Jones, faced with the task of establishing several sound hypotheses as to the causes of his problem, will attempt to list all the possible causes of his problem that he can imagine as he thinks about his increase in rejects. He will look over the checklists he may have compiled to help him go through the first two steps. He will talk to other qualified persons in his plant and maybe to some of his business acquaintances.

The original list of tentative reasons for the increase in returned products may contain items covering the major areas or aspects of his business, that is, production facilities, product or service produced, methods of distribution of products or services, nature of the market, and policies of the company. Assume that further study of the list and conversations with his associates will eliminate as illogical, too farfetched, or obviously unimportant all of the hypotheses except those dealing with the product.

Let it be assumed, also, that Mr. Jones decides that the facts that must be obtained will be those necessary to substantiate or eliminate these specific hypotheses:

1. My product is less durable than formerly.
2. My product is being made from steel that is inferior to that used formerly.
3. My product is too heavy.
4. Inspection methods of customers have become more strict, and this is the cause of the increase in rejects.

The search for the data necessary to the solution of the problem can now be organized in such a manner as to obtain the required information.

A word of caution should be given here even at the risk of beng repetitious. The process of establishing hypotheses as to the causes of a problem is an extremely important step in research procedure. If for any reason, certain hypotheses are overlooked, they may constitute the very questions that must be answered if a satisfactory solution is to be reached. It cannot be overly emphasized that the search for possible causes of or reasons for a problem must be comprehensive enough to avoid overlooking any conceivably pertinent hypothesis. The person who must obtain the completely correct answers to his problem must realize the great importance of having the knowledge and the courage needed to ask all the essential questions. In the case of Mr. Jones, it was assumed that he knew enough about his firm to be able to look into all of its major areas and that he also had the courage to ask whether his product was as good a it should be.

STATISTICAL HYPOTHESES

Many hypotheses are qualitative in nature since they do not lend themselves to numerical measurement. For example, the attitudes of employees may not be measurable quantitatively. Rating charts are in common usage by government and by large corporations by which supervisors rate employees as to attitude, performance, promptness, and other characteristics using letter grades or simply written sentences. On the other hand, of course, there are aptitude tests which are given to employees which are quantitatively measurable. Nevertheless, many hypotheses in business research are found to be qualitative; and even their solutions may be made only as a result of value judgments concerning courses of action to be taken or decisions to be made.

Statistical hypotheses, however, are quantitative in nature in that they are numerically measurable. Statistics is a system of analysis of numerical information; therefore, it is fundamentally quantitative. Its hypotheses are, therefore, also quantitative.

An example of a statistical hypothesis may be seen in the example in preceding paragraphs in which Mr. Jones posed the hypothesis that his product was less durable than formerly. Providing that the product had been subject to quality-control procedures—which themselves are statistical in nature—the product produced some time ago and possibly still carried in inventory could be subjected to comparative tests with currently produced products. These tests could be used as a basis of determining definitively if the hypothesis should be accepted or rejected. The statistical test involved in this case would have been called a *test of significance* in which the significance of the difference in the two batches of product would have been accepted or rejected at a given level of probability. The same kind of test could be applied to the second hypothesis of Mr. Jones, that is, that his product was now being made from steel inferior to that used formerly. A statistical test of two batches produced at two different periods of time could establish whether or not a significant difference in the two batches occurred, and thus the hypothesis will either be accepted or rejected.

Tests of significance and other types of statistical analysis will receive detailed attention in the latter part of this book and, therefore, will not be discussed in detail at this point. However, the nature of the statistical hypothesis itself can be given some attention. The statistical hypothesis is normally stated as a *null* hypothesis. For example, the hypothesis may be stated: The difference between the two means is zero. This hypothesis is capable of definitive testing. By contrast, consider the hypothesis: The difference between these two means is *something*. This latter hypothesis is incapable of definitive discussion or testing. It is a positive statement while the former statement is a negative or null statement. The reason for the null hypothesis in statistical analysis is, therefore, to make a statement which is capable of definitive testing.

Another point concerning the statistical hypothesis concerns the acceptance or rejection of the hypothesis. These two terms—acceptance or rejection—are used in preference to *proof* or *disproof*. Modern philosophers will maintain that hypotheses cannot be proved in a strict sense since while case after case that is tested may give an affirmative result, there may be one final case untested which would give an unfavorable result. The unfavorable result would disprove forever all of the preceding findings. Therefore, a given hypothesis may give an affirmative result in 100 cases. But in the 101st case a negative result might occur, and this 101st negative result would void all of the preceding affirmative results. Thus, the statistician not only employs the null term in the hypothesis to achieve a definitive test, but, also employs the result of the definitive test in terms of an *acceptance* or a *rejection* of the hypothesis that has been posed.

A CHECKLIST FOR EVALUATING HYPOTHESES

By way of summary, it can be said that if the following questions can be satisfactorily answered about a given list of hypotheses, then the hypotheses can be considered reasonably logical and valid as guides for continuing the research process:

1. Have all the pertinent areas or aspects of the situation been considered in the process of setting up these hypotheses?
2. Do the hypotheses include all the pertinent possibilities as to causes?
3. Have the hypotheses been selected on the basis of their constituting actual possibilities as to causes or reasons?
4. Have the hypotheses been selected without fear or bias in regard to the possibility that they may be substantiated or not substantiated?
5. In general, have the hypotheses been selected under conditions that allowed the researcher to set up all hypotheses that were considered to have real bearing on the problem?

DATA AND ANALYSIS PLANNING

When the problem has been accurately defined and hypotheses as to the possible causes or solutions have been established, the researcher is ready to begin compiling a written list of the specific information necessary to substantiate or reject the hypotheses. The exact data that will be sought must be decided on in the light of the problem as defined and the hypotheses or questions that it has been carefully determined must be tested and answered if the difficulty is to be remedied.

All information that could be pertinent to the project should be considered. At the same time, the prospective information must be evaluated on the basis of its possible value in the solution of the problem as defined. Only the data that are of real value to the solution should be left on the list of the data to be sought when the collection procedure begins. It sometimes happens that much data of some value will have to be left off the list even though the information would be interesting and perhaps, at an indefinite future time, might be of considerable usefulness.

The kind of analysis to which the data are to be subjected in testing the hypotheses must be related to both the methods of collection of the data and to the hypotheses themselves. The analysis, while usually statistical in nature, may be qualitative, involving value judgments and the experience of the analyst rather than the numerical analysis of quantitative variables. In either case, whether the hypotheses have been stated in qualitative or quantitative terms, the methods of analysis must be considered in the light of the definition of the problem, the hypotheses that have been formed, the plans for data collection, and the nature of the data themselves.

DATA COLLECTION PLANS

The items on the list of data to be collected should all be evaluated in terms of the tests represented by such questions as these:

1. Will this information be of sufficient value in the solution of the problem to warrant the cost in time, effort, and money of obtaining it?
2. Will this information be sufficiently accurate if it is obtained?
3. Will this information be as valuable as other information that could be obtained in its place?
4. Is it reasonably certain that this information can be obtained?
5. Can this information be collected within the time period that it must be if it is to be used?
6. Can the data be tabulated or classified meaningfully after they are collected?
7. Does the researcher have or can get the qualified personnel and the facilities necessary for the collection of this information?
8. Is this information all that will be required for the solution of the problem?

If all of these questions can be answered in the affirmative, it is reasonably certain that the information listed is that which is actually necessary. There may be useful data that are available, but to collect them might require more money than the researcher has to spend on the project. In addition, the time that would be required to collect the data might be so great that the pending managerial decision would have to be delayed too long if it were to be held up until the facts were reported. Under such circumstances, the acquisition of the information in question would not be considered feasible.

It often happens that important information may be completely unavailable. Less satisfactory data, consequently, will have to be relied on instead, merely because the most important facts cannot be secured. A few years ago, a study was made of changes in the volume of sales in different types of retail stores during a certain five-week period. The researcher could not obtain figures on the dollar volume of sales in each store, although it was possible to get the figures from each store manager in regard to the percentage of change in sales that occurred during the period. The managers also were willing to report the number of employees in the stores. It was decided that since the more accurate dollar volume figures were unavailable, the less accurate but available data on number of employees in each store would be collected for the purpose of weighting the percentage changes in sales in the different types and sizes of stores. The availability of data, then, determined the kind of information that was collected. The availability factor also influenced the collection technique used.

A careful listing of the information needed to solve the problem under study sometimes goes a long way toward determining whether the research project can be undertaken successfully with the personnel and facilities available in the firm. If not, outside research specialists may have to be brought in, at least for part of the project. For example, the manager of a retail store may, after thorough analysis of the situation, come to the decision that he needs information about the nature of his market area that he is unable to obtain himself. He could decide to call on a research organization with the experienced personnel and facilities required to conduct such a survey.

The research methods to be used are largely dependent on the nature of the information needed. If it is established that the opinions of several hundred homemakers must be obtained, this will probably call for some sort of survey in which the information will be obtained by personal interviews or telephone inquiries or perhaps questionnaires sent out through the mail. In later chapters, there will be considerable discussion of the most appropriate data-collecting techniques for obtaining different types of information. It will also be shown how important it is to know exactly what information is desired before the process of obtaining the data is decided on and put into operation.

In certain instances, information may be collected, but it will be found that for some reason, it is impossible to tabulate and classify it in a form to enable it to be studied sufficiently to reach meaningful conclusions about it. An example could be a survey of opinions of persons that resulted in the collection of answers that were so varied or so vaguely stated that classifying and tabulating them was not practicable. Such data would have little real value.

A whole research project may be a failure if certain data are overlooked. An illustration is the case of the firm that had a research study made to determine the feasibility of establishing a factory in a West Coast city. Many significant data were collected, but information about the availability of labor was omitted. The board of directors of the firm, therefore, was unable to reach a decision because of this oversight in the planning of the research project.

The following outline shows the major types of information-gathering procedures and sources discussed in this and several of the following chapters.

1. Searching for data in published information
   a. In libraries: public, educational institutions, private
   b. Outside of regular libraries: private persons, business firms, others
2. Searching for data in unpublished information and records
   a. Company records
   b. Government agency records
   c. Private individual and other records

3. Observation
   a. By personal senses: sight, sound, odor, taste, touch
   b. By mechanical means: yardstick, camera, scales, thermometer, counter, etc.
   c. Combinations of (a) and (b)
4. Experimentation
   a. In a laboratory
   b. Controlled field projects
   c. Combinations of (a) and (b)
5. Interviewing and other survey techniques
   a. Mail questionnaires
   b. Personal interviews
   c. Telephone inquiries
   d. Motivational research
   e. The panel

The reader should remember that more than one of these methods may be used in a given research project. The nature of the project will determine which method or combination of methods will be needed. It should also be mentioned that some of these procedures may overlap in certain cases.

Each of these items will now be described briefly. Detailed discussion will be reserved for later chapters.

(1) **Searching for data in published information.** Systematic study in libraries is one of the methods of gathering information that will often result in helping to gain background data as well as to bring out the pertinent experiences of other persons or firms with the kind of problem under consideration.

Published materials are numerous, however, and a busy manager may have difficulty in finding the time to locate and read the printed matter that will be of greatest value to him. Libraries usually contain far more books, magazines, newspapers, and pamphlets on most subjects than can be read by any one person. A wide variety of significant information is available and can be used by researchers as sources of data. The investigator must be careful not to overlook the pertinent published facts that are already in existence and which, therefore, should not have to be collected again by expensive and time-consuming original research.

An increasing proportion of firms, individuals, businesspeople, and organizations of businesses and professional persons possess carefully selected books, magazines, and other types of printed materials. Some of the collections have been so carefully planned and filed by the owners that they can correctly be called libraries. When problems arise in the firm, often much helpful information can be located quickly in these private collections of publications.

(2) **Searching for data in unpublished information and records.** Most organizations today keep records which will contain information that can usually be of value in the study of problems in those establishments. Such records should be kept in mind as a source of information. A rather common practice of management, nevertheless, is to make only minimum use of such data. For example, records required for tax and other govern-

mental reporting and for creditors of various types are often used for those purposes alone. Many of these records could serve as sources of information for other purposes as well. The amount and kind of records kept will depend on the size and type of firm and on the manager's knowledge about and use of such records.

Among the various records of one kind or another that can be found in a business are those pertaining to accounting, personnel, production, purchasing, inventory, marketing, and sales. If the records are accurate and reasonably complete, a researcher who knows the importance of such information to the situation being studied can, therefore, often find a considerable amount of pertinent facts in the files of a business.

Certain kinds of information can be found most completely and accurately presented in the official records kept in the offices of federal, state, and local government agencies. Building activity in a city, for example, will be shown in the files of the department in charge of issuing building permits. A large number of other data will be found sometimes only in government records. Government records, therefore, should not be forgotten when the researcher is considering data-collecting methods and sources of information to be used.

In some instances, the private papers, records, or letters of a person may be a source of pertinent information in a study. If, for example, a certain important person may have been a proficient record keeper and letter writer, files containing these records, when available, may contain much of value.

(3) **Observation.** Certain types of information can best be collected by systematic observations made by persons who use appropriate techniques. Effective observation requires that the investigator know exactly what he is looking for, how he is to recognize it, and how to record his findings. If these conditions are met, personal observations can often constitute a method of data collection that is effective.

It will be found in many instances that mechanical devices can obtain measurements more accurately and rapidly than would be possible by the use of the personal senses. A mechanical means of observing and recording also may be less expensive than personal observation, although this is not always the case. The person who is in charge of collecting data by observation may decide to use a combination of personal and mechanical means.

Suppose that it was desired to observe the effects of music played in a factory for the benefit of the employees. Mechanical devices might be used to measure such results as changes in volume of output of workers, strength of goods being produced, or even constancy of color in, say, a cloth material that was being turned out. Personal observations might be used to collect information about whether employees seem happy or disturbed during the period of the project.

(4) **Experimentation.** It is possible in some instances to create certain desired conditions in a laboratory in order that these conditions may be studied and tested before they are put into operation on the large, expensive scale that would be necessary in actual use in a business. Laboratory experimentation under appropriate circumstances can be a quicker, less costly way of collecting accurate data than any other practicable method.

Consequently, whenever laboratory experimentation is feasible, it should be seriously considered as a method of obtaining required information.

If certain parts of a process or surrounding conditions can be controlled, sometimes a quite effective method can be set up for collecting data from actual operations in the business world. For example, suppose that the proprietor of a beauty shop wished to determine whether she should keep the shop open on Thursday evenings until 9:00 instead of closing at the regular hour of 6:00. She could decide to conduct an experiment in which she would keep the shop open for two Thursdays in successive weeks and then close at 6:00 the following two Thursday evenings. Everything else about her shop and services would be kept unchanged. She would then observe and record any customer reactions in the form of favorable or unfavorable comments. She would also compare the number of customers in the weeks in which the shop closed at 6:00 P.M. to those in the weeks the shop closed at 9:00 P.M. on Thursdays. This constitutes a somewhat overly simplified controlled field experiment, but it does illustrate the process. In actual practice, the experiment probably would be continued for more than just two periods of two weeks each.

A combination of laboratory and controlled field experimentation will be advisable in some cases. Suppose that the manager of a factory that makes golf clubs wants to know why his sales of clubs have declined in the last year. He could put his clubs and other comparable brands through certain laboratory tests to determine their performance qualities. At the same time, he might set up a controlled field experiment in which he would ask a representative group of golfers to use his clubs along with other brands in actual golf games. The golfers would then be asked to report their experiences with the clubs and their opinions about the relative merits of the clubs used. The reports could supply significant comparative data. The combined use of both laboratory and controlled field experiments can often give more valid results than the use of either type of experiment by itself.

(5) **Interviewing and other survey techniques.** The researcher will find that certain kinds of information can be obtained only by direct conversation with the types of persons who will have the desired information. This means that direct personal interviews will be required. In most such surveys, the questions to be asked will have to be prepared carefully and probably duplicated on questionnaires. When properly constructed, such questionnaires can be an effective device for securing information.

When the use of the mail can bring reasonably acceptable results, mail questionnaires may be the best method of obtaining information from a representative group in which the investigator is interested. Mail questionnaires are more economical than personal interviews.

The telephone can be a quick and effective device for collecting information if used in appropriate situations. If only a small amount of data is needed from each respondent, telephone inquiries may be the best technique for securing information.

Motivational research attempts to learn actual reasons, the underlying causes, for human behavior. Both direct and indirect questions are asked, discussions ensue, and the interviewer, usually a psychologist, interprets the results. Motivational research is expensive, but has been applied, particularly in market research.

The panel technique involves obtaining a representative group of persons to agree to supply periodically certain information about their actions over a period of time. The panel in practice has usually been composed of families that are asked to send in weekly reports about types of products purchased. These "diaries" can be used to compile various kinds of information about consumer preferences and practices.

✓PLANS FOR ANALYSIS OF DATA

The following outline shows the major types of statistical analysis that will be discussed in this and several of the following chapters in this book.

1. Classifications and cross-classifications
    a. Classifying data
    b. Chi-square tests
    c. Statistical distributions
2. Inference analysis
    a. Averages and dispersions
    b. Inferences for means
    c. Inferences for percentages
    d. Analysis of variance
3. Sampling procedures
    a. Adequacy and representativeness
    b. Sampling techniques
4. Correlation and regression
    a. Linear correlation, with addendum on multiple correlation
    b. Regression and prediction
5. Trend analysis
    a. Prediction over time
    b. Leads and lags

It would appear that these classifications of analytical techniques are all quantitative in nature. However, it should be remembered that even when qualitative hypotheses are involved and, therefore, qualitative data have been gathered and are being considered by a researcher, the researcher will normally place such qualitative information in some kinds of classifications. He may cross-classify such information to yield new facts. He may place such information in tables. For example, in a study of attitudes of employees by a personnel department in which ratings by letter grades A, B, C, D, E and F are included, the ratings may be counted, then classified and cross-classified into whatever classifications the researcher desires. Thus, these cross-classifications may be able to yield new facts. The researcher would be expected to place the results of his counting of such qualitative measurements in tables for summarization purposes and for purposes of writing his final report and recommendations.

Obviously, these classifications of analytical techniques are not mutually exclusive. Several of them may be combined in one research project. For example, classification of the data into various subcategories may be necessary as a prelude to computing percentages, and this may act as a prelude to computing averages and dispersions. Further, if the study is a sampling study, inferences may then be made to the universe of data from the evidence of the sample as analyzed.

(1) **Classifications and cross-classifications.** In any particular research project, a number of classifications of data may be derived from the original information collected. For example, in a questionnaire survey, if there are twenty questions on the questionnaire, there may be yielded as many as fifteen to twenty classifications; therefore, each subject would be listed under each of the fifteen or twenty. Some of these classifications, when they are related to each other, for example, by income level or by age group or by some other *leveling* factor, may require cross-classification to bring out further relationships.

Classifications may be reduced to percentages of the total by dividing each subgroup by the total of the group, thus yielding percentage distributions. Percentage distributions often show a picture of the relationships of the items in a classification not yielded by looking at the raw data. Percentages are sometimes cumulated either from top to bottom or from bottom to top, thus yielding the heaviest groups at one end or the other or enabling the researcher to pick out the point in the classification which breaks the distribution into halves and thus enables him to locate the *median*.

A test that is often used in statistical analysis to compare an *observed* distribution to a *theoretical* distribution, the latter constructed on some rational basis, is called a *chi-square test*. The chi-square test is a test of significance since it rates the significance of the difference between two distributions. For example, assume that a self-study by the operating employees of a given department of a company in respect to their productivity is undertaken. The validity of the findings could be verified by testing a distribution of grades assigned to themselves by the employees with a distribution of grades assigned to those same employees by their supervisors. In this case, the distribution of grades assigned by the supervisors of the employees would be considered the theoretical distribution against which the observed distribution would be tested. The chi-square test would give a definitive answer to the question as to whether the two distributions differ significantly, thus testing the findings of the employees' self-rating study.

(2) **Inference analysis.** Inference analysis involves determining the characteristics of a universe from the evidence of a sample. The universe is delimited, of course, by the bounds of the problem being investigated. The universe of data may be too large for the investigator to cover in a 100 percent study. It may take too long to study, or it may be too costly to study. Sampling techniques will permit gathering the data in the form of a sample which, collected at random, will yield a miniature picture of the universe. When this sample is analyzed, it yields estimates of the characteristics of the universe; thus, inferences about the universe can be made from the evidence of the sample.

The most common measurement involved in inference analysis is the *arithmetic mean*, called simply the *average* by the layman. The average, of course, is usually accompanied by a measure of dispersion; and the usual measure of dispersion is the standard deviation. Both of these measures, as well as others involved in the classifications discussed, will receive detailed attention in following chapters. Inferences of proportions in a universe are of importance. Averages and proportions are probably the most usual characteristics studied in a universe by analyzing a sample of that universe.

The analysis of variance tests the significance of the difference among the means of a number of samples simultaneously. It may be used when two, three, four, or more samples have been collected or subgroups or treatments have been given in an experiment, and it is desired to learn if the samples, the groups, or the treatments differ from each other. For example, it would furnish a definitive test of the question as to whether the commissions earned by the insurance agents in five different field offices are alike or differ significantly.

(3) **Sampling procedures.** In all cases where inference from a sample to a universe is involved, the nature of the sample must receive attention. The sample must be selected in such a manner that it is representative of the universe, and it must be of a size adequate to represent the universe. Thus, both the data-collection method of the sample and the specific size of the sample must be given careful thought.

(4) **Correlation and regression.** Correlation deals with the association of variables. Later in this book, simple correlation is presented involving two variables whose association could be described mathematically by a straight line. This straight line describing the association is called a *regression line*.

Where a high degree of correlation is discovered, represented by a high correlation coefficient approaching plus or minus one, then, if it is known that one variable causes the other to react, the dependent variable may be predicted on the basis of known facts about the independent variable. This prediction is accomplished by extending, in effect, the regression line. Thus, correlation and regression are closely associated in statistical analysis.

(5) **Trend analysis.** Trend analysis is one of the most important aspects of the analysis of time series of data. It deals with the analysis of time-series data over long periods, usually several years. Its general nature consists of fitting curves to data over past time periods, then projecting the curve which fits the data best into the future and thus enabling predictions and forecasts to be made. This is a common and standard technique for forecasting for inventory purposes, for expansion or contraction of the firm's activities, for capital acquirement, for personnel acquirement and training, and for many other important purposes in the business firm.

Trend analysis may also involve testing for leads and lags as between or among several time series of data. If it can be established that a given time series occurs at a regular interval before a second time series, then the second series of data can be predicted from the first. Such leads and lags are studied in respect to economic barometers or indicators, some of which are published by the federal government.

LEVELS OF DATA MEASUREMENT

There are four levels of data measurement: nominal, ordinal, interval, and ratio. The level of data measurement affects, and is affected by, the kind of analysis called for.

Nominal

This level of measurement is illustrated in exhibit 3-2, which shows a cross-classification. The categories are mutually exclusive and possess no order, i.e., the order of the categories is meaningless. Nominally scaled data are analyzed by nonparametric methods—methods which make no assumptions as to the universe from which the sample came—and are also called *distribution-free*.

Probably the most notable analysis employed with nominal data is chi-square analysis, a nonparametric technique. The chi-square test of independence of classifications is applied to the data of exhibit 3-2 in chapter 8.

EXHIBIT 3-2
Characteristics of the Population
14 Years and Over — South Phoenix, Arizona

	Male	Female	Total
"Anglo"	2,900	3,100	6,000
Mexican-American	4,300	5,000	9,300
Non white	4,000	4,900	8,900
All classes	11,200	13,000	24,200

Source: "An Estimate of the Cost of Unemployment in an Area of Phoenix," *Arizona Business Bulletin,* February, 1968, Vol. XV, No. 2, p. 27 (Bureau of Business Research and Services, College of Business Administration, Arizona State University, Tempe, Arizona), original data from unpublished tabulations of Bureau of Labor Statistics on file with Arizona State Employment Service.

Ordinal

Ordinally scaled data are illustrated in exhibit 3-3. The order of the classes is of significance, but the distances between the ordered classes are not equal: an F is not precisely the same distance below E as B, for example, is below A. This example is used in a chi-square test of homogeneity in exhibit 8-6.

EXHIBIT 3-3
Self-Ratings by Secretaries

X Grades	f Number of Ratings
A	27
B	40
C	68
D	32
E	12
F	6

Source: Secretarial Self-Study, June 1977.

Nonparametric tests are proper for analyzing ordinal data. Ranked data are ordinal. Spearman's coefficient of rank correlation *rho* is applied to such ranked data in exhibit 11-4. However, sometimes the median, a parametric measure of central tendency, is used with ordinal data, since it is simply the middle value in an ordered series. The arithmetic mean or other parametric measures should not be applied to ordinal data because the resulting statistics may be biased by the unequal distances between categories.

The ordinal scale includes the nominal characteristic of mutually exclusive categories, but is a *higher level* because order is required in the classification.

Interval

The interval scale includes the mutually exclusive categories of nominal data and the requirement of order of ordinal data, and adds equality of the distances separating the ordered categories. It is, thus, a higher level than the ordinal scale. Exhibit 3-4 illustrates interval data.

EXHIBIT 3-4
Frequency Distribution of Average Orders of Salespersons
in the Southwestern District

X Average Daily Orders	f Number of Salespersons
10 to 19	8
20 to 29	22
30 to 39	13
40 to 49	7

Source: Sales Summary, June 1977.

All statistical tests, parametric and nonparametric, are applicable to interval-scaled data. The assumption of a normal distribution of observations in the universe is often made, making possible analyses by parametric techniques: inferences for the arithmetic mean, standard deviation, correlation, regression, and trend analysis. Nonparametric techniques, such as, chi-square tests and rank correlation, are also proper.

The arithmetic mean and the standard deviation are computed from the data in exhibit 3-4 in exhibit 9-2.

Ratio

The *highest level* of data measurement is the ratio scale. It includes the characteristics of nominal, ordinal, and interval: mutually exclusive categories in equidistant orders. In addition, it possesses a true zero point; for example, scales in ounces, pounds, other weights, or mass have a true zero. The ratios of the measurements of two objects on two scales are the same; therefore, transformations of the data are possible.

The *geometric mean* is an example of a parametric measure properly used for ratio data. Ratio charts, also called *semilog charts*, and *geometric line charts*, have data plotted on a ratio scale. Such charts are shown in exhibits 12-11 and 12-12.

Although all arithmetic operations are applicable to ratio-scaled data, the occurrence of such measurements is rare in business and economic data.

SOURCES OF DATA

The sources of data may be classified as (1) primary, and (2) secondary. These are the usual classifications. A *primary* source is often defined as a publication that contains the first material on the subject that is put into print. For example, the volumes published by the U.S. Government Printing Office that are the official U.S. Bureau of the Census volumes can be called primary sources as the term is used here. After these census data have been published in these final volumes (or in the earlier preliminary pamphlets that are usually issued), various authors will write about these census data in books, magazines, and newspapers. These latter publications constitute *secondary* sources.

It should be pointed out that in general usage, *primary* and *secondary* when applied to sources of information may have a somewhat different meaning than that given in the preceding paragraph. Primary material may refer to the first recording of the information involved. For example, original accounting and other records of a firm, longhand notes written by an investigator, and completed schedules or questionnaires would be called primary sources. Secondary sources would refer to any copied or printed matter based upon or taken from the primary source.

The significance to researchers of the distinction between primary and secondary sources lies in the fact that a primary source is likely to contain more complete and accurate data than may be found in a secondary source. The reason for this is that the primary source contains all the original data in unaltered form. The secondary source may contain only part of the original data, and what is included may have been selected to convey a special meaning. It is also possible that the writer of the secondary source material may have misinterpreted the data in the primary source. Researchers, therefore, should strive to get data or information from primary sources instead of secondary whenever it is feasible to do so.

The discussion of the sources of data that follows will classify data as (1) published information, (2) unpublished records, and (3) originally collected data.

PUBLISHED INFORMATION

A preliminary activity to a research project may be a search of the existing literature regarding the subject matter. At times, a massive amount of literature is encountered, enough to preclude completion of the task. In such a case, an automatic information retrieval system could be of great help. At times, the search of the literature will reveal that the subject matter has already been adequately—even profusely—investigated. Sometimes the search indicates that a primary research project must be undertaken; perhaps the basic numerical data on which to construct the project have never been gathered. Occasionally facts or inferences uncovered in the literature will have the effect of changing the nature or the direction of the planned research.

A search of the literature naturally begins in a library—often in a university library, although sometimes a public library or specialized library may be used. The library holds the information sought in an investigation of the literature. The investigation may be for the purpose of summarizing what is known of a given subject matter, or perhaps of making new inferences about the subject matter. The investigation may be for the purpose of locating data—usually numerical—to be subjected to analysis in an effort to expand knowledge.

The library is truly a storehouse of knowledge, but its functions go far beyond this fundamental description. The library exercises selection in building the most useful collection of published works within its capabilities. It classifies materials as to subject, title, and author, called *cataloging*. It circulates publications and maintains an effective recording system. The library gives *reference service*, answering questions, furnishing bibliographies, and even making special studies of topics when requested.

BOOKS

The oldest classification system in use by libraries in the United States is the *Dewey decimal classification*. It is still widely used. The main classifications are as follows:

000	Generalities
100	Philosophy and related disciplines
200	Religion
300	The social sciences
400	Language
500	Pure sciences
600	Technology (applied sciences)
700	The arts
800	Literature and rhetoric
900	General geography, history, etc.

Each of the main classifications is subdivided. The subdivisions are carried out, using decimals, to find enough gradations to identify any given book. The most useful general classifications for research in economics and business are the "300 The social sciences" and the "600 Technology (applied sciences)." All of the books under a given classification are located together in the library, thereby facilitating investigation. The *call number* of a given book is listed in three locations called *card catalogs*.

The three card catalogs are the subject catalog, the title catalog, and the author catalog. Thus, knowing any of the three facts makes it possible to locate the book.

The *Library of Congress classification* is another system used by many libraries in the United States, including, of course, the Library of Congress. This system is growing in use, particularly in university libraries. The main classifications are as follows:

A	General works—Polygraphy	M	Music
B	Philosophy—Religion	N	Fine arts
C	History—Auxiliary sciences	P	Language and literature
D	History and topography	Q	Science
E-F	America	R	Medicine
G	Geography—Anthropology	S	Agriculture—Plant and
H	Social sciences		animal industry
I	Economics—Sociology	T	Technology
J	Political science	U	Military science
K	Law	V	Naval science
L	Education	Z	Bibliography and library
			science

The Library of Congress system contains more than twice as many basic classifications as the Dewey system and uses letters rather than numbers. Its possibilities for expansion are much greater. This classification system is used in some very large libraries, including many university libraries, in the United States. The classifications "H Social sciences" and "I Economics—Sociology," are most useful for research in business and economics.

The card catalog of a library will contain records of all books held in the library; however, the researcher may desire to search out all books in print regarding the subject matter. The *Cumulative Book Index* is a record listing by author, title, and subject of all books published in the English language since 1928. A monthly supplement keeps it current. Before 1928, this record bears the name *The United States Catalog*. Another publication, *Publishers' Weekly* is a trade journal of the publishing industry which lists all books as they are released and, also, contains information about pamphlets and other paperbacks.

Books not in a given library may be obtained on *interlibrary loan* from a library that has them. This reciprocal procedure is practiced by libraries in the United States and makes it possible to secure practically any book in print for the price of the postage involved.

PERIODICALS

Libraries maintain a *periodical index*, which is a card catalog listing the periodicals by name that are held by the library. Such a catalog is useful for locating a given periodical, but the articles within a periodical which are of interest to the researcher must usually be found by referring to one of the bibliographical publications. *The Industrial Arts Index* (before 1958) lists articles in the fields of business and economics, among others, by title, which in the case of articles is usually nearly equivalent to a subject index.

The reference will give the name, volume, issue, and date of the periodical in which the article appears as well as the author's name. In 1958, *The Industrial Arts Index* was split into two bibliographies: *Business Periodicals Index* and *Applied Science and Technology Index*.

The *Readers' Guide to Periodical Literature* is a general bibliography, listing articles by both subject and author. The *International Index*, named the *International Index to Periodicals* before 1955, lists articles by subject and author, including foreign as well as United States periodicals, but is useful chiefly in the humanities and the sciences.

There is a large number of important periodicals in business and economics. These may be general in nature, like *Business Week* and *Fortune*, or concentrated in a given field as in personnel, accounting, marketing, economics, or insurance. The researcher investigating the literature pertinent to his project should examine the specific periodicals relating to the subject matter as well as consult the bibliographies.

OTHER PUBLICATIONS

Much information may be obtained from reports, pamphlets, monographs, and other materials published in other than book and periodical form. Such miscellaneous materials are produced by trade associations, quasi-governmental agencies, and research organizations of various kinds. The *Vertical File Index* is a bibliographical aid which catalogs pamphlet materials by subject matter, giving reference to their nature and location. Another bibliography, the *Bulletin of the Public Affairs Information Service*, lists chiefly economic and public affairs materials.

For governmental publications, the principal bibliographical reference work is the *Monthly Catalog of U.S. Government Publications*. This bibliography lists all publications of the federal government. The proceedings of the U.S. Congress are published in the *Congressional Record*. Information published by state governmental authorities will be classified somewhat differently as among different states. All of the states, however, make the hearings and other proceedings of the governmental units available to the public.

Some private firms have libraries for the use of their staff. In certain instances, these libraries may be used by outsiders under appropriate circumstances. Bureaus of business research in universities often publish research reports as well as issue current periodical publications that contain data of use to businesspersons. These bureaus may also be able to supply information in reply to requests for data on subject matter that may have been collected and filed for such informational services.

Chambers of commerce or similar oganizations in many cities have libraries that may contain information of definite value to businesspersons. A number of chambers now serve as depositories for a considerable quantity of U.S. Department of Commerce publications of assistance to small business. Two sets of such reports that may be particularly useful to smaller businesspersons should be mentioned. The "Establishing and Operating Series" of pamphlets offers much valuable advice on how to set up and operate various kinds of smaller businesses. "U.S. Government Research Reports" briefly describes thousands of scientific and technical research projects that have been financed by governmental expenditures of over $2 billion yearly. In addition, the nearest field office of the U.S. Department of Commerce will have hundreds of pamphlets and booklets on a great variety of problems faced by business and industry. These may be obtained at reasonable prices by mail.

Government departments and agencies at all levels from school districts up through cities, counties, states, and the federal government publish reports. Some of these are special reports, but many are the official annual or biannual reports of agencies or departments. The U.S. Government Printing Office is the central publishing office for nearly all federal documents, including the business, agriculture, and population censuses. The Superintendent of Documents, Washington, D.C. 20402, is the place to write when ordering publications of the federal government. Lists of available publications in various subject matter fields may be obtained by interested persons.

Trade associations frequently publish trade journals and reports of research of particular interest to members. There is also a considerable number of publishing firms which specialize in trade periodicals in one or more fields. Every businessperson should be acquainted with the trade journals as well as the professional journals in his field of interest.

EVALUATION OF PUBLISHED INFORMATION

One of the major problems of the reader searching for accurate information is to decide which of the innumerable books, pamphlets, and magazine articles are most authentic and of high enough quality to make them worth-while sources of information to be used in a research project.

The following is an outline of some of the major aspects of the problem of evaluating published material.

1. Nature of publication
   a. Popular
   b. Semipopular
   c. Trade journal
   d. Semiprofessional
   e. Professional
2. Type of persons on board of editors
   a. Specialists in choosing material of interest to general readers rather than technical or professional groups
   b. Professional persons or technical experts in subject matter included in publication
3. Publisher or sponsor of publication
   a. Commercial companies specializing in publications of various kinds
   b. Trade associations and other specialized organizations
   c. Professional associations
   d. Publishers specializing in promoting certain viewpoints

4. Author
   a. Other writings (publications)
   b. Occupational and economic connections (at time of writing)
   c. Educational or other qualifications (experience, etc.)
   d. Memberships in professional organizations
   e. Listings in pertinent directories and Who's Who's, etc.
5. Characteristics of the writing
   a. Contents
   b. Actual purpose
   c. Choice of words
   d. Reasoning used
   e. Documentation
   f. Date of writing

Discussion of the points in the preceding outline will be sufficient to show the significance of the five main headings.

(1) **Nature of publication.** If the reason for reading a publication is to gain accurate, reliable information, the professional publication would nearly always be preferable. The exact nature of the publication can be determined usually by turning to the pages in the front that provide such information as that given in the next two headings in this outline.

(2) **Type of persons on board of editors.** A board of editors composed of recognized authorities in their profession can serve as an invaluable screening group for manuscripts before they are accepted for publication. It can ordinarily be expected that the evaluation, editorial advice, and selective functions performed by such a board will result in the final publication of accurate and significant material in the books or magazines involved.

(3) **Publisher or sponsor of publication.** In addition to regular commercial publishing firms, trade associations and other types of business organizations often sponsor or publish directly authentic material that has been carefully collected, written, and edited to serve the needs of members of the sponsoring groups. Various organizations of professional persons have official publications of their associations. These professional journals contain articles that may have great value for researchers because the manuscripts have been carefully selected by qualified members of the professions.

(4) **Author.** Has the author written other articles or books? If he has, they may be helpful in evaluating the writer. The occupational and economic connections of an author at the time of writing, if known to a reader, can indicate the possible interests and probable prejudices that may have influenced the writer. The education and college degrees of an author serve as a partial guide to his qualifications. The amount and nature of experience he has had in the field about which he is writing is important.

A writer who is discussing a subject dealing with a profession will probably be a member of one or more associations in that profession. Many of the experts in the various fields of human activity today will be listed in one or more directories of persons who are considered as accepted practitioners in their area of specialization. There are directories or Who's Who's for each of the various fields of activity. Most of the leading professional associations also publish directories which list their members and provide pertinent information about them.

The task of looking into the qualifications of an author may seem quite formidable. It can be; but, in the typical checkup, usually most of the items mentioned in the preceding paragraphs can be found in a library. A search through the author card catalog will usually show whether the writer has written other books. Most of the questions raised in the other items about the author can be satisfactorily answered in the pertinent directories or Who's Who's. Some books and journals give significant data about the authors of the material in each issue.

(5) **Characteristics of the writing.** The contents or subject matter of the writing itself obviously would have to pertinent to the needs of the reader. The stated purpose of the author is an important characteristic of a publication. When the actual purpose differs from the stated purpose, as is the case sometimes, the reader may be misled. It is often impossible to determine accurately whether the stated or apparent purpose is the same as the actual purpose. If the purpose is to inform the reader accurately of all facts, that is one thing. On the other hand, if the real purpose is to present only certain data supporting one viewpoint, that places a different light on the material.

Most writers and speakers indicate their attitudes and knowledge about a subject by the statements they make and the words they use. The qualified author who is striving to present an accurate discussion will avoid statements which are too general or inclusive. Necessary qualifications will be included in the interests of making the statements correct. Oversimplifications are tempting at times, but they can be dangerous. Adjectives will be used sparingly by the writer who is presenting a factual, balanced discussion. If accurate statistical data are available, they will be cited instead of using only vague references such a "many," "a great number," "small," or "majority." The clearest and most exact words will be employed throughout. Any word that has an incorrect meaning when used in certain ways will not be used under those conditions. Words which appeal to emotions and biases will be discarded for words that are neutral, unambiguous, and exact.

The art of presenting information by the use of pictures and charts has reached an advanced state of development. Unfortunately for the reader who is searching for factual information, pictures can be incorrectly titled, retouched, or taken in such a manner as to misrepresent or to omit certain parts of a scene. A "picture is better than ten thousand words" only if it is an accurate picture taken by a photographer who knows the significance of the photograph he is obtaining and is interested in presenting a true picture. Charts and graphs, also, may be inaccurately constructed and presented. In a later chapter, there will be a discussion of the use of charts and graphs in the presentation of information.

The clarity of the reasoning used by a writer should be watched carefully. He should reach his conclusions in a logical step-by-step manner. The data and assumptions on which he bases his final contentions should be made known to the reader. Gaps in reasoning or jumps to conclusions should be avoided. The sources of information used should be carefully cited. Documentation should be presented to substantiate and support all major points.

The date of the writing, that is, the time at which it was prepared, can be of importance if the subject involves conditions which may have changed significantly since the material was written. The researcher, however, should not assume that more recent material is always superior to older publications. This is an oversimplification that may lead to seriously erroneous results.

RETRIEVAL SYSTEMS

New developments in the storage and retrieval of information have linked the electronic computer to the tasks of compilation of sources and descriptions of references. The general nature of the improvements is to reduce storage space and access time. The individual researcher, working with or without the help of the professional librarian, can use large amounts of time for little gain in searching related literature when he uses the original documents in the library. The use of microfilm has become standardized in U.S. libraries, cutting down considerably on storage requirements and time lost in searching out documents.

Computers have been used for both storage and retrieval of information, but this use has been principally directed at numerical information. The *IBM Ramac* disc-type memory unit is probably the best known. It has been used for military inventories and for commercial and industrial purposes. Employment of such high-capacity *random access* memory units has vastly reduced access time to digital data.

Many recent developments have been made in the use of visual scanning of printed documents to increase input speed and thus to permit rapid access to information in language form. One of the formidable difficulties in this effort is to read the different type faces and sizes. Resolving this difficulty will make possible a wider adoption of automatic information retrieval systems by libraries.

Among the possible benefits of computerized library search procedures is the improvement in existing recording and search techniques. Improved communications between libraries, as well as between researchers and documents, have resulted from developments in automatic information retrieval.

One of the criticisms of automatic retrieval systems by scholars and librarians is that they inhibit the *by-product* results of human, manual library searches. Such human searches commonly turn up relatively unrelated materials which may change the subject or nature or direction of the existing research or may suggest new projects. The value of these by-product results often transcends that of the original project.

An example of recent developments in facilitating library search procedures is *Datrix* (Direct Access to Reference Information: a Xerox service). Datrix is a search procedure of information in doctoral dissertations carried on by the University Films Library Services, Xerox Education Division, Xerox Corporation in Ann Arbor, Michigan 48106. Datrix combines computerized search of scores of thousands of dissertations with microfilm and Xerox reproduction and processing.

Another example is *Eric* (Educational Research Information Center) sponsored by the Office of Education, U.S. Department of Health, Education, and Welfare. A number of Eric information clearinghouses have been established at major universities to facilitate search for educational and education-related information.

UNPUBLISHED RECORDS

Internal records are one of the first sources of information to which an investigator should turn when he is searching for the facts about a firm. These unpublished records, however, are often overlooked or used very little when a problem is being studied. Often records are used by management only to the extent dictated by governmental tax and regulatory laws or by bankers and other creditors of a firm. There is a tendency for the inexperienced researcher to believe that the facts of most value will nearly all have to be located outside of the business being studied. Managers sometimes think that they already know all the "inside" information about their organization; and, therefore, the places to look for the answers to their problems are outside the company.

It will often be true that much, or even most, of the needed data may lie outside the firm. At the same time, internal records may still contain much information of value; and, in a significant proportion of research projects, internal sources of information will supply most of the facts needed to solve the difficulty being studied.

One example of the use of records of a firm is found in the marketing research technique called *sales analysis*. This type of investigation involves, along with other appropriate techniques, the careful study of whatever pertinent records are available about the sales of the business concerned.

The sales information sought can take numerous forms. The major types of data desired can be classified as follows:

1. variations in the types of products or services sold
2. variations among different teritorial areas
3. variations among customers (by groups and individuals)
4. variations in timing by seasons, in business cycles, and long-run movements or trends

In short, a firm's managers may need to know these things about its sales: what is sold, where, to whom, when, and how. A well-kept set of records can be expected to supply a great deal of information about these matters.

The following brief list of types of internal records is presented, not as a complete list, but merely to suggest the great variety of such records:

1. accounting and other related financial records
2. personnel records
3. marketing-sales-customer records
4. production records
5. inventory control records
6. purchasing records
7. special reports on the preceding or other items
8. interoffice memoranda
9. official minutes of conferences, board meetings, etc.
10. files of letters

The types of records kept by a firm will depend upon the nature and size of the organization as well as the preferences and practices of management personnel. In many companies, the accountant or a person who is responsible for the financial aspect of the establishment will be the keeper of most of the records. In othe concerns, the manager or perhaps his secretary or administrative asistant will compile and/or keep many of the records.

Ordinarily, record compilation will be the responsibility of various persons who are found in the different divisions of the firm. Certain offices, such as that of the chief accountant or the comptroller, may or may not keep a central set of records. Regardless of who compiles the records and keeps them, the researcher will need to locate them and use them if they can aid in the analysis and solution of a problem which is under investigation.

The exact meaning of the information contained in records must be ascertained before any use is made of them. Serious errors can occur if records are assumed to mean one thing when they actually mean something else. Sometimes records have a bias or perhaps a constant margin of error that may be known to the persons who have been compiling them or to other persons who have used these records in the past.

The possible correct uses to which these records can be put must also be established. Any interpretation which the investigator tentatively decides to put on records should, if it is at all practicable, be presented to persons familiar with the correct meaning of the records. If such persons agree that the assumed meaning and proposed uses of the records are correct, then the researcher will be justified in so using the records.

Unfortunately, when research is started in a firm, one of the early discoveries may be that certain records are missing or incomplete and some that are available are faulty in one or more respects. These conditions make it unlikely that a fully satisfactory investigation can be conducted. On the other hand, the findings about the weaknesses in regard to the records may lead to significant recommendations about how the system of records should be improved. This result can go a long way, in some instances, toward making the research project worth-while.

UNPUBLISHED DATA OUTSIDE THE FIRM

Such groups as trade associations and nonprofit research organizations, in the process of conducting research, may sometimes collect a great deal more information than they have the time or money to break down completely and publish in all of its possible ramifications. This unpublished material may contain data that could be obtained for legitimate use by an individual business that could provide personnel or funds to compile the pertinent facts. If these records are available, their use could result in a considerable saving to the interested firm.

The federal government secures a tremendous amount of information in the censuses that are conducted by the U.S. Bureau of the Census. These census records are kept confidential in regard to the identity of persons or companies. But for a reasonable fee paid to the Bureau of the Census, it might be possible for a firm to obtain some detailed unpublished data, as for example, the population and economic characteristics of a geographic area in which the firm is interested. Such a possibility should be explored if a research problem should arise in which this method of obtaining information seemed likely to offer real advantages.

Some private businesses, such as, public utilities, as well as some other firms, may be willing to supply certain information from their records to researchers who have an acceptable reason for needing such data.

GOVERNMENT RECORDS

Governments of all levels in the course of operation necessarily collect a great volume of information about people and economic conditions in the areas served by the governments. Most of the unpublished records of the federal government are relatively unavailable to the average business because the material is located in Washington, or some other city far removed from the home town of most firms. Even the official records of state governments are often considered to be too far away when kept in the state capital. In some cases, however, the data in state records are worth a trip to the capital city. A letter or telephone call to the appropriate state official can often supply enough information about a set of records to determine whether they warrant a visit to the office in which they are kept.

The accessibility of federal and state government records is much greater in those cases in which branch or local offices of the government agencies are located in the city in which the researcher lives. The local telephone directory will contain the names and addresses of the governmental offices in the city. The persons in charge of these offices can supply some records and can inform the investigator about the availability of information in other offices elsewhere in the nation. Local offices of state employment services and of the U.S. Weather Bureau are illustrations of state and federal agency offices easily accessible in various cities.

Official records of cities, counties, and school districts usually contain information that may be of much value. The data are near at hand and are mostly available for use by researchers. Among the various indicators of current local business activity to be found in local government records are: bank clearings, building permits, tax data (including sales and property taxes), warranty deeds, postal receipts, utility meters, telephones, employment conditions (as shown in city, county, or district offices of the state employment service), number of school-age children and school attendance, automobile registrations, freight movement, airport passenger volume, foreclosures, repossessions, marriages, births, and meteorological data.

ORIGINALLY COLLECTED DATA

Data may be originally collected through (1) observation; (2) experimentation; and (3) surveys. The details of collecting original data by these methods are covered in ensuing chapters.

Chapter 4, "Observation and Experimentation," not only explains observation procedures and experimental methods, but includes the collection of data by these methods. Chapter 5, "Survey Techniques," includes the collection of data by mail questionnaires, personal interviews, telephone inquiry, motivational research, and panels. Further, chapter 6, "Constructing and Writing Questionnaires," and chapter 7, "Aids in Administering Surveys," describe data collection by questionnaire methods.

SUMMARY

Locating and defining the problems a business faces may involve some study. Problems can often be found: (1) by studying the records and reports of a firm; (2) by careful observation of conditions in a firm; (3) through purposeful conversations with qualified persons; (4) by careful observation of the procedures and techniques of the most effective firms in the industry; (5) by reading pertinent published material; (6) by using checklists to evaluate the operations of a firm; (7) by brain storming—intensified discussions within a group of experts.

Defining and delimiting the problem itself may be facilitated by the use of checklists. Checklists are detailed listings of all of the areas of operation of a business firm. They may prove to be valuable aids because: (1) constructing the checklist stimulates thinking about problems; (2) use of the checklist results in more complete consideration of all aspects of problems; (3) use of a checklist results in more complete identification and definition of problems; (4) a checklist assists in establishment of hypotheses; (5) a checklist aids in deciding on the data required for solution of problems.

The actual process of preparing a checklist can be summarized as follows: (1) Write out a list of ideas, questions, or comments pertaining to problems. (2) Investigate records of the firm that would seem pertinent to the questions or comments. (3) Talk to other persons, inside the firm or outside, if necessary. (4) Browse thrugh pertinent publications. (5) Evaluate the written notes made so far to arrive at a logically arranged list of points or considerations. (6) Discuss the checklist with other qualified persons. (7) Revise the checklist as it seems necessary.

After determining and delimiting the problem area—probably as a result of establishing a checklist—the hypotheses concerning the problem may be formed. An hypothesis is a tentative statement of cause and effect relating to a problem. The hypotheses may be in the form of statements of condition, usually involving causal factors. Sometimes specific statistical hypotheses may be posed, for example, the difference between the means is zero. This hypothesis lends itself to testing for possible rejection. If it is rejected, the difference is not zero, and the means came from universes that are dissimilar. A checklist for evaluating hypotheses follows: (1) Have all of the pertinent aspects of the problem been considered? (2) Do the hypotheses include all of the relevant possibilities as to causes? (3) Have the hypotheses been selected on the basis of their constituting actual causes or reasons? (4) Have the hypotheses been selected without bias in respect to whether they may be substantiated? (5) Have the hypotheses been selected under conditions that allowed the researcher to set up all hypotheses that were considered to have a real bearing on the problem?

Following the selection, definition, and limitation of the problem, the making of a checklist, and formulating of hypotheses, the plans concerning data collection and analysis can be considered. A written list of the procedures, plans, and the kind of effort to be made in collecting the data should be drawn up. The following questions should be asked: (1) Will the data be of sufficient value to warrant the cost in time, effort, and money to collect it? (2) Will the information be sufficiently accurate? (3) Will the information be as valuable as other information that could be collected in its place? (4) Is it reasonably certain that this information can be obtained? (5) Can the information be collected in the time allotted? (6) Can the data be tabulated or classified meaningfully? (7) Does the researcher have the qualified personnel and required facilities available? (8) Are the data all that are required for solution of the problem?

When plans have been made for collecting the data, plans for analysis must be formulated. It must not be thought that these are completely separate steps—of course, the kinds of analysis have a bearing on the kinds of data needed and on the collection of the data. They are separated in the discussion only to show that they are separate kinds of activities. The analyses of the data are usually statistical analyses. The following kind of analyses will be explored in this book: (1) classifications and cross-classifications, including chi-square tests; (2) inference analysis, involving averages, dispersions, and percentages; (3) sampling procedures, including sample size, representativeness, and sampling collection methods; (4) correlation and regression, whether for studying associations or making predictions; (5) trend analysis, for the purpose of forecasting.

The four levels of data measurement are nominal, ordinal, interval, and ratio, including, respectively, the characteristics of mutually exclusive categories, order, equidistant ordered categories, and a true zero point. These levels of data measurement limit the techniques employed, nonparametric and parametric.

The sources of data are often classified as primary and secondary. They can also be classified as (1) published information; (2) unpublished records; (3) originally collected data.

Published information may consist of books, periodicals, and other publications, and should be evaluated if used. Unpublished records, such as, accounting, personnel, and sales records of a firm, as well as unpublished data from trade associations and governments, may be used. Originally collected data through observations, experimentation, and surveys, will be described in chapters 4, 5, 6, and 7.

EXERCISES

1. The firm itself can provide information leading to the discovery of problems: (1) its records and reports; (2) the conditions in the firm; and (3) conversation among officers and experts in the firm. Give examples of these sources.
2. How can studying other, successful firms, and studying publications of the industry help uncover problems?
3. *Brainstorming* is often fruitful in uncovering problems. What is it? Why may it be effective?
4. Why are checklists important in uncovering problems?
5. Explain how checklists may be drawn up, and how they may be used.
6. Devise a checklist for a manufacturing company relative to production alone; or for a retail firm in respect to its market position.
7. What are hypotheses? How are they set up?
8. What are the characteristics of a statistical hypothesis?
9. Describe in your own words a checklist for evaluating hypotheses.
10. In data and analysis planning, explain the association of the *data* and *analysis*, using examples.
11. What points should be covered in data collection plans?
12. Write a two-page paper describing the five major types of data-gathering techniques.
13. Write a two-page paper describing the major types of statistical analysis for business research.
14. What is meant by *classification* and *cross-classification*? How may these be useful? How important are they in respect to other techniques?
15. Define *inference analysis*. Why is it important?
16. What is the association between regression and correlation?
17. Give an example of each of the following: trend analysis, inference analysis, chi-square analysis.
18. In an essay, distinguish among the four levels of data measurement.
19. Give an example of each of the four levels of data measurement.
20. Distinguish between primary and secondary data.
21. Why are libraries important to the business researcher? What services do they provide?
22. Explain how a researcher can evaluate published information.
23. Give three examples of data from unpublished records inside the firm, and three examples of data from outside the firm.

SELECTED REFERENCES

Balsley, Howard L. *Basic Statistics for Business and Economics*. Columbus, Ohio: Grid, 1978.

Murdick, Robert G. *Business Research: Concept and Practice*. Scranton, Pa.: International Textbook, 1969.

Tull, Donald G., and Hawkins, D. I. *Marketing Research*. New York: Macmillan, 1976.

4

Observation and Experimentation

Observation and experimentation techniques can often be used to advantage in business research. One of their main virtues is that the personal element can ordinarily be reduced to the minimum. Greater objectivity usually can be obtained by these techniques than is possible in most questionnaire surveys. Mechanical measuring and recording devices can be relied on rather extensively. And even when the human senses and judgment must be used in observation and experimentation, the systematic procedures followed place less reliance on the human factor in the investigator or the persons being studied.

Business researchers are making increasing use of observation and experimentation. In this chapter, there will be a description of some of the main principles and possible applications of these techniques in the solution of business problems. It should be realized that in actual research both techniques will often have to be used on a project, as well as other techniques that may be found to be effective.

A great deal can often be learned by carefully watching what is happening, or by looking to see what conditions exist at the present time. The information that can be gained by observation may be more accurate, complete, and economical to collect than if it had been obtained by asking questions or by other techniques.

OBSERVATION PROCEDURES

The things that are to be observed must be decided on definitely before the observation is attempted. These items must be determined to be the ones that are essential to observe in order to collect the information required in the particular research project being undertaken. Suppose that the purpose of a survey was to learn about the physical characteristics of a representative sample of stores of a certain type. Unless the exact objects to be located and observed are known, the observer will find that he sometimes looks for certain items in a given store, while in the next store, he may forget to look for these same items or at least fail to observe all of the same items. This practice will lead to incomplete, haphazard results.

Of course, the observation and recording of unexpected and unforeseen conditions of importance to the purpose of the survey should not be excluded, but such conditions must be kept to a bare minimum by careful planning of the observation procedure.

It is not always easy to recognize every condition to be tabulated. Carefully prepared and sufficiently detailed instructions and descriptions must be supplied to the investigator. Practice or trial observations in the field under actual field work conditions may be desirable. Sometimes the observer may be supplied with pictures of a thing to be observed; or, a sample or model may be presented.

Accurate results require that, as a first step, the total situation or set of conditions to be observed must be divided into small and simple parts that can be easily seen and correctly recorded. Then each part or item should be separately observed, and the result marked on the schedule. Unless this procedure is followed, the observation and the recorded results are likely to be inaccurate due to the fact that the observer gets confused impressions when he attempts to look at too many items at one time.

REPORTING OF OBSERVATIONS

The preparation of the form on which observations are to be recorded is subject to many of the same principles as those for the construction of questionnaires. It is necessary to have a well-prepared form in order that (1) the observations will be accurate and complete, and (2) the results will be recorded in a manner such that they can be effectively tabulated and analyzed. The forms used may be designated by various names, such as, *schedule*, *score cards*, and *observationnaires*.

The form to be used in a particular investigation will need to be constructed in such a manner as to make it possible to record the necessary information easily and correctly. Here are several rules to keep in mind in preparing observationnaires:

1. Provide for the correct identification of each case observed and of the investigator who recorded the results in order to facilitate the interpretation of the findings and the checking of any errors or omissions on the part of the field worker who did the original observing and recording.
2. Each form should as nearly as possible contain all the explanatory data necessary to enable it to be filled out by the observer and interpreted by the compiler of the final research results. If the observer has to refer frequently to a set of separate instructions, the observing process is slowed seriously. In situations in which use is made of the

panel technique of asking for *self-observations* to be recorded by the cooperating panel members, it is especially important that the recording sheet contain all the necessary instructions.

3. Separate places should be provided for recording the results of observations for each item; there must be blanks for each aspect observed and each result that may need to be recorded. Observations sometimes need to be rather detailed and numerous. A well-prepared schedule, however, that may seem quite complicated at first glance, may actually be more easily and quickly filled out than a shorter form because the briefer form may not contain sufficient explanations or have enough places to record all the kinds of conditions seen. Therefore, more time-consuming writing and improvisation of ways to record the various data will be necessary on the shorter sheet than on the longer one.

4. The items on the forms should appear in logical groupings and in the order in which the observer usually would observe them, thus speeding up the observation process, and making for a more complete and systematic coverage of the cases under study. In addition, tabulating and interpreting the results of the field work will be facilitated.

5. The greatest accuracy in recording what is seen will be attained if each observation is recorded at the time it is made. Every moment of delay between the observation and the recording tends to decrease the accuracy of the recorded results. If some delay is unavoidable, the facts determined about any item should be recorded as soon as possible, certainly before the next case is observed.

An example of an observationnaire is given in exhibit 4-1. Field workers conducting this survey would carry a tape measure, lightmeter, and room thermometer. The observers would be instructed how to recognize, measure, and record the characteristics to be measured. Practice observations probably would be conducted under the supervision of the research director before the actual survey is started.

MEASURING OBSERVATIONS

A well-prepared observationnaire or recording form is one of the most helpful devices for aiding the investigator in making measurements. It should be so arranged that results can be quickly and correctly indicated with a check mark, a number, encirclement of an item, or a minimum of words if they are required.

The objectivity and exactness of appropriate mechanical devices make their use especially desirable if it is feasible to employ them. Some measuring and recording instruments are: rulers; scales; small counters held in the hand; highway cable traffic counters; photoelectric-eye counters; still, motion, sound, color and time-lapse picture cameras augmented by light filters, films sensitive to different light and heat rays, microscopic and telescopic lenses; tape, disc, and wire recorders; thermometers; barometers; hygrometers; clocks; speedometers; one-way screens and mirrors; closed-circuit television; lightmeters; pocket calculators.

EXHIBIT 4-1

Physical Characteristics of Rooms Occupied by Business Offices

Code number for office_____ Date of observation _____

Time of day_____ AM, PM   Signature of observer _____

Dimensions of room (in feet and inches):

    Floor space: Length_____ Width_____

               Total square feet _____

    Height of ceiling_____

Windows: Height_____ Width_____ (in inches)

         Glass: Clear_____ Tinted_____

         Panes: Single_____ Double for temperature control_____

         Frames: Wood_____ Metal_____

Lighting: Fluorescent _____ Incandescent _____

         Intensity reading on lightmeter: In lightest work area _____

             In darkest work area_____ (excluding storage and dark rooms)

         Direct_____ Indirect _____

Temperature control:

         Heating: Central heating system for building _____

               Space heater for office only _____

         Cooling: Central cooling system for building _____

               Space cooler for office only_____ None _____

         Temperature of office at time of observation:

               Your thermometer at floor level _____

               48 inches above floor_____

         Thermostat reading if one is located in office area _____

Floor covering: Wood_____ Carpet, wall-to-wall_____ Carpet, partial_____

         Linoleum_____ Concrete_____ Other (specify) _____

CONDITIONS OF EFFECTIVE OBSERVATION

Such intangible items as personal opinions, states of mind, and motives cannot be accurately measured and recorded by observation alone, although observation might be used in conjunction with other data-collecting techniques. Facial expressions and actions of children, it is true, are much better indicators of their thoughts or states of mind than is the case for adults. Also, the actions of a person who does not know that he is being watched may be a more nearly correct reflection of his state of mind than would be the case if he knew he was being watched. Nevertheless, observation is highly limited in its applicability to such things as the quality and quantity of mental processes.

Observation must be done under conditions which will permit accurate and complete results. Persons who are observing must be in a position to see clearly the items or conditions for which they are looking. The distance and the light must be satisfactory. Discomfort and fatigue must be kept from interfering with the investigator. If mechanical devices are used, they must be carefully checked to see that they are in good working order, and they must be kept that way throughout the periods that they are in use. The devices must be operated by persons who know how to use them properly.

Observations must cover a sufficient number of cases. In research projects in which only a part of all the cases in existence can be observed, the question will arise as to how many cases should be observed. The answer will be that the number of cases that will need to be observed will depend on the nature of the universe (all the cases in existence) and the degree of heterogeneity of the cases being studied. The number of cases, in general, will be considered large enough as soon as a true, complete picture of the universe has been obtained. The number is too small if the picture is still developing and changing to a significant degree as additional observations are recorded. The matter of the adequacy of size of a sample will be discussed in detail in later chapters.

Observations must cover a representative cross-section of the universe. When sampling is required, if only certain types of cases in the universe are observed, the sample will be distorted; consequently, the observations will need to be made from various different positions or locations, at various times, and under all the types of conditions which might be of importance in the interpretation of the findings. Such conditions as the following might be significant: times of day, days of week, different sides of the street, types of weather, seasons of the year, and so forth. Ideally, every case in the universe should be given an equal chance of being included in the sample if the cases that are observed are to stand a reasonable chance of being representative of the universe.

Recorded results must be checked for accuracy and completeness. It is essential that the results be correctly observed and recorded. If personal observations have been the technique used, a certain number of the cases could be observed again by another investigator, and the results compared with those on the first observation sheets. A separate set of mechanical devices could be used on the rechecking tests for mechanically observed and recorded results. Sometimes it may be feasible to use two separate investigators and sets of instruments in all or some of the original observations. The results of each investigator or set of instruments could then be compared to see if there were any discrepancies.

Observers must be adequately trained and instructed. Satisfactory results can be expected from observations only if the field workers know exactly what they are supposed to do and how to do it. Every part of the observation sheet should be explained to them. They should be shown how to locate, identify, and observe the items to be studied, and how to record their findings. Their instructions should cover every detail of how to operate any mechanical devices to be used. If sampling is necessary, the exact method of selecting the cases to be studied must be explained to the field workers. Finally, if at all feasible, trial observations should be conducted before the regular field work begins.

The need to train observers can be demonstrated easily by asking untrained persons to tell about a certain situation that they all have observed recently. The descriptions will vary in many important details because people tend to "see" what they want to see, have seen elsewhere, are familiar with, or have heard others describe. Only a trained observer who knows exactly what and how to observe and the correct way to record his findings can be expected to do a satisfactory job of observation.

ADVANTAGES AND DISADVANTAGES OF OBSERVATION TECHNIQUE

The major *advantages* of the observation technique include these points:

(1) The element of human error can frequently be reduced considerably in comparison with some other data-collecting techniques. For instance, more accurate data can often be obtained when careful, systematic observations of visible conditions is the procedure used instead of interviews and word of mouth or copying from records written by other persons.

(2) Mechanical measuring, testing, and recording devices can be used in many situations to secure more accurate data. In fact, some types of data cannot be obtained unless a mechanical instrument is used. Mechanical recording devices also can be used for making continuous observations over rather long periods of time without encountering the crippling effects of human discomfort and fatigue.

(3) Observations can be made of actual cases as they really exist. The most elaborate and expensive laboratory experiment ordinarily cannot exactly duplicate the conditions of real life.

(4) There is relatively little work and expense involved in checking the accuracy of the reports of field workers in many types of projects in which observation is the data-collecting procedure used. It is particularly easy to check reports when the objects observed have a permanent location, and therefore, in the checking process a certain number of them can be found and observed by another investigator.

The major *disadvantages* of the observation technique include the following:

(1) Certain types of psychological data, such as, opinions and motives, are ordinarily impossible to ascertain by observation alone.

(2) When the condition being studied occurs infrequently, observation may not be practical.

(3) Observation naturally is not an appropriate technique when the information needed pertains to possible future conditions which cannot be observed now because they do not presently exist.

(4) Some mechanical measuring and recording devices are expensive to buy or rent and to operate and maintain.

(5) Complicated instruments may require operators who need considerable training and experience.

(6) Mechanical devices needed for certain types of measurements may be too large to transport to the locations at which the observations should be made.

(7) Permission to conduct observations may be difficult and expensive to obtain in certain cases.

(8) The process of rechecking the reports of field workers is difficult, if not impossible, when the objects observed have no permanent location and cannot be found again for a second observation.

The observation technique should always be given careful consideration when the ways of collecting data are under study. Although it has its limitations, it is often superior to alternative techniques. It should be used alone or in conjunction with other procedures in those circumstances in which such a research plan will obtain the best results. Usually when the problem is to discover what people do or buy, the most accurate indication is to observe their actions or the results of their past actions. When it must be known what physical conditions exist, systematic observation is likely to be an essential procedure. It must be admitted that some of the mechanical measuring and recording instruments are quite complicated and expensive. There is a large variety of observations, however, that will require only the more common and relatively inexpensive devices.

APPLICATIONS OF OBSERVATION TECHNIQUE

Although the following paragraphs do not consist of a complete listing of possible applications of the observation technique, they do offer a number of suggestions and illustrations of actual applications.

Counting persons, transportation vehicles, and other items. It may be necessary to learn the number of persons who daily walk by a store location; volume of street traffic passing a possible site for a garage, filling station, or other type of establishment; or the percentage of the persons who pass a store who enter the building. A quick, rough measure of the number of patrons in the several community shopping areas of a city may be made by counting automobiles parked in the adjacent off-street parking spaces and by noticing the number of persons per car as they arrive or leave.

Determining the physical, sociological, and economic characteristics of persons. It may be desired to know such physical facts as approximate age; height; weight; facial appearance or expression (as an indication, for instance, of whether the person has the weathered skin of rural or other outdoor persons; or is pleased or displeased with what they have just seen or heard); sex; racial or nationality characteristics; and apparent health. Some of the sociological characteristics might be whether a young couple were married (note absence or presence of wedding ring); whether persons seemed to be in family groups or in other groups, or alone; whether persons spoke in words that helped to place them in educational level, social relationship, and background or region of the nation. Economic status of the persons observed might be indicated in a general way by their clothing, jewelry, condition of hands, personal care of hair and face, vehicle in which they ride, and environment in which they are found (types of stores, offices, homes, and parts of town).

Experienced observers, when given certain specific items or conditions to observe, may be able to make usable estimates of some rather intangible characteristics of persons, as well as tangible ones. Of course, the findings will be merely approximations, and they should be used with this limitation in mind. These estimates should be utilized mostly to make rough comparisons among groups of persons instead of being considered as measures of absolute conditions. For example, the persons who patronize airlines may be compared with persons seen in bus depots. Or the guests in the lobbies of different hotels may be observed for purposes of determining the possible differences among the hotels studied. "Casual" personal interviews might be used to help establish apparent intelligence or education.

Still photographs taken at set intervals in several hotels under study could supply pictures showing types of clothing worn and other characteristics of patrons. These pictures could then be studied systematically by trained observers. The persons in the photographs could be compared in regard to certain specific things such as, apparent age, sex, type of clothing, and so forth.

General occupational classification of persons. Suppose that in a group of persons being observed the purpose is to estimate the percentages that fall into each of these general occupational classes: (1) factory or operative types of workers; (2) office, clerical, or sales workers; and (3) professional and managerial types. These three broad groups can probably be fairly well identified and counted for some purposes by noticing characteristics mentioned in the preceding paragraphs.

Flow of traffic and parking problems. These matters can be observed from tall buildings and helicopters and by driving around on the streets. Less than capacity use of parking facilities has been discovered in cities that were experiencing congestion and apparent parking shortages. Better direction of traffic and more publicity about parking lots were then carried out.

Determining procedures of workers on the job. Motion and time studies to find out exactly what movements are made and the time required have long been an accepted practice. The facts obtained by these observations have been used to improve the efficiency and reduce the fatigue of workers. The movements of the most proficient workers can be photographed by motion picture cameras and then projected at regular or slower speeds. The films can be shown enough times to other workers to help them as part of a training program to become more proficient.

Determining how materials or products move through a plant. A person watching with a counter or pencil and observation sheet can observe much of importance. Still photographs or motion picture films can be used to obtain pictures. Bottlenecks in materials may be discovered; overworked or under-utilized workers or equipment may be found.

Making an inventory or count of types of equipment and facilities in a factory or other type of establishment. The types of machines, fuel, lighting, and transportation used in the factories in a given industry may be determined accurately by systematic observations in various plants. Also, the kinds of display fixtures and other physical features of retail stores can be noted and recorded. Perhaps the purpose would be to observe only the better stores to draw up an ideal store plan for a new business. The types of store front signs used by hardware stores in several neighboring cities were ascertained in a recent research project. The findings were used to determine the number and types of signs in use, and to discover, among other things, if there was any relationship between the apparent profitability of a store and its type of sign.

"Comparative shopping" of retail firms in a given line to determine their pricing and certain other policies. To enable a store to obtain information that will enable it to keep in step with the other firms in the market area, it may sponsor a research project in which observers may pose as shoppers in order to note various conditions in the establishments being visited.

"Shoppers" sent into stores to observe actions of sales personnel. Observers acting as customers may actually enter and buy merchandise from a store to see how the sales personnel are performing. The research reports can then be used as the basis of sales training courses and instructions to improve performance, or to check on whether past training programs have been successful.

Suppose that it was desired to determine how well the attendants at gasoline filling stations were carrying out their assigned duties. The investigators or observers could smudge the windshields of their automobiles, let enough air out of a tire to make it noticeably low, and have the gas tank one-fourth full. Then, the investigator would drive into a filling station and systematically watch how the attendants acted. Certain specific physical aspects of the station could then be compared to the desired standards of performance and appearance. *Before* and *after* observations could be made to measure the effectiveness of personnel training programs.

Determining how customers actually shop. Examples of some of the things that may be observed are: how long customers take to reach decisions; whether they handle products and read labels, ask advice of sales persons, have any difficulty in finding items, have shopping lists with them which they refer to in buying, stop and look at particular displays; how they dress, whether men or women do the shopping, usual route traveled in moving through store; physical and economic characteristics of customers in general and in particular departments of the store; types of cars driven as indicated by parking lot observations; and so forth. Cameras that take still pictures at frequent time intervals and motion pictures can be used to help record these conditions in the store.

Obtaining audience reactions to programs of entertainment or political speeches. Careful observations recorded to show how each part of the program affected the audience can be useful in improving the program. Cameras, especially the motion picture type, can be highly useful in recording the reactions. The film must be synchronized with the program in order that the actions of the audience can be related to the part of the entertainment being watched throughout the running of the motion picture. Pictures may even be taken in darkened auditoriums by the use of film that is sensitive to infrared light which can be thrown on the objects to be filmed without being visible to the human eye. Laughter and other audience noise, as well as the words spoken in the program, can be sound recorded for future interpretation.

Determining percentage of persons wearing or using various types or brands of products. Ordinarily the types or brands of products being worn or used by people are reasonably accurate indicators of their practical preferences and actual practices. If 42 percent of a representative sample of men observed on the streets in a city, going to and returning from work, at baseball games, and at various other places, are wearing straw hats, this percentage can probably be considered as a fairly good indication of the proportion of men in the city who wear such hats. Other examples of items that can be observed are various types of outer clothing, including colors and some kinds of fabrics; relationships between sex or age and clothing worn; relationship between place or activity of persons and their clothing.

In some instances, it is possible to observe such things as brands of foods, beverages, cigarettes; magazines or newspapers; types of accessories on automobiles; brands of golf clubs and other sporting goods. The makes of cars driven by the persons who live in certain neighborhoods, trade in a given shopping district, or attend a certain kind of event can be determined by observing the cars parked in the areas involved. Quite useful indications about economic status, as well as certain attitudes and habits, of people can be obtained by observing the sizes, types, and conditions of their houses and yards.

A trip down alleys is often revealing about the habits and cleanliness of the occupants of the dwellings. Possible need, if not effective demand, for house painting materials and labor in a city may be estimated by observing the exterior of residences. An observer who knows the plumbing procedures in a given city may be able to tell how many bathrooms a house contains by looking for a certain kind of pipe coming out of the roof. These pipes can usually be seen from the alley.

Systematic observations in homes can be made of such items as household furnishings, equipment, color schemes, and lighting arrangements. Diplomatically conducted visits may allow observation of brands of food products on pantry shelves, makes or brands of household appliances, and so forth.

EXPERIMENTATION

Experimentation is a widely accepted research process in the physical and natural sciences as they are applied in business. Its usefulness has often been regarded as quite limited, however, in the study of the social or human aspects of a firm. But today, managers are finding increasing uses for experimentation outside of the traditional types of research in applied chemistry, physics, and engineering. Various problems which executives must face in such matters as personnel relations, production control, plant layout, marketing, and public relations, can often be at least partially solved by experimentation.

An experiment consists of the testing of a hypothesis under controlled conditions, the procedures defined by an experimental design, yielding valid results. The hypothesis may be a statement or an assumption, but it is in a form such that it may be tested. For example, a hypothesis may be stated statistically as, "the difference between the averages of the two groups is zero." Such a hypothesis is capable of disproof; its truth may be tested. The *controlled* conditions refer usually to the control of the procedures—the scientific method, discussed in chapter 2 is mandated. The experimental design, the definition of the procedural method involving the analysis to be executed, may be one or more of the specific techniques discussed in this section. The final element in the preceding definition of an experiment, *validity*, refers to the question of whether the experiment yields results that pertain only to the experiment.

VALIDITY AND RANDOMIZATION

The quality *validity* is usually considered to be achieved if extraneous variables that might have had an influence in the experiment have been eliminated or handled in such a way that only pertinent variables—those variables whose effects it is desired to measure in the experiment—are in fact the variables that have been measured and have contributed to the results.

In laboratory experimentation, the effects of extraneous variables may be *eliminated*, because close controls over the subject variables are possible. Thus, effects of fungus and disease and insects in botanical experimentation may be eliminated. Where the effects of extraneous variables cannot be eliminated, they may often be *equalized*, by organizing subsamples of, say, the control group and the experimental group, so that each subsample is homogeneous with the others in respect to the extraneous effects, and, therefore, the effects are "equalized" throughout the samples. Sometimes *balancing* is practiced, in which case an attempt is made to arrange the experiment so that heterogeneous subsamples will cross all the extraneous effects for both the control and experimental groups, thus "balancing" the effects of the extraneous variables between the control group and the experimental group. A fourth method of achieving validity through managing the effects of extraneous variables is *randomizing* in the selection of the observations constituting the samples.

A random sample is one containing items selected so that each item in the universe had an equal chance of being chosen; thus, also, each possible sample of the given size had an equal chance of being chosen. Sample items selected from a numbered universe by employing a table of random numbers, such as, the *Table of 105,000 Random Decimal Digits* published by the Interstate Commerce Commission, or by computing the numbers with one of the standard random number generator programs available as subroutines at computer centers, will yield random samples. Appendix E of this book contains the first three pages of the ICC table. The table is used by employing a systematic plan: every number in order, or every fifth number, etc., may be selected, as desired; using double columns increases the usefulness of the table to universes of 10-digit size. For smaller universes, in the hundreds, for example, the first three digits of each number may be used, or the middle three, or the last three.

By employing randomization in the selection of samples, the occurrence of the effects of extraneous variables is relegated to chance. Chance effects are measurable in terms of statistical error, called the *standard error*, which is explained in detail in chapter 9. It is possible, therefore, to compute the error due to chance effects, and allow for it in inference, for example, in the decision, "the difference in the averages of the control and experimental groups is significant at the 5 percent level," which means that only 5 out of 100 times would this decision be mistaken.

Among the advantages of randomization is that no knowledge of the extraneous variables need exist. In attempting to achieve validity by elimination, by equalizing, or by balancing, an extraneous variable must be a known quantity. Not so with randomizing; indeed, it is not even necessary to know if any extraneous effects exist at all for the practice to be effective. It is a fact that business researchers are confronted with the task of taking into consideration the likelihood that not only known and uncontrolled conditions, but also unknown conditions, may contribute to the effects being measured in an experiment. This is one of the main difficulties that must be faced in the use of experimentation in business and other fields of human affairs; namely, the difficulty of holding all conditions constant except the ones that are to be tested. Randomization permits a solution to this difficulty.

EXPERIMENTAL DESIGN

The design of an experiment may have been the first consideration in the research project. The definition of the problem, the formulation of the problem and the hypotheses, the plans for, and collection of, the data, and the organizing and classifying of the data into a form for analysis, would all depend on the central consideration of the experimental design to be used in the project.

In an experiment, the hypothesis to be posed will be one of a statistical nature, such as: the difference between the means is zero. This is a *null* hypothesis, stated in this manner so that a definitive test may be made, a test of *rejection* or *disproof*. The hypothesis is tested in terms of probability, providing that random selection of sample items has occurred; thus, the effects of extraneous variables have been relegated to chance. The testing of the hypotheses is described in detail in chapter 9.

Simple Randomized Design

The most basic design of experiment is one involving a control group and an experimental group. A control group may consist of persons, retail stores, production runs of product, or any such subjects, in a *controlled* condition, to serve as a base against which to measure the changes that occur in the *experimental* group. The experimental group is identical to the control group except that the experimental variable to be tested has been included in it. Thus, after the experiment has been completed, the difference in the control group and the experimental group can be attributed to the effect of the experimental variable. Such a design is known as the *simple randomized design*. As an example, a group of employees may take an in-service course of instruction to improve performance. A measure of the effectiveness of the course may be secured by comparing the average score made on an examination of the experimental group to the average score made on the same examination by a like group of employees, a control group, who have not taken the course.

The simple randomized design includes not only the control group-experimental group test, but also the before-after test. In the before-after experiment, the same group is tested before and after the application of the experimental variable. While there may be some unfortunate effect due to *conditioning* when persons are used in such a test, because of knowing they are being experimented with, and thus bias entering the results, the before-after experiment is useful because the control is so exact. The same group of people, products, systems, or other subject is used in both the *before* and the *after* situation. The use of this method is highly recommended, particularly when human beings are not the subjects to be tested, for example, tests of products for corrosion-resistance before-after application of a preventive treatment; or spoilage before-after a treatment to reduce bacteria growth.

The measurement of the experimental effect may be accomplished by computing the significance of the difference in the means of the two groups, whether the control-experimental plan or the before-after plan is used, to test the hypothesis: the difference between the means is zero. The test will determine whether the experimental variable has had the expected effect or not.

The simple randomized design is depicted in exhibit 4-2. Design A shows the control-experimental plan; design B shows the before-after plan. The techniques of computation of the test are explained in detail in chapter 9.

EXHIBIT 4-2
Simple Randomized Design

A			B	
Control Group	Experimental Group		Before	After
X	X		X	X
X	X		X	X
X	X		X	X
X	X		X	X
X	X		X	X
	X		X	X
			X	X
			X	

Completely Randomized Design

While the simple randomized design is a *two-sample* design, since only two samples are used, the completely randomized design permits testing when more than two samples are involved; it is, thus, a *k-sample* design.

Three or four or more treatments may be tested simultaneously for significance of the difference among their means. The technique involved is called the *analysis of variance*. In this test, the *F*-distribution is used (Appendix D). With this distribution, two variances are tested: the variance among the means against the variance within the data, the latter variance measuring the *chance error*, called the *experimental error*. An explanation of the analysis of variance technique is included in chapter 9.

Assume that four different treatments in processing frozen foods are to be tested for resistance to contamination. Samples of contamination counts would be taken under each of the four treatments. The significance of the difference among the four means would be computed by the analysis of variance, and the results stated in terms of *probability*. The experimental design is the *completely randomized design*. A diagram of the design is given in exhibit 4-3.

EXHIBIT 4-3
Completely Randomized Design

Treatment A	Treatment B	Treatment C	Treatment D
X	X	X	X
X	X	X	X
X	X	X	X
X	X	X	X
X	X		X
	X		X
			X

Replicated Randomized Design

A change in the basic designs described in the foregoing paragraphs may be effected by taking subsamples of each group or treatment. Each subsample would be chosen independently by random methods; each subsample would have the same number of observations. For example, in the simple randomized design, the control and experimental groups may consist of two or three independent, random samples each, with each having an identical number of observations. A new design, the *replicated randomized design*, is the result. Another example might include replications of the completely randomized design, in which there are four treatments with, say, three samples for each treatment. Exhibit 4-4 illustrates this situation.

The replicated randomized design includes a larger total number of observations than otherwise might be taken. Beyond that, however, it permits more coverage of geographical area, for example, and improves the control of extraneous effects by making it more certain that all chance effects are included. Sometimes repetitions of an experiment are defined as replications, in which separate repetitions take place at different times and places, but under as identical conditions as possible.

The number of replications for an experiment usually consists of from two or three to about ten. Deming suggests these numbers.[1] For usual purposes in business research, two or three replications are most commonly used. In situations in which the experiment is critical or sensitive, for example, experiments for studying dangerous drugs, ten replications might be desirable.

The analysis of variance is applied to this design, but its complicated nature is such that it is usually applied using computer analysis. The details of this complication of analysis of variance are not described in chapter 9. Most business experiments are conducted by the simple randomized design or the completely randomized design. Therefore, the more complicated analysis of variance is not included in this book.

Factorial Design

The foregoing three experimental designs have involved only one classification each, whether in groups or treatments. Such designs are said to have *one basis of classification*.

Where there are *two bases of classification*, two classifications are tested, so that one experiment will include two tests involving the *F*-distribution: one test will test for significant difference in the column classification, the second for significant difference in the row classification. A diagram of this design would be identical to the diagram for the replicated randomized design, except that the row classification would replace the replications. For example, with three different treatments for the column classification of fertilizers, the row classification may be three different grain crops: wheat, barley, rice.

EXHIBIT 4-4
Replicated Randomized Design

	Treatment A	Treatment B	Treatment C	Treatment D
Sample 1 (replication)	X X X X X	X X X X X	X X X X X	X X X X X
Sample 2 (replication)	X X X X X	X X X X X	X X X X X	X X X X X
Sample 3 (replication)	X X X X X	X X X X X	X X X X X	X X X X X

The *factorial design* employs the same analysis of variance employed for the replicated randomized design. In each case there will be two *F*-tests: for the column classification and for the row classification. This design is called *two bases of classification with more than one observation in each class*.

PROCEDURES IN EFFECTIVE EXPERIMENTATION

Experimentation, although it should be scientific in method, to a large extent still must depend for success on the researcher's imagination and insight into each particular problem under study. A wide variety of experimental techniques is required to handle the many types of problems that must be investigated. New ways of solving problems must be developed continually to meet the ever changing and emerging conditions in business and the other social sciences. Consequently, it is not possible to present here an all-inclusive list of principles or procedures in experimentation. The items discussed in this section are offered to give the reader some knowledge of the types of experimental methods and techniques that have proved reasonably effective in helping to solve problems in business firms.

Three-fold classification of experimental plans, based on types of controls. Various possibilities exist for setting up experiments in which conditions are to be studied. A simple but useful classification of techniques of experimentation based on types of controls is as follows: (1) one case plan; (2) parallel or equivalent cases plan; and (3) rotation of cases plan. In the *one case plan*, a single store might be studied by noting what happened when certain practices were tried while all other practices and conditions were held constant.

The *parallel or equivalent cases plan* could be illustrated by the situation in which two highly similar stores were used in the experiment. The conditions in one store would be kept unchanged in order to have a way to measure the results of the changed practices tried out in the second store. This procedure is sometimes referred to as the *matched cases* technique. The ideal arrangement, of course, would be to use stores that were identical in all respects. In actual practice, the stores must be nearly enough alike that any of the differences in results observed in the stores during the experiment must obviously be due to the test conditions created and not to any original differences in the stores involved. The store in which conditions were kept unchanged would be designated as the *control* store. The store in which the experimental changes were put into effect would be referred to as the *test* store.

The *rotation of cases plan* would call for first trying the new practice in one store and then trying it in the second store. Each store would be used once as a *test* store and once as a *control* store. Of course, more than two stores may be used, and the tests may be rotated any number of times considered necessary to reach an accurate conclusion.

If feasible, tests or measurements in experiments should be repeated several times to assure accuracy of results. The repetition, or *replication*, of tests is often needed in order to be sure that (1) all major real life conditions have been included in the experiment, and (2) results have been correctly observed and recorded. Repeating the tests may be especially necessary in experiments in which there are important conditions that are beyond control. Added reason for repetition exists in cases in which it is thought that there may be unknown conditions that may be significant. Suppose that the shop foreman in a plant wants to find out whether men or women could assemble a given product more rapidly. The experiment should be conducted over a long enough time to allow a sufficient number of tests and measurements of output per certain time periods to be sure of the results. Of course, all controllable conditions must be kept the same except the sex of the workers.

It is possible in this example that women might be more or less productive than men at the beginning of the experiment, but that their productivity would change later. Outside or other uncontrollable conditions such as beginning or ending of school sessions and family needs may complicate the process of reaching final conclusions. The number of tests may have to be quite large and the period of time rather long in order to enable the experiment to cover all possible kinds of conditions that could influence the results.

Unfortunately, in some business problems, repeating an experiment may be very costly and sometimes impossible. If the first or second trial does not bring dependable results, no further tests may be practical. If, for instance, it was desired to know whether a self-service filling station would be profitable in a certain city, a full-sized experimental station could be built. But if the results were inconclusive, repetition of the experiment by building another such station might be too costly for the businessperson concerned. One possible way to handle this difficulty is to conduct an experiment on a smaller scale than the regular size of the type of establishment being investigated.

Experimental conditions should be as nearly the same as the expected real life conditions as it is possible to make them. Exact, complete duplication would be the ideal. In actual practice, it will ordinarily be expected that the experimental conditions must merely be similar enough to real life conditions to make the findings sufficiently accurate to make it possible to reach an acceptable solution of the problem under study.

In some instances, the conditions tested in an experiment can be more numerous and severe than the real life conditions that are likely to be met. This possibility can constitute an important reason for using experimentation in certain cases. At the same time, it should be remembered that unless the conditions of laboratory experiments can be kept reasonably similar to those that will exist in actual practice, the whole research project may fail in its function of supplying accurate information on which managers can base their operational decisions.

Because of the difficulty of duplicating the real life conditions in laboratories or in smaller-than-actual-size models, it is sound procedure in many experiments to conduct them in real life situations. When this is done, however, it is necessary to follow the correct experimental procedures outlined in this chapter. This requirement is mentioned because it is sometimes forgotten that systematic, scientific procedures should be used in projects conducted in the field as well as those carried out in the laboratory.

Records of prior conditions may be essential. If experiments to show the results of the use of a new machine or technique are to be conducted in a certain firm, the results of the experiments, no matter how accurately observed and recorded, can be of maximum value only if they can be compared with conditions and results in the firm before the experiments were conducted. It is imperative, therefore, in planning an experiment to have correct records of past and present conditions. Sometimes experimenters overlook this requirement. If records do not exist, some may have to be accumulated during a period that must be allowed to lapse before the experiment is conducted or any experimental changes are put into effect.

In interpreting results, consider all possible causes, and attempt to determine what surrounding conditions might have changed unexpectedly between the experimental trials or tests. The experimenter must be willing to consider all the plausible reasons that could be assumed for his findings. No possible cause should be overlooked. This is an ideal, however; the researcher must at some point get on with his work, lest he be continually unable to say what he has found.

In such a social science as business, it should be remembered that certain conditions may have changed unexpectedly during the experiment. These uncontrolled or unforeseen changes, instead of the controlled changes applied by the researcher, may have been the cause of the results observed. For example, in the interpretation of the results obtained from the operation of an experimental self-service filling station, it might be assumed that an increase in gallons sold was due to the lower price charged. Actually, causes for the results might conceivably been such unaccounted for or uncontrolled conditions as an unusually good manager, growth of the population in the trade territory, or the construction of a new highway by the location.

The experimenter in business may even find that conditions which have been controllable or at least constant in the past, may become uncontrollable, and may change to an extent that could not have been predicted. Habits and ideas of persons are mostly rather slow to change. But businesspersons have found that wars and threats of wars can bring quick, drastic changes in the minds of people. With the various media of communication available today, news and ideas travel across a nation or around the world in a short time, sometimes bringing rapid alterations in attitudes of consumers, workers, and business executives.

Throughout the experiment the investigator should follow the appropriate steps in the scientific method. The *scientific method* in research was described in detail in chapter 2; therefore, its discussion in connection with experimentation can be brief. The points that should be stressed here are that the problem must be accurately defined, and the process of investigating it must be such that the correct information and solution will be obtained. The surest way to secure a satisfactory outcome is to follow the scientific method of research. It must be added, of course, that a happy conclusion cannot be guaranteed, nor can a solution be assured in all cases. The use of the scientific method is presented in this book as merely the procedure that is most likely to bring accurate results.

ADVANTAGES AND DISADVANTAGES OF EXPERIMENTATION

The major *advantages* of experimentation include these points:

(1) The element of human error is reduced to the minimum. No other method can ordinarily equal experimentation in objectivity.

(2) Control of the conditions being tested can be exercised more completely than in any other method of research.

(3) Experimentation is often less time consuming than other techniques. The conditions to be tested can sometimes be created rather quickly by the researcher instead of having to wait for real life situations to arise or for a questionnaire survey to be planned and conducted.

(4) Tests in experiments can usually be repeated until results are definitely determined.

(5) More conditions may be created and tested in experimentation than may be possible in surveys or in projects relying on observation alone.

(6) Experimentation may allow for the setting up of margins of safety in specifications of products or predictions of possible results. The controlled tests may be deliberately made more extreme than most real life conditions under which the product may be used. Consumer and producer goods often need such margins of safety. Experimentation in some cases also may be less dangerous than other techniques.

(7) Experimentation in certain instances may be less costly than other techniques.

(8) Experimentation in physical or technical problems can now be performed for a fee in specially equipped and staffed research laboratories. This practice frees the ordinary businessperson from the necessity of obtaining expensive equipment and personnel for a project.

In addition, since observation is a necessary part of experimentation, many of the previously mentioned advantages of observation apply to experimentation as well.

The major *disadvantages* of experimentation include these points:

(1) For some research problems, it is not possible to set up and control the conditions to be tested for the following reasons: (a) Experimentation is often not possible because groups of persons or individuals cannot be manipulated, controlled, and made to react in conformity with experimental test requirements. (b) Some experiments require very costly equipment that must be operated by scarce and high-salaried experts. (c) Some necessary equipment may be relatively immobile because of large size and/or scarcity of fuel sources.

(2) Artificiality in an experiment may be tolerated if it is not too great, but it may be difficult to keep it from being excessive. There may be no satisfactory measure of whether the artificiality is greater than can be allowed if the results are to be applicable to the solution of real life problems.

(3) Experimentation is of limited use in determining opinions of persons, their motives, reasons, and possible future opinions and actions.

Finally, as is true in the case of the overlapping of the advantages of observation and experimentation, many of the disadvantages of observation, as listed earlier, also apply to experimentation.

Experimentation is generally conceded to be a valuable research method. In those situations in which it is feasible to solve problems by experimentation, it is usually considered superior to alternative research procedures. The objectivity of the testing techniques, the exactness of the measurements made, the possibility of repeating tests under controlled conditions, all add to the accuracy and dependability of the results of experimentation. To a certain degree, then, it can be contended that progress in business research can be measured in the developments in new and improved ways of applying experimental techniques to various kinds of business problems.

APPLICATIONS OF EXPERIMENTAL TECHNIQUES

The reader should keep in mind that experimentation would ordinarily be used in conjunction with other techniques in research projects dealing with the types of problems mentioned in this section. The examples given here, however, are situations in which experimentation would constitute a major part of any appropriate research plan.

Testing of materials and products in laboratories. Goods and materials can often be put through tests in laboratories that can show results that for all practical purposes are the same as those that would have been found in actual use. In some instances, laboratory tests can be set up to subject articles to performance tests that may exceed the requirements for ordinary use. Margins of safety for the consumer, or industrial user, for example, can thereby be provided for such things as foods, drugs, and appliances; or chemicals, metals, fuels, and other items produced and used in industry. Assurances of the possession of certain qualities not needed in normal use but considered as desirable for some purposes by a maker or user of a product may also be provided by laboratory experimentation and testing of products.

Testing of materials and products in experiments involving actual consumer or customer use. Certain persons or firms who are actual or prospective customers can be supplied with the items to be tested and be informed to use them as they normally would. The results can be systematically observed and recorded for them to be analyzed correctly. Care must be exercised by the investigators in selecting items to be tested because only average or typical products or materials should ordinarily serve as the test items. Also, the customer users of the items must be selected in such a manner as to make them truly representative of customers in general.

Sometimes, to keep the users from acting abnormally because they know they are testing a product, the individual users are not told that they are part of an experiment for the specific purpose of seeing what experiences they have with the test products. Of course, the cooperating customers would not be asked to use any potentially dangerous or harmful products. They could be informed later that their assistance was appreciated, and could be compensated in those instances in which any expenses or costs had been incurred by them.

Test marketing. The process of reaching decisions in regard to what marketing practices should be followed on a large scale can often be aided appreciably by a type of experimentation called *test marketing*. Pilot studies or tryouts of the marketing practices under consideration are first conducted in one or more test markets. These test areas are cities that are considered to be acceptably representative of the types of market areas in which the full-scale marketing will be carried on. The types of testing that may be done can include such things as the following: most effective advertising appeals or media; consumer acceptance of a new product or changes in an old one; effect of price changes of a product on volume of sales and profits; most effective package for a product; economic and sociological characteristics of consumers of a product.

A multiplant or chain type of organization may institute experimental changes in procedures in certain units only. The results in a test plant or store may be compared with the results in the rest of the units in an organization. The test units, of course, must be carefully selected to be representative of all units.

Trade associations may use certain members as experimental units. This situation would enable smaller businesses to enjoy some of the research advantages usually thought to be available to larger firms only. The procedure could be to select certain representative members of the association as the units in which certain new procedures or equipment would be tried and the results recorded. The operational results in the rest of the members in the association would be used for comparison purposes. The costs of these experiments could be borne by the association and the findings could be made available to all members.

Testing advertising copy and layout, window displays, etc. Experiments may be set up in which, for example, five possible advertisements in dummy form may be shown to a representative group of persons. All aspects of the advertisement could be kept the same except the characteristics that it is desired to test. The viewers could be asked to indicate which advertisement they like best.

In the *split-run* technique for testing, say, two proposed advertisement layouts, the procedure could be as follows: Half the copies of a newspaper or magazine for a given issue will contain one proposed layout of an advertisement; and the other half of the issue will contain the second possible layout of the advertisement in the same position and on the same page. The purpose is to determine which layout is most effective as evidenced by the number of inquiries or visits of customers at the sponsoring store that can be attributed to each layout of the advertisement. It will be noted that all conditions about the advertisement, such as, size, position in publication, and date of appearance, are held the same. The layout or internal content is the only variable, and it is what is being tested. Both layouts of the advertisement could contain an identical but inconspicuously keyed coupon to be brought or mailed to the store to obtain a small gift. The layout that caused the most coupons to be turned in could be considered the more effective. To assure bona fide responses, the gift offer may be buried in the text of the advertisement.

Displays with different arrangement plans or themes may be rotated in a store window or placed in similar windows on the same day. The number of persons who stop to look at each display can be recorded, as well as the length of time they spend looking. Identical products could be shown in the different window displays and a record kept of the sales of these products made in the store on the days when each test window display is used. Customers requesting an item could be asked in which window they had seen it displayed.

Experimenting with retail store merchandise arrangement. Display counters of different items may be placed side by side for a test period to determine if sales of the two items tend to move up and down together. Competing brands of the same products may be placed on a counter and a record made of the number of items of each which are sold during a test period. A certain product may be placed simultaneously in, say, three locations in the store for a given period of time to determine at which location the largest volume of sales occurs. The best height from the floor for displaying a product or the more effective of several ways of stacking or arranging products on shelves or in display cases may be established. The order in which items of different kinds should appear as the customer moves through his usual route in the store may also be partially determined by systematic experimentation.

Experimentation to determine most efficient arrangements for machines in factories or equipment in offices. Machines can be set up in various arrangements to determine which is most productive or reduces unit costs to the lowest level. In larger plants, there may be test areas composed of a small part of the total machines in the factory. In offices, arrangements and locations of desks, filing cabinets, business machines, and even drinking fountains may be experimented with to discover the best of several possibilities. Heights of working tables, seats; types of lighting facilities; noise levels; and effects of different temperatures, may constitute other subjects for experimental research.

Making scale models or smaller-than-actual-size experimental machines or pilot plants. Constructing scale models is often helpful in visualizing and experimenting with arrangements of items, such as, layouts of machines in a plant, floor plans of a store or warehouse, and furniture arrangements in offices or homes. The models may be small ones with non-moving parts, or they may be working models that approximate the actual item in behavior.

Models may also be useful in experimenting with products that are in the process of being designed and developed. In some instances, such large items as buildings and even factories may be partly planned by the use of models of paper or other materials. The parts may have been made so that they could be moved around into various patterns simulating operation flows and arrangements. Sometimes bottlenecks, wasted spaces, or inefficient arrangements can be seen in such a model in time to save much money and effort. Experimentation with different locations for items in an existing plant may also be facilitated by construction and use of small models of the plant.

Smaller-than-actual-size experimental machines or pilot plants often can provide results that for all practical purposes are the same as those that would be experienced in a machine or plant of regular size. These experimental setups can be large enough to enable the researcher to obtain the necessary information but without the added expense of building a full-scale machine or plant.

Using selected real life cases to provide the experimental setup. Suppose that it was desired to know whether the drive-in movie theaters with playground facilities for children had more customers than the drive-ins without these areas. An experimental plan could be developed to provide for the observation of the number of cars parked in representative theaters with and without play facilities. The drive-ins chosen would need to be highly similar in all physical- and entertainment-offering respects except the playground characteristic.

Experimentation to determine best procedures or techniques for workers performing certain tasks. The study of procedures can often be set up in such a manner as to call for experiments to determine which movements and methods of performing a given piece of work are most efficient in terms of output per units of effort, time, and cost. In some instances, the workers considered most productive may be chosen for careful observation. Their techniques will be recorded, and perhaps put on motion picture film. These *best* techniques will then be taught to average workers, and the *before* and *after* performances noted. Experiments may be feasible to determine whether tall or short men are more effective on given jobs, young or old persons, men or women. Even clerical and sales personnel may be studied advantageously by experiments that will turn up better ways of accomplishing tasks.

The reader will recall that motion and time studies of workers were also cited as a type of use of the observation technique in research. There is an obviously close relationship and an intermingling of the techniques of observation and experimentation in research.

Unusual occurrences and emergencies sometimes provide opportunities for experimentation. The experimenter in business and the social sciences often cannot cause people to get themselves into certain conditions that the experimenter might desire to create for test purposes. If these conditions should happen, however, a wide-awake researcher may be able to collect information that is of considerable value. For example, studies may be made of the way persons react to news or actual occurrences of wars, airline tragedies, fires, and floods. Is there, for instance, any change in the number of passengers on airlines after a serious plane crash? Does a fire loss in a city increase the sales of fire insurance? What kinds of items do consumers tend to rush to buy when there is a threat of war? And after the war is over?

An incident that illustrates the possibility of research based on emergency conditions occurred several years ago in the Southwest. All the retail stores in the cities in the region were forced to close for one weekday on two occasions without prior announcement. The cause was lack of the supply of gas for heating of business buildings. These two "holidays," which occurred within a five-week period, were used as part of an experiment to help determine which unexpectedly postponed consumer purchases of various types would be made later. More specifically, the purpose of the research was to determine as far as possible the percentage of retail sales that were "impulse" sales and the percentage that were due to planned purchases of consumers. The assumption was that items that spurted upward in sales temporarily after the stores were opened following the "holidays" were items that consumers tended to plan for rather than to buy on impulse or as the result of quick on-the-spot decisions. If impulse had been the trigger for these purchases, they would not have increased significantly after the stores opened, but instead would have continued at about the same daily volume as before.

SUMMARY

Effective observation procedures require that a comprehensive list of the items to be observed be drawn up before observations begin. In the reporting of observations, an observationnaire is often used. The following are rules in preparing observationnaires: (1) provide for correct identification of each case and each observer; (2) contain the explanations necessary to filling it out correctly; (3) provide separate places for recording each tem; (4) items appear in logical groupings, in order of the observations.

Many methods of measuring observations exist: rulers, scales, counters, cameras, and other mechanical devices. Certain conditions are required for effective observation: (1) conditions permitting accurate and complete results; (2) must cover a sufficient number of cases; (3) must cover a representative cross-section of the universe; (4) the recorded results must be checked for accuracy and completeness; (5) observers must be adequately trained and instructed.

Certain advantages of the observation technique may be listed: (1) human error can be reduced; (2) mechanical devices can secure more accurate data; (3) observations may be made of actual, real conditions or occurrences; (4) little effort and expense occurs in checking the results of observations.

However, certain disadvantages of observation exist: (1) opinions and motives cannot be obtained; (2) infrequent occurrences may be impossible to obtain; (3) not appropriate when future judgments or predictions are needed; (4) some mechanical devices needed are expensive; (5) complicated instruments may require expert operators; (6) mechanical devices may be too large or fragile to transport to the site; (7) permissions to conduct observations may be difficult or impossible to obtain; (8) supervision and rechecking may be difficult or impossible when there is no permanent location of the observed items.

A listing of applications of the observation technique follows: (1) counting persons or vehicles; (2) determining physical, sociological, or economic characteristics of persons; (3) classifications of occupations; (4) traffic and parking conditions; (5) procedures of work; (6) movement of materials or products; (7) taking inventory of equipment and facilities; (8) *comparative shopping*; (9) actions of sales personnel; (10) shopping habits and actions; (11) audience reactions to entertainment or political events; (12) percentages of persons wearing types, brands of products.

Experimentation is a widely used research process in business. It permits studying a universe by using a relatively small sample; it permits the testing of hypotheses; it permits inferences as to results.

Validity may be achieved in an experiment if the effects of extraneous variables are eliminated or managed so that only the effects of pertinent variables are measured. This may be done by (1) eliminating extraneous effects; (2) equalizing extraneous effects; (3) balancing extraneous effects; (4) randomizing extraneous effects. If samples are selected by a random method, extraneous effects can be made a matter of chance; this chance effect is measurable in inference, and may be allowed for in terms of probability.

The experimental designs of experiments discussed are (1) simple randomized design, and (2) completely randomized design. Other, more complicated designs exist, such as, replicated randomized designs and factorial designs.

Certain procedures exist for effective experimentation: (1) experimental plans based on types of controls; (2) repetition (replication) of experiments to achieve accuracy; (3) make experimental conditions as near to real life conditions as possible; (4) records of prior conditions may be essential or desirable; (5) all reasonable causes and results should be considered; (6) follow the steps of *scientific method*.

The advantages of experimentation are listed as follows: (1) Human error is reduced. (2) Control of the test may be maximized. (3) It is often less time consuming than other methods. (4) Experiments can usually be repeated. (5) More different conditions can be created than by other methods. (6) It permits setting up margins of safety for specifications, by creating extreme conditions to be tested. (7) It may be less costly than other methods. (8) It may be purchased by contract with experimental laboratories.

There are disadvantages to experimentation, however: (1) In some projects, controls may be difficult or impossible to establish. (2) The artificiality of an experiment may be too great. (3) It is of practically no use in determining opinions or judgments.

A listing of applications of experimentation follows: (1) testing of materials and products; (2) testing of products involving customers; (3) test marketing; (4) multiplant or chain tests in selected units; (5) selected members of trade associations may be tested under various conditions; (6) testing advertising layout and display; (7) merchandise arrangement; (8) machine and equipment arrangement; (9) use scale models and pilot plants; (10) use selected real life cases; (11) procedures or techniques of workers; (12) unusual occurrences and emergencies can sometimes be used.

EXERCISES

1. Five rules are given in the text for preparing observationnaires. Describe them in your own words.
2. Prepare an observationnaire for one of the following studies: showroom for merchandise; office for a typing pool; machine shop; sales office.
3. Write a two-page paper describing the conditions of effective observation procedure.
4. Compare and contrast the advantages and disadvantages of the observation technique.
5. Describe an observation procedure for counting shoppers at a downtown intersection.
6. Select one of the *applications of observation techniques* described in the text, and plan the procedure of effective observation.
7. How does the observation technique differ from experimentation?
8. Define experimentation in your own words, including the important elements of the procedure.
9. How does a researcher obtain validity in his experiment?
10. Of the four methods of achieving validity in experimentation, which is most important? Why?
11. What are the important effects of randomizing in selecting samples?
12. What is the *null* hypothesis? Explain.
13. "The simple randomized design of experiment includes not only the control group-experimental group test, but also the before-after test." Compare these two tests.
14. How does the completely randomized design differ from the simple randomized design?
15. Write a two-page paper on the procedures in effective experimentation.
16. Compare and contrast the advantages and disadvantages of experimentation.
17. Select one of the *applications of experimental techniques* as described in the text, and plan an experiment with that technique. It should be detailed and specific.

SELECTED REFERENCES

Balsley, Howard L. *Quantitative Research Methods for Business and Economics*. New York: Random House, 1970.
Mendenhall, William; Ott, Lyman; and Shaeffer, Richard L. *Elementary Survey Sampling*. Belmont, Calif.: Wadsworth, 1971.
Parten, Mildred. *Surveys, Polls, and Samples: Practical Procedures*. New York: Cooper Square, 1966.
Raj, Des. *The Design of Sample Surveys*. New York: McGraw-Hill, 1972.
U.S. Bureau of Labor Statistics. *BLS Handbook of Methods for Sampling and Studies*. Bulletin 1910. Washington, D.C., 1976.

ENDNOTE

1. W. Edwards Deming, *Sample Design in Business Research* (New York: Wiley, 1960), chapter 21.

5

Survey Techniques

At first thought, it may seem that if there is a need for information, it is only natural and logical to ask for it. In other words, if it is necessary to know what people think about certain issues or products, it may appear that the easiest and quickest way to find out is to interview people. A great deal of such surveying is being done today. More of it will occur in the future as businesspersons and others strive to get more facts to guide their decision making. Therefore, it is imperative that sound survey techniques be understood and used.

Surveys can result in valuable findings if correct procedures are followed. The use of well-worded, satisfactorily pretested questionnaires administered by trained and instructed interviewers who follow sound patterns for selecting respondents can result in the collection of useful information that would otherwise be unavailable. On the other hand, when poorly planned and conducted, the questionnaire survey technique is unlikely to be a satisfactory device for securing data.

Certain conditions must exist before a satisfactory survey can be planned. Among the most important of these conditions are:

1. It must be decided definitely and specifically what information is needed in view of the purposes of the project and the uses to which the findings are to be put.

2. It must be determined that the questionnaire survey technique is the best information-collecting technique available for the particular problem under study.

3. Certain characteristics of the universe must be known; that is, the geographical area and the persons and/or the other types of cases or units in which the researcher is interested must be decided upon.

4. It is necessary to establish which type of questionnaire survey technique is most appropriate in this particular project—mail, personal interview, or telephone.

The process of collecting information, regardless of the technique used, requires that the collector must first decide what facts he needs to obtain. These facts must be those that are necessary to the solution of the problem under study, and they must be set forth as specifically written statements which describe and explain exactly the information required. If it is decided to obtain the information by a questionnaire survey, the questionnaire can then be constructed with questions that are carefully worded and arranged in such a manner as to obtain the specific data needed.

Fact finding should always be accomplished by the techniques that are most efficient in the light of the problem being investigated and the time and financial limitations involved. There is no general rule that can be given for deciding when and where the questionnaire survey technique will serve best. The researcher will have to decide which technique or combination of techniques would be most efficient for each particular research project.

The universe, or population, is all the persons or cases in which the researcher is interested. For example, if it were necessary to know what brands of canned foods are purchased by the homemakers of a city, the universe would be all the homemakers in that city. The questionnaire would then need to be prepared in such a manner as to elicit the desired information from such persons. The geographical location of this particular universe would probably make it possible to reach the respondents by personal interviews; consequently, the questionnaire would be constructed with that method of distribution and approach in mind. The homemakers of the city would include all levels of education, age, family sizes, and economic status. The questions asked them, therefore, would have to be worded so that they could be correctly understood and answered by all these types of persons.

An example of the importance of knowing some of the main characteristics of a universe occurred a few years ago when a used car dealer in a city in the Southwest discovered that he needed to know more about what makes of cars to stock. It was decided that a questionnaire survey would be conducted among his present and potential customers. This dealer specialized in selling cars that were four to six years old.

Preliminary study of the problem brought out the fact that in this city, the buyers of such cars constituted a group of people who lived mostly in certain sections of town and had certain racial, nationality, educational, and occupational characteristics. With this knowledge in mind, the questionnaire was constructed in such a manner as to be meaningful and effective with this kind of universe. Unless these facts about the universe had been known, the questions used in the questionnaire could well have contained words or terms that would have been unclear to many of the respondents. It is even possible that words that meant one thing to the typical person in that city might have had a different meaning to the particular group in which the used car dealer was interested.

There are situations in which the universe cannot be satisfactorily delimited before the survey begins. Sometimes this situation may call for a questionnaire with one or more *filter questions*, which are asked first to determine whether the respondent is actually a member of the universe in which the researcher is interested. Suppose that the manager of a taxicab company desired to know the characteristics of the persons who ride regularly in taxicabs and why they use this means of transportation. If he already knew where such persons lived, he could go to their residences and interview them with a questionnaire that was appropriate for these kinds of persons. But if he does not know who these people are, he may have to visit all types of residences to find the regular riders. The first question could be the *filter*: "Do you usually ride in a taxicab at least once a week?" A person answering yes to this question might be considered a "regular rider." The regular riders only would then be asked the rest of the questions on the questionnaire. Filter questions usually are not a satisfactory substitute for the process of carefully establishing the characteristics and location of the universe before a survey is started. When it is not feasible to do this, however, filter questions may be an acceptable device.

The nature of the survey will determine which method of distributing the questionnaires and obtaining replies will be best. There are certain types of projects that may be most efficiently handled by mail questionnaires, others call for personal interviews, while some kinds of data can be collected satisfactorily by telephone inquiries. The advantages and disadvantages of each of these three ways of conducting surveys will be discussed in this chapter. The conditions which favor the use of each technique will be pointed out, and the conditions under which each would be inadvisable will be described.

MAIL QUESTIONNAIRE TECHNIQUE

The postal system offers a valuable avenue for distributing and receiving questionnaires. The advantages and disadvantages of this technique should be carefully weighed before a final decision is made about the survey technique to be used.

ADVANTAGES OF A MAIL QUESTIONNAIRE

(1) Mail questionnaires can be sent to persons in widely scattered locations covering a large geographical area.

(2) Prospective respondents can be reached at relatively low cost.

(3) Respondents can be reached in their homes or offices where they read and answer the questionnaire.

(4) Mail questionnaires can be answered more carefully than personal or telephone questionnaires because more time can be allowed for thinking through the answer.

(5) No interviewer is present to bias the answers or to make mistakes in recording information.

(6) Certain personal and economic data may be given more completely and accurately in an unsigned mail questionnaire. Data about personal fi-

nances, age, and some kinds of personal opinions may be refused in face-to-face interviews or in telephone conversations.

DISADVANTAGES OF MAIL QUESTIONNAIRE

(1) A relatively large percentage, even 50 percent to 90 percent, of mail questionnaires will usually not be returned.

(2) Answers to certain questions may be omitted or the questions may be incorrectly answered because they are misunderstood.

(3) Mail questionnaires can be sent only to persons who can read and write.

(4) Even among persons who can read and write, some persons are less likely than others to respond to a mail questionnaire. Ordinarily, persons who are less well educated, those who are away from their homes much of the time, persons whose occupation does not call for much writing, or people who have little spare time on their hands, are all less likely to answer questionnaires.

(5) In order to induce respondents to return satisfactorily completed questionnaires in sufficient quantity to constitute an adequate number and percentage of replies, certain cost-raising steps may have to be taken: (a) premiums may have to be offered; (b) special care and time may be given to the preparation of an effective questionnaire; (c) it may be necessary to use expensive paper, pictures, and printing; (d) a low response rate may require that follow-up letters be sent out; and (e) in some cases, personal interviews may be necessary to obtain replies from certain persons and/or to learn if nonrespondents will keep the sample from being representative.

(6) A mailing list that contains up-to-date addresses of the persons it is desired to reach may be difficult and expensive to obtain.

(7) Much valuable information that could be obtained by observation during personal interviews cannot be secured by mail questionnaires.

(8) Degree of representativeness of a sample obtained by mail may be difficult to determine. Certain visual checks on the characteristics of the respondents and their surroundings as they might shed light on the consistency, honesty, and accuracy of the replies cannot be applied in mail questionnaires.

WHEN TO USE THE MAIL QUESTIONNAIRE

The mail questionnaire is an effective technique when used under appropriate conditions. Some of these conditions are listed in the following paragraphs.

When the type of information required can be obtained in satisfactory form by a mail questionnaire that can be answered easily and quickly. Answers that can be stated correctly in the form of a yes or no, a check mark, or a number after a checklist of choices are types that meet these requirements.

When the information is possessed by persons who are able and willing to respond through the mail. Persons who have at least a high school education are more likely to reply. Clerical workers and white collar workers in general are usually more accustomed to writing and filling out forms. These persons will, therefore, be more willing to fill out and return mail questionnaires than will less-educated persons. Questionnaires sent to such articulate groups as business managers and lawyers, doctors, accountants, and club members are more likely to be completed and returned than questionnaires sent to nonprofessional persons less accustomed to writing and expressing their opinions on paper.

When the universe is composed of a relatively homogeneous group of persons with similar interests, education, economic and social backgrounds. A questionnaire directed exclusively to truck drivers, for example, could contain questions of particular interest to such a relatively homogeneous group. The words and terms used in the questions could be those that were of special significance and clarity of meaning to truckers. Consequently, a larger percentage of replies could be expected.

A universe composed of a heterogeneous group of persons with widely different interests, educational levels, economic and social characteristics is difficult to sample by mail. It is difficult to construct a mail questionnaire that will be clearly and uniformly understood by such a varied universe. Also, the subject matter of the questionnaire may not be of equal interest to all types of persons in the group; and, therefore, the percentage of returns from each type of respondent may be quite different.

A mail survey that is sanctioned by a professional or other type of association and is conducted among the membership of such a relatively homogeneous group will usually bring in a high percentage of satisfactorily completed questionnaires. Another situation in which a mail survey might be appropriate could be represented by the case of the editor of a magazine who wanted to survey its subscribers. Its list of addresses might compose a reasonably homogeneous universe, at least to the extent that all the subscribers were apparently interested enough in the types of the material in the publication to pay the subscription price. Some magazines request certain information from their subscribers at the time or soon after they start taking the publication. This provides the magazine with some valuable information that could be used in the compilation of a mail questionnaire and in the analysis and evaluation of returned questionnaires.

When up-to-date, satisfactorily complete, and reasonably priced mailing lists are available. Membership lists of various types of organizations can be obtained for a fee for appropriate uses. Telephone directories that are revised at least once a year will contain the names and addresses of the persons with telephones in their homes and other establishments. The address of the person may be used to locate him by type of neighborhood and, consequently, give some indication of his economic and social characteristics.

In larger cities, there will usually be a city directory that is prepared by a company that specializes in this activity. This directory will contain the names and addresses of persons and establishments by streets. Such data as the occupation, home ownership status of occupants, and whether they possess a telephone will often be given. These directories can be used to compile mailing lists for different types of universes or populations.

In many cities, there are firms that specialize in compiling mailing lists for various purposes. These can be purchased by an interested researcher. Certain types of mailing lists may be compiled under appropriate conditions from official records in state and local government offices.

If the universe happens to be the customers of the business sponsoring the mail survey, the mailing list should be immediately available. The records of the firm, if well kept, will contain the names and addresses of the persons or firms in which the researcher is interested.

The nearest public or college library will have several directories and other publications that contain lists of names of persons or establishments in certain fields. The researcher should inquire at these libraries about the types of mailings lists that might be compiled from available materials. The local chamber of commerce will be likely to possess several publications of possible value to anyone desiring to develop a mailing list.

Before a mailing list is used to send out questionnaires, it must be determined whether the addresses are those of persons who compose the universe in which the researcher is interested. The mailing list must contain all, or at least be highly representative of all, the persons or establishments which constitute the universe that is being studied. A mailing list should not be used if it contains only an unrepresentative part of the population or only the portion that is in certain income groups or are members of an association whose membership does not contain all or even a representative portion of the persons in the field. Mailing lists must be revised frequently to be reasonably up to date.

When mail questionnaires can be used in conjunction with personal interviews or telephone inquiries in order to reach certain respondents more economically or effectively than they could be reached by either technique alone. In some surveys, certain types of respondents may be able and willing to supply information by mail but not in personal or telephone interviews. If such persons compose part of the universe, it may be sound and economical procedure to use mail questionnaires to obtain the desired information from them.

Some surveys use a combination of personal interviews or telephone calls and mail questionnaires. The purpose of the personal interviews and telephone inquiries may be to elicit interest and to introduce or explain the nature of the information required. As much information as possible will be obtained during the conversation. But if it is not possible to obtain all the desired data at this first meeting, the unfinished parts of the questionnaire or an extra copy will be left with the respondent or sent to him to be completed and mailed as soon as possible. Another possibility is represented by the plan of first attempting to reach and obtain usable replies from all persons by mail. Personal interviews, and in some instances telephone calls, would then be used to reach those persons who did not respond to the mail questionnaires.

It is essential to realize, however, that when a survey employs more than one technique to reach the respondents, the replies from persons contacted by a given technique may not always be comparable to the responses of those persons contacted by different techniques. For instance, it is possible that a certain question asked in a telephone inquiry may be answered somewhat differently than it would in either a personal interview or a mail questionnaire. This possibility of lack of strict comparability of replies obtained by different survey techniques should always be kept in mind when a survey is being planned, when techniques are being pretested, and finally, when the returns are being tabulated and analyzed.

When sufficient funds are available for the completion of a satisfactory mail questionnaire survey. A successful survey by mail requires that the questionnaire, before it is finally mailed out, be carefully prepared, pretested on the types of persons to whom it is to be sent, and revised in the light of the pretest results.

A well-worded cover letter will be needed to introduce the questionnaire, briefly explain the purpose of the survey, and, most important of all, induce the respondent to fill out and return the questionnaire form. For best results, this letter should appear to be an individual letter, and, in many instances, it should be signed personally. The use of pictures and color may be found advisable.

The questionnaire form should be sent as first-class mail and should include an addressed and stamped return envelope. When a relatively large number of questionnaires is being sent out, it may be more economical to use return-postage-guaranteed envelopes for the replies. Postal cards may be used in surveys which ask only a few questions about subjects that would not be considered confidential or embarrassing to the respondents. A folded double card may be used. The folded-in half could contain the return address on one side and the questionnaire on the other. In many cases, however, the use of a card may cause the respondents to believe that the survey is of too little importance to be worth the trouble of replying.

Attention in some instances is attracted to letters that are addressed in longhand and contain an individually affixed stamp instead of a metered stamp. The metered stamp, even though first class, appears much like non-first-class mail. It is exceedingly important that the letter containing the questionnaire be noticed. The letter must be one that will be opened immediately or else there is a definite possibility that it will be forgotten and thrown away unanswered.

Sound sampling procedure often requires that follow-up letters should be sent out to at least a portion of the persons who do not respond to the first letter. Also, personal interviews may be necessary with a cross-section of the nonrespondents to determine if they are the same types or are different types of persons than the ones who returned the mail questionnaires. If these nonrespondents are found to be different from the respondents, they may need to be interviewed in sufficient number to have them adequately represented in the general sample.

When sufficient time can be given for the replies to be received from the respondents to a mail questionnaire. The data-collecting process in a mail survey can be expected to require three weeks to a month, including the time required for follow-up letters to the persons who do not send back the first questionnaire. If the survey must be conducted in a shorter time than this, personal interviews or even telephone calls may have to be considered to determine if they could be completed satisfactorily within the time available.

Letters can be sent out at times that will cause them to reach the respondent on days when smaller amounts of mail are received; and, consequently, the mail questionnaire will have a better chance to be seen and answered. The middle days of the week are better than weekends or Mondays. The first of the month is crowded with bills for many families. Days just before or after holidays and vacation periods should be avoided.

PERSONAL INTERVIEW TECHNIQUE

Correctly conducted personal interviews constitute one of the most satisfactory survey techniques. Ordinarily, unless there are clearly evident reasons for not using this technique, the personal interview is the generally suggested procedure for carrying out questionnaire surveys.

ADVANTAGES OF PERSONAL INTERVIEWS

(1) Presence of an interviewer greatly increases the percentage of interviews that will result in satisfactorily completed questionnaires.

(2) A well-trained interviewer can increase the accuracy and completeness of responses by explanations and by checking over the questionnaire form before leaving the place of the interview.

(3) The interviewer by observation can collect certain information that might be refused by the respondent in answering questions. This is especially true for the types of facts that might embarrass the respondent or be considered confidential. For example, if necessary, ages of persons can be estimated for some purposes within reasonably narrow brackets. Approximate economic level may be determined within general groupings from observation of the size, type, and condition of the house, furniture, automobile, lawn, and the characteristics of the neighborhood. Appearance of the clothing worn and apparent educational or intellectual level of the respondents may also help in classifying respondents and interpreting their replies.

(4) Personal interviews can often result in obtaining a more representative sample of the universe than is possible with a mail survey or telephone inquiries. The problems resulting from low response rates of all or certain types of persons in surveys not using the personal interview technique can usually be reduced greatly when personal interviews are employed. Interviewers can go wherever the persons in the sample live instead of being confined to reaching only those individuals on an available mailing list or those who possess a listed telephone.

(5) Personal interviews can provide for certain measurements or tests of the accuracy and dependability of the answers obtained. The honesty and consistency of the replies can be checked by observing the interest and attention of the respondent. The apparent knowledge of the person about the subject can also be observed and used to help evaluate the correctness of his answers.

DISADVANTAGES OF PERSONAL INTERVIEWS

(1) When persons to be interviewed are scattered in locations that are long distances apart, personal interviews may require too much time and money. If it is desired to interview only a few persons in each of certain cities, the time and expenditures required for travel, interviewer recruiting, training, and supervision may be excessive.

(2) Poorly trained interviewers may bias the answers of respondents by hurrying too rapidly through the interview or by recording replies incorrectly. Prejudices of the interviewer can have definite influences on the person being interviewed. Interviewers can affect answers if they have a tendency to get restless, shuffle their feet, sigh, or clear their throat when a question is being considered. On the other hand, if they act particularly interested in a given question, show no tendency to want to move quickly on to the next question, offer an opinion, or give examples, they can influence replies in another direction.

(3) The costs per completed questionnaire are usually higher for personal interviews than for mail questionnaires and telephone inquiries. This is due to the expenses involved in recruiting, training, and supervising interviewers as well as their compensation and expense accounts. The comparative costs of personal interviews and mail and telephone techniques appear considerably less unfavorable to personal interviews, however, when the amount and the quality of the information collected per interview are compared.

It should be kept in mind that an appreciable amount of added data can be observed and recorded in personal interviews. Also, the accuracy and completeness of the replies can usually be established more satisfactorily in face-to-face interviews. It may often be the case that the costs per item of usable information obtained by personal interviews may not be higher and may even be lower than in either mail surveys or telephone inquiries. The research planner must study the comparative costs in the light of these quantity and quality considerations before he decides which technique to use.

(4) Certain types of personal and financial information may be refused in face-to-face interviews. Such information might be supplied more willingly and accurately on mail questionnaires, especially if they are to be unsigned.

(5) Personal interviews may reduce the cooperation of respondents because the interviews may be considered an intrusion.

(6) Certain types of information cannot be supplied accurately in the time allowed in the usual personal interview. The respondent may need time to look up data or to confer with other persons before answering a question.

WHEN TO USE THE PERSONAL INTERVIEW TECHNIQUE

It will bear repeating that, in general, the personal interview technique is considered the best survey procedure. Ordinarily, it is employed unless there are definite advantages that can be established for the mail technique or telephone inquiries. One of the reasons why the advantages and disadvantages of mail and telephone surveys should be clearly understood by the researcher is due to the fact that he needs to know when to use or not to use the personal interview technique. Some of the main conditions favoring the use of personal interviews exist when the following situations prevail:

• When personal interviews can be used in conjunction with or as supplements to other survey techniques.

• When the quality of information needed requires that personal interviews be used.

• When a sufficient number of qualified interviewers can be obtained.

• When there are adequate funds and time to recruit, train, supervise, and compensate the personnel required in the use of the personal interview technique.

• When the questionnaire requests no embarrassing personal or financial information that might be refused in a face-to-face interview.

• When the respondent will have sufficient time during the interview to obtain and give the information asked for.

• When depth interviewing is required. *Depth interviews* are those in which the interviewer asks a series of probing questions in order to draw out and fully develop the ideas and reactions of the respondent. The original question in the series may be the only question on the subject listed on the questionnaire sheet. The probing questions must be decided upon by the interviewer and asked in such a manner and sequence as the interviewer finds necessary to obtain the desired information. Therefore, it can be seen that the type of information desired when depth interviews are considered appropriate can best be obtained by personal interviews.

It should be pointed out, however, that depth interviewing cannot be done satisfactorily by the ordinary interviewer. Specially trained and experienced persons are required for such interrogation. An interviewer without these qualifications should not attempt to use this type of questioning because of the danger involved in prejudicing the respondent by the probing questions and by the overemphasis or underemphasis that may be given by the interviewer to certain aspects of the subject.

• When the universe is composed of areas sufficiently compact geographically to make personal interviews feasible. If the persons to be interviewed all live in a given city or are distributed in several cities each of which contains, say twenty-five or more respondents for the usual consumer survey, personal interviews are usually practical. If the persons to be questioned live in rural areas but on good highways and near enough together to keep travel costs reasonably low, again personal interviews may be feasible. The problem of recruiting, training, and supervising interviewers in their field work is increased, however, if there are several cities involved, especially if the cities are some distance apart or are located a long way from the city in which the director of the survey is stationed.

A considerable number of research firms now maintain a standby panel of experienced supervisors and interviewers in various representative cities and areas across the nation. These field workers are used periodically as the need arises to supervise and conduct interviewing surveys in their home areas. This arrangement makes it feasible to carry out nation-wide or regional surveys in which some interviewers may be asked to obtain as few as ten or fifteen interviews in a particular survey. These part-time field workers are willing to engage in such projects, however, because they usually can stay at home overnight and can expect other small survey jobs from time to time as well as large ones now and then. Other research companies may also use these same field workers. The research firm and its clients benefit from these arrangements because recruiting and training costs and travel expenses can be kept at an acceptable level.

TELEPHONE INQUIRY TECHNIQUE

The telephone has a definite, though limited, place as a device for collecting information. Its advantages, disadvantages, and the situations in which its use is appropriate will be discussed briefly.

ADVANTAGES OF TELEPHONE INQUIRIES

(1) Information can be collected in a relatively short period of time. Between 15 to 20 calls can usually be made per hour. This means that from 120 to 160 calls can usually be made in eight hours. For certain surveys, this may be a large enough sample for the purposes of the project.

(2) Telephone interviews can be timed to occur at any specific period. For example, if it is desired to know whether people are listening to or viewing a particular radio or television program, the calls can be placed at the time that the programs are on the air.

(3) Interviews can be completed at a relatively low cost.

(4) The names and addresses of the persons in the universe are easily accessible—an increasing number of dwelling units have telephones in both urban and rural areas.

(5) The addresses listed in the telephone directory can be used to show in what type of neighborhood the respondent lives.

(6) The telephone directory provides a well-prepared listing of the persons in the universe from which a correctly balanced probability or random sample can be obtained. The procedures for constructing appropriate sampling patterns will be discussed in detail in later chapters.

(7) Telephone inquiries can be used to reach certain persons who will not answer mail questionnaires or cannot be interviewed face to face. Phone calls, therefore, can, under appropriate conditions, also be used to supplement the other techniques.

DISADVANTAGES OF TELEPHONE INQUIRIES

(1) Telephone inquiries are limited to persons with listed telephones. The sample will be distorted if the universe includes some persons who cannot be reached by telephone. In general, the persons whose names are listed in a telephone directory are in the upper economic levels and are also the more permanent, longer-time residents. If all groups in a city must be included in the sample, the telephone survey will not obtain a representative cross-section. Persons without telephones will have to be reached by other techniques.

(2) The telephone questionnaire can ask for a relatively limited amount of information. Usually a call cannot last over two or three minutes, and not more than five or six questions can be asked.

(3) The type of information is limited to that which can be given in simple, short answers of a few words or with a yes or no.

(4) An adequate amount of classification data may be impossible to obtain in telephone surveys. The respondent cannot be seen, his voice may be misleading, his surroundings cannot be observed, and in the short period of two or three minutes, little or no time is available to ask questions in order to obtain information to be used in the analysis of the replies.

WHEN TO USE THE TELPHONE INQUIRY TECHNIQUE

In spite of its limited usefulness, the telephone inquiry technique should sometimes be employed. Its usefulness is indicated in the following paragraphs.

When the universe is composed of those persons whose names are listed in telephone directories. The telephone technique will often be appropriate for a survey to be conducted among those persons whose incomes place them in, say, the upper 50 or 60 percent of the residents of the area covered by a directory. This statement is based on the assumption that telephones would be found mostly in the middle- and upper-income homes. The percentages in these income levels will, of course, vary from one city or one part of a city to another. In some relatively prosperous cities, as many as 80 to 90 percent of the dwelling units may have listed telephones. A researcher will need to determine whether telephone subscribers in the geographic area in which he is interested constitute the universe from which he desires to collect information.

The actual universe will often not be confined entirely to telephone subscribers, but for certain types of surveys they may be acceptably representative of the kinds of persons it is desired to survey. Suppose that the purpose of the survey was to find out what percentage of the homes had such expensive appliances as electric dishwashers, color television sets, or central air-conditioning systems. It could be assumed that nearly all such homes would have telephones; and, therefore, the universe, for all practical purposes, could be considered as composed of the occupants of the homes listed in the telephone directory.

When only five or six easily answered questions need to be asked. Telephone inquiries are appropriate if the questions can be answered accurately with a simple yes or no or at the most with an easily recalled two- or three-word response. Such questions as, "Do you own a color TV set?" "Are you listening to your radio?" or "How many automobiles do you own?" are examples of questions which can be answered easily and quickly.

When the survey must be conducted in a relatively short period of time. As has been pointed out in the discussion of the advantages of the telephone inquiry, from 120 to 160 interviews can be completed by one person who spends all his time calling during an eight-hour period. This is several times more respondents than can be contacted by any other technique in an equal amount of time.

When the subject is so interesting or important to respondents that they will be willing to stay on the telephone long enough to answer more than the usual five or six short-answer questions. Although the telephone inquiry technique must usually be confined to surveys which require only five or six short, simple answers, in a few situations, it may be employed to obtain answers to longer questionnaires. For example, a trade or professional association may decide to conduct a survey among a representative sample of the members of the organization. If such a survey covered a subject of considerable importance to the members, it may be possible to ask a relatively large number of questions.

When it is unnecessary to observe the respondent and his surroundings to obtain classification data to aid in interpreting answers. While it may usually be desirable to obtain classification information about a respondent during an interview, it may not be essential in certain instances. First, the added facts may not be needed in the interpretation of the replies. For instance, the purpose of a survey may be to determine quickly whether there are enough of a new kind of household appliance in a city to warrant the expense to a firm of sending several repairpersons away to take a course in repairing the appliances. Perhaps all the data needed are the approximate number of such appliances in town and their ages, brands, and sizes.

Second, if classification and interpretive data are needed, there may be more effective ways of obtaining them. The name, telephone number, and address of the persons to be called must be written down on a recording sheet before the telephoning begins. If a well-prepared city directory is used to obtain the list of respondents to be called, such added information as occupation and ownership status of occupants can be placed after each name. Even in telephone directories, the address of the respondent may provide a helpful guide to his socio-economic status because of the known characteristics of the neighborhood in which he lives.

In addition, the address can be used to show where the respondents live who answer in certain ways. For example, in the analysis of the findings from a telephone survey, it may be found that the greatest percentage of homes with air-cooling units are located in the sections of town in which the highest income families live. Also, the house numbers in the addresses may show that more than twice as many houses facing south have air conditioners than is true for houses facing north. This could be determined, for instance, if it were known that most streets ran east and west and the odd numbers were on the north side of the street and even numbers on the south.

The telephone inquiry technique can sometimes be used effectively when several hundreds or thousands of persons may first be interviewed in brief two or three minute calls. After the calls have been completed, the various neighborhoods of the city may be visited and the chief classifying characteristics of each noted. The homes of a representative sample of the persons telephoned may also be observed and certain data recorded about them. This information can then be used in the interpretation of the answers obtained in the telephone calls.

When telephone inquiries can be used in conjunction with or to supplement mail questionnaires and personal interviews. Telephone calls may be made to persons who have not responded to a mail questionnaire or to an attempted personal interview. Or telephone inquiries may be used in conjunction with the other survey techniques in such a manner that each technique will be used to obtain information under the conditions most appropriate for each type of person to be reached.

RECRUITING AND TRAINING INTERVIEWERS AND INVESTIGATORS

The process of obtaining qualified interviewers and field investigators will be discussed under two headings: (1) recruiting, and (2) training, instructing, and supervising. The comments which follow apply to field workers who will be expected to ask questions of persons as well as to investigators whose main job will be to observe and record information concerning certain specified conditions.

RECRUITING INTERVIEWERS AND INVESTIGATORS

Teachers in all levels of school and graduate students in colleges may be efficient interviewers or investigators. The superintendent in the public school system can often supply names of teachers who are on the substitute list. In summer or other vacation periods, regular teachers may be interested in doing field work. Clubs or organizations will usually have some members who are willing and qualified to do satisfactory interviewing on a part-time basis.

In many cities, there are persons who do field work now and then for one or more research firms. These persons usually will be reasonably well qualified. Their experience will enable them to do better work in most instances than could be done by persons who are recruited for one job only. Research companies ordinarily know the names of such field workers. These persons, therefore, compose a national pool of local interviewers throughout the United States. A smaller firm without a regular research department may be able to locate these interviewers by placing advertisements in the local newspapers.

Major Qualifications of Interviewers and Investigators

Willingness to work is necessary because personal interviewing requires considerable walking and physical, as well as nervous, energy. A person who is interested in this kind of work and who wants the income from it will usually be willing to put forth the effort required. These two characteristics should be sought in the persons employed to do interviewing.

A person who is careless about reading and following instructions should not be used in field investigations. His interviews or observations are unlikely to be accurate or complete. The quality of the factual base of the research findings depends largely upon the complete honesty and accuracy of the collector of the original data. Any hint of dishonesty in an interviewer or investigator can destroy the value of his work.

There are various other qualifications that may be of importance, such as, age, sex, personal appearance, general education, and experience. Persons under twenty-five, for example, may be too young for interviews with older persons. Women are usually considered superior for interviews with women, especially in homes, and men are ordinarily used for interviews with businesspersons.

The more effective interviewers seem to be those who do not dress too expensively. They often are rather average looking and act like individuals of average intelligence and not as expertly informed persons. Experienced investigators, if all other qualities are equal, usually are better than inexperienced ones.

In summary, the interviewer should have those characteristics that make it likely that people will be willing to answer honestly and completely the questions the interviewer asks. This means that the interviewer should be a person with a quiet, pleasant manner and appearance. An investigator who is too timid or too aggressive, too low or too high in apparent intelligence will be relatively ineffective in getting information from other persons. In the final analysis, the interviewers employed should be individuals who will be most likely to do satisfactory work in view of the type of persons to be interviewed and the kind of information that is sought in the survey.

Compensation

The field worker must be correctly instructed in regard to the following:

1. The rate of pay for field work.
2. The expenses that will be paid and exactly how they are to be computed.
3. The reports that must be kept and sent in to show time worked and expenses incurred.
4. When payment will be made.

The strategic importance of the data-collecting process performed by research field workers is so great that it is imperative that the compensation be adequate to attract the type of field worker needed. In general, it can be said that interviewers and observers should be paid the prevailing wage in their community for the average skilled worker and/or white collar worker below the supervisory level.

It is true that pay alone does not assure that efficient persons will be obtained and satisfactory field work performed. A sound program for recruiting, training, and supervising is also essential. In addition, the morale of the workers must be maintained by a feeling that they are really considered to be important persons who are performing a vital part of the research process. Research firms that have a panel of part-time field workers located in various cities may have a policy of keeping in touch with these workers. This can be done by newsletters, periodic visits by supervisory or training personnel, and sometimes by regional conferences.

Ordinarily the compensation should be based on the time spent by the field worker on the assigned job. It is of prime importance that the interviews or observations be done correctly. If payment is measured by the number of completed questionnaires or schedules sent in, a premium is placed on speed; and, consequently, the quality of the field work may suffer.

Trial interviews will have been conducted as part of the planning for the survey. The approximate amount of time required to complete interviews can, thereby, be ascertained. The interviewer can be instructed that such pilot interviews have shown that the typical interview can be completed satisfactorily in, say, ten minutes, and that about four interviews can be obtained in an hour, including necessary travel time between interviews. It should be emphasized that completeness and accuracy of recorded responses should still be considered as of greatest importance.

TRAINING, INSTRUCTING, AND SUPERVISING FIELD WORKERS

Any program of training and instruction of field workers should be carefully planned and conducted. The ideal situation would be to hold several training conferences personally led by an experienced field supervisor. Each session would last two or three hours, and there would be one or more sessions depending on the complexity of the field work to be done. The prospective interviewers or investigators would be paid for attending these training sessions and for studying the written instructions during and after the sessions. Before the field work begins, trial interviews would be conducted under the close supervision of the field supervisor.

If such training sessions are not feasible in actual practice, the instruction of the field workers must be provided by written information sent through the mail. The interviewers are usually encouraged to write, wire, or telephone collect for any added information or clarification that might be needed before or during the interviewing period. Some research organizations have their prospective field workers take brief written examinations over the instructions given to them. The grades on these tests help to evaluate the field personnel. The results of the tests can also be used to improve instructional procedures in the future.

When a research firm has recruited and trained a panel of part-time field workers in cities across the nation, these interviewers can usually be given instructions by mail sufficient to enable them to carry out field work in subsequent surveys. Supervisors from the central office can be sent out now and then to visit and confer with the various field workers stationed over the country. Some research firms train certain field workers to serve as supervisors in the communities in which these field workers live.

Regardless of whether the training program is carried out in personal conferences or handled by mail, there are certain points that should be covered in any training procedure. These points should be written down to be followed in the instructional periods. Copies should be given to each field worker for his guidance during the training sessions and afterward in his field work. More detailed written explanations will ordinarily be required if the instructions are to be mailed to the field workers instead of being presented to them in face-to-face training sessions.

A summary of the suggested points to be included in a set of instructions for training field workers is included in the following paragraphs.

Purpose of Project

Enough should be explained about the purpose of the project to convince the field worker of the importance of doing accurate work. Usually, the whole purpose of the survey need not be described. Certainly, the intended use of the findings, if they should be kept confidential, need not be divulged. An interviewer, in fact, may do more impartial work if he does not know, for example, the name of the company that is paying for the research or the brand name of a product that is the primary subject of the research.

The imperativeness of collecting only accurate information must be stressed. The field worker should be convinced that bias and partiality are two of the greatest dangers to be faced. The following points should be stressed: The facts, even though they may make unpleasant reading, nevertheless, are what must be obtained. The company paying for the survey is paying to get the facts, whether pleasant or unpleasant. The work of the field workers will be judged primarily on two bases. Did they carry out the interviewing according to instructions? And did they impartially and accurately collect the requested information? In short, everyone concerned with the research project has an overriding interest in obtaining all the pertinent facts whatever they are.

Interviews or Observations

The instructions must cover such things as the number of interviews or observations to be completed; when the field work is to begin and when it is to be completed; where the interviews or observations are to occur; the exact geographical location of the area to be covered including the boundaries, such as, streets, roads, or buildings and landmarks to follow. Maps may be supplied with the areas to be covered marked distinctly.

Who or what is to be interviewed or observed and how they are to be selected must be carefully described. For example, it might be that only married women between the ages of approximately forty to fifty-five compose the universe which is to be sampled. The instructions to the field workers should designate these types of women and give suggestions as to how to recognize such persons. Or suppose that the universe was all the retail gasoline filling stations within the city limits of certain towns. The instructions should tell how to identify these stations and whether garages and small grocery stores which sell gasoline should be included.

The exact procedure for selecting the prospective respondents should be explained in detail. A selection system that eliminates the judgment or opinion of the field worker should be presented. The importance of having a selection system that removes interviewer bias in the sampling process will be discussed in a later chapter. It is mentioned here, however, because of the ever-present danger that the validity of the whole survey can be brought into question because interviewers were not adequately instructed in the matter of selecting respondents. In some of the better planned surveys, the field workers are given the actual names or addresses of the persons or businesses to be interviewed or observed. If substitutions are necessary, the specific method for making them is explained.

The approach and introduction must be explained satisfactorily. Interviewers should be instructed about how to greet prospective respondents and how to introduce or explain briefly the purpose of the visit. One or two pretested greetings and brief introductory explanations may be given to the interviewers to be committed to memory. The material should be well enough learned, however, that it does not sound mechanical or artificial.

The advantage of such memorized material is that it can be tried out and perfected to accomplish the best results possible for the majority of the interviews. Further, time can be saved, and the interviewer will avoid poor openings and misleading or inaccurate explanations. Interviewers usually welcome a carefully prepared and pretested introduction that they can learn and have ready without the worry and uncertainty that they might experience if they had to learn an introduction during time-wasting experiences of their own.

In some surveys, it may be found necessary to make an early comment to the effect that the interviewer is not selling anything nor will anyone attempt to sell the respondent anything later as a result of this interview. Letters of introduction and identification cards with their photographs may be supplied to field workers to help them if needed in their introductions.

The inexperienced interviewer may find it helpful to stand before a mirror and observe how he appears when he speaks. His facial expressions, the way he stands, what he does with his lips and hands may bear study and improvement. The correct amount of a pleasant smile will often be a useful addition to the approach.

Interviewers should be given some advice about the appropriate way to dress to make the most effective impression. The kinds of clothing to wear will depend on the particular type of respondents to be approached in the survey. Either overdressing or dressing too casually should be avoided. In general, the field worker should dress as one in his job should be expected to dress. Usually this will mean that he will dress about as his prospective respondents ordinarily dress when they are paying a friendly visit to a home or the usual call to a business establishment.

The cooperation of respondents will be increased if they are convinced that their opinions and answers are important. The interviewer must pay careful attention to the statements made by the person being interviewed. The interviewer should realize that, in a sampling survey, each respondent represents perhaps hundreds or thousands of persons of his type. Therefore, his answers are not merely to be considered in the light of one person only. The respondent can be told in the introduction that he has been chosen as a good representative of his group. This statement can be so worded that he does not feel that he is "just an average person," which he probably is not, but instead that he is a "good representative" of the type of people who are his friends and associates.

It also is advisable to inform the respondent that a good deal of money and time is being spent to obtain this important information from the people most qualified to give it: the persons who have been selected for these interviews. Finally, it should be made known that the facts collected in this survey will make a difference in decisions to be made in the future.

The Questionnaire or Schedule

The meaning of each question and part of a schedule must be thoroughly explained to interviewers. All questions or items must be discussed in such detail that every word and phrase is clearly understood.

What constitutes a complete and adequate answer to each question must be explained and illustrated. The exact way that information is to be recorded on the survey forms must be explained and illustrated. If the interviewer is to record the answers himself, he must be cautioned to record the exact words used by the respondent in order to avoid the tendency of the interviewer to use general stereotypes or to substitute his opinions or thoughts for those of the respondent. The interviewer should be instructed to obtain full answers and to write comments in margins or on backs of sheets if necessary. A well-prepared questionnaire or schedule provides ample space for answers whether they are to be written by the respondent or the interviewer.

It should be pointed out that each questionnaire or schedule should be edited by the field worker before the interview or observation process is terminated. The field worker, before moving on to the next respondent, must look over the form that has just been filled out to determine if it has been completed correctly, clearly, and without omissions. Any needed additions and changes should be made before leaving the place of the interview or observation.

In many surveys of homemakers, the respondent will not be concerned about seeing the questionnaire. When this is the situation, it is probably best for the interviewers to ask the questions and record the replies. Only in situations in which the fullness and accuracy of answers will be improved by having the respondents write down their own answers should that procedure be followed. On the other hand, some respondents, especially businesspersons and professional persons, are reluctant to answer questions unless they can see the entire questionnaire and read each question. In other cases, the respondent may merely want to glance over a copy of the questionnaire form and perhaps keep one before him as he answers the questions which are asked and recorded by the interviewer on another copy of the questionnaire.

There are exceptional instances in which the process of filling out the questionnaire will have to be delayed until after the interview has been completed. Suppose that it was considered necessary to conduct the interview as a casual conversation and that it would be unwise to be busily recording information during the visit. The interviewer would have to be instructed, therefore, to memorize the questions and to record the answers immediately after he has left the respondent. This type of interview calls for a well-qualified interviewer, and it should not be attempted unless absolutely necessary.

Practice Field Work

The ideal arrangement would be to provide for practice field work under the same conditions that would prevail in the actual survey. Even as few as five or six trial interviews can lead to worth-while improvements in procedure. In some cases, the practice interviews can be satisfactorily held in the room in which the training session is taking place. The trainee can practice on other prospective interviewers or on the person who is conducting the training session.

If the telephone inquiry technique is to be used, the voice of the interviewer must be heard over a telephone before his suitability can be established. A few practice calls can be made between the prospective field worker and the supervisor.

The ideal arrangement, also, would provide for supervision and guidance of the field work during the actual process of collecting the information. This practice is often not feasible. In any case, inspection or authentication of the field work after it has been completed is necessary.

Inspection of Field Work

Field workers should be informed that, as a matter of sound research procedure, the work of each interviewer or observer will be authenticated. It should be pointed out that this is no reflection on the field workers; instead, it is merely standard practice.

The advantages of telling field workers beforehand that their work will be inspected include:

1. Better field work will be accomplished.
2. Worker is not upset as he would be if he were to learn later that his work has been secretly checked.
3. User of the findings can be convinced that the work has actually been done.
4. The efficient, honest field workers know that their good work will be observed.

To start the process of inspecting field reports, a randomly selected group of completed questionnaires can be pulled out. The respondents whose names appear on the questionnaires will then be either visited personally, telephoned, or sent a letter of inquiry through the mail. These respondents will be asked certain questions to determine if they have been actually interviewed and, perhaps, if their answers have been recorded correctly. The purpose of the inspection may also include a test of the accuracy with which the interviewer followed his instructions. As can be seen, all field workers must be instructed to put their names on each questionnaire that they turn in. Also, the name and address of the respondent must be recorded except in situations in which this might violate a promise of complete anonymity.

If anonymity is promised respondents, a list of the names and addresses of the respondents can be made on a separate sheet by the interviewer. Some of the persons listed can then be contacted later to establish at least whether they have been interviewed by a field worker on the subject covered in the questionnaire used in the survey involved. The respondents contacted in this inspecting process could be informed that their names had been drawn at random from a general list of all the persons who had been interviewed and that their individual questionnaires were not identifiable in any way.

The percentage of completed questionnaires that need to be authenticated can be quite small, perhaps less than 5 percent. But if any interviewer turns in a single falsely completed questionnaire, all his work is suspect; and he should not be used in future surveys. It should be remembered, however, that it is possible that some respondents may not recall that they have been interviewed. Sometimes the interview was with a respondent who did not mention it to the member of the family who is reached in the authenticating procedure. These possibilities should be kept in mind by the inspector.

MOTIVATIONAL RESEARCH

Businesspersons are interested in why customers, employees, stockholders, or other businesspersons act as they do. Knowing what these persons do is of major importance, of course, but in some instances that is not enough. If it is desired to change or to conform to the things that people do, it is often necessary to know the reasons for their actions, i.e., what motivates them.

But, can researchers find out why a person buys toothpaste instead of tooth powder? Or why a worker is unhappy on his job? Or why stockholders are selling or buying the stock of a company? Or why other businesspersons in the industry are expanding (or contracting) their output at a given time? Some researchers believe that there is little of value that can be learned from persons by asking them why they do what they do. It is contended that people are unable to give their actual reasons because basically human beings are irrational creatures. According to this view, a person should be asked only for facts that can be quickly established and can be given mostly in simple yes or no answers. Such facts, for example, as occupation, marital status, or whether the respondent owns a car are held to be the types that can be best asked on a questionnaire.

There is considerable justification for this reluctance to attempt to learn by direct questions why people behave as they do. Such information when obtained in personal interviews, it must be admitted, is often subject to a large margin of error. Nevertheless, if it is necessary to obtain information about reasons for the actions of persons and some measure of the relative importance of the different reasons, it is altogether possible that some useful results can be secured by a correctly conducted questionnaire survey.

The conditions that cause difficulties for the investigator who wishes to determine why an individual acts or fails to act in a certain way include the following possibilities:

1. There is usually no one reason for an action; instead, there are several reasons.

2. Consequently, the respondent, when he is asked to give his "main reason," is faced with a task that is not easy because he must decide which one of several reasons he should give. Several of the reasons may be of almost equal importance; hence, it is exceedingly difficult for the respondent to say which is most important. To rank them correctly may be practically impossible.
3. For some actions, the individual will have irrational or subconscious reasons that he does not recognize himself.
4. Some real reasons that are recognized by the respondent will not be given because the reasons are not socially acceptable, intellectually flattering, or are considered to be of a confidential nature.

Even with these admitted difficulties, *why* or motivational research when conducted properly can obtain valuable results. It is important that the limitations be understood and the *why* questions be confined to the situations in which they can be used with a reasonable degree of success. When these limitations are recognized however, the researcher will be able to make some use of such questions in certain surveys.

The process of attempting to learn why persons act in certain ways is designated by some researchers as *motivational research*. Attempts to learn the actual reasons for human behavior in economic matters are not new phenomena. But due to continuing interest in the subject of personal motivation, particularly in the fields of market and opinion research and in personnel management, a great deal has been done in recent decades in the development of techniques to be used in the study of motives.

SOME TECHNIQUES USED IN MOTIVATIONAL RESEARCH

Several relatively complex techniques of obtaining information about motives have been developed. These techniques include:

1. depth interviewing
2. word association
3. sentence completion
4. reactions to pictures
5. others: story completion, thematic apperception tests, and focused group interviewing

These techniques are examined in detail in more specialized books. The use of these devices requires professional personnel experienced in the fields of psychological research. In this book, only a brief description of the techniques will be given.

(1) **Depth interviewing.** Depth interviewing is a process of asking probing questions that delve deeply into the reasons or motives of the respondent. An expert, experienced interviewer must do the interrogation in order to ask the necessary questions and at the same time avoid unduly influencing the answers.

(2) **Word association.** The reaction of persons to each word in a carefully chosen list is recorded. The assumption is that the reactions will indicate how the person feels about certain matters. If the word *marriage*, for

example, calls forth a happy word in the few seconds allowed for the reaction, this could be interpreted to indicate that the respondent is favorably inclined toward marriage. This answer may be due to experiences in marriage or to contemplation of marriage. Some practical applications of the word association technique might be to determine which words to use in advertising copy, in a talk to the employees of a firm, or in a political speech. Another application is to *match up* persons whose reactions to the words indicate sufficient similarity of interests and opinions to make them satisfactory coworkers on particular jobs.

(3) **Sentence completion.** The respondents are asked to complete a sentence. What is given in the completion process is assumed to show how the respondent would react to a given situation or what his experiences would cause him to believe would happen. An insight into why he thinks or acts as he does may be uncovered by a qualified analyst who studies the completed sentences.

(4) **Reactions to pictures.** Pictures are shown to persons who are asked to give their reactions to the pictures. The story that the picture suggests may be asked for. Sketches may be shown in which the comments of one character are given while the space for the answer of a second character is left blank to be filled in by the respondent. The responses given by the persons being interviewed are then assumed to be useful indicators of how they would react to the situation pictured. A person who might not be willing to tell how he felt or thought might be willing to indicate how the person in the picture would react. This response can possibly be considered as a reflection of what the respondent himself thinks.

(5) **Story completion, thematic apperception, and focused group interviewing.** Story completion and thematic apperception techniques rely on the same general assumptions as the word association, sentence completion, and the pictorial reaction techniques. The thematic apperception technique involves showing the respondent a series of ink blotches or abstract figures. The respondent is asked to tell what these figures bring into his mind. Certain shapes may elicit pleasant thoughts, others unpleasant ones. A practical use of this technique might be to discover pleasing designs for fabrics or wallpaper. Another use might be to discover the possible similarities or dissimilarities of the thoughts and interests of two or more persons. This would be done by comparing the ideas or images of things that are suggested to these persons by various ink blotches. If the blotches called forth comments about sports from several persons, this might be interpreted to mean that these persons were all interested in sports; and, consequently, they might get along reasonably well working together in the same shop.

Dr. Lyndon O. Brown described a procedure which he referred to as "Focused Group Interviewing."[1] The plan is to have a trained psychologist interview a group consisting of six to twelve representative persons. The interviewing or discussion follows a predetermined outline which focuses the conversation and reactions on the desired subject matter. The possible peculiar value of this technique is that it determines how people respond in groups in which a subject is discussed by different persons and the statements of each person are heard by several others. This situation may constitute, in some instances, a more usual condition than exists in single personal interviews. The responses actually have been found to be different in these two situations.

THE PANEL

The basic characteristic of the panel technique for collecting information is that a selected group of persons is requested to supply information periodically to the researcher. The same persons compose the reporting group or panel over extended periods of time. The panel may consist of homemakers, businesspersons, professional persons, or other groups or combinations of persons it is desired to cover and who can be induced to supply regularly the information needed.

Panel members are asked to report on prepared forms or in *diaries* immediately after an event has occurred such matters as the following:

1. Brands of various kinds of food or other items purchased, including date, price, store where purchased, and quantity.
2. Movies attended.
3. Television and radio programs watched or heard.
4. Books, magazines, or newspapers read or subscribed to.
5. Various other actions, including in some instances opinions in regard to certain matters.

The specific information that will be requested will, of course, be determined by the purposes behind the creation of the panel and the uses which will be made of the data supplied in the reports of the panel members. The amount of information will be limited by the fact that requests for an excessive quantity of data will cause prospective members of a panel to decline to cooperate, and many of the persons who do send in reports for a while will drop out later.

The types of information collected will also be limited to those things that persons are able and willing to report accurately and completely. Only by careful trial runs of panels and pretesting can it be determined exactly what sorts of information can be obtained from the members of any particular panel. Experience has demonstrated that, ordinarily, best results are obtained when requested reports do not cover too many different items nor require considerable self-analysis on the part of the respondent.

The types of persons on a panel will depend on the purposes of the research project. The usual panels have been composed of consumers who could supply information about their preferences in regard to brands of products and indirectly about the effectiveness of advertising or other selling programs. But panels can also be constructed to include more specialized groups, such as businesspersons, professional persons, or other economic or occupational groups. On the other hand, if the purpose of the panel is to keep track of changes in public opinion, the panel will have to be widely representative of all persons in the geographical area covered by the universe.

A *static panel* is one in which the membership remains the same throughout the life of the panel, except for the members who drop out.

These dropouts are not replaced. In a *dynamic panel*, to keep the panel representative of the current population in the area covered by the universe, replacements are found for the members who quit.

The static panel is appropriate when the purpose is to study changes in a given group of persons over a period of time. The main weaknesses of the static panel are that, due to dropouts, it ceases to be representative of the original universe after a time and the size of the reporting panel may become too small for satisfactory results.

The dynamic panel is most useful when it is important to keep the panel membership highly representative of the population of an area at all times. The main problem connected with the use of the dynamic panel is the expense and difficulty of recruiting new members to replace the dropouts.

ADMINISTRATION OF PANELS

The investigator may have to make visits to prospective panel members to obtain full understanding and cooperation. Explanations must be given about the report forms or diaries to be filled out. Clear instructions must be presented in regard to how often reports are to be sent in and the importance of promptness, both in recording items and mailing in reports. Reports are often sent in frequently, sometimes each week. The cooperating panel members will be supplied with reporting forms and stamped and addressed return envelopes.

The matter of compensation for the cooperating members of the panel may be of considerable importance. The payments often are in the form of coupons and stamps redeemable in premiums. The coupon payments can be sent to the panel members at the regular times that new batches of report forms are mailed to them.

The average amount of time that the panel member would have to spend on the reports could be determined in pilot studies. This average time then could be used as the base for setting the value in coupons to be paid periodically to each cooperator for satisfactorily completed reports.

The classification data needed in the interpretation and validation of the reports are obtained mostly in the interviews which are held in the process of recruiting panel members. Such information ordinarily can be more extensive than it could be in the usual single-contact personal interview survey, because the interest of the respondent in a possible panel can be aroused due to the fact that he or she has the prospect of receiving compensation for their time. The field workers can also become fairly well acquainted with the panel members in the course of subsequent visits; therefore, a considerable amount of additional information can be asked for as well as observed.

The types of classification data needed for the interpretation of reported information depend on the nature and purpose of the panel. Careful analysis of the reasons for setting up the panel and the possible uses of the reported data of all kinds are necessary before the exact items to be obtained can be determined. For example, suppose that the major purpose of a research project was to determine the effectiveness of advertising on television. The types of data needed for interpreting the panel reports could include the favorite television programs or at least whether there is a television set in the home. The reports from nontelevision homes then might show that a product that was advertised exclusively on television was purchased by a much smaller percentage of these nontelevision homes than was the case for homes with television sets. The conclusion could be that the television advertising was influencing families to buy the product involved.

The administration of a panel requires carefully selected and well-trained field workers. To obtain the continuing cooperation of panel members, periodic visits may be needed in homes of members. Those who are sending in incomplete or inaccurate reports will need special attention. Persons who indicate that they intend to drop off the panel may have to be "resold" on the idea of participating. Perhaps an adjustment in their compensation will be necessary.

The process of recruiting new panel members to replace those who drop out will take a considerable amount of time and ability on the part of the research personnel in the field. It will be necessary to find new panel members who are like those who are dropping out.

The field workers in the operation of some panels may have to become well acquainted with the habits and attitudes of the panel members assigned to their supervision in order to make the necessary adjustments to the individual differences of the panel members. Some panel members, for example, may be able and willing to report through the mail. Others may need the encouragement involved in personal visits during which the reports will be picked up.

Panels constructed to obtain small amounts of easily recalled information may be administered almost entirely by telephone if a representative sample can be reached by that means. An example would be a case in which the answers to but ten or fifteen simple questions were needed, none of which required much use of memory. Perhaps the questions would be mostly about the present status of ownership or use of a product or state of mind about a given issue. Suppose that the information requested had to do with the actions of the respondents that they had been asked to jot down on a prepared form at the time that the events had occurred. In this case, it would be easy to supply data over the telephone that otherwise might be difficult to remember. The telephone call under these conditions could be a quick and inexpensive way to collect the desired information.

ADVANTAGES OF PANEL TECHNIQUE

(1) Regular, periodic reports from the members of the panel can show changes that are occurring in the types and brands of products purchased, in other kinds of actions, and in opinions. No other technique of collecting information can supply such an up-to-date picture of current developments. For example, the effect of public relations or advertising campaigns can be measured quickly, sometimes almost concurrently, with the campaign. It is also possible to make comparisons in regard to conditions before, during, and after the campaign.

(2) The panel technique provides information that can be used to show the changes in the relative rank in popularity and consumer use of various brands of products. Much of the information collected through panels

could be obtained for the products of a particular company by use of the records of the company concerned. But these data would not show what was happening to the brands of other producers or dealers. Without information about consumer purchases of various other brands, a change in the volume of purchases of one brand cannot be evaluated adequately. A change in the medium used to advertise brand A of a product, for example, may be accompanied by an increase of 10 percent in the purchases of that brand. A careful study of the panel reports, however, may show an equal increase in the purchases of all brands of this particular product. The change in advertising medium, therefore, could not logically be said to be the only or even the main cause of the increase in purchases reported for brand A.

(3) Relatively greater accuracy of the information collected can be expected because the action is recorded soon after the act has been performed or the occurrence of the event reported. Reliance on memory is kept to a minimum. The diary method of regularly writing down the required data decreases the chances of mistakes.

(4) Panel reports can come from final consumers; therefore, they give a more complete and ultimate measure of the actions and purchases of the public. Data collected from manufacturers, wholesalers, or retailers may be incomplete because some of these respondents cannot be contacted and others will not supply the necessary information. Also, there may be a relatively long time lag between changes in final consumer purchases on the one hand and the production of manufacturers and the stocks of goods in warehouses on the other.

(5) Panels can supply data that can be subjected to a considerable amount of analysis because a relatively large amount of classification data are usually obtained in the process of recruiting the panel members. Such data as economic or occupational status, home ownership, possession of various household facilities, age, family characteristics, types of automobiles driven, preferences in entertainment, and published material in the home, can all be used to classify and interpret the data supplied by reporting panel members.

(6) Panels can be constructed to be representative of any of a variety of different groups. They may be composed of members of a certain profession or of farmers or truck drivers, for instance. The membership may include almost any type of persons who can be induced to make satisfactory reports.

(7) Effects of certain "outside" or generally influential occurrences can be seen. General changes in the economic outlook or in the political or military picture may have repercussions in the reports sent in by panel members. For instance, decreases in purchases of certain types of goods and increases in other goods may be noted.

(8) Depth interviewing may be facilitated by the panel technique because the panel members will become fairly well acquainted with the field workers and will be willing to allow rather searching and probing interviews from time to time.

DISADVANTAGES OF PANEL TECHNIQUE

(1) Panels are expensive to establish and to administer. The cost per co-operating panel member will be relatively high even though the mail is used for transporting the reports and most of the information is recorded by the panelist. The recruiting of members of the panel, the payment of premiums, periodic visits by supervisors, and the costs involved in replacing dropouts, all call for expenditures that can add up to a relatively high total cost.

It should be pointed out, however, that the relatively high cost of the panel technique may be reduced for any given business user of the results if the research program can be financed by several firms. This spreading of cost is ordinarily what is done, because most panels are set up and administered by a research organization, which then sells reports of findings to various interested companies. When the number and frequency of reports are taken into consideration, the cost per item of information obtained by the panel technique may be relatively low in many situations. Smaller establishments may, through a trade association or through other jointly financed projects, set up a panel that would supply needed current information for all the sponsors. The cost for each firm could, therefore, be kept within reasonable limits.

(2) It is often difficult to set up a representative panel and to keep it representative. Many persons may be unwilling to participate in such a project. A considerable amount of work and money will be needed to recruit the members and to retain them. The types of persons most willing or unwilling to cooperate will need to be determined by pilot studies in each community, and then special effort will be required to obtain and retain a continually representative panel.

(3) There is a definite possibility that the panel members may begin, sooner or later, to give "conditioned" answers. The knowledge that they will report certain of their actions may cause them to act differently than they would otherwise. Both their actions and answers may be changed somewhat—conditioned—because they are members of the panel. These persons, therefore, cease to be representative of their neighbors and friends. If this conditioning effect is thought to be strong for some types of acts, reports on these acts should be discontinued. Acts that may reflect on the social prestige or intelligence of the panel member are especially subject to this difficulty. It may be necessary to gain this information in single-contact interviews, by observation, or by other means.

(4) Reports may be carelessly, inaccurately, and incompletely prepared. Special attention will need to be given to instructing the panel members in the correct way to fill out the reports. Poor reporting may increase due to decreasing interest after a panel has been in operation for some time. Visits by field workers will be necessary. Cheating may be a problem in some cases. In other cases, the investigator will have to collect all the reports during the personal visits and interviews.

(5) There is the danger of attempting to collect too much information from the panel. Because of the time and money spent in recruiting and maintaining the panel, there is a temptation to ask for more information than can or will be supplied accurately.

(6) Persons who are unable to read and write cannot make written reports. If such persons are to be included on the panel, the relatively expensive practice of personally interviewing them regularly will be required.

THE NATIONAL LONGITUDINAL SURVEY

There has been in operation in the United States since 1966 a nationwide panel, the National Longitudinal Survey (NLS), originally containing more than 20,000 persons composing a probability sample of persons in the labor force.[2] Interviews are conducted once a year with members of the panel. The original general panel contained slightly over 5,000 persons in each of the following four labor force groups: men forty-five to fifty-nine years old; women thirty to forty-four; men fourteen to twenty-four; and women fourteen to twenty-four. The attrition rate due to deaths and other causes during the years has reduced the sizes of the panel groups; however, these reductions are not considered large enough to destroy the representativeness of the samples. In each of most of the years, the members of the panel have been personally interviewed, but in a few of the years they were contacted by mail or telephone. The information requested concerns the labor market experiences of the persons in the panel. Specifically, information is obtained about on-the-job experiences, earnings, unemployment, and other experiences including changes in opinions or in outlook as the years pass.

The value to businesspersons of such a nation-wide panel depends on the type of information obtained. Information about changes through the years in actions and attitudes of customers, employees, the public (voters), and stockholders concerning economic, political, and business conditions might be of considerable value to business managers over the course of several years. Some of the possible users of the longitudinal survey are larger companies, members of trade associations, and local, regional, and national chambers of commerce.

In addition to the NLS, the concept and variations of the concept of the panel technique are widely used by the federal government in collecting such information as data concerning changes in the population, the labor force, employment, unemployment, and consumer prices. For examples, see last two items in the selected references at end of chapter.

SUMMARY

Surveys are often the only method by which information can be acquired. Survey techniques include such procedures as personal interviews, mailed questionnaires, telephone inquiries, motivational research, and the use of panels. For surveys to be effective, certain conditions must exist: (1) The information needed must be defined specifically in view of the purposes of the project. (2) It must be determined that the survey is the best method of collecting the information. (3) Certain characteristics of the universe must be known: its geographical area, the persons/subjects to be investigated. (4) It must be established which type of survey technique is to be used: personal interview, mail, telephone, for example.

There are certain advantages to the mail questionnaire technique: (1) They can be sent to widely scattered locations. (2) Respondents can be reached at a low cost. (3) Respondents can be reached at their homes or offices. (4) They can be answered at leisure, and may be more complete. (5) No interviewer is present to bias the answers. (6) Certain data concerning personal or economic facts may be forthcoming from an unsigned, unidentified questionnaire.

There are, however, some disadvantages to mail questionnaires: (1) A large percentage of the questionnaires may not be returned. (2) Answers to certain questions may be omitted by respondents. (3) Only persons who can read and write can give answers. (4) Some groups may not return questionnaires because they are not used to reading or writing, or they may have little time to answer. (5) Premiums may be needed to induce replies. (6) Mailing lists may be difficult or costly to obtain. (7) Some information may not be obtained through the mail. (8) The representativeness of the sample is difficult to establish.

Mail questionnaires are effective where used under the proper conditions: (1) when the information needed can be answered easily and quickly on questionnaires; (2) when the information is possessed by persons willing to respond by mail; (3) when the universe consists of a homogeneous group; (4) when complete and reasonably priced mailing lists are available; (5) when mail questionnaires can be used as supplements to personal interviews or telephone inquiries; (6) when sufficient funds are available for a satisfactory mail questionnaire study; (7) when sufficient time is available for the lengthy process of collecting the data through the mail.

The personal interview technique is often used when rather complete and comprehensive replies are needed. Some advantages of the personal interview technique are: (1) The presence of the interviewer increases the percentage of returns. (2) The interviewer can add explanations and observations. (3) The interviewer can collect information about items that might be objected to, through observation. (4) A more representative sample of the universe may be obtained than by mail questionnaires. (5) Tests of accuracy, by check questions or observations, may be included.

However, some of the disadvantages of personal interviews are: (1) When the respondents are dispersed over a wide geographic area, the cost and time of travel may be great. (2) Poorly trained interviewers may bias answers. (3) The costs of interviewing are high. (4) Personal or financial information may not be obtained. (5) Personal interviews may be considered an intrusion by respondents. (6) Some information may take too long for reply to be included in the interview.

There are times when the personal interview technique is by far the best technique to use: (1) when the quality of information needed requires personal interview; (2) when a sufficient number of interviewers is available; (3) when there are adequate funds and time to recruit interviewers; (4) when the questions to be asked are not embarrassing or objectionable; (5) when the respondent will have sufficient time during the interview to answer adequately; (6) when *depth interviewing* is called for; (7) when the universe consists of areas that are compact geographically; (8) when personal interviews can be used in conjunction with, or as supplements to, other survey techniques.

The telephone inquiry technique is often used when only brief answers are required, and a telephone conversation can supply the needed information. The advantages are: (1) Information can be collected very quickly. (2) The interviews can be timed to occur at a certain hour of the day. (3) Interviews can be completed at a low cost. (4) The names and addresses of respondents are easily accessible in the telephone book. (5) The addresses can be used to show the kind of neighborhood in which the respondent lives. (6) The telephone directory provides a listing of respondents in the universe. (7) Persons who are unavailable for personal interview or who will not answer mail questionnaires may be contacted by telephone.

However, there are some disadvantages to using the telephone inquiry technique: (1) The inquiries are limited to persons having listed telephones. (2) Only a very few questions can be asked in the limited time available. (3) The information must be limited to questions that can be answered by yes or no, or very briefly. (4) An adequate amount of classification data may be difficult or impossible to obtain.

There are times, however, when the telephone inquiry method is the most effective one to use: (1) when the universe is composed of respondents listed in telephone directories; (2) when only five or six questions at the most will elicit the needed information; (3) when time is a limitation; (4) when the subject is of interest enough to cause respondents to be willing to cooperate; (5) when observation is unnecessary; (6) when telephone inquiries can be used in conjunction with other survey techniques.

The recruiting of interviewers has problems connected with it. Persons must be selected as interviewers with qualifications for interviewing effectively. It may be necessary to select interviewers of a given age bracket, of a given sex, or of a given educational level. The matter of compensation must be considered. The field worker must be paid sufficiently to warrant his efforts in being trained, instructed, and supervised. They should be told the purpose of the project so they will appreciate the need for the survey. The conduct of the interviews must be explained. The habits and appearance of the interviewer must be explained. Some practice must be given the beginning interviewer. Supervision must be provided.

One of the modern techniques of survey is called *motivational research*. Motivational research involves attempting to get at the underlying motives or causes of responses. Some of these motivational techniques are: (1) depth interviewing; (2) word association; (3) sentence completion; (4) reaction to pictures; (5) others, such as, story completion, thematic apperception tests, and focused group interviewing.

The panel is a modern technique in wide use today. Panel members may be homemakers, businesspersons, factory workers, or any other segment of the population whose responses are desired. These panels consist of a group of people who may be paid regularly and employed regularly in the testing of products and packaging. Panels have problems of their own. In the administration of panels, the decision as to the group to be reached, the methods of reaching the groups, the compensation of the panel members, and the periodic updating and interviewing constitute expensive and difficult procedures.

There are certain advantages to the panel technique: (1) Regular, periodic reports are available, indicating changes occurring in products, opinions, mores. (2) Panels provide information of changes in ranks of products or persons. (3) Accuracy of information is high. (4) Rather complete measures of actions and of purchases of the public are obtained. (5) Panels can supply data that can be subjected to considerable analysis, because a large amount of classification data are available. (6) Panels can be constructed for any kind of group in society. (7) General changes in the economic outlook or the political situation have repercussions in reports, and these can be recorded and analyzed. (8) Depth interviewing may be facilitated by using panels.

There are some disadvantages to using panels: (1) They are expensive to establish and to administer. (2) Often it is difficult to organize a representative panel, and to keep it representative. (3) The panel members may begin sooner or later to give "conditioned" answers. (4) Reports, after some time, may be carelessly and incompletely prepared. (5) Attempting to collect too much from the panel may discourage membership. (6) Only persons who can read and write may become panel members.

The National Longitudinal Survey conducted by the U.S. Department of Labor is a nation-wide panel. The panel technique is used by the federal government to collect data on population, labor force, employment, and other economic conditions.

EXERCISES

1. The text lists certain preconditions for a satisfactory survey. Describe these in your own words.
2. What is the *universe* for any particular survey? Is it always specifically delimited? Why or why not?
3. Compare and contrast the advantages and disadvantages of using mail questionnaires.
4. What conditions are necessary for effective use of mail questionnaires? Give an example.
5. Compare and contrast the advantages and disadvantages of personal interviews.
6. Under what circumstances are personal interviews desired?
7. Describe the advantages and disadvantages of the telephone inquiry technique.
8. List the conditions necessary for effective use of telephone inquiries.
9. What points must be kept in mind—what questions must be asked—when recruiting interviewers and investigators?
10. Write a two-page paper on the training of field workers, detailing how it should be done.
11. Is supervision of field workers always necessary in the survey procedure?
12. Write a two-page paper on motivational research, covering the specific techniques employed.
13. Define the panel technique in your own words.
14. What problems are met in the administration of panel surveys?
15. Compare and contrast the advantages and disadvantages of using panels.
16. What is the purpose of the National Longitudinal Survey? How is it conducted?

SELECTED REFERENCES

Balsley, Howard L. *Quantitative Research Methods for Business and Economics*. New York: Random House, 1970.

Mendenhall, William; Ott, Lyman; and Shaeffer, Richard L. *Elementary Survey Sampling*. Belmont, Calif.: Wadsworth, 1971.

Parten, Mildred. *Surveys, Polls, and Samples: Practical Procedures*. New York: Cooper Square, 1966.

Raj, Des. *The Design of Sample Surveys*. New York: McGraw-Hill, 1972.

U.S. Bureau of Labor Statistics. *BLS Handbook of Methods for Sampling and Studies*. Bulletin 1910. Washington, D.C., 1976.

U.S. Bureau of Labor Statistics. *Consumer Expenditure Survey: Diary Survey, July 1972–June 1974*. Bulletin 1959. Washington, D.C.: Superintendent of Documents, U.S. Government Printing Office, 1977.

U.S. Bureau of Labor Statistics. *How the Government Measures Unemployment*. Report 5505. Washington, D.C.: U.S. Bureau of Labor Statistics, 1977.

ENDNOTES

1. Lyndon O. Brown, *Marketing and Distribution Research*, 3d ed. (New York: Ronald Press Company, 1955), chapter 18.
2. U.S. Department of Labor, *The Pre-Retirement Years*, Vol. 4, Manpower R. & D. Monograph 15 (Washington, D.C., 1975), pp. iii and 1–9. (Also see Monographs 16, 21, and 24).

6

Constructing and Writing Questionnaires

The first essential condition in the process of constructing a questionnaire is to decide what information is required. A list containing all conceivable items of information that might be helpful in the solution of the particular problem being studied should be compiled. While this list is being written, the purposes of the survey must be kept constantly in mind. The compiler need not on the first writing be concerned about the matter of logical order or the composition of sentences. Instead, he should give rather full rein to his insight and imagination. Perhaps during or immediately after the first rough listing, he may consult with other qualified persons.

When the first original list of possibly important items of information has been drawn up, it should be studied carefully to determine which items seem to be of greatest importance and pertinency to the purposes of the survey. A revised list will then be prepared from the original. This second list, and any further revised lists that it is necessary to compile, will be considered intensively with the aim of preparing a final list containing the exact items of information that must be obtained in the survey.

It may be found that, after the list of the exact items of information needed has been compiled, the list will show that the particular information needed can be collected more efficiently by techniques other than the questionnaire survey. Usually, if the questionnaire survey is not the best technique, this fact will have been discovered earlier in the research project. But this final review will still be a worth-while safeguard leading to the selection of the best technique.

The goal of the first draft of the questionnaire should be to compose questions that will obtain all the information that is listed as necessary. The first draft of the questionnaire, therefore, should be studied carefully to see if it asks questions that, when answered, will have supplied every item of information needed.

It may be necessary at this point to decide whether any *filter* questions are needed to help locate and identify the respondents. Suppose one purpose of the survey was to find out what homeowners thought about the zoning regulations in a city. The first, or at least one of the first questions, asked could be, "Do you own or rent your house?" The answer to this question could be used to *filter out* the homeowners for further questioning. Sometimes the purpose of the filter question will be to determine which of two sets of questions should be asked of the particular respondent. In the example just given, the homeowners might be asked a certain series of questions, while the renters would be asked a different series of questions.

The questionnaire should be long enough to contain all the essential questions which must be asked to obtain the information needed. Ordinarily, the questionnaire should not take over ten or fifteen minutes to complete. These two points can be contradictory on certain surveys in which the questions which are considered essential would require much more than fifteen minutes to answer. If the questionnaire is restudied, and it is found that no questions can be eliminated, the survey plan may have to provide for interviews longer than fifteen minutes. Longer interviews are sometimes possible if the questionnaire is well worded and the interviewing is done skillfully. Interviews of an hour or longer have been conducted successfully. Appointments may be necessary in these cases, and sometimes more than one session of interviewing may be needed to complete a questionnaire. On the other hand, if fifteen minutes per interview is the maximum amount of time that can be used, reappraisal of the questionnaire will have to be undertaken to decide which questions will be omitted.

WRITING THE QUESTIONS

The actual composition of the questions to go into a questionnaire must be done with care and thoughtfulness. General rules for questions are that they should be brief and simple in construction, having no compound phrases; they should be clear, having few or no adjectives; and they should be positive rather than negative. A detailed discussion of most of the characteristics of questions and the difficulties of writing the questions is presented in this chapter.

KINDS OF QUESTIONS

The following paragraphs describe the kinds of questions appearing on questionnaires: open, dichotomous, multiple choice, and declarative. A discussion of questions to avoid is also given.

Open Questions

An open question is one that leaves the answer open to whatever kind of reply the respondent decides to give. An example would be:

What do you think about the general retail sales tax? _____

_____

_____

_____

The respondent can answer in whatever way he pleases; no checklist of possible answers is supplied. Freedom of response is maximized. It is imperative that there be ample space provided for the reply. Perhaps four or five blank lines or more may be needed. Too little space discourages answering.

The *advantages* of the open question would include:

1. Free expression is encouraged.
2. Responses are not biased by a list of possible answers that might suggest replies that were not true reflections of the thoughts of the respondents.
3. Open questions may be used to get an interview started with a general question to arouse interest.
4. Open questions are an effective way to start a depth interview in which the interviewer then will keep asking further probing questions to develop the thinking of the respondent.

Some of the *disadvantages* of open questions are:

1. Respondents often will not answer fully or at all when faced with such a general discussion type of answer.
2. The interviewer may bias the answers with his probing or encouragement to fuller answers.
3. Ordinarily, only experienced, expert interviewers can successfully administer open questions.
4. Open questions are not so clear to the respondent as are more specific questions which ask for either yes or no answers or a checking of choices from a list of possible answers.
5. The compilation, classification, and interpretation of answers to an open question often present a difficult problem.

Dichotomous Questions

The dichotomous question is one that can be answered in one of two ways, such as, yes or no. The two possible answers may be definitely indicated by appropriately labeled spaces to check. In other cases, the wording of the question itself may show that only two answers are possible. For example, this question may be asked in two forms:

Do your own your house? _____
    or
Do you own or rent your house?   Own _____   Rent _____

The second form of the question would usually be considered superior because it makes the meaning of the question and the possible answers more definite. In addition, the tabulation of the results can be accomplished more easily and quickly.

It is necessary to realize that many questions that apparently can be answered accurately with one of two choices really cannot be correctly answered in this manner by all respondents. An example of such a question is:

Will you take a vacation this summer?

There are three choices needed for the answers:

Yes
No
Undecided
  or
  Don't Know

In constructing dichotomous questions, therefore, the third possible answer should be allowed whenever the subject of the question makes this third choice a possibility. The respondent should never be forced to answer in terms of only two choices when actually neither is accurate in his case. If a person "does not know," has "no opinion," or is "undecided," these are the answers that he should be allowed to give.

When correctly constructed and used under appropriate conditions, dichotomous questions have the following *advantages*:

1. They can be answered quickly.
2. The replies can be easily and accurately tabulated.
3. They are clear as to meaning.
4. When a question can be answered simply and accurately with one of two possible choices, with a third "don't know" type of possibility for some of the respondents, the dichotomous question is ordinarily the best type to use.

The major *disadvantages* of dichotomous questions stem from the following conditions:

1. Many questions cannot be answered accurately by two choices only, even when a third "don't know" or "undecided" type of choice is allowed.
2. Opinion questions often require the possibility of various degrees of approval or disapproval.
3. Questions which seek to find out why a person does a certain thing usually can be answered in considerably more than two or even three ways.

Multiple Choice Questions

This is a type of question for which several choices of answers are allowed. The replies may be recorded by placing a check mark or number in the appropriate blank or by encircling the correct words. An example of this kind of question is:

What are the two main reasons that you trade at the grocery store at which you now buy most of your food items? (Please check your *two main* reasons.)
_____ Can always find a parking space
_____ Wide variety of merchandise
_____ Economical prices
_____ Within easy walking distance of home
_____ Store gives trading stamps
_____ Pleasant sales personnel
_____ Merchandise conveniently arranged
_____ Others, please specify _____

The question may be asked by the interviewer who will then check the appropriate answer. Or, the respondent may be shown the list before either he or the interviewer records the replies. The main advantage of not showing the checklist to the respondent is that his answers are more likely to be strictly his own. If he has seen the list of choices, he may be influenced to answer in a somewhat different way than he would otherwise. Also, the interview can ordinarily be completed more quickly if the interviewer merely asks questions and checks the appropriate choices. If the answers are to be recorded by the interviewer, he should be cautioned to check the choices that exactly fit the respondent's meaning. When the reply must be placed in the "Others, please specify" blank, the answer should be written in the exact words of the respondent and be stated completely enough to convey its full meaning.

There are, on the other hand, some advantages to the practice of letting the respondent see the questions and the choices of answers. The questions will be made more clear and specific. Therefore, the respondent may, in some cases, answer more accurately when he sees an ample checklist of possibilities. The checklist may guide him through the process of a fuller consideration of the question than he might have given if he had not seen the list. If the respondent can see the questionnaire, he may also be more willing to give his answers. When the "Others, please specify" choice is used in answering, the written reply given by the respondent may be more accurate than it would have been if written by the interviewer.

In summary, it can be said that the decision as to whether the questionnaire and the list of choices should be shown to the respondent will depend on the possible effect that either procedure will have on the accuracy and completeness of the replies. The research director will have to decide whether the sight of the questionnaire might unduly distort answers or, on the contrary, increase their accuracy. Pretesting of the questionnaire using both methods will allow a comparison of the answers obtained. If the answers are different, perhaps the replies are being influenced one way or another. A decision will have to be made, then, as to which technique can be expected to get the best results.

An important problem which faces the user of multiple choice questions is how to construct a satisfactory list of answers to a question. The ideal list of answers would contain the following characteristics:

(1) It would be exhaustive, that is, it would contain all the possible choices that respondents would be likely to want to use in replying. Respondents have a strong tendency to check some of the choices given for each question even though none of the choices is exactly what they would like to check. It sometimes happens that the compiler of a questionnaire inadvertently, or even deliberately, omits certain important choices. The result is that the actual choices selected by the respondent from the limited variety given on the questionnaire do not give a true picture of the respondent's opinion.

(2) It would contain no overlapping or unclear choices. An example of overlapping choices is given later, in the illustration about causes of business failures, in which "Bad management" and "Lack of experienced manager" definitely overlap. An example of an unclear choice would be the use of the word *small* to indicate one possible choice of the size of house preferred by the respondent. Small is unclear or ambiguous because it has no definite, uniform meaning. A small house to a person living in a mobile home might be a dwelling unit with 500 square feet of floor space. To a person living in a six-bedroom house, 1,000 square feet could be considered as small.

(3) None of the choices would be so worded as to cause it to be checked or avoided because of the prestige or social approval connotations connected with the wording. Suppose that a question was asked about to what type of radio programs the respondent listened. The answers listed might include "Soap Serials" and "Hillbilly Music." Both of these designations may cause some actual listeners to avoid checking these particular choices because the terms may be considered derogatory or an indication of low taste. More neutral titles such as "Dramatic Serial" and "Western Music" would be advisable.

(4) The choice of "Others, please specify" or its equivalent would be included to allow sufficient freedom of answers to avoid forcing any respondent to answer inaccurately and to make sure that no possible type of reply is overlooked. The words *please specify* must be included or else a meaningless check mark may be all that is recorded. There would be adequate space provided for all the answers, especially to the "Others, please specify" item. This particular choice should not be used, however, as a catch-all for a poorly prepared checklist that forces a large percentage of the replies into this miscellaneous category. As a very rough estimate, it can be said that ordinarily a well-constructed and pretested questionnaire should result in not more than 10 or 15 percent of the replies falling in the "Others" blank.

(5) The choices would be psychologically consistent. The choices would not confuse or intermix causes and effects or items in different psychological classifications. A question that contains a psychologically weak checklist follows:

In your opinion, what are the two main causes of business failures? (Please check two causes only.)

_____ a. Bad management

_____ b. Insufficient capital

_____ c. Lack of experienced manager

_____ d. Bankruptcy

_____ e. Others, please specify _____

Items (a) and (c) overlap, and item (d) is not psychologically consistent because it can be considered a result or merely another name for business failure instead of a cause.

The actual process of constructing a satisfactory checklist for the answers to a questionnaire composed of multiple choice questions could be outlined as follows:

1. Write out a series of open questions that cover the desired subjects.
2. Take this questionnaire to twenty or thirty persons of the type who are to be interviewed in the planned survey. Record their answers to each question.
3. Compose a second questionnaire and for each question provide a checklist containing a classification of the various answers obtained on the first pretest.
4. Use the second questionnaire to conduct another pretest. After the respondents have answered or have failed to answer, ask each if the choice of answers offered actually included the answers they would have preferred to give. A few additional choices that should be in the checklist may be discovered and perhaps some of the original choices will need to be reworded to increase their clarity.
5. The questionnaire will now be revised in the light of the second pretest. As a further safeguard against forcing persons to reply inaccurately, an "Others, please specify" blank should always be included, even though several pretests and revisions have been completed.

Of course, the more complex the subject of the survey, the more pretests and revisions that will be necessary in the preparation of a questionnaire. Here again, the researcher will have to strive for an acceptable balance of accuracy and completeness of results on the one hand, and economy of time and expense on the other.

Declarative Questions

The declarative question is a type of multiple choice question in which the respondent is asked to give his reaction to a series of statements about a given subject. For example, various viewpoints or degrees of favorable or unfavorable reaction to a subject may be offered as the choices of answers. An illustration of a declarative question follows:

Please check the one statement that most fully represents your view about the union shop:

_____ a. It is a bad thing for workers, employers, and the public.

_____ b. It is bothersome to employers and the public, but it is necessary to protect the worker.

_____ c. It is a good thing for workers, and it does not create a hardship for employers and the public.

_____ d. It is a good thing for workers and employers, and it does not bother the public.

_____ e. It is a good thing for workers, employers, and the public.

The declarative question fits the psychology of certain subjects better than any other type of question. When the replies are best expressed in degrees of agreement or disagreement or like or dislike, the declarative approach should be considered. If it is desired to find out how people feel about certain slogans, commonly heard statements about a controversial subject, or whether they are favorably or unfavorably inclined toward a given institution, such as, the income tax, the declarative question may allow a truer set of responses than other alternative types of questions.

TYPES OF QUESTIONS TO AVOID

The compiler of questionnaires should avoid certain kinds of questions that can be designated as leading, misleading, ambiguous, double, or uninformative.

Leading Questions

A leading question is one that is worded in such a way as to strongly influence the respondent to give a certain answer. It practically leads the respondent to a particular reply. A leading question is ordinarily a poor question because it usually does not elicit an accurate answer or one that correctly represents the viewpoint of the respondent. Examples of leading questions follow:

You would like to own a new refrigerator, wouldn't you?
Don't you think that the last book by that author was thrilling?

Except in some instances as an introductory question to serve as a pleasant way to start the respondent talking, leading questions should be avoided.

Misleading Questions

Misleading questions are those that are deliberately leading. The purpose of the misleading question is to force the respondents to answer questions in the way that the compiler of the questionnaire wants them to be answered. An ordinary leading question may be an honest oversight, but a misleading question is the result of bad faith. The user of misleading questions is not really conducting research. Instead, he is trying to support some preconceived notion, to "prove" something rather than to find out whether it is true.

Misleading questions are usually "loaded" with words that compel the respondent to reply in a certain way or else give an answer that only a foolish person would give. Here are examples of misleading questions that are "loaded":

Do you believe that organizations of business firms should coerce the federal Congress to lower taxes on excessive profits of corporations?
_____ Yes _____ No
Have you ever tried to get special favors from a business establishment by pressuring them?
_____ Yes _____ No

In the first question, the word *coerce* definitely stacks the cards against a yes answer. The phrase *excessive profits* makes a yes answer seem foolish. In the second question the respondent cannot answer yes without putting himself in a bad light.

Ambiguous Questions

An ambiguous question is one that does not have a clear meaning. It may be understood to mean different things. An example of such a question would be as follows:

Are you interested in the small imported automobiles?

Such a question can be understood to have at least two meanings: Would the respondent like to buy a car? Or, would he wish merely to see one, or to drive one?

Ambiguous questions are more likely to creep into questionnaires than either leading or misleading ones because ambiguous questions are often difficult to recognize as such. One of the chief reasons for pretesting a questionnaire before finally using it in a survey is to discover and correct any questions that are unclear or permit the respondents to interpret them logically to mean different things.

Double Questions

A double question is a type of ambiguous question. This type is found so frequently, especially in the first draft of a questionnaire, that it is mentioned separately here. The double question is one which really contains two questions or more. For example:

Would you like to own a comfortably riding, high-speed car?

This is actually two questions, one about "comfortably riding" and the other about "high speed." The question should be made into two questions because some persons might want only one of the characteristics rather than both.

Uninformative Questions

An uninformative question is one that supplies meaningless or unreliable information when it is answered. Some questions calling for simple, one-word answers can be so quickly answered that the respondent will reply without much thought, especially if he thinks there is no possibility that the accuracy of his answer can be checked. An example of an uninformative question is:

Do you know a considerable amount about the game of golf?
_____ Yes _____ No

This might be termed an *empty question* because the respondent may find it equally easy to answer yes or no. Also, even though he attempts to give an accurate reply, he probably cannot because he has no way of determining whether what he does know about the game should be called *a considerable amount*.

Employment agencies have learned that it is often useless to ask a man a simple direct question, such as:

Are you a journeyman carpenter?

Instead, several questions about the tools and operations of the trade are asked. The answers to these questions will be much more informative because the wording would be such that only an experienced carpenter would know how to answer them correctly.

THE WORDING OF QUESTIONS

The precise meaning of words and the effects of their use should be known or determined by the compiler of a questionnaire. Unfortunately, the actual meaning of words to various persons and groups differs; and the dictionary definition may not be the same as the connotations that the words have in day-to-day usage in a particular community. No universally applicable rules about word usage in questionnaires can be given. Nevertheless, survey experience has contributed considerable knowledge about the matter of the types of words to be used or avoided in constructing questionnaires.

In general, the types of words that should be used in questionnaires would have the following characteristics:

1. uniformity of meaning
2. preciseness of meaning
3. freedom from undue influence of prestige or bias
4. freedom from tendency to arouse irrational or extremely emotional responses

A word should mean the same thing to all persons who are to be interviewed. The word *evening*, for example, has two meanings in some parts of the South. To some persons, it means from 12:00 noon to 6:00 or 7:00 P.M. For others, it means the period after 6:00 P.M. The reader can probably think of many words that have different meanings to different persons or in different usages. The variety of meanings of words is especially great in communities that contain many different social and economic classes or persons from several parts of the nation or world.

Preciseness of meaning is closely related to uniformity of meaning. It is mentioned here to bring out the additional characteristic of having an exactness and, consequently, a usability that will enable replies to be recorded, measured, compared, and totaled in the process of interpretation. Such words as *small*, *frequently*, *good*, *beautiful*, *tall*, and *quality* mean somewhat different things to practically every person. When they are used in a question, the responses will be almost impossible to evaluate and use in arriving at an accurate comparison and interpretation.

Suppose that the purpose of a survey was to determine what sizes of houses were the most likely to be preferred by the prospective home buyers in a city. The building contractors need the information about sizes to be given in specific terms, such as, so many square feet of floor space. The words *small*, *medium*, and *large* would not be sufficiently definite and exact. Even sizes stated in number of rooms would be highly indefinite.

Undue influence of prestige or bias can result in inaccurate answers. Certain words will cause prospective respondents to answer in a way that does not truly represent their thinking or preference. For example, the following questions are "loaded" with words that practically force the respondent to answer in a certain way:

Do you approve, in general, of the way that the capable, patriotic governor of this state has been conducting the government?
Would you patronize a high-class cafe that served clean, nourishing food at reasonable prices?

A tendency of a word to arouse irrational or extremely emotional responses will result in replies that incorrectly reflect the respondent's attitude. Words should be avoided if they cause tempers or emotions to flare up and distort the more usual reaction that the respondent would have to the subject of the question.

The type of words that should be used might be designated as *neutral* words. These would be words that are free from the distorting influence of fear, prestige, bias, or the upsetting effect of excessive emotions. Such words should be preferred by the compiler of questions, even though in reality they may be difficult to find. When the subject of the survey is charged with controversy and emotional repercussions, a considerable amount of time and effort will be required in the selection of words and in the construction and pretesting of the questionnaire.

ORDER OF QUESTIONS

The decision in regard to the position and order of questions in a questionnaire should be guided by certain considerations including:

1. Need to arouse and hold interest of respondent.
2. Influence of one question on another.
3. Best position for more important questions.
4. Determination of place at which fatigue should be recognized as a problem.

The need to arouse interest may dictate that easy and interesting questions should be placed at the beginning of the questionnaire. Later in the questionnaire, such questions may be needed again to revive interest. Sometimes a relatively unimportant question will be asked merely because it is interesting and attracts the attention of the respondent. For example, in a recent survey of homemakers, the beginning question was, "Does anyone in your family own a saddle?" The question was not directly related to the general survey subject, but it did cause smiles and started the respondent talking about a leather product. This resulted in a pleasant lead into the subject of leather handbags and luggage, which were the actual items with which the survey was concerned.

The influence of one question on another can be of considerable importance. Suppose there was a survey made to determine the opinion of the public in regard to the choice of politics and government service as a lifetime profession. If the first question in the questionnaire asked about the activities of a well-known but unethical government official, the respondent would probably keep thinking about politicians in an unfavorable vein throughout the rest of the questionnaire. The responses would probably have been much different if the unethical official had not been mentioned first. In the pretesting of the questionnaire, several arrangements of the order of questions may need to be tried to see if some questions are influencing the answers to others.

A striking example of the influence of one question on others occurs when a survey is being made to determine the relative popularity of a certain product or brand of product. If an early question mentions the name of a product or in any way indicates that the makers of a particular brand are interested in the findings, all the answers to the remaining questions are likely to be biased. The usual bias will be toward favoring the brand mentioned because, ordinarily, respondents would prefer to be pleasant rather than unpleasant to the interviewers. It is extremely important that no questions be asked that will prejudice the answers to the rest.

If it is considered necessary to mention a specific product or brand name that might prejudice the answers to any following questions, it is imperative that the bias-creating questions be asked at the end of the questionnaire in order that they cannot influence the answers to other questions.

The best position for the most important questions would be at that place in the questionnaire at which they would be answered most accurately and completely. The best place for a question will vary from one questionnaire to another. In some questionnaires, the most important questions should be asked first because interest then may be highest and fatigue has not appeared. In other questionnaires, the most important questions should be asked somewhere near the middle or end, after interest has been gradually built up and the respondent has had time to think the subject through to the point that he is ready to give an accurate answer. Again, it must be realized that only by pretesting can the best position be determined in a particular questionnaire.

Determination of the place in the questionnaire at which fatigue may become a distorting influence is important because respondents are likely to become inaccurate and uncooperative when they get tired. If interest cannot be revived and fatigue reduced to the point that it is not troublesome, the interview may have to be terminated. The offer of a small gift or a coffee break may lessen fatigue. The interjection of an interesting question may help, also. Trial interviews will be necessary to guide the compiler of the questionnaire in his determination of when and where fatigue will constitute a serious problem.

QUESTIONS CAUSING DIFFICULTY

Knowledge that certain kinds of questions cause difficulty for respondents and, therefore, also for the analyst will make it possible to keep them out of the questionnaire when it is designed. Such questions may be inadvertently included, however, and will usually be revealed in the pretesting procedure. Questions that respondents are unable to answer should be excluded, as well as questions that many respondents will be unwilling to answer. Unnecessary questions should be avoided since they add length to no purpose and may cloud the results. Questions that overlap in meaning and questions that include more than one meaning should be rewritten. The following paragraphs elaborate on these points.

Questions Respondents Are Unable or Unwilling to Answer

Questions with the following characteristics should be avoided as much as possible:

1. Rely heavily on the memory of the respondent.
2. Too general.
3. Require considerable amount of self-analysis on the part of the respondent.
4. Require considerable amount of thinking before an accurate answer can be given.
5. Ask for information that is too personal.
6. Ask for replies that are too closely associated with prestige-endangering matters.

Memory is a tricky quality of mind. Most persons have a difficult enough time remembering those things that they really want to remember, not to mention the various matters that they might be asked about in a survey. If memory must be relied on, the general rule would be to ask about the most recent events possible and to confine the question to the most easily recalled facts. The process of aiding the respondent to remember will be discussed in more detail in the next chapter.

Questions that are too general are difficult to answer. Suppose that the following open question was asked: "What do you like about advertising?" This question would be difficult to answer because it would require a long discussion; also, it is not entirely clear what aspects or kinds of advertising are involved. Such a question as this would actually have to be either narrowed in its scope or broken into several specific questions that are clear in meaning and are, therefore, more easily answered.

For example, suppose that the actual purpose behind the preceding general question about advertising was to determine whether the respondent had seen the newspaper advertisement of Early Bird breakfast food. The question should have been made more specific by wording it somewhat as follows: "What brand of breakfast food have you seen advertised in the local newspaper within the last two weeks?" This is an illustration of the *aided recall* technique, which will be discussed briefly in the following chapter in connection with procedures for helping the respondent to remember.

Questions which require a considerable amount of self-analysis on the part of the respondent present a difficult task for the person who is expected to reply. The reasons why a person does a certain thing, for example, are often only partially known by the person himself. To ask him to give this information to a stranger in a few seconds or minutes of time is asking a great deal more from the typical respondent than can ordinarily be expected. If such information is essential, some useful amounts of it may be obtained under certain conditions by the use of carefully constructed questionnaires and/or observation and experimentation techniques. Some specific ways of aiding the respondent to answer *why* questions will be given in the following chapter.

Questions that require a considerable amount of thinking and, perhaps, the use of arithmetic before they can be answered are obviously unlikely to be successful in the majority of surveys. Here again, the likelihood of obtaining answers to these questions can be increased if they are broken into several specific, more easily answered questions. Pretesting a questionnaire often uncovers one or more questions of this type.

Questions that ask for personal or other types of confidential data may run into a stone wall through the refusal of the respondent to divulge such information. The ages of persons, the income of persons or businesses, and the consumption of certain products are examples. If such facts are to be secured, special care may be necessary by way of explanations of the importance of the data and assurances that the data will be kept confidential. Ordinarily, these devices will have only limited effectiveness; and the personal or confidential types of information will either have to be estimated during observation or obtained from other sources.

The question that asks about information that involves social prestige is closely related to the confidential data type of question. If a person is asked what magazines he reads, his social or intellectual status is reflected in the reply he gives. He will have a tendency to remember only the publications with high prestige value and to "forget" the other kinds. Usually, information that may indicate social and intellectual status will have to be obtained by the use of indirect questions.

Unnecessary or Overlapping Questions

The following tests should be applied to each question:

1. Is this question necessary—will the information it will bring be of definite value in accomplishing the purpose of this survey?
2. Will the inclusion of this question make the questionnaire so long that another more significant question will have to be omitted?
3. Are there other more important questions that should be asked instead of this question?

If two questions ask for essentially the same information, the less effective question should be omitted. Exceptions to this rule would exist if the two questions were intentionally asked either to measure the consistency or accuracy of the replies of the respondent or to help substantiate the answers to a question of major importance in the survey. For example, the main purpose of the survey may be to determine what is the most important characteristic of an automobile that causes people to buy it. The intentionally duplicating or overlapping questions might be as follows:

What is the main characteristic of your present automobile that caused you to buy it?
If your present car is a different make than you owned before, what was it about your other car that made you decide not to buy another of that make?
What is the chief characteristic you will look for in the next car you buy?

These questions probably would be placed in different parts of the questionnaire. If the same characteristic is mentioned in each of the three answers, the possibility of its actual importance is strongly indicated, if not fully substantiated. If the answers to the three questions do not conform, this lack of agreement probably means that the responses were not accurate. Of course, there is the possibility that the reasons given for buying (or not buying) a particular make of automobile could still be correct even though each was different from the other two. This could logically happen if in the time between the purchases, the economic condition of the respondent had changed sufficiently to cause him to look for different characteristics in his automobiles. Perhaps, in the example given here, the questionnaire would need to ask for certain information about the changes between purchases of cars that may have occurred in the economic status of the respondent.

When a respondent is faced with a complex question that must be answered with the use of qualifications and the setting forth of exceptions, he is unlikely to be willing to give an answer. The compiler of a questionnaire, therefore, must break down each subject into questions that are consistent, clear in meaning, and easily answered. It is a common experience in the construction of questionnaires to discover that what at first seemed to be a bit of information that could be obtained by one or two questions, actually is a complex subject that requires a considerable number of questions. The scope of many surveys has had to be narrowed to the most essential aspects because of this condition.

CLASSIFICATION AND VALIDATION QUESTIONS

Classification data are information about respondents, such as, sex, age, and occupation. These data help to classify the respondents into different groups, aiding in the analysis of the findings of a survey. For example, suppose that the purpose of this survey was to locate skilled male workers within the age group of twenty-five to thirty-five who would go to Alaska to work. Let it be assumed that 85 percent of the yes answers to the question "Would you be willing to take a job in Alaska?" were given by men between the ages of twenty-five and thirty-five who were unskilled workers. These findings, then, could be interpreted to mean that most of the workers who were interested in a job in Alaska were men in the desired age limits, but they were not skilled.

Classification data usually are a necessary part of the facts that should be acquired in a survey. The exact facts that will be of most help in interpretation and in reaching conclusions will depend on the particular research project. The compiler of the questionnaire should carefully consider which kinds of classification data would be most pertinent to the problem under study and which of these data can be obtained in the survey.

Validation data are facts about the respondents in a sample that can be compared with the same facts as they exist in the universe. The purpose of the comparison of these validation data in the sampled cases with the existence of these same facts in the universe is to determine whether the sample constitutes a representative cross-section of the universe. For instance, if the average age of the persons in a city was 31.3 years and the average age found on the questionnaires was also 31.3 years, the sample could be considered as representative of the universe in regard to age. The chapter on sampling procedures contains a detailed discussion of validation procedures.

PRETESTING THE QUESTIONNAIRE

All questionnaires should be pretested before they are put into final use. The pretest should be conducted by using the questionnaires in interviews with the types of respondents who will be interviewed in the planned survey. The interviews should also be conducted under the same kinds of conditions that will exist in the actual survey. If possible, experienced interviewers should be used in these trial interviews because they will be more likely to recognize the changes that may be needed in the questionnaires. On the other hand, when the trial interviews have as their main purpose the determination of whether typical, ordinary interviewers can successfully conduct the survey, the interviewers selected may need to be those who are considered to be average in ability.

The number of pretest interviews required will depend on the nature and complexity of the questionnaire under consideration. Often only fifteen or twenty pilot interviews will be sufficient to turn up most of the revisions likely to be needed in a relatively simple questionnaire. As few as five or six trial interviews may even be enlightening. In larger, more complex surveys, the number of interviews in the pretests may run into the hundreds; and the number of times the questionnaire may have to be pretested and revised may be as high as six to eight or more.

Inexperienced researchers often begrudge the time and money spent on pretesting. But experienced investigators know that pretesting, in the long run, actually saves time, effort, and money. The saving results from time saved in the regular survey in explaining ambiguous questions, in going back to obtain information missed in the first interview, and sometimes in having to do the whole survey over again because of a faulty questionnaire used in the first one.

Pretests not only result in the discovery of improved ways to word and arrange questions, but entirely new questions or subjects may be suggested. For example, in a pretest of a questionnaire to be used in a survey on types of heaters preferred in automobiles, it was found that several respondents in the trial interviews mentioned that they needed a device to warm milk when they attended drive-in movies. A question therefore was added to the original questionnaire, and the replies to it proved helpful in the final analysis and recommendations.

QUESTIONNAIRE EXAMPLE

The questionnaire in exhibit 6-1 was designed and used for a survey of the demand for housing by married students at Texas Tech University. The survey was part of a study of the feasibility of constructing low-cost housing by a private promotional combine. It was necessary for the questionnaire to include a large number of questions concerning rooms, rentals, furnishings, carports, a swimming pool, floor coverings, location, lease arrangements, laundry, etc. A sample of 463 students was randomly selected from 1,852 male married students enrolled. Nonrespondents were dropped after one call-back plus one telephone call followed by determination of unavailability (dropped from college, moved, etc.). The final number of completed questionnaires was 304.

EXHIBIT 6-1
Questionnaire Example

HOUSING STUDY — TECH MARRIED STUDENTS

We are trying to learn the attitudes of Tech married students concerning housing facilities. Will you help us find these attitudes by answering a few short questions?

Interviewer's Number _____
Address of respondent _____

1. Which would you prefer:
   _____ To live in an apartment with all married Tech students?
   _____ To live in an apartment with nonstudents?

2. What is your present housing situation?
   _____ Own
   _____ Rent
   _____ Other

3. How many bedrooms do you now have?
   _____ 1   _____ 4 or more
   _____ 2   _____ Efficiency
   _____ 3

Source: Dr. John A. Ryan, Dean, College of Business Administration, Lamar University, formerly Professor of Marketing, Texas Tech University, kindly granted permission to reprint the questionnaire.

EXHIBIT 6-1 (*continued*)

4. How many children do you have living with you?
   _____ 0
   _____ 1
   _____ 2
   _____ 3
   _____ 4 or more

5. Is your present home:
   _____ Completely furnished?
   _____ Furnished with major appliances only?
   _____ Unfurnished?

6. Do you pay all of your own utility bills?   _____ Yes _____ No
   Do you pay part of your utility bills?   _____ Yes _____ No
       If yes, which do you pay?
       _____ Electricity
       _____ Water
       _____ Gas

7. How much rent did you pay during the month of November, 1962? $_____

8. Did you rent housing in Lubbock during the months of June, July and August, 1962? _____ Yes _____ No _____ Rented for part of this period

9. Do you own a car? _____ Yes _____ No

10. What are your means of conveyance to and from the campus?
    _____ Private vehicle
    _____ Public vehicle
    _____ Walk
    _____ Other

11. Does your wife work?
    _____ Yes   If Yes: _____ Part-time
    _____ No   _____ Full-time
    Is your wife a student?
    _____ Yes   If Yes: _____ Part-time
    _____ No   _____ Full-time

12. If you were to rent another apartment would you want it to be:
    _____ Completely furnished?
    _____ Furnished with major appliances only?
    _____ Unfurnished?
    _____ Other (Specify) _____

EXHIBIT 6-1 (*continued*)

13. What type flooring would you want?
    _____ Tile (If type specified, circle one: Rubber Asphalt Plastic Terrazzo)
    _____ Carpet

14. If a carpeted apartment cost $3 per month more than one with tile floors, which would you prefer?
    _____ Tile
    _____ Carpet

15. If you were to rent another apartment, which would you prefer?
    _____ Built-in range   Check one choice for 'range'
    _____ Free-standing range
    _____ Built-in refrigerator   Check one choice for 'refrigerator'
    _____ Free-standing refrigerator

16. Here are some floor plans I would like for you to examine.
    If you were looking for another apartment today and these were available at the rates indicated, which would you be most likely to take?
    _____ Efficiency, Unfurnished, $50
    _____ Efficiency, Major Appliances Only, $54
    _____ Efficiency, Furnished, $60
    _____ One Bedroom, Unfurnished, $60
    _____ One Bedroom, Major Appliances Only, $64
    _____ One Bedroom, Furnished, $70
    _____ Two Bedroom, Unfurnished, $70
    _____ Two Bedroom, Major Appliances Only, $74
    _____ Two Bedroom, Furnished, $85

17. In rank order, which *four* of the following extras do you most desire at an added cost? (1 is highest rank, 2 is second highest, etc.)
    _____ Nursery Building   _____ Carpet
    _____ Playground   _____ Swimming Pool (unheated)
    _____ Recreation Room   _____ Swimming Pool (heated)
    _____ Air conditioning   _____ Carport

18. Considering the floor plans, furnishings, and all extras you have indicated, what would you consider a fair rental value with bills paid?
    _____ $51 to $60
    _____ $61 to $70
    _____ $71 to $80
    _____ $81 to $90
    _____ $91 to $100
    _____ Over $100

EXHIBIT 6-1 (*continued*)

19. By the choices you have indicated, would you be interested in renting an apartment in the Tech Married Student Housing?
    _____ Yes
    _____ No
    _____ Undecided (Specify any reservations)

20. If the apartment you have specified were available now, what is the maximum distance from the Tech campus you would consider?

    _____ 1 – 5 blocks   _____ 26 – 30 blocks
    _____ 6 – 10 blocks   _____ 31 – 35 blocks
    _____ 11 – 15 blocks   _____ 36 – 40 blocks
    _____ 16 – 20 blocks   _____ 41 – 45 blocks
    _____ 21 – 25 blocks   _____ 46 – 50 blocks
                                   _____ over 50 blocks

21. Which would you prefer:
    _____ to live in an apartment building where children *are* allowed?
    _____ to live in an apartment building where children are *not* allowed?

22. Would you be willing to *lease* the apartment for one year at a 5% reduction in the monthly rental rate?
    _____ Yes
    _____ Yes, but only if I could sub-let the apartment during summer months
    _____ No

SUMMARY

Several drafts of a questionnaire may be required before the final product is acceptable. The goal of the first draft is to compose questions in a form that will obtain all the information necessary. The kinds of questions can be classified as follows: (1) open questions, which permit a short, unstructured answer; (2) dichotomous questions, which may be answered by yes or no; (3) multiple choice questions; (4) declarative questions, in which statements are answered.

Certain types of questions should be avoided in the construction of a questionnaire: (1) leading questions, which influence the answer; (2) misleading questions, which deliberately lead; (3) ambiguous questions, which do not have a clear meaning; (4) double questions, which have two questions in one; (5) uninformative questions, which supply useless information.

The wording of questions is important. The words going into the questions should have certain characteristics: (1) uniformity of meaning; (2) preciseness of meaning; (3) freedom from undue influence of prestige or bias; (4) freedom from a tendency to arouse irrational or emotional responses. In other words, neutral words should be used.

Usually a certain order of questions is desirable. The following considerations will guide in organizing the order of questions: (1) the need to arouse and hold interest; (2) the influence of one question on another; (3) the best position for the most important questions; (4) the determination of the point at which fatigue of the respondent may occur.

Certain questions in questionnaires may cause difficulty: (1) questions respondents may be unable or unwilling to answer; (2) unnecessary or overlapping questions.

Classification or validation questions may be incorporated into the questionnaire. These are questions for which the answers can be classified and compared to already known characteristics existing in a population. For example, if the average age of persons in a city was 31.3 years, and this age was also found in the survey, representativeness of the survey would be indicated.

Usually questionnaires are pretested. This means that, after the final copy of the questionnaire is produced, it will be tested in the same kind of a universe for which it is designed. A small subset of the normal sample would be used to test the questions for order, ambiguity, bias, etc. The pretest may result in the rewriting of some questions, in deleting some, possibly in adding some. The final questionnaire may not be changed at all, of course.

EXERCISES

1. Certain necessary conditions must be met before actually writing the questions for a questionnaire. List these conditions.
2. Classify the kinds of questions that may appear on a questionnaire, describing each briefly.
3. In writing multiple choice questions, the answers listed must have certain characteristics. What are they?
4. Write out two examples of the following types of questions:
   a. dichotomous
   b. multiple choice
5. List and describe types of questions to avoid. Then, write one example of each.
6. Explain briefly the characteristics of the types of words that should be used in questionnaires.
7. Why is the order in which questions appear on a questionnaire of importance?
8. What kinds of questions are respondents unwilling to answer?
9. Give three examples of overlapping questions.
10. What are classification questions? What are validation questions? Compare the two kinds.
11. Why may pretesting the questionnaire be important?
12. Write a critical evaluation of exhibit 6-1.
13. Construct a questionnaire for one of the following surveys:
    a. homemakers opinions of refrigerators
    b. political affiliations of college students
    c. ratings of the U.S. Congress by businesspersons
    d. lawyers' opinions of advertising legal services

SELECTED REFERENCES

Interviewer's Manual. rev. ed. Ann Arbor: Survey Research Center, Institute for Social Research, The University of Michigan, 1976.

Parten, Mildred. *Surveys, Polls, and Samples: Practical Procedures*. New York: Cooper Square, 1966.

7

Aids in Administering Questionnaire Surveys

The preceding chapter explained in detail the writing of satisfactory questions for questionnaires and gave examples of successful question construction. The current chapter considers administration aspects of the construction of questionnaires, specifically (1) techniques of aiding the respondent to reply and (2) aids to final interpretation of replies. Finally, a summary of the characteristics of a good questionnaire is presented.

TECHNIQUES OF AIDING THE RESPONDENT TO REPLY

It is important to reduce to a minimum the time and effort required by the respondent in supplying the information required. At the same time, the replies must be kept as accurate as it is feasible to make them. The persons who are being interviewed must be made to feel that the survey techniques have been carefully planned and the questionnaires skillfully constructed to obtain the desired information as correctly and easily as possible.

When the respondent is asked to answer questions, the main difficulties which he may face are: (1) difficulty in remembering the information requested, (2) possible embarrassment if the answer is given correctly, and (3) difficulty in expressing ideas. In this section, various ways of overcoming each of these blockages to correct replies will be described.

AIDS IN REMEMBERING

The central purpose of most of the techniques for aiding a respondent to remember is actually to reduce to a minimum the amount of reliance that must be placed on memory.

Make the question as concrete as possible. For instance, instead of asking a worker how many pairs of cloth work gloves he buys in a year, ask him how long a pair lasts him. He will not need to remember back over a whole year. The interviewer can quickly calculate the approximate number of pairs purchased in a year on the basis of the life of the gloves given.

Make the question as specific as possible. This technique is somewhat related to the preceding point about making the question as concrete as possible. The respondent may be able to remember the information desired more completely and correctly if he is asked a specific question that makes it unnecessary for him to recall a large amount of information. For example, suppose that the safety engineer of a manufacturing company wanted to ask the employees of the firm about the existence of unsafe conditions in the plant. One thing he desired to know was what unsafe conditions the workers had noticed. The question could be worded as follows: "Have you seen any unsafe conditions in this plant?" This is a general question, however, that will be more difficult to answer than a more specific one, such as, "Have you seen any unsafe conditions within the last month in the department in which you work?"

A word of caution should be given about the use of this *aided recall technique*, as it has been designated. The aids or hints given to the respondent should not be so revealing as to suggest answers that do not represent the true reactions or thoughts of the respondent. That is, the question should not become a leading one. For instance, the worker in the safety survey should not have been asked, "Have you noticed that the nailing machine was vibrating dangerously?" The aid to recall, instead, should merely be sufficient to make the question clear and to enable the respondent to answer accurately.

The aided recall technique has probably been used most frequently in surveys to measure effectiveness of advertising. An example, taken from a survey in that field, will help to illustrate more fully the use of this technique. As part of a market study, a television retail sales and repair shop wanted to know the percentage of the persons in its trade area who could remember having seen a series of advertisements of the shop. The advertisements had appeared weekly in the local neighborhood newspaper over the last month.

Several other retail firms handling television sets had also been advertising in the neighborhood paper. The questions needed to be worded in such a way as to let the respondent know what types of establishments were concerned and what medium of advertising was involved. At the same time, the name of the particular television shop for which the survey was being conducted should not be mentioned because to do so would bias the replies. With these conditions in mind, the following questions were asked:

1. Have you seen any newspaper advertisements recently of any retail stores
   featuring TV sales and repair services?
   _____ Yes _____ No _____ Do not recall
   (If answer is yes, ask next question.)

2. What were the main ideas or things about the advertisement that you can recall?

_____

_____

The purpose of the first question was to aid recall and response by making the question as specific as possible. This was accomplished by designating the type of sponsors of the advertisements and the medium used. The second question was asked to determine whether the advertisement recalled was actually one that had been sponsored by the particular television shop for which the survey was conducted.

Ask about the last purchase made.   The *theory of the last purchase*, as a technique for determining preferences of persons, is based on these two assumptions: (1) The type of product most recently purchased is ordinarily a reasonably accurate reflection of the marketplace preferences of persons in general. (2) The most recently purchased article can be remembered more correctly than can articles bought in the more remote past.

For example, a person may be asked, "What type of movie did you attend most frequently during last year?" This question will require a considerable amount of thinking back over the year in an attempt to recall the various movies attended. Also, the phrase, "types of movies," will present difficult classification problems for the respondent. A much easier and more accurate reply could be given if the question were stated as follows: "What was the name of the movie that you last attended?" This second question puts considerably less reliance on memory; and, in addition, the name of the last movie attended can be used by the researcher, by reference to trade journals, to determine the type of movie named.

It is true that there will be certain individuals who will have attended a movie not of the type that they usually attend. But in a survey covering several hundred persons in a community with a sufficient number of movie theaters to provide each day a fare of various kinds of pictures, the type last seen by the most respondents will quite likely be the most popular type among the persons interviewed.

The "theory of the last purchase" can be applied not only to purchases of products and services but to other actions, as well, which indicate preferences or perhaps merely usual behavior patterns. Suppose that a business firm and the traffic control division of the city desired to know what streets the employees of the firm usually traveled in getting to and from work. The workers could be asked what routes they took in coming to work "this morning" and when they went home "last night." Of course, in this situation, they could also be asked if these routes were the ones they ordinarily used.

Ask questions along the time line of memory or occurrence.   Memory can sometimes be refreshed and events recalled if the respondent is asked several questions about what he was doing and what he did next, step by step, in regard to the events leading up to or leading back to the particular thing that it is desired for him to remember.

Suppose the proprietor of a recreation lodge located several hundred miles from the city in which the respondents live wanted to learn where he should place roadside signs to advertise his lodge. The questions in the questionnaire could be arranged in a *time line* order, say, about as follows: "Did you take a vacation trip in your car last year? If so, where did you go? What highway did you take? What was the name of the first town of fairly large size that you passed through? What was the next town?" Etc. The purpose of these questions is to refresh the memory of the respondent and to get him to remember what route he traveled, assuming that he went in the general direction of the recreation lodge in which this researcher is interested. The routes mentioned most frequently in the survey would then be the ones along which the proprietor should place his signs. It is obvious in this case that respondents could also be shown road maps on which they could be asked to trace their routes as they recalled them.

AIDS IN AVOIDING EMBARRASSMENT

While the questionnaire from its inception should be designed to elicit a favorable reaction from the respondent relative to his participation in the survey, specific attention must often be given to avoiding embarrassment to the respondent. There are occasions when the nature of the product or the use of the product, or the need for the information or the nature of the questions themselves may tend to cause embarrassment. In these circumstances, effort must be given to establishing methods of avoiding or minimizing the embarrassment. The following techniques will help.

Ask indirect questions. An indirect question that is skillfully worded may enable the respondent to supply information that is needed without being embarrassed by the reply. Suppose that the manager of a department store that had a fine reputation wanted to know whether the people in his trade area thought his store sold only high priced goods. Perhaps he is concerned about the possibility that some prospective customers are not buying at his store because they believe that all the merchandise is higher priced than at least some of it really is. Since the store has such a good reputation, many persons in the community would not want to indicate that they might not trade in the store because they believed that it handled only the lines in the top price levels.

Suppose a direct question is asked, such as:

Do you believe that store X handles high priced goods only?
_____ Yes _____ No

Some persons in the trade area of the store would possibly be reluctant to answer yes to this question. The main reasons for this reluctance could be that the respondent might not want to give an answer that is in any way derogatory to store X or to admit that he cannot afford the higher prices of good quality merchandise. Direct questions in this situation would, therefore, call for answers which if given correctly would embarrass some of the respondents. Inaccurate replies, therefore, could be expected from such persons.

An indirect question which could be substituted for the direct one in the preceding paragraph might be constructed as follows:

Please indicate the percentage of the shoes sold by store X which you believe fall in each of the following price brackets. (Encircle the appropriate percentage figure in each price bracket.)

Price Bracket	Percent of All Shoes Sold That Fall in Each Price Bracket										
$ 4.95 to $ 7.95	5%	10%	20%	30%	40%	50%	60%	70%	80%	90%	100%
7.96 to 12.95	5	10	20	30	40	50	60	70	80	90	100
12.96 to 15.95	5	10	20	30	40	50	60	70	80	90	100
15.96 to 22.95	5	10	20	30	40	50	60	70	80	90	100
23.96 and over	5	10	20	30	40	50	60	70	80	90	100

If the respondents encircled the percentages that were approximately the same as were shown by a study of the actual records of the store, then the persons surveyed had an accurate knowledge about the level of prices charged in the store. On the other hand, if on the questionnaires, the estimates of the percentage in the upper-price brackets were too high, the manager of the store would have evidence that his store was considered to be a higher priced store than it really is. This belief might then be a contributing factor to the failure of some persons to buy in the store.

Ask comparative questions.   Use can be made of comparative questions to obtain some kinds of potentially embarrassing information. For example, the manager of a store might want to know what his customers think of the sales personnel in his store. Many customers would not want to be embarrassed by being asked to answer a direct question, such as:

Do you think my salespersons are reasonably polite?
_____ Yes _____ No

Instead, a less direct comparative question of the following type might be asked:

How do you believe my salespersons compare in politeness with the salespersons in similar stores in this city? (Please check one.)
_____ Much more polite
_____ Somewhat more polite
_____ About the same in politeness
_____ Somewhat less polite
_____ Much less polite

This question can be answered in degrees, and the respondent is not forced to reply in either of the extremes that the salespersons "are" or "are not" polite. The answers "somewhat less polite" and "about the same in politeness" may be checked more frequently than the manager of the store might like to have them checked. But he is much more likely to get a true picture with this comparative question than he would have with the simple question with the "yes" or "no" choices only. Many respondents who actually do not believe the salespersons are reasonably polite would, nevertheless, answer that they were rather than have to give the completely opposite answer. The comparative question, since it allows a more nearly correct representation of the opinion of the respondent without unduly embarrassing him, is superior to the direct question.

Another method of using comparative questions is to ask the same questions about each case that is of interest to the researcher. The answers to these questions can then be compared; and the degree of favorableness or unfavorableness to the various cases can be studied. For example, in the survey on customers' opinions about politeness of salespersons, the same question could be asked about each of the several stores of this type in the city (without the respondent being told which particular store was sponsoring the survey). Then, the answers for the stores could be compared to determine how the stores ranked in the minds of the respondents.

Ask respondent about actions of other persons. Instead of asking the respondent what he has done, it is sometimes possible to get practically the same information about persons of his type by asking him to tell what other persons have done or would be likely to do. Suppose it was desired to find out beforehand whether people in a certain city would be likely to buy a certain brand of garden water hose if their children were offered a chance to win a Shetland pony. Many adults might be ashamed to admit they would decide to buy such an item as a garden hose because their children would get a chance to win a small pony. The same persons, however, might well be able without embarrassment to answer whether they thought other persons of their acquaintance would be induced to buy by such an offer.

Keep respondent from knowing name of sponsor of survey. Often, if the respondent knows that a certain person or company is backing the survey, the answers given will be more favorable to this sponsor than they would be otherwise. The typical respondent will tend to experience some embarrassment in giving an answer that is somewhat adversely critical of a person or organization that is paying the interviewer for his work.

For example, suppose that a polite young male interviewer approached a dwelling and the homemaker answered the door. The young man was wearing a uniform with "Purewhite Ice Cream" written across the front. He then proceeds to ask the homemaker several questions about her preferences in regard to different brands of ice cream. If the respondent in this case is a typical person, it is unlikely that she will want to give answers that are unfavorable to Purewhite Ice Cream. Consequently, a true picture of the respondent's opinion about the different brands of ice cream cannot be obtained under these circumstances.

Allow respondent to "save face." Often a question can be worded and presented in such a way as to allow the respondent to avoid embarrassment in his answer. For example, instead of asking simply, "What movie did you last attend?" or "Do you read the magazine *Passionate Confessions*?," the same questions might be asked with face-saving qualifications. The respondent might not want to answer these particular questions with yes because he could be considered to be admitting that he preferred this type of movie or magazine. The face-saving qualifications can often be reasonably effective, even though they are relatively minor additions to a question. For instance, the movie question could be prefaced by some such apparently casual statement as "Often persons with time on their hands will attend the most conveniently located movie theater." The question would then follow, "What motion picture did you happen to attend last?" The word *happen* in the preceding question also helps to convey the idea of casualness rather than deliberateness of action. Answering this question, therefore, would not seem to mean to the respondent that he was being asked to state the type of movie he usually attended.

The magazine question could be introduced with a comment to the effect that "There certainly are a lot of magazines that a person comes across almost everywhere he goes today." Then this question could be asked, "Have you ever happened to read anything in the magazine *Passionate Confessions?*"

To summarize, the purpose of these statements before the questions are asked and the changed wording of the questions is to let the respondent feel that even though he gives an affirmative answer, he still is merely admitting a casual, half-accidental action, certainly not one that indicates his regular preference or actions. It must be realized, of course, that such somewhat roundabout questions should be used only when it is considered necessary to secure answers to questions which would not be answered with reasonable accuracy otherwise.

AIDS IN EXPRESSING REACTIONS

The persons being interviewed may be willing to give the desired information. They may not feel any embarrassment, either. Still, they may have trouble expressing themselves. For instance, such matters as preferences in tastes, colors, odors, and sounds are difficult to put into words. Where a man's feet hurt is perfectly clear to him, but he would find it difficult to tell in words alone the exact location of the pain. A woman cannot tell an interviewer what kind of a hat she prefers. She will have to see and try on a hat before she can accurately express her reaction. It soon becomes evident to a researcher interested in obtaining the opinions of people that in a considerable number of situations, specially prepared questionnaire techniques will be needed to help the respondent supply the required information.

Several of these techniques are discussed in the following paragraphs. Some of the types of questions, it will be seen, have been described before in connection with the problems of aiding the respondent to remember and to avoid embarrassment. The types of questions, however, which will be presented in the present discussion will be in the forms appropriate to the particular situation involved.

Ask indirect questions. As has been mentioned before, a person can in some situations supply information more accurately when asked an indirect instead of a direct question. Whenever an answer to a direct question would require a large amount of self-analysis on the part of the respondent, careful consideration should be given to the possibility of using an indirect question. For example, instead of asking a man such a direct question as, "Are you an avid sports fan?," he could be asked how frequently he attends sports events in terms of times per week or month. The actual frequencies of attendance at such events could be tabulated for each respondent. The degree of "avidness" could be more accurately determined in this manner than by asking the direct question.

Suppose it is desired to know whether the respondents in a survey would be likely to patronize a new bowling alley in their part of town. The direct question, "Would you patronize a new bowling alley?," would draw a relatively large percentage of yes replies, especially from persons who know how to bowl or like to watch bowling. These replies might be sincere, but they would not be accurate measures of the probable amount of fee-paying attendance at a new bowling alley. What the proprietor of the prospective alley needs to know is what percentage of the persons in the trade area of the proposed site of the establishment are active bowlers and how frequently they bowl. The best indicators of whether there will be sufficient patronage, therefore, will be obtained by the less direct but more effective questions, such as:

Do you bowl? _____ Yes _____ No
How many times each week or each month do you bowl?
_____ Times per week   or   _____ Times per month

Ask comparative questions.   For instance, it may be desired to know the relative rank of milk among various foods in the minds of the consumers in a given community. The respondent might be at a loss as to how to express his actual opinion in regard to milk as compared to other foods. The standing of milk might be established by asking the respondent to show how he believes milk compares in nourishment with each of certain selected foods. The comparative question could be constructed as follows:

How do you believe a pint of milk compares in food value with each of the following quantities of foods:

Kind of food:	Food value compared to milk:		
½ pound of beef steak	_____ More	_____ Less	_____ About same
2 eggs	_____ More	_____ Less	_____ About same
Etc.	Etc.		

If the actual nourishment of these portions of food were all equal to that of a pint of milk, the answers would show whether consumers knew the facts about these foods. Even if the portions were not equal in food value to the milk, the responses would still indicate how milk compared with each of the other foods in the opinions of the respondents.

Obtain realistic answers.   Ordinarily in business research the preferences of prospective customers must be determined in terms of actual or probable purchases in the marketplace. Preferences must be in realistic terms, not in terms of wishful thinking. Suppose that a man was asked, "What kind of automobile would you like to own?" His answer might be on the level of a daydream, that is, he would give the name of a car that he believes he "would buy if he had a million dollars." What the manufacturers and his dealers need to know is what kind of car the man is really likely to buy.

It is because of this need for realistic answers that the respondent should be asked such a question as, "What make of car do you now drive?" The car that he last purchased is probably the best indication that it is possible to obtain of what kind of car he actually can buy. In general then, for most practical purposes, the realistic preferences of people are best shown in the products that they currently own and use. And it is usually true that the kind of item last purchased is a good indication of the kind that will be purchased next time. It can be seen, therefore, that the "last purchase" type of question may provide an effective way for the respondent to express himself accurately.

Show samples, models, or actual products to help respondents to decide. When it is desired to learn what persons think about a product, often the best way to enable the respondents to answer questions accurately is first to show them a sample of the product. For instance, a man might have some difficulty in describing the shape of pipe he prefers; but, he probably could quickly indicate which one in a display of pipes has the shape he likes best. The samples used should be as nearly like the real product as it is feasible to make them. In fact, the ideal in testing customer preferences would ordinarily be to let the respondent see and make normal use of the actual product concerned.

In a survey in which this technique is involved, the researcher is actually making use of some aspects of the experimental and observational techniques. These will be discussed later, but it can well be mentioned here again that in setting up research plans for collecting information, the procedure should include the techniques or combinations of techniques which will be most effective. Usually this means that in most research projects, use will be made of more than one of the various techniques described in this book.

Sometimes the product being asked about is so large or expensive that it is not practicable to use the real product to show prospective respondents in the questionnaire survey. Small, portable models might be constructed for this purpose. For example, a building contractor or an association of builders might desire to know what kinds of houses prospective buyers prefer. Scale models of various types, styles, shapes, and color combinations could be used. Furniture manufacturers might be able to use models in interviewing persons about their preferences in color and other features of furniture.

Models may be necessary, also, when the product being asked about is not yet in existence. Perhaps it is being planned and designed. The purpose of the survey could be to aid in the designing of the product. Suppose the manufacturer of materials that go into fences around residences wanted to know what designs would be likely to be most popular. This information would enable him to take advantage of the lower costs of producing in quantity the component parts of the most popular types. In this situation, a representative group of prospective fence buyers might be able to supply quite helpful information about their preferences if they were shown some models of fences.

It should always be remembered, however, that small models are not likely to cause exactly the same reactions as the actual product itself. Because of this fact, whenever it is feasible, the real product should be shown. For instance, if the building contractors mentioned in a preceding paragraph could have taken representative potential buyers on conducted tours through actual houses of various types, instead of showing them models only, the replies of the respondents would have been more realistic. In the case of the furniture survey, the respondents might have been transported to store buildings, warehouses, or into homes in which the actual furniture could be seen.

Ask question after trial use of product. This technique will merely be mentioned here since it was discussed in greater detail as an aspect of experimentation. It should be recognized, however, as a possible way of aiding the respondent to reply more realistically to questions pertaining to his reactions to a certain product.

Let respondent taste, smell, feel, or hear the product before replying. These points also were described in the chapter on experimental techniques. Here it need only be mentioned that it would often be impossible for a person to describe in words alone his preferences in regard to the taste, odor, or the "feel" of an item or the sound of, say, a stereo set. But he could tell, for instance, which of several tastes or odors that he liked best after he had tasted or smelled them and which musical numbers or instruments he preferred after he had heard them played.

Let respondent see pictures of the product before replying. If it is not feasible to show respondents actual products, samples, or even models, pictures in some cases will be useful substitutes. In a recent survey for a large music store, one of the main purposes was to find out what kinds and styles of pianos prospective buyers would purchase next. Each respondent was shown pictures to help him give a clear indication of what kinds and styles he would buy. Pilot interviews had shown that many persons with a piano in their home had only hazy notions about actual kinds and styles available.

Care must be exercised in using pictures to keep everything about the pictures the same except the variations of the product to be asked about. For example, suppose that the picture of some of the pianos had been on a larger scale or were in more pleasing colors than was the case for the rest of the pictures. Then, the more impressively pictured pianos would have been given a better chance than the others of being selected. The replies would have been distorted. The pictures used must, of course, be accurate pictures of the products involved. Often it will be desirable to have a capable photographer make photographs of the same size and under identical conditions for each article covered in the survey.

Make ranking of choices as easy as possible. When the respondent is asked to indicate which is his first choice in a list of possible answers, he has been presented with a problem which may require considerable thinking and evaluating. If he is requested not only to show his first choice but his second, third, fourth, and so on, he may face a task that is so difficult and time consuming it may not be possible to obtain his cooperation. Therefore, any ranking of choices which must be required of the respondent should be made as easy as possible for him to do.

Here are some of the techniques for making ranking of choices easier as well as more effective:

(1) Never ask the respondent to rank any more than three choices unless it is absolutely necessary. When a person is asked to indicate his choices of, say, from first to tenth place, he is confronted with an extremely difficult job. A person may be able to decide rather easily what are his first two or three choices, but beyond the third the decisions may be very hard to make. Deciding which is fifth and sixth, for instance, may be asking for an evaluation of choices that are so nearly equal that no accurate ranking is possible.

(2) Ranking may be accomplished reasonably satisfactorily when a sizable number of respondents are interviewed by merely asking for a check mark after, say, the two (or three) main choices out of the ten listed. When the replies to all the questionnaires are tabulated, the check marks after each choice can be totaled to determine the ranks of the ten choices. The process of deciding which two (or three) of the ten to check has required the respondent to give a usable ranking to the choices listed.

(3) If the checking of the choices listed is expected to concentrate on, say, three choices only, then the respondent may have to be asked to place the number 1 after his first choice, 2 after his second, and perhaps 3 after his third. Suppose that out of a list of ten possible choices of answers to a question, all the checks were placed after the same three items. These items would have an equal number of checks; and, therefore, ranking them would be impossible. If it does not confuse the respondents being interviewed, some time can be saved by instructing them merely to put a 1 after their first choice and a check after their second and third choices.

(4) Always inform the respondent that he is to check only the stated number of choices out of the total listed. Unless this instruction is given, the respondent may check all or nearly all of the choices; and he will, therefore, not have indicated his ranking of the items.

(5) Make use of the "more, less, or same" type of question when it is appropriate. This is a type of question which is useful in readership or audience surveys or in any survey concerned with how a fixed amount of space or time should be utilized. The respondent is asked whether he would like to read, hear, or see more, less, or about the same amount of different types of published material or types of entertainment in the movies or on radio and television. It is relatively easy for a person to indicate how he feels about a certain type of article or program when all he has to do is tell whether he would like to read, see, or hear more of that type, less of that type, or about the same amount as is presently available.

If a newspaper editor wanted to know whether his types of editorial material were considered by his readers to be well balanced, he might conduct a questionnaire survey among his readers. He would first need to decide what types of material carried in the paper could be increased or decreased in amount. Then these types of material could be identified with a name or phrase that would be clear to the readers to be interviewed. The "more, less, or same" kind of questions that could now be constructed might be as follows:

Please look at the following types of articles that the *New Town News* now carries. Then check whether you would like to have more or less or about the same amount of these kinds of items as now appear in the paper.

Type of article:		What do you want:	
Sports	____ More	____ Less	____ About same as now
Business news	____ More	____ Less	____ About same as now
National and world news	____ More	____ Less	____ About same as now
Local social news	____ More	____ Less	____ About same as now
Woman's page news	____ More	____ Less	____ About same as now

AIDS TO FINAL INTERPRETATION OF REPLIES

An important characteristic of a satisfactory questionnaire is that the questions have been constructed in such a manner as to facilitate the interpretation of the replies.

MORE, LESS, OR SAME INDEX

The "more, less, or same" type of question as used in the mythical *New Town News* survey was described in the immediately preceding paragraphs. The *more, less, or same index* can be a particularly helpful aid in the interpretation of the replies to such questions.

The formula for computing the more, less, or same index, in longhand form, is: Subtract the total number answering "less" from the total number answering "more" and divide the result by the total number of replies. In short form, this could be written as:

$$\text{more, less, or same index} = \frac{\text{"more's" minus "less's"}}{\text{total number of replies}}$$

The persons answering "same" should not be considered in the formula except to add them to the "more" and "less" replies to arrive at the "total number of replies." Persons who could not make up their minds or answered that they "did not know" would be counted as having replied "same."

The most favorable index number that a type of article could obtain would be +1.00. This would have occurred if all persons in the *New Town News* survey had answered "more." The lowest or least favorable index number possible would be −1.00. In this case, all persons would have answered "less." It is possible for the index number to be 0.00 if either all persons wanted the "same" or if an equal number checked each of the three possible choices or an equal number checked "more" and "less." If the index number were near 0.00, any change in the amount of this type of article would displease about as many persons as it would please; therefore, probably no change should be made. In the use of the results, the type of article that received the highest index number, or one of the highest, would be given more space and this space would be taken from a type with one of the lowest index numbers. A shortcoming of this technique is that there is no measure provided for the amount of change that should be made in the spaces involved. It would be possible, however, to conduct periodic surveys to see the effects of previous changes in space allotments in terms of bringing the index numbers into line for the various types of space usage.

RATING SCALES

Rating scales are a complex and costly but relatively accurate technique for enabling persons to express their attitude toward a certain condition, product, or idea. The "more, less, or same" type of question employs the basic principles of rating scales. The latter, however, offer more choices of responses to each respondent than are found in either the single question or the "more, less, or same" question techniques.

In the use of rating scales, the persons in the survey may be asked to indicate whether their attitude is "favorable" or "unfavorable" toward, say, each of five statements about a carefully stated or defined condition (idea or product). The five statements will have been systematically selected originally by a group of persons who have been asked to rank these statements as to how favorable or unfavorable they seem or appear to be in regard to the stated condition being studied. The statement that is least favorable to the stated condition will be placed at one end of the list (scale) of statements to be shown to the respondents when the final survey is conducted, and the most favorable statement will be placed at the opposite end of the list. The other three statements will be placed in their correct order in between.

Each statement can be assigned a scale weight depending on its degree of favorableness or unfavorableness to the condition under consideration. For example, the least favorable of the five statements could be assigned a weight of 1 and the most favorable a weight of 5. Each "favorable" and each "unfavorable" reply by a respondent will be multiplied by its weight, then the "favorables" will be totaled and the "unfavorables" will be totaled. The weighted averages of the "favorables" and the "unfavorables" are sometimes used.

A major use of rating scales is to determine what changes, if any, occur in the scores of ratings given by respondents between two surveys. The general score or rating for all of the respondents combined can be computed by adding the score of each respondent to obtain a grand total. The grand totals secured in this manner in each survey can be compared to show the change that has occurred between the two surveys.

Suppose that it is desired to determine whether an educational campaign, sponsored by a civic group, would favorably change the attitude of people toward the question of financial support for city public schools. The research procedure called for could be as follows: One survey among a representative sample of persons will be conducted before the campaign is started. A second survey will be made after the campaign has been under way for a long enough period of time for it to have had a reasonable chance to cause a change in the attitude of the public. The scores on the first and second surveys could then be compared to see what change, if any, in attitude had occurred.

The favorable and unfavorable replies are weighted (the weights are at the left of each statement) and totaled, then divided by the grand weighted total of both (and multiplied by 100) to change them to percentages for comparison purposes.[1] Further, the unweighted percentages of favorable and unfavorable for each individual statement may be computed, in order to compare the statements to each other as well as to the total unweighted percentages of favorable and unfavorable for the questionnaire.

The questionnaire, used in both surveys, might be as follows:

1. Our city public school system should be financed by a combination of property tax plus tuition.

 _____ Favorable _____ Unfavorable

2. Our city public school system should be financed by a combination of property tax plus a city sales tax.

 _____ Favorable _____ Unfavorable

3. Our city public school system should be financed solely by the property tax.

 _____ Favorable _____ Unfavorable

4. Our city public school system should be financed by a combination of property tax plus state aid.

 _____ Favorable _____ Unfavorable

5. Our city public school system should be financed 100 percent by state aid.

 _____ Favorable _____ Unfavorable

Another scale rating technique—called a *Likert scale*—that is useful in some projects requires that the selected and rated statements be shown to a sample of persons who are asked to indicate the extent to which they agree or disagree with each statement.[2] The choices could be "strongly agree" (approve), "agree" (approve), "neither agree nor disagree" (undecided), "disagree" (disapprove), and "strongly disagree" (disapprove). In some situations, the appropriate categories may be "like very much," "like," "indifferent," "dislike," and "dislike very much." Each choice of answer is assigned a weight according to its degree of favorableness to the condition being studied. Where five choices are offered, the most favorable could be given a weight of five and the least favorable a weight of one.

Consider an example of a mail questionnaire sent by a department store to its customers because of a suspicion that customers may be dissatisfied with certain services of the store. Customers were requested not to sign the returned questionnaires in order to preserve anonymity in the hope the replies would therefore be more reliable. The questionnaire follows:

	Strongly agree (5)	Agree (4)	Unde- cided (3)	Dis- agree (2)	Strongly disagree (1)
Returns of merchandise for exchange or credit are made promptly.	___	___	___	___	___
Adjustments to account mistakes are made promptly.	___	___	___	___	___
Major appliance service is performed when promised.	___	___	___	___	___
Major appliance service is satisfactory.	___	___	___	___	___
Deliveries are made when promised.	___	___	___	___	___
Other complaints are handled effectively and fairly.	___	___	___	___	___

The returns from the survey are totaled, and the totals for each category multiplied by each respective weight. The grand total of the products is divided by the total number of returns to find the average weight. Suppose the results of the survey are as follows:

	Weight	Questionnaire returns	Weight times returns
Strongly agree	5	30	150
Agree	4	25	100
Undecided	3	15	45
Disagree	2	10	20
Strongly disagree	1	10	10
		90	325

325 divided by 90 = 3.6 (average weight)

The average weight is 3.6, a score slightly more than midway between 3 (undecided) and 4 (agree). This score of itself may have meaning for the department store executives in attempting to arrive at a decision relative to customer satisfaction or dissatisfaction with services. The score may be compared with scores of other surveys of a like nature, or to standards secured from, say, a trade association.

In this kind of survey, the scores of individual statements may be compared with each other. For instance, a score of 2.7 on the statement, "Returns of merchandise for exchange or credit are made promptly," compared to a score of 4.2 on the statement, "Adjustments to account mistakes are made promptly," would indicate superior handling of problems by the accounting department relative to the returns department. These scores on individual statements may also be compared to the average for all statements (3.6) to see if they are above or below the average.

INDEXES OF FAME AND POPULARITY

The *index of fame* is a device that can be used for ranking the notoriety or fame of a personality in the social, political, sports, or entertainment worlds. Especially in the fields of sports and entertainment, a high index of fame may be of great importance. Whether or not the person is liked more or less than others in the field, the person may prove to be the largest drawing card because he or she is more famous or notorious than other figures. The *index of popularity* is a device to show the rank of an individual in regard to how well people like him or her. Some persons with a high index of fame may have a low index of popularity, and vice versa.

It is important for the compiler of a questionnaire to know whether he wants to determine the relative popularity or the notoriety of the type of persons about which he is asking. If, for example, the purpose of the survey is to provide a measurement of fame or notoriety, the question asked about a heavyweight wrestler would need to be stated in some such manner as this:

When heavyweight wrestlers are mentioned, what name comes to your mind first?

If popularity is the desired characteristic to be determined, the question could read about as follows:

What heavyweight wrestler do you admire the most?

The method of computing the indexes of fame and of popularity is the same. The names mentioned by the respondents in a survey are listed in the order of the number of times each name was given. The number of times each name was recorded should be shown beside each name.

Name of wrestler	Number of times mentioned	Index number
"Rocky" Ricardi	80	100
"The Bat" Jones	65	81
"Sweet Allen" Simpson	25	31
"Baby" Brown	20	25
"Curly" Sampson	15	19
Etc.	Etc.	Etc.

In the preceding table, the base of 100 was the 80 times that "Rocky" Ricardi was mentioned. Any other base could have been chosen, but "Rocky" Ricardi's score was selected as the base because he received the most "mentions." All other scores are made relative to his score by dividing each of them by Ricardi's 80, and multiplying by 100. Thus, 65 divided by 80 times 100 equals 81; 25 divided by 80 times 100 equals 31; etc. In the example shown, the number of wrestlers was intentionally kept small to keep the illustration simple. With only five names listed and the total number of "mentions" as small as shown, there may be little need for computing index numbers to show the ranking of the wrestlers. But, the use of index numbers can make comparisons much easier when the survey results include the names of scores of participants, and the "mentions" run into such large numbers that the relative rankings are difficult to see clearly in the raw totals.

If a wrestling match promoter knew the indexes of fame, preferably in his city, of the various wrestlers he might obtain for bouts, he could attempt to book only the performers with the highest indexes. Of course, it might be contended that the drawing power of a sports personality can best be determined by the box office receipts that he will draw by having him on some wrestling bout cards. This statement may be true, but it would be an excessively costly and slow way to learn if, instead, it is possible that an index of fame covering a variety of available wrestlers can be derived from a relatively inexpensive questionnaire-type survey. Several hundred dollars spent on such a survey may supply information that can direct the promoter to bookings that will mean thousands of dollars more in net receipts.

SUMMARY OF CHARACTERISTICS OF A GOOD QUESTIONNAIRE

The construction and use of questionnaires has been discussed at length in this and the preceding chapter. A summary of some of the main characteristics of a satisfactory questionnaire will be given here.

(1) It asks for and obtains the information needed in the light of the purposes of the research project.

(2) All questions included are pertinent and no unimportant questions are asked. Every question has a specific and significant purpose, because the time required to complete an interview must be kept at a reasonable level, usually not to exceed fifteen minutes.

(3) No information is asked for that can be more accurately, economically, and quickly obtained by other data-collecting methods, including observation by the interviewer.

(4) It asks for sufficient classification and validation data to (a) allow for adequate interpretation of the replies and to (b) provide for the testing of the sample for representativeness and accuracy of information obtained.

(5) Questions asked require no more reliance on memory than is essential for the purposes of the survey. If memory must be relied on, the appropriate techniques for aiding the respondent to remember are used.

(6) It contains no open or discussion questions unless they are absolutely necessary. The types of questions required in depth interviews are used only when qualified interviewers are available.

(7) It contains no questions that are unclear, ambiguous, double, leading, misleading, or uninformative.

(8) It contains questions that can be answered as quickly, easily, and with as little writing as is feasible. Answers that can be recorded by check marks, numbers, or in one word, such as, yes or no, are used whenever it is

appropriate to do so. Questions that require a considerable amount of self-analysis on the part of the respondent are avoided unless they are absolutely necessary.

(9) It does not restrict the questions and possible answers or choices of answers to an extent that biases and distorts replies given or otherwise forces the respondents to answer inaccurately.

(10) All checklists of choices of answers have been constructed in such a manner that they have all the characteristics of an adequate checklist.

(11) It asks embarrassing or prestige impact questions only when they are absolutely necessary and then, if at all possible, by the use of indirect and other types of questions that eliminate or reduce to a minimum embarrassment to the respondent.

(12) The questions are constructed in such a way and presented in such a manner as to make it easy for the respondent to express himself accurately. When appropriate, pictures of products, models, or actual products are shown to the respondent for him to use or at least to see, taste, smell, feel, or hear before he answers questions about the product. Indirect and comparative questions may be asked.

(13) Filter questions are used if needed.

(14) Adequate space is provided for answers.

(15) Questions and choices of replies appear in the correct psychological order to elicit accurate answers.

(16) Positional bias of questions has been eliminated by pretesting or by rotating the positions of questions in the questionnaire or items in checklists of answers.

(17) Overall size and shape is made as convenient to handle as is practicable. Appearance of size and length is reduced, if necessary, by using legal length sheets that are folded and by numbering only the main questions. Other questions may be lettered and printed in a lighter ink or in smaller letters.

(18) It is constructed in such a manner as to make the tabulation and interpretation of replies as easy and accurate as possible. Questions and answers have been or can be coded if it is considered helpful for mechanical processing.

(19) Mail questionnaires are accompanied by a clear, effective letter of introduction and explanation. Personal interview and telephone questionnaires are presented with appropriate introductions as needed.

(20) The entire questionnaire has been adequately pretested and revised to meet the qualifications of a satisfactory questionnaire for the particular survey in which it is to be used.

SUMMARY

There are techniques that may be applied to aid the respondents to reply to a questionnaire. Certain aids in remembering may be included: (1) Make the questions as concrete as possible. (2) Make the questions as specific as possible. (3) Ask about the last purchase made. (4) Ask questions along the time line of memory or occurrence.

There are aids for avoiding embarrassment of the respondents: (1) Ask indirect questions. (2) Ask comparative questions. (3) Ask respondents about the actions of other persons. (4) Keep respondents from knowing the name of the sponsor of the survey. (5) Allow the respondent to "save face."

Certain aids exist for aiding the respondents to help in expressing reactions: (1) Ask indirect questions. (2) Ask comparative questions. (3) Ask questions that will result in realistic answers. (4) Show the respondent samples or models. (5) Ask questions after trial use of products. (6) Let respondents see or handle the products before replying. (7) Let respondents see pictures of the product before replying. (8) Make the ranking of choices as easy as possible.

Certain aids will help the analyst in the final interpretation of replies. These are techniques making interpretation and classification easier: (1) Use a "more, less, or same" index. (2) Employ rating scales for the questions. (3) Use indexes of fame and popularity where they are applicable.

A summary of the characteristics of a good questionnaire follows:

1. Obtains the needed information.
2. Questions are pertinent and important.
3. No information is sought that can be better collected another way.
4. Includes sufficient classification and validation questions.
5. Requires as little reliance on memory as possible.
6. Keeps open questions at a minimum.
7. Contains no unclear, ambiguous, double, leading, misleading, or uninformative questions.
8. Questions can be answered quickly and easily.
9. Does not restrict choices to an extent that bias occurs.
10. All lists for check choices are adequate.
11. Avoids embarrassing or prestige-impact questions.
12. Aids respondents in expressing choices.
13. May use filter questions.
14. Provides adequate space for answers.
15. Has correct order of questions.
16. Pretesting of questionnaire for positional bias has occurred.
17. Size and shape of questionnaire is convenient.
18. Constructed to aid in interpreting and tabulating data.
19. Appropriate introduction and explanation are included.
20. Pretesting and revision have occurred to make the questionnaire fit the purpose of the survey.

EXERCISES

1. Among the techniques of aiding the respondent to reply are *aids in remembering*. List and describe these aids in your own words.
2. The *aided recall* technique has advantages and disadvantages. What are they?
3. Explain the *aids in avoiding embarrassment* as listed in the text. Why are these aids important?
4. Give four examples of aids in avoiding embarrassment in administering a questionnaire survey.

5. Describe in your own words the *aids in expressing reactions*.
6. How can the use of samples or models aid in getting reactions from respondents?
7. Describe in your own words the techniques for making ranking of choices easier for the respondent.
8. What is a *more, less, or same index*? How is it constructed? How is it used?
9. What are the uses of rating scales? How are they applied?
10. What is a *Likert scale*? Explain.
11. Describe in your own words the *index of fame*.
12. Write a two-page essay summarizing the characteristics of a good questionnaire.
13. Class project: Prepare a questionnaire to survey students on a current economic topic (like inflation, unemployment, job seniority). Pretest and revise. Conduct the survey. Then, evaluate the questionnaire using the characteristics of a satisfactory questionnaire.

SELECTED REFERENCES

Interviewer's Manual. rev. ed. Ann Arbor: Survey Research Center, Institute for Social Research, The University of Michigan, 1976.

Parten, Mildred. *Surveys, Polls, and Samples: Practical Procedures*. New York: Cooper Square, 1966.

ENDNOTES

1. Whether the difference in two such percentages is significant or not in terms of probabilities may be determined by techniques presented in chapter 9, in the section "Inferences for Percentages."
2. Named after Rensis Likert, Director of the Survey Research Center, University of Michigan.

8

Constructing and Analyzing Classifications

Classifying information is a preliminary step to any kind of analysis. The classification problem may be relatively simple, with few classifications involved, or complicated, requiring many classifications, cross-classifications, and possibly testing or analyzing the relationships revealed by the cross-classifications. The work may be preliminary to sophisticated statistical analysis, such as, correlations or regression or analysis of variance. This chapter explores the difficulties and practices in constructing and testing classifications effectively.

ORGANIZING INFORMATION

After information has been collected, it must be organized into classifications. The classifications may have been determined even before the data were collected; this procedure probably prevails in most cases. It is usually necessary to have the organizations of the data in mind in the planning stage so that the collection of the data will result in securing the kinds and classifications of information desired, and the work of classification and tabulation will be facilitated.

The data may be organized into logical classifications for one or both of two purposes: (1) to make possible the preparing of tables or charts for presentation in a report, or (2) to prepare the data for analysis and synthesis through the application of statistical techniques. The data must be classified properly and with minimum effort; the mass of data must be separated into groups which will make possible either the direct preparation of a report or will further the statistical refinement of the data.

EDITING DATA

Collected data are usually edited before organization or classification, whether the data consist of schedule reports, or of interview questionnaires, or of questionnaires returned through the mail, or if the data have been gathered from records within a firm. The editing of data is ordinarily necessary to insure accuracy and uniformity in reporting and to attain the maximum information from the data.

Omissions. An enumerator, whether working from a schedule or from individual questionnaires, may sometimes fail to record some answers; thus, the total on the schedule sheet may not tally, or blanks may appear in some questionnaires. In such an event, the enumerator is often able to reinterview the subject or to telephone the subject to gain the desired information. In some cases, the information may be unattainable and must be omitted. Some effort, however, should be made to correct such omissions.

When mailed questionnaires are used, some will be returned with a few of the blanks not filled in; such omissions are a normal occurrence. If too much information is missing, the questionnaire itself may be discarded; or, in the event it can be salvaged, the entry *N.R.* (not reported) is sometimes made in the blanks that have not been filled in by the respondent. It is hardly to be expected that every return in a mail questionnaire campaign of any considerable scale would contain complete answers from every subject. It is apparent, therefore, that in many cases omissions must be accepted by the collector of the information.

Inconsistencies. Returned questionnaires from a mail questionnaire campaign occasionally contain inconsistencies in the information. For example, if an individual proprietor lists his labor force as twelve common laborers and lists his weekly payroll as $10,280, it is obvious that he has made a serious error. Such inconsistencies may be corrected if enough information is obtained from the questionnaire to make a change possible. Sometimes the correct interpretation is impossible to make, and in such cases it is probably best to delete both answers. Sometimes enumerators, whether working from a schedule or from individual questionnaires, may be able to catch such inconsistencies during an interview at the time of their commission. For example, if a person gives her birthdate as 1912 and her age as 22, it is obvious to the enumerator instantly that a gross inconsistency exists. He can correct it then by a question to the subject. Sometimes questions may be included in a survey, the answers to which will serve as a check on the answers to other questions; such questions are often included in order to verify important statements.

Mistakes. Sometimes mistakes in mathematical computation will occur. When the subject is required to use arithmetic in answering a questionnaire, he often makes mistakes. People answering questionnaires which require computations frequently make mistakes with percentages. Whenever any computation is required in a questionnaire, the supervisor or statistician should check each computation on every return in order to insure maximum accuracy. Reports of records from accounting departments, operating departments, personnel departments, or from other sources inside a firm should be checked for accuracy.

Lack of uniformity. Enumerators' reports of interviews must have uniformity or a lack of unity in the study will result. For this reason, detailed instructions are normally given so each enumerator will ask the same questions, ask them in the same connotation, and interpret answers in the same way. On questionnaires to be sent through the mail, it is necessary, from the very beginning, to design the questions as carefully as is humanly possible in order to preclude any misunderstanding on the part of the subject answering the question. In spite of such care, however, the answers to at least one question in almost every mailed questionnaire of any length will reveal that the question has been misunderstood by many persons. Sometimes the nature of the misunderstanding is clear, and an adjustment can be made in the returns. At other times, the misunderstanding may be so serious that the answers to that question must be discarded. In every case, there should be some examination of returns, whether interview returns or mailed questionnaire returns, to determine whether there has been any misunderstanding of questions, and to determine the possible degree of seriousness of such misunderstandings.

Illegibility. When a mailed questionnaire provides for answers by a yes or no or by a check·in a blank or box, there is no difficulty in deciphering such returns. However, when a mailed questionnaire requires a written phrase or requires computations, a word in the phrase or a number in the computations is sometimes illegible. Every effort should be made to decode such undecipherable words or numbers. Since, in the interview method, the enumerator makes all of the entries, if undecipherable phrases or numbers appear, they can be corrected by consultation with the enumerator.

SUMMARY QUESTIONNAIRES

One of the first steps in the compilation of the answers to a questionnaire is to tabulate the number of replies recorded for the different parts and possible choices of answers for each question. It often will be found that it is quite logical that the compiled totals be placed in the appropriate blanks on a copy of the questionnaire form that was used in the field during the survey. This constitutes a *summary* or *master* questionnaire. The same procedure may be followed in the case of a survey in which information has been collected by means of observations which have been recorded on schedules or observationnaires.

In some research projects, there will be survey forms or schedules that will contain some questions that have answers which cannot be tabulated numerically on the survey form. The totals for these data, therefore, will not be shown on the regular copy of the form. Instead, in the answer space on the form there will be a notation as to where the tabulation, discussion, or summary of the answers can be found in the report. Usually this information will be on a sheet accompanying the summary questionnaire.

In other instances, the actual survey form used in the field work may not contain enough space to record the totals and summaries of some of the answers. In such a case, it may be necessary to construct a special summary questionnaire form that is identical to the original in all respects except for the larger amount of space for recording data and totals allowed on the summary form. If the answer space on the copy of the regular survey form is large enough to record all but a few of the data collected, special *overflow sheets* may be used to record the few sets of data that require too much space to be placed on the regular form.

Ordinarily, in a summary questionnaire, the most useful and meaningful arrangement of the totals for the answers to multiple choice questions is the exact order in which the choices appeared on the actual form used in the field during the survey. When, however, the ranking of the totals for these choices is of particular significance in the interpretation of the findings, it may be wise in the construction of the summary questionnaire to make certain adjustments in the survey form that was used in the field. For example, on the summary questionnaire, the choices may be listed in the order of the size of the total number of answers for each choice. Another procedure is merely to add on one side of the list of choices a column of numbers designating the rank of each choice. (See exhibit 8-1, question 3.) If the list of choices recorded in the field work exceeds the number of choices on the form, the overflow may be placed on an attached sheet.

EXHIBIT 8-1
Example of Summary Questionnaire

Opinions of Homemakers About Trading Stamps

Based on 251 personal interviews in a representative sample of homes in Bluton, Nebraska; conducted during period of October 15 to November 1. Numbers shown in brackets [15], etc., refer to pages in report in which the data are described and analyzed.

No. Ans'g
Ques.

251   1.   Do you save trading stamps? Yes *225* (89.6%) No *26* (10.4%) [15]

251   2.   How many persons are there in your family? *Average* 3.35 for 251 homes [10]

225   3.   What kinds of trading stamps do you save? [17]

		Rank			Rank
Pioneer	*72* (32.0%)	2	Economy	*107* (47.6%)	1
P & Q	*36* (16.0%)	3	Bonder's	*5* (2.2%)	4

Others, please specify *Miller 4 (1.8%) Olton's 1 (0.4%)*

225   4.   Are you saving stamps for a particular premium or item? [20]
     (a) Yes *88* (39.1%)   No *137* (60.9%)
     (b) If 'Yes,' what? (See accompanying overflow sheet for answers.)

223   5.   What do you believe a book of stamps is worth in terms of the monetary value of the items it will buy in the redemption center?
Average $2.61 [29]
For 223 Answers

Overflow sheet containing the summary of the answers to question 4(b): Are you saving stamps for a particular premium or item? If "yes,' what?

Item		*Times Mentioned*
Luggage	*22.*	*25.0%*
Clock	*17.*	*19.3*
Iron	*15.*	*17.1*
Camera	*12.*	*13.6*
Dishes	*8.*	*9.1*
Lamps	*5.*	*5.7*
Others	*9.*	*10.2*
	88	*100.0%*

Exhibit 8-1 provides a brief illustration of most of the possibly desirable features of a summary questionnaire. There are no exact rules on how to construct such a summary form. The nature of the material and the uses which are to be made of it should determine how it will be compiled. In most instances, however, the following procedures will help to maximize the usefulness of such a summary.

(1) If at all feasible, the summary questionnaire should be compiled on a copy of the actual form used in the field work. Modifications such as have been mentioned earlier may be necessary, but to the extent that the original form used in the process of collecting the data can be used, there are strong reasons for using this original field form. Among these reasons are:

a. The exact wording of the questions asked is given.
b. The order in which they were presented to the respondent is shown.

These conditions are important because the wording and order of questions have a great deal to do with what they mean to the respondents and, therefore, how they will be answered.

(2) The exact title of the research project should be placed at the top of the summary questionnaire. Any clarifying or descriptive terms needed should be added.

(3) Basic facts about the methods of collecting the data shown in the summary questionnaire should be placed at the top of the first page or at the bottom as a footnote. This brief statement supplies some information about the following:

a. Data-collecting techniques, including sampling, number of cases, and survey techniques.
b. Universe and types of cases, including political and geographic area covered.
c. Dates showing period during which the data were collected.

(4) The number of persons answering each part of each question should be entered in the space for answers provided on the questionnaire. Immediately following this number should be a figure showing what percentage of all answers to this question were answered in this way.

(5) Beside the number of each question, down the left-hand side of the page or in another appropriate place, the number of persons replying to each question should be shown. This figure will be the base number for any percentages that are calculated for the responses to each part of a question; from it can be computed what proportion of the persons interviewed gave a reply to the particular question. Such proportions are often important in the analysis of the responses. For instance, if a certain question were answered by only 10 out of a possible sample of 200 persons, the responses would probably have to be considered insufficient to serve as the basis of any significant conclusions.

(6) The number of the answers to each part of a question must add up to the same total as the total number of persons who answered the question. Also, the percentages answering the different parts of a question must add to 100 percent, with allowance for rounding to the nearest figure up to one or two decimal points.

An exception to the matching requirement for the totals occurs in those cases in which the respondent is instructed to answer more than one part of a question. For example, if each respondent was instructed to check two possible choices to a given question, then the total number of answers should be two times the total number of persons replying to the question. Such a situation as this should be clearly indicated on the summary questionnaire. The percentage figures must be compiled and interpreted with this condition in mind.

(7) When necessary, overflow sheets should accompany the summary questionnaire. (See the bottom portion of exhibit 8-1.) These sheets can be used:

a. To show data that take up too much space to be placed on the regular summary sheets.
b. To allow for the rearrangement of listings to conform to relative rankings of the answers to multiple choice questions.

(8) Brief citations to pages in the research report that contain discussions of the data shown may be placed after the questions in a summary questionnaire. These citations can be useful references to places in the final report where the findings are interpreted in detail, and perhaps graphically presented to bring out relationships and implications otherwise not apparent.

(9) Any adjustments in the copy of the questionnaire form used in the field in order to incorporate the preceding eight features in the summary questionnaire should not change the wording or sequential order of any of the material on the original form. The added material in the summary questionnaire should be in a different style of printing or in color, if this is feasible, to distinguish it from the material on the original form. The reader of the summary will then still be able to see the exact wording and sequence used in the process of asking questions in the actual survey.

It should be pointed out again that nearly all of the main features and advantages in the use of summary questionnaires also apply, with appropriate modifications, to summary observation schedules or observationnaires.

A summary of the main reasons for constructing and using a summary questionnaire or observationnaire follows:

1. Presents a concise summary statement of the basic statistical findings of the survey.
2. Facilitates the comparison of the replies to the different questions on questionnaires, or of the data tabulated on observationnaires.
3. Assists in the accurate interpretation of the findings by presenting the exact wording and position of the questions or items as they appeared on the form used in the actual survey.
4. Provides a brief statement showing the purpose of the project, research methods used, and the date of the survey.
5. Contains page citations placed by each item to direct the reader to the various parts of the final research report on which there is discussion and analysis of the data shown.

CROSS-CLASSIFICATION AND CHI-SQUARE

The purpose of cross-classification is to obtain and to present more information than can be obtained from single classifications. A listing of seven products produced by a factory with the total production of each gives a certain amount of information. When the production of each of the seven items is listed according to the eight machines that produced the product, then the output of each individual product from each individual machine can be seen, as well as the total production. This example would reveal, therefore, that a cross-classification consists of a matrix of cell values which represent one variable in the rows and another variable in the columns. However, cross-classification may contain more than two variables. For example, an age classification of animal breeding stock undergoing experimental treatment may be cross-classified by "male, before-after," and "female, before-after." Thus, three variables would be shown in the data within the cells.

The data in the cells of cross-classifications are nearly always reduced to percentage figures for ease in making comparisons. Sometimes cross-classifications will include both the original figures and the accompanying percentages.

Sometimes the testing of cross-classifications is necessary in order to reveal further the relationships of the variables involved. Such a test is given by chi-square, which is essentially a test for determining the *goodness of fit* of an observed distribution to a theoretical distribution. The theoretical distribution may be constructed from the original observations, it may be given by the problem itself, or it may consist of a standard mathematical distribution to be fitted to the original observations. Chi-square tests can be considered as tests showing the independence of two variables or showing the homogeneity of two variables as well as testing the goodness of fit of an observed distribution to a theoretical distribution. However, whatever the hypothesis that is set up to be tested, the basic technique is the same; and its essential nature is that of comparing the significance of the difference between an observed distribution and a theoretical distribution that has been derived or organized on some rational grounds to serve as an *ideal* against which to compare the original observations.

The following discussion will give examples, first, of cross-classifications, explaining how these cross-classifications improve understanding and widen knowledge and, second, of the computation of chi-square showing how it is used and how it is interpreted.

CROSS-CLASSIFICATIONS

Exhibit 8-2 presents the characteristics of the population fourteen years and over in a section of South Phoenix, Arizona. The data presented in the cells are cross-classified by ethnic characteristic and sex. In reading this table, it is immediately noticed that the total of the male and female for each of the three classifications of ethnic characteristic is given at the right and the grand total then is given. Observing the total of male and female, it is apparent that there are more females than males in this section of South Phoenix. This fact is true for each of the three ethnic groups.

EXHIBIT 8-2
Characteristics of the Population
14 Years and Over — South Phoenix, Arizona

	Male	Female	Total
"Anglo"	2,900	3,100	6,000
Mexican-American	4,300	5,000	9,300
Non-white	4,000	4,900	8,900
All classes	11,200	13,000	24,200

Source: "An Estimate of the Cost of Unemployment in an Area of Phoenix," *Arizona Business Bulletin,* February, 1968, Vol. XV, No. 2, p. 27 (Bureau of Business Research and Services, College of Business Administration, Arizona State University, Tempe, Arizona), original data from unpublished tabulations of Bureau of Labor Statistics on file with Arizona State Employment Service.

Exhibit 8-3 gives the same data but reduced to percentage terms. This percent distribution of characteristics of the population fourteen years and over in South Phoenix, Arizona, shows the relationships somewhat more clearly than the raw data. The "percent of total" column at the far right shows the percents of each of the ethnic groups, and it is seen instantly that the "Anglo" group is only one fourth of the population of the district. The other two ethnic groups are approximately evenly divided in the total. Referring to the "male," "female" columns, in each case, the percentage of females exceeds the percentage of males. It is apparent, however, that the differential in the percentage of male-female is smaller for the "Anglo" group than for the other two ethnic groups. The other two ethnic groups show a considerably broader spread, that is, a considerably larger proportion of females to males.

EXHIBIT 8-3
Percent Distribution of Characteristics of the Population
14 Years and Over — South Phoenix, Arizona

	Male	Female	Total	Percent of Total
"Anglo"	48.3	51.7	100.0	24.8
Mexican-American	46.2	53.8	100.0	38.4
Non-white	44.9	55.1	100.0	36.8
				100.0

If the male-female proportions in the general population of the United States is 50-50, then the problem of the male-female proportions in South Phoenix, Arizona, is a problem requiring investigation. It undoubtedly has implications in the unemployment problem of the area. The possible impact of rules or restrictions on child welfare payments where an able-bodied male in the family exists might help account for the difference. The existence of better employment opportunities for males elsewhere may help account for the difference. Better opportunities for females in the given district of South Phoenix may help account for the difference. In any case, the investigation of the reasons for the discrepancy between the male-female percentages of the population of these ethnic groups is required. The cross-classification technique brought to light new information as well as suggesting problems for investigation and possibly pointing out directions to be taken in investigation.

In exhibit 8-4, a list of selected attractions to tourists in Georgia and in national park areas is presented, and cross-classified by the percent of annual attendance during the four seasons. This cross-classification enables the seasonal pattern of attendance at these attractions to be compared. It is noted that at "All National Parks" and "All National Recreation Areas", the percentages of attendance in winter are low, doubling in the spring, increasing in the summer, and then decreasing in the fall. The summer attendance is more marked in the national parks than in other national recreation areas. Examining other attractions reveals somewhat similar patterns. The Smoky Mountains, for example, go from the smallest attendance in winter due to the closing of parts of the Smoky Mountains Park to a considerable increase in the spring, exceedingly heavy attendance in the summer, and somewhat of a decline in the fall. This pattern is followed in most of the attractions listed. However, when the Everglades are examined, it is apparent that the heaviest attendance is in the winter, followed closely by spring. The lightest attendance is in the fall, and there is a somewhat light attendance in the summer. Such a difference is undoubtedly due to the fact that Florida is a winter vacation land. The pattern at Cumberland Island, which was the subject of the investigation in which this analysis occurred, follows the general national pattern, although not as markedly, going from 12 percent in the winter, doubling in the spring, practically doubling again in the summer, and dropping off in the fall.

EXHIBIT 8-4
Seasonal Variation in Attendance at Selected Attractions in Georgia and National Parks Service Areas

	Percent of Annual Total			
	Winter	Spring	Summer	Fall
Cape Hatteras	6.9	19.4	53.8	19.9
Everglades	33.2	31.2	21.6	14.0
Shenandoah	6.5	14.9	46.8	31.8
Smoky Mountains	2.7	14.0	61.3	22.0
All National Parks	6.2	13.3	60.8	19.7
All National Recreation Areas	10.7	21.2	47.6	20.5
Fort Frederica	15.4	26.6	42.0	15.9
Fort Pulaski	13.8	24.8	39.7	21.7
Jekyll Island	14.1	26.2	36.1	23.6
Cumberland Island	12.0	24.0	45.0	19.0

Source: William B. Keeling, "Cumberland Island as a National Seashore," *Georgia Business,* April, 1968, Vol. 27, No. 10, p. 11 (Bureau of Business and Economic Research, Graduate School of Business Administration, The University of Georgia, Athens, Georgia), original data derived from statistics of the National Park Service and reports from individual attractions; Cumberland Island estimate by Bureau of Business and Economic Research.

CHI-SQUARE TESTS

As explained in previous paragaphs, the essential nature of the chi-square test is to compare an observed statistical distribution with a theoretical statistical distribution, the theoretical distribution having been arrived at on the basis of some rational grounds. It is, thus, a test of the significance of a difference between two sets of observations, that is, two distributions. The actual hypothesis that may be involved in a chi-square test may be a hypothesis concerning the homogeneity of two distributions or the independence of two distributions, or indeed, simply the significance of the difference between an observed and a theoretical distribution. The test itself is identical regardless of the hypothesis which it attempts to test. Sometimes the chi-square test is used in place of correlation analysis, and indeed, it is often called a kind of correlation analysis. The reason for this can be seen in the test involved in exhibits 8-6 and 8-7, which will be discussed in later paragraphs.

The formula for the chi-square test is as follows:

$$\chi^2 = \Sigma \left[\frac{(f - f')^2}{f'} \right]$$

where: f = observed frequencies of each class
f' = theoretical frequencies of each class

It is apparent upon examining this formula that the difference between the observed and theoretical frequencies for each class is taken and squared. Each squared difference is then divided by the theoretical frequency of each class. The resulting values are added, and therefore, it becomes apparent that chi-square is an *additive* value. The larger the number of classes, the larger the value of chi-square becomes. Therefore, in the test of significance, allowance must be given for the number of classes involved in the test. This is done in the table of theoretical chi-square values which is used in determining the significance of the difference between the observed and theoretical distributions.

Exhibit 8-5 shows one way of deriving a theoretical distribution from observed data. The data for the observations were taken from exhibit 8-2 which presented the characteristics of the population fourteen years and over in South Phoenix, Arizona. The middle column of exhibit 8-5, "Proportions of Totals," was computed by dividing each of the totals for the ethnic groups by the grand total consecutively. These calculations follow:

$$6,000 \div 24,200 = 0.247934$$
$$9,300 \div 24,200 = 0.384298$$
$$8,900 \div 24,200 = 0.367768$$

EXHIBIT 8-5
Derivation of Theoretical Distribution for Chi-square Test

	Observed			Proportions of Totals	Theoretical		
	Male	Female	Total		Male	Female	Totals
"Anglo"	2,900	3,100	6,000	.247934	2,776.9	3,223.1	6,000
Mexican-American	4,300	5,000	9,300	.384298	4,304.1	4,995.9	9,300
Non-white	4,000	4,900	8,900	.367768	4,119.0	4,781.0	8,900
	11,200	13,000	24,200	1.000000	11,200.0	13,000.0	24,200

The hypothesis of the chi-square test for the problem presented in exhibit 8-5 provides the basis for the derivation of the theoretical distribution. The hypothesis to be tested is that the male-female distribution is independent of the ethnic distribution. That is, the ethnic groups are, in effect, not different from each other in respect to male and female proportions. In testing this hypothesis, then, the proportions of totals already computed should give the proportions of the total of male and of the total of female that should be distributed to each of the ethnic groups. If upon completing the chi-square test, it is found that the proportions of the totals are different from the proportions of the ethnic groups as between male and female, then the male-female distribution differs as among "Anglo," Mexican-American, and Nonwhite ethnic groups. Such a finding would give a basis for further investigation.

To continue the actual derivation of the theoretical distribution, the proportions of totals for each of the ethnic groups is multiplied by the total of the male, the total of the female, and the results listed as theoretical values under male-female. The following computations were accomplished:

Male	Female

Male	Female
.247934 × 11,200 = 2,776.9	.247934 × 13,000 = 3,223.1
.384298 × 11,200 = 4,304.1	.384298 × 13,000 = 4,995.9
.367768 × 11,200 = 4,119.0	.367768 × 13,000 = 4,781.0

Examination of exhibit 8-5 shows the insertion of the preceding computed values. The totals of the theoretical values, male-female, for each ethnic group are given at the right in the exhibit. It should be noted that all totals of theoretical columns equal all totals of observed columns. The equality of totals is a requirement in chi-square testing.

So far in the analysis, the theoretical values have been derived from observed values, the theoretical values being based on the hypothesis which had been posed for testing. Next, the actual testing of the hypothesis employing the chi-square test is to be accomplished. The difference in each equivalent cell for observed and theoretical values must be taken, the differences squared, then divided by the theoretical cell value, and the resulting values added for all cells. In exhibit 8-5, there are six cells, three for male and three for female. Thus, there are six sets of computations to be added in the final calculation of the chi-square value. The actual calculations appear as follows:

$$\chi^2 = \Sigma \left[\frac{(f - f')^2}{f'} \right]$$

$$\chi^2 = \frac{(2,900 - 2,776.9)^2}{2,776.9} + \frac{(4,300 - 4,304.1)^2}{4,304.1} + \frac{(4,000 - 4,119.0)^2}{4,119.0}$$

$$+ \frac{(3,100 - 3,223.1)^2}{3,223.1} + \frac{(5,000 - 4,995.9)^2}{4,995.9} + \frac{(4,900 - 4,781.0)^2}{4,781.0} .$$

$$= \frac{15,153.61}{2,776.9} + \frac{16.81}{4,304.1} + \frac{14,161.00}{4,119.0} + \frac{15,153.61}{3,223.1}$$

$$+ \frac{16.81}{4,995.9} + \frac{14,161.00}{4,781.0}$$

$$= 5.457 + .004 + 3.438 + 4.702 + .003 + 2.962$$

$$= 16.566$$

Since chi-square is additive in nature, the greater the number of cells in the problem, the larger will be the value of chi-square. Therefore, the computed value of chi-square must be interpreted in terms of the theoretical chi-square distribution, the values of which are included in Appendix C, "Values of the Chi-square Distribution." The number of cell values or number of classes, where class intervals are involved, provide the *degrees of freedom*. The degrees of freedom are simply the number of cells or the number of classes less the number of constraints that have been placed on the data in deriving the theoretical distribution. In exhibit 8-5, there were six cells. However, there were column totals and row totals. If the column totals and row totals are to remain intact, as they must, then the analyst is "free" to change only two of the values in the cells. All of the others would be given in order for the totals to remain intact.

A rule for matrices, that is, columns and rows, is given as follows: The number of rows less one, multiplied by the number of columns less one, will give the number of degrees of freedom remaining. This may be stated in formula as follows: $(r - 1)(c - 1)$. In exhibit 8-5, this means $(3 - 1)(2 - 1) = 2$. The degrees of freedom remaining for the problem in exhibit 8-5 are, therefore, two. This number of degrees of freedom must be used in ascertaining the value of chi-square from the theoretical distribution in Appendix C for the given level of significance that is desired. Referring to this table for a 99 percent probability of accuracy, the theoretical value of chi-square is 9.210; for a 95 percent level of accuracy, the theoretical chi-square value is 5.991. The usual way of writing these theoretical values is as follows: $x^2_{.99} = 9.210$ and $x^2_{.95} = 5.991$. The 99 percent and the 95 percent probability levels are the most commonly used.

When the computed chi-square value from the problem is less than the theoretical chi-square value at the selected level of significance from the appendix table, the original hypothesis is accepted. When the computed chi-square value exceeds the chi-square value at the chosen level of significance from the theoretical chi-square distribution, the original hypothesis is rejected. In the case of the problem of exhibit 8-5, the computed chi-square value of 16.566 exceeds the chi-square value both at the 99 percent probability level and at the 95 percent probability level. Therefore, the original hypothesis must be rejected. It will be remembered that this hypothesis was that the male-female distribution was independent of the ethnic groups. Rejection of the hypothesis means that the male-female population is *not* independent of the ethnic groups; in other words, the male-female distribution is affected differently by different ethnic groups. The analyst, having discovered definitively this fact, may turn back to his original data to examine the reasons for the rejection of this hypothesis. Examining the original observations as they appear in exhibit 8-5 or in 8-2 does not reveal the differences in male-female proportions for the three ethnic groups nearly as well as exhibit 8-3 in which they had been converted to percentages. An examination of exhibit 8-3 reveals that the "Anglo" group is very close to a 50-50 male-female distribution: in other words, close to the national distribution; whereas, the Mexican-American and the Nonwhite groups are very close to each other in their distributions, but the spread between female and male is considerably wider than it is for the "Anglo" group. Thus, the preponderance of females in South Phoenix, Arizona, exists almost exclusively in the Mexican-American and Nonwhite groups, not in the "Anglo" group. This fact now may bear investigation by the analyst.

Another example of chi-square testing is given in exhibit 8-6. The situation that had occurred in a firm was that the 185 secretaries had conducted a self-study program for the purposes of studying their own attitudes, habits, work performances, and other aspects of job performance with a view toward improvement, both in their work and in their relations with superiors and other members of the firm. It was felt by the secretaries that, if the ratings they gave themselves were substantiated by equivalent ratings given them by their supervisors, this fact would lend credence to their study. On the other hand, if their self-study ratings were unreal and did not conform to the ratings assigned to them by their supervisors, then the study, indeed, would be of little value. Therefore, it was decided that not only would the secretaries rate themselves by giving themselves grades, but their supervisors, separately, would rate the secretaries, and these results would be recorded and then tested. Chi-square analysis was to be used as the basis for making the tests.

EXHIBIT 8-6
Secretarial Ratings by Secretaries and by Supervisors

X Grades	f Observed Frequencies (Assigned by Secretaries Themselves)	f' Theoretical Frequencies (Assigned by Supervisors of Secretaries)
A	27	25
B	40	35
C	68	75
D	32	35
E	12	10
F	6	5
	185	185

Source: Secretarial Self-Study, Marietta Corp., June, 1977.

In this situation, it is apparent that the ratings of the secretaries by the supervisors were to be accepted as a set of theoretical frequencies, this theoretical distribution being arrived at on rational grounds. The self-study ratings of the secretaries were to constitute the observed distribution that was to be tested against the theoretical. Thus, unlike the problem presented in exhibit 8-5, there were no computations involved in the derivation of the theoretical distribution. The theoretical distribution was given; it consisted of the frequencies assigned by the supervisors of the secretaries.

Exhibit 8-6 lists the ratings by both secretaries and supervisors. Exhibit 8-7 shows the calculation of the value of chi-square. The entire calculation of the chi-square value is shown in exhibit 8-7, and the result is chi-square = 2.384. This value is considerably below the chi-square value of the chi-square distribution at the 99 percent probability level for five degrees of freedom, which is 15.086. Since the chi-square value at the 0.95 probability level for five degrees of freedom is 11.070, the hypothesis must be accepted at either significance level. The hypothesis of homogeneity, that is, that the two distributions are identical, must be accepted. Having determined this result, the secretaries may proceed with their self-study with assurance that their own self-ratings have been substantiated by separately recorded ratings of the secretaries by their supervisors. Thus, the validity of the self-study has been improved.

EXHIBIT 8-7
Calculation of Value of Chi-square

X	f	f'	$(f - f')$	$(f - f')^2$	$\dfrac{(f - f')^2}{f'}$
A	27	25	+2	4	.160
B	40	35	+5	25	.714
C	68	75	−7	49	.653
D	32	35	−3	9	.257
E	12	10	+2	4	.400
F	6	5	+1	1	.200
	185	185			2.384

$$\chi^2 = 2.384$$
$$\text{d.f.} = 6 - 1 = 5$$
$$\chi^2_{.99} \text{ at 5 d.f.} = 15.086$$
$$\chi^2_{.95} \text{ at 5 d.f.} = 11.070$$

In the problem of exhibits 8-6 and 8-7, the degrees of freedom were given as $6 - 1 = 5$. There were six classes of information, and therefore, six original degrees of freedom to begin with. However, one degree of freedom was lost in the equality of the observed and theoretical distributions. Since the observed and theoretical frequencies must always be equal, there will always be at least one degree of freedom lost. This problem required no other computations in deriving the theoretical frequencies, and therefore, no more degrees of freedom were deducted.

There are certain requirements for chi-square analysis to be effective that should be listed. These are as follows:

1. Original observations must be used, not percentages or relative values.
2. There should be five or more observations in each cell or class. Generally, this statement is made of the theoretical frequencies, rather than the observed frequencies.
3. The degrees of freedom are computed from cells or classes, not from the total observations n.
4. The totals of the observed and theoretical distributions must be equal, and n should exceed fifty.

The preceding rules are not always absolute. For example, sometimes fewer than five observations are accepted when there are a large number of degrees of freedom. On the other hand, when there are only a few degrees of freedom, such as, one or two, very often analysts will require ten or more observations in each cell or class. The fact is, the listed requirements should be adhered to if at all possible. It should also be pointed out that the foregoing discussion is not completely comprehensive or exhaustive; there are other formulas and techniques for handling chi-square tests. When the number of degrees of freedom exceed thirty, the formula given is not used. However, for the student who seeks further information, the references given at the end of this chapter will give detailed and complete coverage of the chi-square distribution and chi-square testing.

STATISTICAL DISTRIBUTIONS

A statistical distribution is an organization of data for the purpose of statistical analysis. The two chief classifications of statistical distributions are the *array* and the *frequency distribution*. Statistical distributions may be contrasted to mathematical distributions, sometimes called *theoretical* distributions. Mathematical distributions are ideal distributions of mathematical variables, for example the binomial distribution, the Poisson distribution, the chi-square distribution, and so on. Statistical distributions, however, as has been explained, are simply arrangements of data for analysis.

THE ARRAY

Exhibit 8-8 presents an alphabetical listing of the names of employees in a machine shop with their ages listed. The exhibit also shows those same ages placed in an array. An array, as is apparent, is a numerical listing in order. It may be from smallest to largest or from largest to smallest. Every individual value is listed, regardless of how many times it occurs. The array lends itself to statistical analysis, for the middle value will be the *median*, the most frequently occurring value will be the *mode*, and the sum of the values divided by the number of values will yield the *arithmetic mean*. It is the simplest form of statistical distribution and one of the most effective.

EXHIBIT 8-8
Ages of Employees in a Machine Shop

Alphabetical Order of Name		Numerical Array
Name	Age	Age
Allen	60	22
Burton	43	25
Carson	25	30
Dupree	48	37
George	40	40
Martin	43	43
Peters	22	43
Roberts	30	48
Smith	37	50
Waters	53	53
Yalt	50	60

Source: Personnel Department, Marietta Corp., August, 1977.

THE FREQUENCY DISTRIBUTION

Exhibit 8-9 presents a frequency distribution of manufacturing employees classified by the wage rate. This exhibit actually shows more than one kind of distribution. At the left, the wage rates show the groupings into which the variable, "Wage Rate," has been divided. The column "Employees" lists the frequencies of occurrence of each classification of wage rate. The total number of employees given is 2,410. Those two columns normally constitute a frequency distribution. In exhibit 8-9, however, a percentage distribution is also shown. Such a distribution might accompany the frequency distribution itself or might be shown as a separate percentage frequency distribution. The percents of the total have been computed by dividing each group of employees by the total of the employees, yielding the percents.

EXHIBIT 8-9
Manufacturing Employees of Marietta Corporation
Classified by Wage Rate

Wage Rate	Employees	Percent of Total	Cumulations Downward (Less Than)	Cumulations Upward (More Than)
$1.50 to $1.74	122	5.1	5.1	100.0
1.75 to 1.99	130	5.4	10.5	94.9
2.00 to 2.24	284	11.8	22.3	89.5
2.25 to 2.49	534	22.1	44.4	77.7
2.50 to 2.74	608	25.2	69.6	55.6
2.75 to 2.99	322	13.4	83.0	30.4
3.00 to 3.24	184	7.6	90.6	17.0
3.25 to 3.49	164	6.8	97.4	9.4
3.50 to 3.74	62	2.6	100.0	2.6
	2,410	100.0		

The last two columns in exhibit 8-9 show cumulations of percentages. The first of these columns is cumulated downward, and the second of the columns is cumulated upward. These percentage cumulations allow further analysis by observations. For example, referring to the downward cumulation of percentages, 69.6 percent of the workers earn less than $2.75 per hour; 90.6 percent of the employees earn less than $3.25 per hour. Referring to the upward cumulation, 94.9 percent of the employees earn $1.75 per hour and more. Only 9.4 percent of the employees earn $3.25 per hour and more. It is apparent that percentage cumulations enable observations to be made quickly that could not be made otherwise. Such cumulations, it is repeated, may accompany an original frequency distribution as is shown in exhibit 8-9, or they may be shown separately.

The frequency distribution also lends itself to statistical analysis since there are formulas permitting the calculation of all of the averages and the measures of dispersion from frequency distributions. However, the arithmetic mean and the standard deviation, the two most widely used measures of average and dispersion, require for best effectiveness that the classifications be equal in size, that is, the class intervals be equal as they are in exhibit 8-9. Further, the ends must be *closed*; this means that the ends may not be *open*, in other words, the bottom end showing "$3.50 and over," for example. Such open-end distributions preclude the computation of the arithmetic mean and the standard deviation since these two measures require determining the value of the midpoint of each of the classifications. The midpoint of an open-end class interval cannot be determined. The analyst interested in statistical analysis of his data, therefore, will attempt to have equal class intervals and closed ends in his frequency distribution. These characteristics are not always attainable, however, because some types of data are so scattered that the class intervals must be made unequal in order to have values in the intervals. For example, with income distributions, if income groupings were of equal-sized class intervals of, say, $1,000, there may be some class intervals with zero frequencies and other class intervals with very large frequencies. Such a distribution would be awkward to work with and would not likely yield the information desired. Therefore, analysts are sometimes faced with the necessity of constructing frequency distributions with unequal class intervals and sometimes with open ends because exact values cannot be determined for the final ends of the data.

Discrete Frequency Distributions

A discrete frequency distribution is one whose classifications do not consist of groups but consist of single individual values. Exhibit 8-10 shows a discrete frequency distribution in which the defects per lot are listed at

EXHIBIT 8-10
Occurrences of Defects in 100 Lots in Bar Process Shop

Defects Per Lot	Number of Times Defects Have Occurred	Relative Frequency
0	37	.25
1	52	.35
2	32	.21
3	16	.11
4	13	.08
	150	1.00

Source: Production Records, Bar Shop, Marietta Corp., August, 1977.

the left, and the frequencies consist of the number of times defects have occurred. The third column consisting of "Relative Frequency" does not always appear with a discrete frequency distribution. It is shown because it is often computed in problems involving defects in production or other types of production problems. When these relative frequencies, which are records of past results in the experience of the process undergoing investigation, are adopted as probabilities that are likely to occur in the future, then a *probability distribution* may be constructed. The probability distribution would consist of the column at the left, "Defects Per Lot," and a column "Probabilities of Occurrence," in which the identical values would be listed that are shown in the column for "Relative Frequency" in exhibit 8-10. This probability distribution may serve as the basis for establishing quality control procedures as well as the decision rules for workmen to follow in the quality control process.

SUMMARY

After information has been collected, it must be organized into classifications, either to make possible the preparing of tables or charts, or to prepare the data for analysis by statistical techniques.

Collected data are edited for the following: (1) omissions; (2) inconsistencies; (3) mistakes; (4) lack of uniformity; (5) illegibility.

Summary questionnaires may be constructed to be used in classifying the data from questionnaires. Often the summary questionnaire is a copy of the original questionnaire. The following procedures help maximize the usefulness of such a summary: (1) If possible, the summary should be on a copy of the original form. (2) The exact title of the project should be listed. (3) Basic facts about the collection method should be listed (techniques, number of cases, dates). (4) The numbers and percentages of each part of each question should be listed. (5) Beside the number of each question, the number of replies may be shown. (6) The number of replies for each part, or each question, must add up to the proper totals. (7) *Overflow* sheets may be used with the summary. (8) Citations to pages of the research report may be given. (9) Any adjustments of the copy must minimize any changes in questions on the questionnaire copy used.

A summary of the main reasons for using a summary questionnaire follows: (1) It presents a concise summary statement of the statistical findings. (2) It facilitates comparisons. (3) It assists in interpretations of findings. (4) It provides a brief statement of the purpose, methods, and dates of the survey. (5) Page citations may be given for ready reference.

The purpose of cross-classification is to present more information than can be found in a single classification. It contemplates combining two or more classifications, so that the cross-effects are shown in cells of a matrix. They may be converted to percentages to make comparisons easier.

A form of cross-classification may be used in chi-square tests. The chi-square test compares an observed statistical distribution with a theoretical statistical distribution, the theoretical distribution having been arrived at on some rational grounds. When the test is made, the following formula is used:

$$\chi^2 = \Sigma \left[\frac{(f - f')^2}{f'} \right]$$

The result is determined in the light of the probability of the difference occurring through sheer chance, read from a chi-square table. Either rejection or acceptance of the hypothesis may occur: the difference between the observed and theoretical distributions is zero.

Certain requirements exist for chi-square analysis: (1) Original observations must be used, not percentages or ratios. (2) There should be five or more observations in each cell. (3) The degrees of freedom are computed from the number of cells, not the number of observations. (4) The totals of the observed and theoretical frequencies must be equal, and n should exceed fifty.

There are two statistical distributions that constitute the chief classifications of data arranged for statistical analysis: (1) The array is a listing of observations by magnitude. (2) The frequency distribution is a quantitative distribution, in which frequencies are listed in groups of the variable.

The frequency distribution itself may be further classified into two kinds: (1) continuous frequency distributions; (2) discrete frequency distributions.

EXERCISES

1. What are the purposes of classifying data into logical arrangements?
2. List and describe in your own words the items to be covered in editing data.
3. Why are summary questionnaires useful in a questionnaire survey?
4. Certain procedures are desirable in maximizing the usefulness of summary questionnaires. What are these procedures?
5. Summarize in your own words the chief reasons for constructing and using a summary questionnaire or observationnaire.
6. Explain how cross-classification of data can reveal additional information.
7. Describe the essential nature of the chi-square test.
8. How are theoretical distributions derived for chi-square tests?
9. What is the hypothesis for chi-square tests?
10. What are the requirements for chi-square testing? Explain in your own words.
11. Of the total contacts by industrial salespersons, the ratio of successes to failures necessary to satisfy sales management requirements is 60:40. Records for the past year show firm sales of 1,080 and lost sales of 672. Using chi-square analysis, test to see if the requirement is being met.
12. For an assembly process to be kept *in control*, defects in diameter, length, hardness, and color must be in the ratios 10:8:4:2, respectively. One day's production yielded defects of 27, 18, 9, and 6, respectively, totaling 60. Is the process in control, tested by chi-square analysis?
13. Permanent residents of a town with a large transient population took a sampling of plans to build or purchase homes. Using chi-square analysis, test to see if such plans are independent of permanent-transient status.

	Plan to build or purchase	Do not plan to build or purchase
Permanent residents	280	460
Transients	100	360

14. A manufacturing company management suspects that a profit-sharing plan would meet with approval by older workers, but not by younger workers. A

sampling of attitudes yielded the following results. Test by chi-square whether management is right.

Age	For	Against
30 and under	11	10
31 to 40	22	18
41 to 50	30	15
Over 50	10	4
	73	47

✓ 15. A binomial distribution is fitted to a sample of defects; if it fits the observations, a decision rule employing the binomial function could be derived. Test for fit by chi-square. (Note: use $4 - 2 = 2$ degrees of freedom.)

Defects per batch	Observed number of batches	Binomial distribution of batches
0	3	5
1	9	10
2	16	10
3+	2	5
	30	30

16. How does a discrete frequency distribution differ from a continuous frequency distribution?
17. What is a probability distribution? How may it be derived?
18. Make a list of the first thirty New York Stock Exchange common stock closing prices given in the *Wall Street Journal*. Then, place the prices in an array.
19. Construct a frequency distribution of the stock prices listed in exercise 18, using the principles of correct frequency distribution construction.
20. Construct a percentage frequency distribution from the frequency distribution constructed in exercise 19. Then, make "less than" and "more than" cumulations.

SELECTED REFERENCES

Balsley, Howard L. *Basic Statistics for Business and Economics*. Columbus, Ohio: Grid, 1978.
Balsley, Howard L. *Quantitative Research Methods for Business and Economics*. New York: Random House, 1970.
Chou, Ya-Lun. *Statistical Analysis*. 2d ed. New York: Holt, Rinehart and Winston, 1975.

9

Statistical Inference in Business Research

Statistical inference may be defined as inferring the characteristics of a universe under investigation from the evidence of a sample representative of that universe. (The term *population* is often used instead of the term *universe*; they are synonymous in statistical inference.) By far, the most widely employed characteristic in statistical inference is the arithmetic mean. The median is occasionally inferred from the evidence of a sample, and sometimes, the standard deviation. A percentage in the universe is sometimes inferred from the evidence of a sample. In this chapter, inferences involving the arithmetic mean and percentages will be explored to the exclusion of other characteristics, these being the most important for research purposes.

Statistical inference also includes testing hypotheses, that is, testing the significance of a difference between two means either drawn from the same population, or universe, or drawn from two different universes to see if the universes are identical. Such a test of the significance of a difference may also be applied to two proportions as estimated from samples. It is apparent that there are really two areas of statistical inference that will receive attention: (1) statistical estimation, in which the mean or a proportion will be inferred to a universe from the evidence of a sample, and (2) tests of hypotheses involving tests of the significance of the difference between two means or two percentages, the results being inferred to universes from the evidence of samples.

Nearly all experimental studies involve statistical inference since an experiment is a closely controlled procedure involving usually a segment of a universe. Historical studies may or may not be statistical inference studies. *Searches for facts* may involve the entire universe of facts of a firm or may involve a sample of the universe of facts under consideration. In research, the use of statistical inference techniques is widespread and furnishes a powerful tool of analysis. It enables decisions to be made and

191

conclusions to be drawn from studies which could otherwise not be under-taken because of sheer size of a universe, because of prohibitive costs of studying a universe, because of destructive testing in quality control proce-dures thus precluding the studying of all items produced, and because of the length of time often involved in studying a universe.

The results of statistical inference studies are often held open to ques-tion, usually inadvisedly. A small segment of a universe under study as a sample enables the researcher to reduce the possibility of human error in making the study, and for this reason, the observations may be more accu-rate. The error involved in inferring the characteristics of a universe from the evidence of a sample is measurable when a random sample is taken; this measurement, called the *standard error*, is computed and the error of inference allowed for in the analysis. Thus, very often sampling studies give more reliable information than can be obtained from a census or uni-verse study.

The procedures in collecting samples will require investigation. Since the sample must be representative of the universe, procedures must be fol-lowed which will insure that the sample will, therefore, represent the uni-verse properly and will be of such size that such representativeness is assured. The current chapter will discuss the specific techniques of sta-tistical inference; the following chapter will explain the proper sampling procedures to follow in making an investigation by employing samples of universes.

AVERAGES AND DISPERSION

The arithmetic mean, it has been noted, is the most widely used char-acteristic inferred to a universe from the evidence of a sample. The second most widely used characteristic inferred to a universe from the evidence of a sample is a percentage. However, the computations for percentages hardly need review. The computations for the arithmetic mean and for the standard deviation, a measure of dispersion that accompanies the mean, do require review at this point, however. The arithmetic mean and the standard deviation will therefore be reviewed as computed both from an array and from a frequency distribution. It should be kept in mind that the arithmetic mean and the standard deviation as well as percentages are computed from formulas in the same way whether applied to sample data or to universe data. Thus, the formulas described in the following para-graphs are universal in application.

COMPUTATIONS FROM AN ARRAY

The following formulas are for the computation of both the arithmetic mean and the standard deviation, including explanations of each of the components of the formulas:

Arithmetic Mean for Array or Unorganized Data

$$\bar{X} = \frac{\Sigma X}{n}$$

where: $\overline{X}$ = arithmetic mean of a sample, sometimes used for mean of the universe; however, more properly, μ = mean of the universe

Σ = summation

X = the data

n = number of observations in the sample; N for universe

Standard Deviation for Array or Unorganized Data

$$s = \sqrt{\frac{\Sigma x^2}{n}}$$

where: s = standard deviation of a sample; σ for universe

Σ = summation

x = deviation of each observation from the mean $(X - \overline{X})$

n = number of observations in the sample; N for universe

In exhibit 9-1, the computations of the average and the standard deviation of an array are illustrated, employing the data from exhibit 8-8, which listed the ages of the universe of employees in a machine shop. First, the arithmetic mean is shown, being the sum of the values divided by the number of the values, yielding 41. The median is shown as well as the mode. The median is defined as the value of the middle item in an array, having as many items preceding it as following it. In exhibit 9-1, the median value is 43, but since the value occurs twice, there are not the same number of values preceding it as following it. Therefore, the notation is entered in the exhibit that the median is *indeterminate*. Although a median may be indeterminate, it is still useful, of course. The mode, defined as the value of the most frequently occurring item, becomes 43, since 43 occurs twice and is the only value that occurs more than once. The median and the mode are seldom, if ever, used in statistical inference and are shown here only for definitional purposes.

EXHIBIT 9-1
Averages and Dispersion of an Array

X (Age)	x $(X - \mu)$	x^2
22	-19	361
25	-16	256
30	-11	121
37	-4	16
40	-1	1
43	$+2$	4
43	$+2$	4
48	$+7$	49
50	$+9$	81
53	$+12$	144
60	$+19$	361
451		1,398

$$\mu = \frac{\Sigma X}{N} = \frac{451}{11} = 41$$

Md. = 43 (indeterminate)

Mo. = 43

$$\sigma = \sqrt{\frac{\Sigma x^2}{N}} = \sqrt{\frac{1,398}{11}} = \sqrt{127.09} = 11.3 \text{ rounded} = 11$$

The computation of the standard deviation is also illustrated in exhibit 9-1. The computations are straightforward, including the extraction of the square root. The result is rounded, giving the standard deviation as 11. The discussion of the normal curve that appears in the next section of this chapter will make the meaning of the standard deviation clearer. At this point, it can be mentioned that, since the standard deviation measures the dispersion of the data around the arithmetic mean, the smaller the value of the standard deviation relative to the size of the mean, the more valid the average becomes as a representative of the data. In this case, the standard deviation is approximately one-fourth the value of the mean. The analyst would conclude that the mean is a relatively valid representative of these data, the dispersion being as narrow as it is.

COMPUTATIONS FROM A FREQUENCY DISTRIBUTION

The following formulas are for computing the arithmetic mean and the standard deviation from frequency distributions, including explanations of each of the components of the formulas.

Arithmetic Mean for Frequency Distribution

$$\overline{X} = \frac{\Sigma (fm)}{n}$$

where: $\overline{X}$ = arithmetic mean of a sample; sometimes used for mean of the universe; however, more properly μ = mean of the universe

Σ = summation

f = frequencies

m = midpoints of the class intervals

n = number of observations in the sample; N for universe

Standard Deviation for Frequency Distribution

$$s = \sqrt{\frac{\Sigma f(m - \overline{X})^2}{n}}$$

where: s = standard deviation of a sample; σ for universe

Σ = summation

f = frequencies

m = midpoints of the class intervals

$\overline{X}$ = mean of the sample; μ = mean of universe

n = number of observations in the sample; N for universe

In exhibit 9-2, the computations of the arithmetic mean and the standard deviation for sample data in a frequency distribution are presented. The value of the arithmetic mean becomes 28.8 and of the standard deviation, 9.1. It is noted here that each of these values is rounded to one decimal place more than occurs in the raw data as represented by the X-variable, which is a fairly common practice. It does not often occur with ages, which are the subject of exhibit 9-1, but would probably be used with the data of average daily orders which are the subject of exhibit 9-2. The standard deviation, of course, would always be quoted to the same number of decimal places as the arithmetic mean which it accompanies. In exhibit 9-2, it is apparent that the standard deviation is approximately one-third the value of the mean, and again, the analyst would probably conclude that the arithmetic mean is a relatively valid representative of the data of the material in the exhibit. If the measure of dispersion approached the size of the average or if, indeed, the measure of dispersion exceeded the value of the average it accompanied, the value of the average as a representative of the data would be impaired. The dispersion in such a case would be so great that the data, scattered widely about the mean, would not be concentrated enough to allow a single value to represent such data.

EXHIBIT 9-2
Arithmetic Mean and Standard Deviation of a Frequency Distribution of Average Daily Orders of Salesmen in Southwestern District

	Arithmetic Mean			Standard Deviation		
X Average Daily Orders	f Number of Salesmen	m	(fm)	$m - \overline{X}$	$(m - \overline{X})^2$	$f(m - \overline{X})^2$
10 to 19	8	15	120	-13.8	190.44	1,523.52
20 to 29	22	25	550	- 3.8	14.44	317.68
30 to 39	13	35	455	+ 6.2	38.44	499.72
40 to 49	7	45	315	+16.2	262.44	1,837.08
	50		1,440			4,178.00

$$\overline{X} = \frac{\Sigma (fm)}{n} = \frac{1,440}{50} = 28.8$$

$$s = \sqrt{\frac{\Sigma f(m - \overline{X})^2}{n}} = \sqrt{\frac{4,178}{50}} = \sqrt{83.56} = 9.14 \text{ rounded } = 9.1$$

STATISTICAL INFERENCE

Inferring the characteristics of a universe from the evidence of a sample requires some kind of estimate of the accuracy of the inference. This estimate of accuracy is called in statistical terms *reliability*. Reliability is meas ured in terms of probability. For example, the analyst would construct a 95 percent confidence interval around the universe mean as estimated from evidence yielded by the sample; 95 samples out of 100 taken from that universe would yield means falling within that interval. Therefore, he may take a step further and state that there is a 95 percent probability that the true mean of the universe falls within the limits prescribed.

In the discussion of chi-square tests in the preceding chapter, probabilities were employed in determining the significance of the difference between an observed distribution and a theoretical distribution. The confidence levels of 95 percent and 99 percent were used. These confidence levels were probabilities; and they were measures of reliability.

PROBABILITY AND THE NORMAL CURVE

The probabilities employed in statistical inference which thus furnish measures of reliability are derived from the *normal curve*. The normal curve is a representation of the *normal distribution*, a mathematical distribution describing the chance occurrence of a large number of the characteristics of man and of his environment. Chance occurrences of most characteristics in nature, therefore, are described by the normal curve. If a large number of samples should be selected at random from a universe, the occurrence of their means would be a matter of chance, and therefore, a distribution of the means of such a large number of random samples should be described by a normal curve. This normal curve, then, would give the basis for the probabilities used in reliability measures. The probabilities themselves are computed by separating the areas under the normal curve into regions, and these areas furnish the degrees of probability.

The normal curve has certain well-defined characteristics:

EXHIBIT 9-3
The Normal Curve

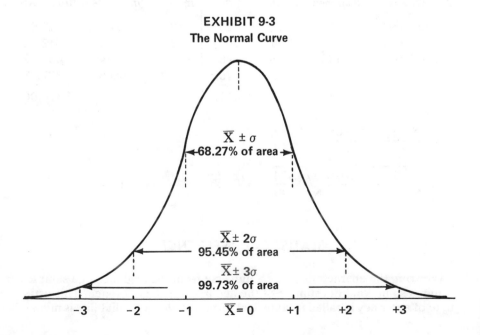

1. It is perfectly *symmetrical*, meaning the two sides would be congruent if folded over.
2. It is bell-shaped with a point of inflection on either side marking the point of the mean plus and minus one standard deviation.
3. The base is *asymptotic*, meaning that the base of the figure never touches the base line on out to infinity.
4. All averages are equal, mean, median, and mode.
5. The standard deviation bears a specific relationship to the normal curve.

Inspection of exhibit 9-3 reveals that where the mean is equal to zero and the standard deviation is equal to 1, the mean plus and minus one standard deviation includes 68.27 percent of the area subtended under the curve; the mean plus and minus two standard deviations includes 95.45 percent of the area subtended under the curve; and the mean plus and minus three standard deviations includes 99.73 percent of the area subtended under the curve.

The statistician, however, does not use probabilities, such as, 99.73 percent or 95.45 percent. He uses instead probabilities such as 99.9 percent or 99 percent. The fact is, the most common probabilities used, with their equivalent standard deviations computed from the normal curve, are as follows:

$$95\% = 1.96\,\sigma$$
$$99\% = 2.576\,\sigma$$

The probabilities are usually called confidence levels; for example, the 95 percent and the 99 percent confidence levels are referred to. The converse of the 95 percent confidence interval is the 5 percent critical probability, sometimes called the .05 level of significance; the converse of the 99 percent confidence level is the 1 percent critical probability, sometimes called the .01 level of significance. These two probabilities, then, are the most commonly used whether in the form of confidence levels, critical probabilities, or levels of significance for statistical estimation and for tests of hypotheses. Each of these latter two uses will receive detailed attention in ensuing paragraphs.

A "Table of Areas of the Normal Curve" is included in Appendix A of this book. This table shows the area subtended under the curve at successive distances in one-hundredths removed from an arithmetic mean of zero. The areas are 50 percent areas, that is, they are the areas on only one side of the mean instead of on both sides, because both sides are identical. Thus, to get a total area subtended under both sides of a mean, the area value from the table would need to be doubled. The table may be examined to check on the two most common confidence levels: 95 percent and 99 percent. Referring to the column in the table, x/σ, for 1.96, it is found that the area value given is .47500. This area value doubled yields .95 or in percentages 95 percent. Consider the other confidence level: 99 percent. This value .99 divided by 2 yields .495. This value looked up in the table cannot be located exactly. There is one value .49506 and another value .49492. The value of the area in standard deviations is interpolated between the two x/σ values and becomes 2.576. (This value was not actually interpolated; it was computed from the formula for the normal curve. Direct interpolations within values in the "Table of Areas of the Normal Curve" will be inaccurate because of the changing slope of the curve itself.)

It should become apparent that any given statistical distribution whose values are normally distributed could yield probabilities computed in areas under the normal curve. Its mean could be computed; its standard deviation could be computed; the value of x, which is $(X - \overline{X})$, could be computed. Thus, for any given x, that is, deviation from the mean, the area under the normal curve could be computed, and this would become a probability. Consider the following example:

A production run of bronze pump castings, the weights of which are normally distributed since weight variations are due to chance, has an average weight of 24 pounds per casting with a standard deviation of 6 pounds. What proportion of the castings will weigh more than 33 pounds?

$$\overline{X} = 24$$
$$\sigma = 6$$
$$X = 33$$
$$x = X - \overline{X} = 33 - 24 = 9$$
$$\frac{x}{\sigma} = \frac{9}{6} = 1.5$$

Since 1.5 standard deviations equals .43319 from the "Table of Areas of the Normal Curve," it is apparent that 43.319 percent of the castings weigh between 24 pounds, the mean, and 33 pounds, the *cut-off* value. However, the question asked was, "the proportion of castings that would weigh *more than* 33 pounds." Since there is 50 percent of the area under the normal curve above the mean, the 43.319 percent must be deducted from 50 percent. The result is 6.681 percent of the castings will weigh more than 33 pounds.

THE SAMPLING DISTRIBUTION

In the foregoing illustration, probabilities were computed from areas under the normal curve based on the assumption that the data concerned were normally distributed and, therefore, described by a normal curve. Probabilities may likewise be computed from areas under the normal curve for inferences to a universe from the evidence of a sample. In this case, the distribution through which the inference is made is called the *sampling distribution*. The sampling distribution is a distribution of the characteristic under study—for example, the arithmetic mean—that could be constructed from a large number of samples taken from the universe. If a large number of samples were taken from a universe and an arithmetic mean computed from each one, then a separate statistical distribution could be made up of the arithmetic means computed from the samples. This distribution of means, called a *sampling distribution of means*, would be normally distributed and, therefore, described by the normal curve. It would be normal because the occurrence of the differences among the means would be a matter of chance, providing that the samples had been selected by some random procedure. Assuming, then, the random selection of the items to go into each sample and, therefore, the chance occurrence of the differences among the means, the sampling distribution of the means would be normally distributed because the normal curve describes the sheer occurrence of chance values. Since the sampling distribution of means is described by the normal curve, the areas under the normal curve serve for the computation of the probabilities in inferring the characteristics of the universe from the evidence of the sample. (Where *small* samples are taken ($n < 30$) the sampling distribution becomes more *platykurtic*, i.e., flat-topped, the smaller the sample size becomes below 30. In such cases, the sampling distribution is not normal, but is described by Student's *t*-distribution. See following pages for a discussion of the effect of small sample size on statistical inference.)

The probabilities computed from the areas under the normal curve are in terms of standard deviations, of course. The standard deviation of the sampling distribution must therefore be computed. The analyst, however, normally has but one sample; he does not have a large number of samples and, therefore, does not possess a sampling distribution. Consequently, he could not compute the standard deviation of the sampling distribution directly. He may compute it, however, from a formula derived mathematically from the formula for the standard deviation of a sampling distribution. The standard deviation of a sampling distribution of the mean is called the *standard error of the mean*.

THE STANDARD ERROR OF THE MEAN

The formula for the standard error of the mean is given as follows. (The true formula for the standard error is $\sigma_{\overline{X}} = \sigma/\sqrt{n}$; however, in practice the sample estimate (s) of the universe standard deviation (σ) is adopted by point estimation, and the formula becomes: $\sigma_{\overline{X}} = s/\sqrt{n}$.)

$$\sigma_{\overline{X}} = \frac{s}{\sqrt{n}}$$

where: $\sigma_{\overline{X}}$ = standard error of the mean
     s = sample estimate of the standard deviation of the universe;
     σ = standard deviation of the universe
     n = size of the sample; N = size of the universe

Since the standard error of the mean is a standard deviation, it is used to compute the areas under the normal curve which then are used as probabilities in making inferences concerning means. For example, if it is desired to estimate the arithmetic mean of a universe from the evidence of a sample, the mean of the sample is computed, the standard deviation of the sample is computed, then the standard error of the sample is computed. Since one standard deviation above and below a mean includes 68.27 percent of the cases in a distribution when the distribution is described by a normal curve, the mean plus and minus one standard deviation of its own sample would include 68.27 percent of the cases in the sample itself providing that the sample represented a normal distribution. However, the sample mean adopted as the mean of the universe plus and minus one standard error would include 68.27 percent of the sampling distribution of means. This statement would enable the analyst to assert that in 68.27 percent of samples taken from that universe, means would occur that fell between the limits of the sample mean plus and minus the standard error of the mean. The sample mean plus and minus two standard errors would yield a *confidence interval* of 95.45 percent. The sample mean plus and minus three standard errors would yield a confidence interval of 99.73 percent. However, it will be remembered that the analyst usually uses the 95 percent confidence interval or the 99 percent confidence interval. Therefore, if the standard error of the mean were multiplied by 1.96, and the resulting value added to and deducted from the arithmetic mean of the sample, the resulting confidence interval would be an interval within which it would be expected that 95 sample means out of 100 samples taken from the universe would fall. The analyst might extend his statement then, and say: The probability that the true mean of the universe falls between these two limits is 95 percent. Illustrations of this procedure will be given in the following paragraphs.

INFERENCES FOR MEANS

It is apparent that a sampling distribution of sample means being normally distributed permits the use of the areas under the normal curve for computing probabilities of inferences to the universe from the evidence of the sample. The value of the mean in the universe may thus be estimated from the mean of the sample to a given level of probability; this procedure is called *statistical estimation*. The probabilities may also be used to test the significance of the difference between two means: First, the difference between a mean as computed from a sample and thus representing a universe may be compared to a hypothetical mean or a control mean as established in a quality-control procedure, for example, where product produced must meet certain average standards. Second, two means representing two universes or sometimes two parts of the same universe may be compared to determine the significance of their difference. For example, in the case of a desire to compare two products, the mean of a sample of each product would be computed, and then the significance of the difference between the two means tested. These two types of procedures are given the name *test of hypotheses*.

STATISTICAL ESTIMATION INVOLVING THE MEAN

In exhibit 9-2, an illustration of the computation of the arithmetic mean and the standard deviation of a frequency distribution was presented, the data consisting of the daily orders of fifty salespersons in the southwestern district of a company. This problem could be construed as an inference problem, assuming that the company had salespersons in a number of districts other than the southwestern district, perhaps six or seven districts in all. The southwestern district data of average daily orders of salespersons would be considered a sample, and if the daily orders of the salespersons in the southwestern district were to be considered representative of the daily orders of all salespersons in all districts, then this sample could serve to give the average daily orders for the entire company for all of its districts. The value of the mean computed in exhibit 9-2 was 28.8 average daily orders, and a standard deviation of 9.1 daily orders was computed. The following computations show the procedure to be followed in making the inference in terms of a confidence interval constructed in the universe from the evidence of the sample collected.

$$\overline{X} = 28.8$$
$$s = 9.14 \text{ rounded} = 9.1$$
$$n = 50$$
$$\sigma_{\overline{X}} = \frac{s}{\sqrt{n}} = \frac{9.14}{\sqrt{50}} = \frac{9.14}{7.071} = 1.2926 \text{ rounded} = 1.29$$

99% confidence level $= 2.576\sigma$

$$2.576 \times 1.2926 = 3.3297376 \text{ rounded} = 3.33$$
$$\overline{X} \pm z\ \sigma_{\overline{X}} = 28.8 \pm 3.33 = 25.47 \text{ and } 32.13 \text{ rounded}$$
$$= 25.5 \text{ and } 32.1$$

From the information provided in exhibit 9-2, the arithmetic mean, the standard deviation, and the size of the sample were obtained. These were used in computing the standard error of the mean. A 99 percent confidence level was adopted because the analyst felt he wanted that degree of assurance of accuracy or reliability in his results. That level of confidence, of course, yields in standard deviations 2.576, designated z. The confidence level in standard deviations was multiplied by the unrounded standard error value, and the result was added to and deducted from the mean of the sample. The resulting confidence interval, 25.5 and 32.1, is an interval within which the means of 99 samples out of 100 would be expected to fall. In other words, only one sample mean out of 100 taken from this universe would have a value falling outside that interval. Another way of stating this result would be that while the best estimate of the mean of the universe as a single value would be 28.8, the analyst is 99 percent confident that the true mean of the universe does lie between 25.5 and 32.1 average daily orders for the entire company.

Small Sample Size

A small sample is defined as one containing fewer than thirty observations ($n < 30$). While the normal curve describes the chance errors among means of a large number of samples taken from a universe when each sample size is greater than thirty, it was found by W. S. Gossett, a British scholar, that as the sample size for each sample declined below thirty observations, the sampling distribution became more and more *platykurtic*, that is, flatter and flatter as the size of the sample decreased. This phenomenon resulted in a larger and larger standard deviation of the sampling distribution—standard error—as the individual sample size decreased. The distribution of the areas under the small sample curve for each separate sample size is contained in Appendix B, "Table of Student's *t*-Distribution." The name of the distribution, *Student's t-Distribution*, results from the fact that Mr. Gossett made his discovery while he was a graduate student, and his discovery was published in mathematical journals under the pseudonym *Student*.

It is apparent that with a larger and larger standard error occurring with smaller and smaller sized samples, the areas under the small sample curve must be determined in the light of the size of the particular sample. In the table in Appendix B, the left-hand column contains the degrees of freedom remaining after deducting one observation from the number of observations in the sample. One degree of freedom is lost since the total of the sample must be fixed for an inference to be made. Thus, one degree of freedom has been lost. Obviously, the gradations in hundredths of the deviations from the mean of zero that appear in the table of areas under the normal curve in Appendix A could not be presented because of the enormous size of the table that would be required. There would have to be a separate table for each size of sample for thirty observations and below down to one. Thus, only certain levels of significance or confidence levels or critical probabilities are used. These critical probabilities are listed at the top of the table in Appendix B and the headings are self-explanatory. The use of single-tailed tests and double-tailed tests appear in the discussion that follows concerning tests of hypotheses.

An example of the use of Student's *t*-Distribution for small samples would be worth studying. In exhibit 9-1, the computations of the averages and standard deviation of an array were presented. The data consisted of 11 observations of ages of employees in the machine shop of the Marietta Corporation. If it is assumed that the machine shop is representative in ages among the employees of all the maintenance department, which would normally include a pipe shop, electric shop, boiler shop, forge shop, and carpenter shop, the data in exhibit 9-1 may be considered a sample of a universe consisting of the ages of all employees of the maintenance department. The mean age found was 41 years with a standard deviation of 11.3 rounded to 11, and the number of observations was 11, also (which occurred by sheer coincidence). The computations required for making an inference to a 99 percent confidence interval in the universe follow:

$$\overline{X} = 41$$
$$s = 11.3 \text{ rounded} = 11$$
$$n = 11$$
$$\sigma_{\overline{X}} = \frac{s}{\sqrt{n}} = \frac{11.3}{\sqrt{11}} = \frac{11.3}{3.317} = 3.4067 \text{ rounded} = 3.41$$

99% confidence level for small samples: $n = 11$,
degrees of freedom $= 11 - 1 = 10$, thus, $3.169\,\sigma$
$3.169 \times 3.4067 = 10.7958323 \text{ rounded} = 10.80$

$$\overline{X} \pm z\,\sigma_{\overline{X}} = 41 \pm 10.8 = 30.2 \text{ and } 51.8; \text{ rounded} = 30 \text{ and } 52$$

Since there were 11 observations in the sample and one was deducted, the degrees of freedom remaining were 10. Looking up 10 degrees of freedom in the table in Appendix B at the 99 percent confidence level, which is the 1 percent critical probability, the resulting value of the standard deviation was 3.169, designated z. This value, multiplied by the value of the standard error unrounded, yielded a final rounded value of 10.8. The mean, plus and minus this value, yielded a confidence interval. The confidence interval rounded to even years was 30 years and 52 years. The result indicates that in 99 samples out of 100, average ages between 30 and 52 years would be found. In only one sample out of 100 taken would a mean be found that would fall outside those two limits. Thus, the analyst may proceed further and say: My best single estimate of the mean age in the entire maintenance department is 41 years; the probability is 99 percent, however, that the true mean does lie between 30 years and 52 years. It is apparent that this is a rather wide range within which to estimate the mean age. The larger the sample, the smaller the confidence interval would become.

TESTS OF HYPOTHESES FOR MEANS

The first of the tests of hypotheses for means—otherwise called a test of significance—is between a sample mean and a universe mean or hypothetical mean. The situation is often confronted in quality control for production where an average measurement such as a diameter, a length, or a hardness must be maintained. Samples of the production run are taken periodically, the average of each sample taken, and the significance of the difference between the sample average and the control or hypothetical average computed. If the sample average representing a given production run is significantly different from the control average that is required in the quality-control procedure, the production run would be rejected because the hypothesis that the difference between the sample mean and the hypothetical mean is zero would be rejected. If, on the other hand, the significance of the difference between the sample mean and the hypothetical mean were found to be zero, then the production run would be accepted as meeting specifications, and the hypothesis that the sample mean and the universe mean are identical or that the difference is equal to zero, would be accepted. The following formula is used for the test of significance:

$$T = \frac{\overline{X} - \mu}{\sigma_{\overline{X}}}$$

where: T = test of significance
$\overline{X}$ = mean of the sample
μ = mean of the universe or population (hypothetical mean)
$\sigma_{\overline{X}}$ = standard error of the mean

The following example will serve to illustrate the computations involved in the test of significance of the difference between the sample mean and the universe mean.

Assume that a question has arisen as to the ability of the tuner section of the assembly department of a television manufacturing concern to maintain the requirement of 65 completed tuners assembled per hour in order to maintain the production line. The following test is applied: for one 9-hour shift the tuners assembled per hour are counted, the average computed, and the standard deviation computed. The following computations result.

$$\mu = 65 \text{ per hour}$$
$$\overline{X} = 63 \text{ per hour}$$
$$s = 6 \text{ per hour}$$
$$n = 9 \text{ hours}$$

$$\sigma_{\overline{X}} = \frac{s}{\sqrt{n}} = \frac{6}{\sqrt{9}} = \frac{6}{3} = 2$$

$$T = \frac{\overline{X} - \mu}{\sigma_{\overline{X}}} = \frac{63 - 65}{2} = \frac{-2}{2} = -1$$

Hypothesis (H_0): the difference between the sample mean and the universe mean = zero

Confidence level: 95 percent for small sample size 9 yields 8 degrees of freedom; from Student's t-distribution in Appendix B = 2.306

T-value of absolute value of $1 < 2.306$; hypothesis is accepted; the difference between the means is zero

The preceding test yielded the result that the difference between the sample mean and the universe mean was indeed zero since the result of the T-test was less than the value of the confidence level in standard deviations. If the result of the T-test had been greater than the value of the 95 percent confidence level in standard deviations, the hypothesis would have been rejected. In the given instance, the conclusion is reached that the tuner section of the assembly department of the television manufacturer is indeed meeting the requirement of 65 completely assembled tuner units per hour.

The situation in which two sample means are computed and the significance of the difference between them tested arises often in product comparisons. For example, the burning length of two brands of cigarettes may be tested by computing the mean burning length of each of two samples of the two brands. The mileage of two different brands of gasoline may be tested by computing the average mileage yielded by two samples of the two brands. The following formula illustrates the procedure in testing the significance of the difference between two sample means:

$$T = \frac{\overline{X}_{s_1} - \overline{X}_{s_2}}{\sigma_D}$$

where: T = test of significance

$\overline{X}_{s_1}$ = mean of first sample

$\overline{X}_{s_2}$ = mean of second sample

$$\sigma_D = \sqrt{\sigma_{\overline{X}_1}^2 + \sigma_{\overline{X}_2}^2} \qquad \text{(this is the standard error of the difference)}$$

in which: $\sigma_{\overline{X}_1}$ = standard error of the first sample

$\sigma_{\overline{X}_2}$ = standard error of the second sample

Following is an example of the test of significance applied to the difference between two sample means.

Assume that a test of the mileage given by two brands of gasoline, brand A and brand B, is to be made. One gallon of each kind of gasoline is to be tested in each of 25 cars. Since there will be 25 cars in each sample, the total number of observations is 50. In determining the number of degrees of freedom for small samples when the standard error of the difference is to be computed, the two samples are added together and two degrees of freedom deducted. In this case, $50 - 2 = 48$. Therefore, the sample is large, and the "Table of Areas of the Normal Curve" applies rather than the "Table of Student's t-Distribution" for small samples.

Gasolines
1 Gallon in Each of 25 Cars in Each Sample

Brand A   Brand B

$$\overline{X}_{s_1} = 12.3 \qquad\qquad\qquad \overline{X}_{s_2} = 13.6$$

$$s_1 = 2.5 \qquad\qquad\qquad\qquad s_2 = 2.9$$

$$\sigma_{\overline{X}_1} = \frac{s_1}{\sqrt{n_1}} = \frac{2.5}{\sqrt{25}} = \frac{2.5}{5} = .5 \qquad \sigma_{\overline{X}_2} = \frac{s_2}{\sqrt{n_2}} = \frac{2.9}{\sqrt{25}} = \frac{2.9}{5} = .58$$

$$\sigma_D = \sqrt{.5^2 + .58^2} = \sqrt{.25 + .3364} = \sqrt{.5864} = .7657$$

$$T = \frac{\overline{X}_{s_1} - \overline{X}_{s_2}}{\sigma_D} = \frac{12.3 - 13.6}{.7657} = \frac{-1.3}{.7657} = -1.697 = -1.70$$

If the hypothesis that had been posed for the means of the two gasolines, brand A and brand B, had been that the difference between the means was zero, this hypothesis would be accepted at the 95 percent level or indeed, at the 99 percent level since the T-value computed, -1.70, was less than either 1.96 or 2.576. The negative sign to the -1.70, of course, means merely that the second mean was larger than the first and has no bearing on the significance test itself. If the result of the T-test had yielded a value greater than 1.96 or greater than 2.576, the hypothesis would have been rejected at those levels of significance.

It is possible that, in such a single-purpose test as this one, a given critical probability might not have been set up at the beginning, but it had been determined beforehand that the T-value would be interpreted in the light of the actual probability that the difference found between the means was due to sheer chance. Such a computation could be accomplished as follows: The T-value of 1.70 would be looked up in the "Table of Areas of the Normal Curve." The resulting area value is .45543. This value doubled yields .91086. The value .91086 deducted from unity yields .08914 which, multiplied by 100 to secure the percentage, results in an 8.914 percent probability that the difference occurred through sheer chance. Such a difference, 8.914 percent, occurring through sheer chance is fairly large; indeed, statisticians generally consider that if the probability that the difference between two means occurred through sheer chance is greater than 10 percent, there could hardly be any possibility that the difference would be significant—it would indeed be due to chance. Thus, with this large a probability that the difference is due to chance, the statistician would probably accept the difference as being due to chance and, therefore, it would be considered that there was no significant difference between the two means.

One-Tailed and Two-Tailed Significance Tests

The preceding examples dealt with what are called *two-tailed tests* of significance because they dealt with probabilities computed from areas under the normal curve on both sides of the mean. There are occasions, however, when the probability that is desired occurs on only one side of the mean and thus includes the area under the normal curve in only one *tail* of the normal curve. For example, a firm manufacturing motors in which plastic gears were used would require the plastic gears to be of a certain minimum hardness. If it manufactured its own gears, it would maintain the hardness of the plastic gears as it manufactured them within given limits, for gears of too low a hardness would wear out too quickly, and gears of too high a hardness would be too expensive to produce. A quality-control test designed for this production procedure would include a two-tailed test. However, suppose that the firm contracted out the manufacture of the plastic gears. It would no longer be interested in any excess of hardness in the gears; it would be interested only in the minimum hardness of the gears. Therefore, if the subcontractor furnishing the plastic gears went to excess expense producing gears harder than necessary, it would be no concern of theirs. The firm would be interested in a *one-tailed test* of the hardness of the plastic gears simply to insure that the gears met the minimum test for hardness; it would not care how excessive the hardness would be beyond the minimum requirement.

The difference between the two-tailed test and the one-tailed test may be explained somewhat as follows in terms of computing significance levels in standard deviations: For a two-tailed test at the .05 significance level, $1.00 - .05 = .95 \div 2 = .475$ in area yields 1.96 in standard deviations. However, for a one-tailed test at the .05 significance level, $.50 - .05 = .45$ yields 1.645 in standard deviations (approximately). The difference lies in deducting the critical probability or significance level from the total area under the normal curve for a two-tailed test and dividing the resulting area by two, and, in the case of a one-tailed test, deducting the critical probability or significance level directly from 50 percent representing one-half of the normal curve. It is apparent that the two-tailed test and the one-tailed test will yield different results in standard deviations for given significance levels. An example follows:

Assume that the manufacturer previously mentioned produces his own plastic gears requiring a hypothetical mean of 22 pounds per square inch hardness with a standard error of one pound per square inch hardness and has adopted a 5 percent critical probability (95 percent confidence level). With such specifications the region of acceptance of production is determined as $1.00 - .05 = .95 \div 2 = .475$ yields 1.96×1 standard error, then added to and deducted from the mean of 22 yields 20.04 and 23.96 pounds. This is the region of acceptance, and production of the plastic gears must be contained within this confidence interval.

Suppose, however, the firm subcontracts the manufacture of these plastic gears and requires the same specifications. In this case it is interested only in the minimum hardness required. A one-tailed test is now posed: $.50 - .05 = .45$ yields 1.645×1 standard error and deducted from the mean of 22 yields a minimum hardness requirement of 20.355 pounds. This becomes the minimum requirement for acceptance by the firm. It does not care how much harder the plastic gears are.

THE ANALYSIS OF VARIANCE

While the test of the significance of the difference between the sample mean and the hypothetical mean or between two sample means may be for the purpose of testing hypotheses concerning populations, the analysis of variance tests the significance of the differences among several means simultaneously. The T-test, as explained in the preceding section, will not apply where more than two means are involved in the analysis, except, of course, in the situation in which there may be several means, for example, four or five, and the differences between each two of the group are to be studied. In such a situation, the T-test is applicable. However, where the hypothesis posed concerns the significance of the difference among all of the means simultaneously, then only the analysis of variance can be applied to the problem.

An example of a situation in which the analysis of variance was required is as follows: In the city park districts of a large city in Texas, some evidence existed that the valuation assessments of real property surrounding neighborhood parks differed with the distance that the property was located from the park. The property was divided into so-called *rings* around a given park district. The first ring consisted of all of the houses adjacent to the park on all four sides. The next ring consisted of the houses on the next block surrounding the park. The third ring consisted of the houses located on the third block, and the fourth ring consisted of the houses located on the fourth block surrounding the park. The average valuation of each such ring was computed and the analysis of variance applied to testing the significance of the differences among the average valuations of the rings of property. In this particular case, there was found to be a significant difference among the rings, and the hypothesis that the park affected the valuation of property adjacent to it was borne out.

In situations in which the significance of the differences among several means is to be tested simultaneously, the variance among the means is analyzed. The total variation existing in all of the data may be broken into two parts: the variation among the means of the components and the variation within the data. The variation among the means of the data is computed by:

1. computing each mean
2. squaring the difference between each of the means and the grand mean of all of the means
3. multiplying the squared deviations by the number of items making up each mean
4. summing the weighted squared deviations

The result is divided by the degrees of freedom which are computed by simply deducting one degree of freedom from the number of means involved.

The second element of the variation, that is, the variation within the data, is computed by:

1. computing the difference between each item of data and its own mean for each of the components of the problem
2. squaring each of these deviations
3. summing each set of deviations
4. the sums of the squared deviations for each of the elements of the problem are added, and the total is divided by the total of the degrees of freedom computed by summing the number of observations in each of the elements less the number of elements of the problem

The final step in the application of the analysis of variance is to compute the F-ratio, which is the ratio of the variance among the means to the variance in the data. This formula follows:

$$F = \frac{s_1^2}{s_2^2}$$

where: s_1^2 = variance among the means

s_2^2 = variance within the data

It will be recalled that s is the designation of the standard deviation. When this value s is squared, it becomes the variance. Thus, to compute the F-ratio, the variance among the means is divided by the variance within the data. The variance within the data becomes the *experimental variation*, just as in the T-test the standard error of the mean becomes the experimental variation or *experimental error* used as the denominator in computing the ratio for the T-test itself. Thus, while experimental error for the T-test is given by the standard error of the mean, the experimental error in the analysis of variance is given by the variance within the data.

Appendix D of this book contains a table of the values of the theoretical distribution of the F-ratios. This distribution is a skewed distribution and is skewed differently for each of the degrees of freedom of the numerator and the denominator. Therefore, in this table, only two levels of significance are included: the .05 level and the .01 level. These are commonly designated in the literature as $F_{.95}$ and $F_{.99}$. After having computed the F-ratio for a given problem, the analyst turns to Appendix D and looks up the theoretical value of the distribution of the F-ratio for the degrees of freedom for the numerator and the degrees of freedom for the denominator. If his computed F-ratio is greater than the theoretical F-ratio from the table, the hypothesis that the difference among the averages of the elements of the problem is zero is rejected. The difference, in such a case, is a significant difference. If the computed F-ratio is less than the theoretical F-ratio from the table, the hypothesis is accepted which means that the differences among the means of the elements is not significant. It should be pointed out that any time the ratio of the observed computation is less than one, the difference among the means is not significant since the variance among the means is accounted for by the variance within the data. Thus, whenever the observed F-ratio is one or less, there is no need to refer to the table of the theoretical distribution of the F-ratio. It is only when the observed F-ratio exceeds one that the analyst must seek the value of the theoretical distribution of the F-ratio from the table to make the comparison.

An example of the application of the analysis of variance to solving a problem follows:

As part of a research study into the operational efficiency of a four-store discount retail chain, a comparison of the average weekly take-home pay of the employees of the four stores is projected. A random sample of 10 observations for each store is selected within a three-month period. The data are as follows:

Store 1	Store 2	Store 3	Store 4
80	76	100	94
84	90	102	90
108	105	110	88
102	84	70	80
90	77	77	96
94	88	102	92
88	94	80	79
80	110	76	88
90	102	78	94
104	84	85	89

The hypothesis, that the differences among the means equal zero, is to be tested by the analysis of variance.

EXHIBIT 9-4
Testing the Significance of Differences by the Analysis of Variance

Store 1			Store 2			Store 3			Store 4			Totals	
X	d	d²	X	d	d²	X	d	d²	X	d	d²	X	d²
80	−12	144	76	−15	225	100	+12	144	94	+5	25		
84	−8	64	90	−1	1	102	+14	196	90	+1	1		
108	+16	256	105	+14	196	110	+22	484	88	−1	1		
102	+10	100	84	−7	49	70	−18	324	80	−9	81		
90	−2	4	77	−14	196	77	−11	121	96	+7	49		
94	+2	4	88	−3	9	102	+14	196	92	+3	9		
88	−4	16	94	+3	9	80	−8	64	79	−10	100		
80	−12	144	110	+19	361	76	−12	144	88	−1	1		
90	−2	4	102	+11	121	78	−10	100	94	+5	25		
104	+12	144	84	−7	49	85	−3	9	89	0	0		
Σ 920		880	910		1,216	880		1,782	890		292	3,600	4,170
N 10			10			10			10			10	
X̄ 92			91			88			89			90	

$$s_1{}^2 = \frac{[(\overline{X}_1 - \overline{X})^2 \times N_1] + [(\overline{X}_2 - \overline{X})^2 \times N_2] + [(\overline{X}_3 - \overline{X})^2 \times N_3] + [(\overline{X}_4 - \overline{X})^2 \times N_4]}{\text{number of classes minus one}}$$

$$= \frac{[(92 - 90)^2 \times 10] + [(91 - 90)^2 \times 10] + [(88 - 90)^2 \times 10] + [(89 \times 90)^2 \times 1}{4 - 1}$$

$$= \frac{(2^2 \times 10) + (1^2 \times 10) + (2^2 \times 10) + (1^2 \times 10)}{3}$$

$$= \frac{(4 \times 10) + 10 + (4 \times 10) + 10}{3}$$

$$= \frac{100}{3}$$

$$= 33.33$$

$$s_2{}^2 = \frac{\Sigma d_1{}^2 + \Sigma d_2{}^2 + \Sigma d_3{}^2 + \Sigma d_4{}^2}{(N_1 - 1) + (N_2 - 1) + (N_3 - 1) + (N_4 - 1)}$$

$$= \frac{880 + 1{,}216 + 1{,}782 + 292}{(10 - 1) + (10 - 1) + (10 - 1) + (10 - 1)}$$

$$= \frac{4{,}170}{36}$$

$$= 115.83$$

$$F = \frac{s_1{}^2}{s_2{}^2} = \frac{33.33}{115.83} = .28775$$

$F_{.99}$ at 3 and 36 d.f. $= 4.38$ $\qquad$ $F_{.95}$ at 3 and 36 d.f. $= 2.86$

The complete computations for the analysis of variance are shown in ex-hibit 9-4. The computation of $s_1{}^2$ is shown by first presenting the formula for computing the variance among the means. The difference between the mean for each store and the grand mean is computed; each such value is squared and multiplied by the number of observations for each store. The total of these squared deviations is divided by the number of degrees of freedom. The result is shown as 33.33. For the value $s_2{}^2$ the formula is first presented, showing that the difference between each individual value for each store and the mean for each store is taken. Each such individual value is then squared and summed. These sums of squared deviations for each store are in turn added and divided by the total of the degrees of freedom, which have been computed by adding the total observations minus one for each of the four stores. The result is 115.83. The F-ratio is computed as:

$$\frac{s_1{}^2}{s_2{}^2} = \frac{33.33}{115.83} = .28775$$

The final line of the exhibit shows the theoretical F-ratios secured from the table of the F-ratios in Appendix D for the .01 significance level and the .05 significance level. The computed F-ratio of .28775 is less than either of the significance levels from the theoretical distribution of the F-ratio; indeed, the computed F-ratio is less than one. Therefore, reference to the theoretical distribution was really unnecessary. The hypothesis that the difference among the average weekly take-home pay of the employees of the four stores equals zero must be accepted. The difference, in other words, is not significant. The variance among the means is fully accounted for by the variation within the data and, therefore, is accounted for by experimental error.

The analysis of variance can, of course, become much more complicated than is presented in exhibit 9-4. Its essential nature is indicated here, however. For the student or analyst who desires more complicated examples and more complicated treatment of the analysis of variance, selected references at the end of this chapter will give comprehensive treatments of the more complicated problem types and methods of analysis of variance.

INFERENCES FOR PERCENTAGES

Inferring percentages or proportions to a universe from the evidence supplied by a sample is a common procedure in business research. Percentages of manufactured products, percentages of sales, performances rated in percentages, percentage ratings for efficiency, and so forth are commonly computed and inferred for all elements of a business firm or for an industry. Among the difficulties faced in inferences involving percentages is the fact that the binomial distribution describes the theoretical distribution of percentages. The binomial distribution describes the occurrence of *yes-no* possibilities, *go-no go* possibilities, and other such possibilities that can be described as one of two possible occurrences. Such is the situation with a percentage where p equals the percentage, and $1 - p$ equals the remainder of the possibilities between the percentage and unity. When the proportional percentage involved departs widely from 50 percent, the binomial distribution describing it, of course, would need to be skewed. This skewness occurs since a sampling distribution would consist of samples collected from close to one end of a scale from zero through one, with 50 percent being the mean.

However, the normal distribution is adopted as an approximation for the binomial distribution when sample sizes are large, that is, greater than 30, and when the percentages involved do not depart greatly from 50 percent. In the ensuing analysis, the methods applied are to be applied only in the situations in which sample sizes are large and in which the percentages do not depart drastically from the areas around 50 percent. For example, when percent of occurrence, as in defectives in a manufacturing process where the percent defectives may be as small as 1 percent or 2 percent, and small samples are taken, the Poisson distribution, which in some respects may be considered a skewed version of the binomial, is adopted as a theoretical distribution. For the purposes of business research, however, most percentages that are computed are computed from very large samples. Usually, or at least, often, there are several hundred items in the sample and, many times, several thousands. It is common for the percentages to be greater than 25 or 30 and usually less than about 75 or 80. Thus, for most problems in business research, the adoption of the "Table of Areas of the Normal Curve" for the binomial distribution or another mathematical distribution is proper. It is repeated that the analysis in the following pages dealing with inferences for proportions to a universe from the evidence of samples is based on the assumption of large samples plus a departure from 50 percent that is not extreme.

The standard error of the percentage must be computed, of course, to serve as the experimental error just as the standard error of the mean is computed to serve as the experimental error in tests of hypotheses and statistical estimation when the arithmetic mean is involved. Following is the formula for the standard error of the percentage:

$$\sigma_\% = \sqrt{\frac{pq}{n}}$$

where: $\sigma_\%$ = standard error of the percentage
  p = the percentage
  q = one minus the percentage $(1 - p)$
  n = size of the sample

The standard error of the percentage as stated is used in tests of hypotheses involving the significance of a difference between two sample percentages, or in estimating a confidence interval in the universe within which it may be expected that a universe percentage would fall to a given level of probability. In tests of hypotheses involving the significance of the difference between a sample percentage and a known universe percentage, the universe percentage is used in the formula to compute the standard error:

$$\sigma_\% = \sqrt{\frac{P(1 - P)}{n}}$$

where: P = universe percentage

The following example illustrates the use of the standard error of the percentage in a problem involving the significance of the difference between a sample proportion and a *known* universe proportion.

It has been assumed by the regional office of an insurance company that 50 percent of the casualty policies it writes for agriculture contain a hail clause. Since the claims for hail damage seem excessive, the assumption is tested by computing the percentage of hail clauses in a sample of 600 policies; the percentage is found to be 62 percent. Hypothesis: that the universe percentage differs from 50 percent by zero.

$$\sigma_\% = \sqrt{\frac{P(1 - P)}{n}} = \sqrt{\frac{.50 \times .50}{600}} = \sqrt{\frac{.2500}{600}} = \sqrt{.00041667} = .0204$$

$$T = \frac{p - P}{\sigma_\%} = \frac{.62 - .50}{.0204} = \frac{.12}{.0204} = 5.88$$

The result of the T-test of 5.88 exceeds by a considerable amount the largest value of the standard normal deviate from Appendix A, the "Table of Areas of the Normal Curve"; the highest value contained in it is 3.99. Therefore, at any level of probability the hypothesis must be rejected. The universe percentage does not differ from 50 percent by zero; it differs by a significant amount. If the insurance company involved in the study has an agreement with another insurance company operating in the same region that the two companies would split the hail clause inclusions in their agricultural casualty policies in order to minimize their risks, it is apparent that the given company is writing more than its share of hail clauses and thus incurring more losses than it should according to its agreement with the other company. Such agreements are standard practice in hail areas and may involve several insurance companies, who thereby spread the risk of hail loss among themselves. As a further interpretation of the result of the T-test of the 5.88 standard deviations, it may be remembered that the .01 significance level in standard deviations is 2.576, and the .05 significance level is 1.96 standard deviations. The result of the T-test exceeds both, and therefore, at either level the hypothesis must be rejected.

The use of the standard error of the percentage in constructing an interval estimate for the purpose of estimating the interval in the universe within which the true percentage is likely to fall to a given level of confidence is illustrated as follows:

Since the proportion of agricultural insurance policies containing hail clauses is not 50 percent but by point estimation is 62 percent, an interval estimate to a 99 percent confidence level is desired, to establish the limits within which it may be expected the universe percentage lies.

$$\sigma_\% = \sqrt{\frac{pq}{n}} = \sqrt{\frac{.62 \times .38}{600}} = \sqrt{\frac{.2356}{600}} = \sqrt{.00039267}$$

$$= .0198$$

$$99\% \text{ confidence} = 2.576\sigma = z$$

$$z\sigma_\% = 2.576 \times .0198 = .0510048$$

$$\% \pm z\sigma_\% = .62 \pm (2.576 \times .0198) = .62 \pm .051$$

$$= .569 \text{ and } .671$$

yields confidence intervals of 56.9 percent and 67.1 percent

The point estimate yielded in this illustration, of course, is 62 percent. The confidence interval at a 99 percent confidence level is 56.9 percent and 67.1 percent. While the best point estimate of the individual value of the true percentage in the universe is 62 percent, the probability is 99 percent that the true percentage does fall between 56.9 percent and 67.1 percent. There is certainly no doubt that this particular company is writing more than its share of hail clauses in its agricultural policies.

Testing the significance of a difference between two proportions requires the computation of the standard error of the difference just as it is required in testing the significance of the difference between two means when two samples are involved. This situation is illustrated and the computations are shown in the example that follows.

A retail proprietor operates two furniture-appliance stores in different parts of a city. His inventories are procured on the assumption of similar sales patterns for the two stores, but the sales differences between the stores some-times leave him with excessive inventory of some items. To test TV owner-ship in the two areas may, he believes, give him a key to income or spending differentials. A sample of 100 customers of each store yields, for store A, 66 percent ownership; for store B, 71 percent ownership. Hypothesis: the differ-ence in the percentages is zero.

$$\sigma_{D_\%} = \sqrt{\sigma_{\%_1}^2 + \sigma_{\%_2}^2}$$ (this is the standard error of the difference)

where: $\sigma_{\%_1} = \sqrt{\dfrac{pq}{n_1}}$ (standard error of the first sample)

$\sigma_{\%_2} = \sqrt{\dfrac{pq}{n_2}}$ (standard error of the second sample)

Store A	Store B

Store A

$\%_1 = 66\%$

$n_1 = 100$

$\sigma_{\%_1}^2 = \dfrac{pq}{n_1} = \dfrac{.66 \times .34}{100}$

$= \dfrac{.2244}{100} = .002244$

Store B

$\%_2 = 71\%$

$n_2 = 100$

$\sigma_{\%_2}^2 = \dfrac{pq}{n_2} = \dfrac{.71 \times .29}{100}$

$= \dfrac{.2059}{100} = .002059$

$$\sigma_{D_\%} = \sqrt{.002244 + .002059} = \sqrt{.004303} = .0656$$

$$T = \frac{\%_1 - \%_2}{\sigma_{D_\%}} = \frac{.66 - .71}{.0656} = \frac{-.05}{.0656} = -.7622 = -.76$$

Tracing through the computations of the preceding example, it appears that the hypothesis that the difference in the percentages is zero must be accepted. The T-test yields a result of $-.76$. The absolute value of this result is less than the .01 significance level of 2.576 standard deviations and is less than the .05 significance level of 1.96 standard deviations. Therefore the T-value being less than either of the two significance levels, the hypothesis is accepted. The probability that the difference between the percentages occurred through sheer chance may be computed by refer-ence to the "Table of Areas of the Normal Curve." With a standard normal deviate of .76—as yielded by the T-test—the area under the normal curve is found to be .27637. This value times 2 equals .55274. This resulting amount deducted from 1 yields .44726. Therefore, the probability that the difference of 5 percent that was found between the two percentages was due to sheer chance is 44.7 percent, an exceedingly high probability that the difference was due to sheer chance. The conclusion must be reached that the difference was indeed wholly due to chance. Thus, in effect, the difference in the two percentages is zero, and the hypothesis is accepted.

The implication for the retail operator of the two furniture-appliance stores in the example is a reasonable one. His study of TV ownership by the customers of his two stores yields no difference. Therefore, he must turn his attention to other research methods of finding out any possible differences in the customers of the two stores that might account for sometimes a difference in sales of items between the stores which result in an excessive inventory of certain items. He may need to study differences in promotional efforts, differences in sales efforts by salespersons, other differences in income patterns or customer preferences or other aspects of the mores of his customers in the two different sections of town. Certainly his study of differences in TV ownership in the two areas of town yielded him nothing but the information that he must seek elsewhere for data or facts which will help him learn the reasons for differences in sales between the two stores.

SUMMARY

Statistical inference may be defined as inferring the characteristics of a universe from the evidence of a sample. The characteristic under consideration is usually an arithmetic mean or a percentage. Sometimes a standard deviation may be inferred. Statistical inference includes the testing of hypotheses, for example, testing the significance of the difference in two means. Thus, there are two areas of statistical inference: (1) Statistical estimation, in which a mean or proportion will be inferred to a universe from the evidence of a sample; (2) tests of hypotheses, involving tests of the significance of the difference between two means or two percentages.

The arithmetic mean and the standard deviation must be calculated when either or both of them are inferred to a universe. The formulas follow:

From Array

arithmetic mean: $\overline{X} = \dfrac{\Sigma X}{n}$

standard deviation: $s = \sqrt{\dfrac{\Sigma x^2}{n}}$

where: $x = X - \overline{X}$

From Frequency Distribution

arithmetic mean: $\overline{X} = \dfrac{\Sigma (fm)}{n}$

standard deviation: $s = \sqrt{\dfrac{\Sigma f(m - \overline{X})^2}{n}}$

Statistical inference involves an estimate of the accuracy of the inference, called *reliability*. The reliability is given in terms of probabilities determined from areas under the normal curve. The normal curve describes universes when occurrences are in large numbers and occur by chance. The areas under the normal curve can be stated in terms of standard deviations as follows: 68.27 percent of the area is subtended under the curve between the $\overline{X} \pm \sigma$; 95.45 percent of the area is subtended under the curve between the $\overline{X} \pm 2\sigma$; 99.73 percent of the area is subtended under the curve between the $\overline{X} \pm 3\sigma$. The standard deviations, however, usually are quoted for even percentages as follows:

$$95\% = 1.96\,\sigma$$
$$99\% = 2.576\,\sigma$$

These are the most common probabilities used in statistical inference.

In making an inference to a given level of probability, the sampling distribution is involved. The standard deviation of the sampling distribution of all the means that could be collected from all the samples in the universe is defined as the *standard error of the mean*. Following is its formula:

$$\sigma_{\overline{X}} = \frac{s}{\sqrt{n}}$$

where: $\sigma_{\overline{X}} =$ standard error of the mean
$s =$ sample estimate of universe standard deviation
$n =$ size of the sample

In making an inference of the mean of a universe, the mean of the sample is a point estimate of the mean of the universe. An interval estimate of the mean of the universe is computed by constructing an interval within which 95 percent, or 99 percent, of sample means would fall:

$$\overline{X} \pm z\,\sigma_{\overline{X}}$$

where: $z =$ standard normal deviate $(1.96\,\sigma$ for 95%)

Where small samples occur, the "Table of Areas of the Normal Curve" is not used; Student's t-distribution is used when $n < 30$.

For tests of hypotheses for means, the following formula is used:

$$T = \frac{\overline{X} - \mu}{\sigma_{\overline{X}}}$$

$T =$ test of significance
$X =$ mean of the sample
$\mu =$ mean of the universe
$\sigma_{\overline{X}} =$ standard error of the mean

A test of the hypothesis that two sample means differ by zero uses the *standard error of the difference*:

$$T = \frac{\overline{X}_{s1} - \overline{X}_{s2}}{\sigma_D}$$

where: $\overline{X}_{s_1}$ and $\overline{X}_{s_2}$ = the two sample means

and $\qquad \sigma_D = \sqrt{\sigma_{\overline{X}_1}^2 + \sigma_{\overline{X}_2}^2}$ $\qquad$ (the standard error of the difference)

Where more than two means from two samples are to be tested for significant difference, the analysis of variance is employed. Analysis of variance requires using the F-distribution, which gives a value F for the ratio of the variances as follows:

$$F = \frac{s_1^2}{s_2^2}$$

where: s_1^2 = variance among the means
s_2^2 = variance within the data

The decision involving the F-distribution compares the computed F from the test to the F-value from the table of the F-distribution for the degrees of freedom for the numerator and denominator; where it is larger, reject; where it is smaller, accept.

Inferring percentages or proportions to a universe requires the proportion. It may involve comparing two proportions from two universes. The standard error of a proportion is computed as follows:

$$\sigma_{\%} = \sqrt{\frac{pq}{n}}$$

where: p = sample proportion
$q = 1 - p$

Where the universe proportion is known, the following formula is used:

$$\sigma_{\%} = \sqrt{\frac{P(1 - P)}{n}}$$

where: P = universe proportion

The proportion as computed from the sample gives a point estimate of the proportion in the universe. To make an interval estimate, the formula follows:

$$\% \pm z\,\sigma_{\%}$$

where: $\%$ = proportion
z = standard normal deviate ($1.96\,\sigma$ for 95%)
$\sigma_{\%}$ = standard error of the proportion

When a test of significance is made between a sample proportion and a universe proportion, this formula is followed:

$$T = \frac{p - P}{\sigma_{\%}}$$

For a test of the significance of the difference between two sample proportions the formula becomes:

$$T = \frac{\%_1 - \%_2}{\sigma_{D_\%}}$$

where: $\%_1$ and $\%_2$ = the two sample proportions

$$\sigma_{D_\%} = \sqrt{\sigma_{\%_1}^2 + \sigma_{\%_2}^2} \quad \text{(standard error of the difference in proportions)}$$

No small sample theory accompanies inferences for proportions.

EXERCISES

1. What is meant by the term *statistical inference*? Why is statistical inference so important?
2. How does computing the arithmetic mean from a frequency distribution differ from computing it from an array?
3. What is the usefulness of the standard deviation?
4. Describe the characteristics of the normal curve.
5. How are normal curve probabilities arrived at?
6. Define the sampling distribution of means in your own words.
7. What is the standard error of the mean? How is it used?
8. Explain the process of statistical estimation, both for point estimation and interval estimation.
9. What is Student's *t*-distribution? How is it employed? When is it employed?
10. What is the essential difference in a test of hypothesis between a sample and universe mean, and between two sample means?
11. Explain the difference between one-tailed and two-tailed significance tests. Give an example.
12. How does the analysis of variance differ from the *T*-test? How are the two alike?
13. Explain how the standard error of a percentage is used in inference involving percentages. Is this similar to the use of the standard error of the mean in inferences for means?
14. The prices of a name brand of motor oil differ in five supermarkets: $.39, $.42, $.45, $.46, $.48. Compute the mean and standard deviation. Is the dispersion *large* or *small*?
15. Typing errors by the stenographic pool of an investment advisory firm were classified by number of errors per document. Compute the average number of errors per document.

Errors	Documents
0 up to 3	33
3 up to 6	11
6 up to 9	9
9 up to 12	7

16. Two hundred bales of cotton received at a warehouse average 480 pounds in weight with a standard deviation of 10 pounds. How many bales weigh more than 485 pounds? Between 475 and 485 pounds?

17. Diameters of a sample of 100 quarter-inch brass rods average .252 inches with a standard deviation of .004 inches. What is the point estimate? What is the interval estimate at 99 percent confidence?

18. Assume a small sample of 25 instead of 100 for exercise 17, and recompute the confidence interval. What has occurred to the confidence interval as a result of having a smaller sample?

19. The average weight of hundred-pound sacks of grain must be controlled at 100 pounds. Sixteen sacks yield a mean of 101 pounds with a standard deviation of 1 pound. Test the hypothesis that the difference between the sample mean and the hypothetical mean is zero (use 0.001 critical probability).

20. A clothing manufacturer wishes to determine if two brands of polyester yarn, with the same price, have identical breaking strengths; a stronger yarn will have fewer process shutdowns. Test the hypothesis that the difference in breaking strengths is zero at the .05 significance level.

Brand A	Brand B
$\overline{X}_1 = 9.6$	$\overline{X}_2 = 10.8$
$s_1 = 1.2$	$s_2 = 1.6$
$n_1 = 64$	$n_2 = 64$

21. Quarterly records for repairs for two years for major machine shop operations yield the following results. Test the hypothesis of no difference in the repair records by analysis of variance at the .05 significance level.

Quarter	Lathe	Shaper	Drill
I	3	2	4
II	2	2	2
III	4	3	4
IV	2	2	5
I	4	3	4
II	4	3	5
III	3	2	2
IV	4	2	5

22. The following are variations in minutes of four similar operating procedures. Test by analysis of variance, at the .05 level, whether there is a significant difference in time.

I	II	III	IV
2	4	3	5
4	4	4	6
3	5	5	8
7	4		6
4	3		5
4			

23. Sixty percent of orders received by the mail-order department must exceed $10 to break even on shipping and handling costs. A count over a three-month period showed 1,920 orders more than $10 and 80 orders less than $10. Is the requirement being met at the .1 percent critical probability?

24. To test whether labor turnover rates were greater for operations or for administration, samples of 100 of each were taken by an insurance company, with

these results: operations, 18 percent; administration, 12 percent. Is the difference significant at the .05 level? What is the probability that the difference is due to sheer chance?

SELECTED REFERENCES

Balsley, Howard L. *Basic Statistics for Business and Economics*. Columbus, Ohio: Grid, 1978.

Balsley, Howard L. *Quantitative Research Methods for Business and Economics*. New York: Random House, 1970.

Chou, Ya-Lun. *Statistical Analysis*. 2d ed. New York: Holt, Rinehart and Winston, 1975.

10

Sampling Procedures for Business Research

The selection of the items to constitute a sample must be made in consideration of the adequacy of the sample, the representativeness of the sample, and the fact that the sample will be used to make inferences to a universe. A *statistically adequate sample* is one that is of such size that the inferences drawn from the sample are accurate to a given level of confidence. A *representative sample* is one that has been drawn from the universe in such a manner that it is a small replica of all of the conditions in the universe and, therefore, represents all of the factors that exist in the universe. The procedure to be used in selecting a sample that is both adequate and representative is called *probability sampling*.

Probability sampling is any procedure of selecting the cases for each sample that gives each case in the universe an equal chance of being chosen for the sample. Thus, a system of sampling is predicated in choosing these items. If each item in the universe has an equal chance of being chosen, then a given sample chosen from the universe would be one such that every other sample of equal size that could have been constructed from the universe had an equal chance of being chosen. Thus, the *equal chance* of being chosen refers both to the individual cases in the universe and to the samples that could be drawn from the universe.

A simple example will illustrate the probability technique. If men are twice as numerous as women in a given population, a sample of that population would contain twice as many men as women if it is selected by a technique that gives each person in the population an equal chance of being chosen. The probability that a man will be selected each time a person is chosen for the sample is twice as great as the probability that a woman will be selected because there are twice as many men as women in the group. The principle of probability applies, of course, to all of the possible characteristics of any population. This probability principle explains why a probability sample is likely to be reasonably representative of its population.

It has been mentioned that, besides choosing a sample that is large enough so that the inferences made for the universe will be reliable to a given level of confidence and the sample will be representative of the universe, the inferences themselves must be reliable to a given level of confidence. The statistical measures of error, that is, the standard error of the mean and the standard error of the proportion, are defined as the standard deviations of sampling distributions of those respective measurements. The sampling distributions, it will be remembered, were distributions of either the mean or of the proportion that could have been constructed from a large number of samples taken from a universe. Thus, the computation of the standard error, which means the computation of the experimental error existing in the data and accordingly measuring the error in the inference itself, requires that the sample be a probability sample. It is only if the sample is a probability sample that inferences may be made about the universe from the evidence of the sample to a given level of probability, consequently, to a given level of confidence.

ADEQUACY

The subject of adequacy, it has already been explained, refers to the size of a sample, which must be such that the inferences to be made concerning the universe from the evidence of that sample will be reliable to a given level of confidence or probability.

SAMPLE AND UNIVERSE MEANS

Determining the size of a sample before it is taken, of course, requires some knowledge. It requires a decision as to the level of confidence that is desired for the reliability of the inferences: 95 percent confidence level or 99 percent confidence level, for example. The following formula will serve for cases in which the size of sample needs to be determined for either of two situations:

1. To test the significance of a difference between a sample and a hypothetical or universe mean.
2. To estimate a universe mean from the evidence of a sample to a given level of confidence.

$$n = \left(\frac{\sigma}{\frac{\overline{X} - \mu}{z}} \right)^2$$

where: n = size of the sample

σ = standard deviation of the population (known or estimated)

$\overline{X} - \mu$ = estimated deviation of sample mean from population mean; or one-half the estimated confidence interval

z = standard normal deviate (2.576 for 99%; 1.96 for 95% confidence levels)

Examining the formula, it appears that in order to determine the size of a sample, an estimate of the standard deviation of the population is required. Sometimes a standard deviation of the population may be known or it may be possible to compute it from evidence that already exists. In some cases, a foreman on a job knows the amount of dispersion or tolerance existing in the product produced by a given machine, and the analyst will be able to estimate from that information the standard deviation. In other cases, a similar study previously conducted may yield information from which the standard deviation may be estimated. Sometimes the experience of the analyst with similar studies may permit him to make a reasonable estimate.

If the range of the data in the population, i.e., if the smallest value and the largest value occurring in the population, or likely to occur in the population, is known, the standard deviation may be estimated. Referring to exhibit 9-3 in the previous chapter, and the related text, it is apparent that three standard deviations on either side of the mean include 99.73 percent of the area under the normal curve. Thus, if the range is determined, then divided by six, an estimate of the standard deviation will be obtained. This practice rests on the assumption of a normally distributed parent population.

In any case, the standard deviation of the population must either be known or estimated. Next, an estimate must be made of the difference that is to be expected between the sample mean and the universe mean. The standard normal deviate, that is, the level of confidence in standard deviations, must also be decided on. Thus, the sample size will be determined in terms of the *sensitivity* of the difference that the analyst may wish to detect between a sample mean and the universe mean to a given level of probability as indicated by the confidence level. The analyst may pose this phrase to himself: "I wish the size of sample to be such that a difference of \$3 between the sample mean and the universe mean would not occur undetected more than 1 percent of the time." In such a case, he has chosen the 99 percent confidence level to accompany an estimated deviation of the sample mean from the population mean of \$3. If the analyst is dealing with a problem of estimation, he may estimate the confidence interval that he is willing to permit to a given level of confidence and then take half of that estimated confidence interval to insert in the formula. The following example will serve to illustrate the computation of the size of a sample for a problem of estimating the mean of a universe.

The average handling cost of mail orders by a catalog notions store has been assumed to be about \$.25. In order to actually compute the mean to a given confidence level, the size of sample is required. A universe standard deviation of \$.06 is estimated, and a confidence interval of \$.03 in total (\$.015 on either side of the mean) at a probability of 99 percent is selected.

$$n = \left(\frac{\sigma}{\dfrac{\overline{X} - \mu}{z}}\right)^2 = \left(\frac{6}{\dfrac{1.5}{2.576}}\right)^2 = \left(\frac{6}{.5823}\right)^2 = 10.3^2 = 106.1$$

$$\text{rounded up} = 107$$

(Normal rounding procedure would call for rounding 106.1 downward to 106. However, for sample sizes, particularly sample sizes that are relatively small, rounding all fractions upward results in an error on the conservative side. It is considered better to have a sample size slightly too large than one slightly too small.)

A sample size of 107 would be drawn from the universe of mail orders that the store has received, perhaps over a given period of time such as the last month or the last three months. This sample would need to be chosen by some probability technique such as one of those described in later paragraphs of this chapter. Having selected the size of sample and then having selected each of the items to go into the sample by a probability technique, the estimate of the actual mean cost of handling mail orders by the catalog notions store could be computed.

THE ANALYSIS OF VARIANCE

One of the problems that arises in determining sample size is that of determining the sample size for the analysis of variance, in which several means are concerned. It will be remembered that three or four or five or more means may have to be computed as well as the grand mean. The deviation of each mean from the grand mean would be computed; the deviations would be squared, weighted by the number of observations included in each mean, summed, and divided by the degrees of freedom among the means. A suggestion that will yield the minimum size of sample for one class, that is, for one of the columns, would be to proceed as follows: Establish the permitted or estimated difference between one column mean and the grand mean; establish the standard normal deviate, for instance, 2.576 standard deviations for the 99 percent confidence level; and establish the standard deviation to be expected within the column data. These values, inserted in the formula presented in the preceding section, "Sample and Universe Means," would yield the size of sample for one column of data. That minimum size of sample for one column of data could then be used as the minimum size of sample for each column of data in the entire series to be tested by the analysis of variance. Since the analysis of variance yields greater precision than the single T-test of statistical inference, the order of reliability yielded by following this method will be higher than required. However, where a minimum size of sample is desired, this procedure may very well be followed. Attempting to secure the precise size of sample to a given level of confidence for the analysis of variance involves using the F-ratio as a substitute for the standard normal deviate and results in a difficulty that may be called *circular* computation in attempting to arrive at the correct size of sample.

TWO-SAMPLE MEANS

When it is desired to test the significance of the difference in the means computed from two samples, the formula is somewhat different. The formula follows:

$$n = \frac{2\sigma^2}{\left(\dfrac{\overline{X}_1 - \overline{X}_2}{z}\right)^2}$$

where: n = size of the sample

σ^2 = variance expected in each sample

$\overline{X}_1 - \overline{X}_2$ = difference in the sample means (estimated)

z = standard normal deviate (2.576 for 99%; 1.96 for 95% confidence intervals)

This formula assumes a common variance for the two samples as can be seen in the numerator in which the variance is doubled. However, this assumption poses no great difficulty and must be accepted if this formula is to be used in determining the size of the sample. The standard deviation must be estimated and then squared; the squared standard deviation, which is the variance, is doubled. The denominator is formed by the ratio of the estimated difference in the sample means divided by the standard normal deviate, the quantity squared. This formula is illustrated in the following example.

A chemical compound that deteriorates in use in a matter of hours may be purchased from either of two companies. To test which company's product has the longer life, a sampling test is to be run; thus, the size of each sample is required. It is felt that the test must distinguish a difference of 3 hours between the products 95 percent of the time; a variance of 25 hours is estimated $\sigma^2 = 5^2 = 25$.

$$n = \frac{2\sigma^2}{\left(\dfrac{\overline{X}_1 - \overline{X}_2}{z}\right)^2} = \frac{2 \times 25}{\left(\dfrac{3}{1.96}\right)^2} = \frac{50}{1.53^2} = \frac{50}{2.34} = 21.4 = 22 \text{ (rounded up)}$$

The sample size computed for this example is 22. That sample size pertains to each of the two samples. Therefore, when the two samples are added together, a large sample size of 44 results. It will be remembered that where the significance of the difference between two sample means is to be tested, the denominator in the T-test is the standard error of the difference. Therefore, the two samples are added together in determining the total size of the sample.

Sometimes the result will be a small sample, that is, a sample with a smaller total than thirty items in it. Indeed, for the preceding formula for estimating the mean of a universe from the evidence of a sample, or for testing the significance of a difference between a sample mean and a hypothetical mean, a small sample may also result. In such a situation, the standard normal deviate that had been used in the computation of the sample size would not pertain, of course. The sample size would need to be computed a second time, inserting for the standard normal deviate in the formula the Student's t-value from the table of Student's t-distribution (Appendix B) for the particular size sample that had been discovered. A new size of sample would be computed, and a new Student's t-distribution value would be discovered. This may need to be inserted in the formula, and a third computation of the size of sample completed. This procedure is continued until a sample size *stabilizes*, that is, until the size of sample does not change any further by more than one. At that point, the size of sample has been determined, and the Student's t-value from the Student's t-distribution becomes the value of the standard normal deviate to be used in the subsequent analysis and testing to be followed in the problem, substituting for the standard normal deviate from the normal curve.

An example will serve to illustrate the computation of the sample size when small samples are involved.

Consider that, in the preceding example of the chemical compound, the variance had been estimated to be 9 instead of 25, i.e., $\sigma^2 = 3^2 = 9$. The computations follow:

$$n = \frac{2\sigma^2}{\left(\dfrac{\overline{X}_1 - \overline{X}_2}{z}\right)^2} = \frac{2 \times 9}{\left(\dfrac{3}{1.96}\right)^2} = \frac{18}{1.53^2} = \frac{18}{2.34} = 7.69 \text{ rounded} = 8$$

But, 8 doubled = 16, a small sample. The small sample value of z (.05 level) from Student's t-distribution table (Appendix B) for $16 - 2 = 14$ degrees of freedom is 2.145, which is then substituted for 1.96:

$$n = \frac{2 \times 9}{\left(\dfrac{3}{2.145}\right)^2} = \frac{18}{1.3986^2} = \frac{18}{1.956} = 9.2 \text{ rounded up} = 10$$

But, 10 doubled = 20, a small sample. The small sample value of z (.05 level) from Appendix B for $20 - 2 = 18$ d.f. is 2.101, which is substituted for 2.145:

$$n = \frac{2 \times 9}{\left(\dfrac{3}{2.101}\right)^2} = \frac{18}{1.42789^2} = \frac{18}{2.039} = 8.83 \text{ rounded} = 9$$

Now, 9 doubled = 18, a small sample. So, the new value of z, for $18 - 2 = 16$ d.f. is 2.120, to be substituted for 2.101:

$$n = \frac{2 \times 9}{\left(\dfrac{3}{2.12}\right)^2} = \frac{18}{1.415^2} = \frac{18}{2} = 9$$

Since the sample size did not change in the last computation from the preceding one, it has stabilized at 9. This is the sample size that would be accepted for each sample.

SAMPLE AND UNIVERSE PROPORTIONS

The following formula may be used in the following situations:

1. To test the significance of a difference between a sample proportion and a hypothetical or universe proportion.
2. To estimate a universe proportion to a given level of confidence from the evidence of a sample.

$$n = \frac{pq}{\left(\dfrac{p - P}{z}\right)^2}$$

where: n = size of the sample

p = the proportion

$q = 1 - p$

$p - P$ = estimated deviation of the sample proportion from the population proportion; or one-half the estimated confidence interval

z = standard normal deviate (2.576 for 99%; 1.96 for 95% confidence levels)

This formula, it is seen, requires that an estimate of the proportion to be found in the sample be made; if none can be given reasonably, 50 percent is used, and the q becomes thus $1 - p$, which is also 50 percent. (The use of 50 percent maximizes the size of the numerator and thus also the size of the sample; a *conservative* error results. Note: $.5 \times .5 = .25$ for pq, the largest pq possible to obtain.) The value $p - P$ represents either an estimated deviation of the possible sample proportion from the population proportion that is to be detected at a given level of confidence; or it represents one-half of an estimated allowable confidence interval. The standard normal deviate is chosen as before, simply a given level of probability desired for the size of sample and for the subsequent test or estimate. An example of the application of this formula follows.

A department store that conducts frequent sales by using loss leaders wishes to estimate the percentage of secondary sales accompanying the loss leader sales. A percentage of 80 is estimated, and it is desired that any deviation from the true percentage in the universe be detected at 5 percent to a confidence level of 99 percent. What size sample must be taken?

$$n = \frac{pq}{\left(\dfrac{p - P}{z}\right)^2} = \frac{.80 \times .20}{\left(\dfrac{.05}{2.576}\right)^2} = \frac{.16}{.01941^2} = \frac{.16}{.0003767} = 425 \text{ (rounded)}$$

The sample size of 425 represents the number of sales that must be selected at random from a day's sales or a week's sales, whatever has been selected for the research study. They must be selected by some probability technique, of course, to insure representativeness and to make possible the inference as to the percentage of secondary sales actually occurring in the total universe of sales made by the store.

TWO-SAMPLE PROPORTIONS

Where two samples are to be selected and two proportions are to be computed from them for the purpose of testing the significance of the difference between the proportions, the following formula may be used.

$$n = \frac{2pq}{\left(\dfrac{p_1 - p_2}{z}\right)^2}$$

where: n = size of the sample

pq = estimated sample proportion multiplied by 1 minus the proportion: $p(1 - p)$

$p_1 - p_2$ = estimate of the possible differences in the proportions in the two groups

z = standard normal deviate (2.576 for 99%; 1.96 for 95% confidence levels)

This formula requires doubling the pq-value for the numerator. Where no estimate can be made of the proportion that is expected in the universe, 50 percent may be used, and thus 50 percent will be used for both the p and the q. The $p_1 - p_2$ is the estimated allowable difference that needs to be detected at a given level of probability in the experiment or research study. An example follows:

The credit manager of a department store that requires a credit check only on accounts greater than $50 suspects that the smaller accounts—less than $50—actually have a higher delinquency rate. To test his suspicion he wishes to compare the delinquency rates of the two groups, and therefore, desires to know the sample size to use. Assuming an estimated delinquency rate of 30 percent, it is required that the test be sensitive enough to show a 5 percent difference at a 95 percent probability.

$$n = \frac{2pq}{\left(\dfrac{p_1 - p_2}{z}\right)^2} = \frac{2(.30 \times .70)}{\left(\dfrac{.05}{1.96}\right)^2} = \frac{2 \times .21}{.02551^2} = \frac{.42}{.00065} = 647 \text{ (rounded)}$$

The size of sample for each of the two samples is 647 accounts. Thus, 647 accounts smaller than $50 will be selected at random, and 647 accounts larger than $50 will be selected at random or on some probability basis. Having selected the two samples, the test of the significance between the two proportions that are discovered in the two samples will be followed by the usual process, as explained in chapter 9.

WHEN SIZE OF UNIVERSE IS KNOWN

Sometimes in statistical inference studies of either averages or proportions, the size of the universe is known. The techniques and formulas of chapter 9, "Statistical Inference in Business Research," are such that an unknown, and therefore infinite, universe was assumed, because this situation is probably the prevailing one. Further, if an infinite universe is assumed when making inferences, any error of inference would be on the conservative side, resulting in an even higher reliability if a finite, or known size of, universe does indeed exist.

The adjustment for known size of universe in inference is to multiply the computed standard error by the following factor, then proceed with the inference:

$$\sqrt{1 - \frac{n}{N}}$$

where: n = size of the sample

N = known size of the universe

While the use of this adjustment is not necessary, or possibly even desirable, in statistical inference itself, its use in determining sample size may be necessary. For instance, referring to the example of the credit manager of a department store wishing to test the delinquency credit rates in the immediately preceding section, "Two-Sample Proportions," suppose that, with a sample size requirement of 647 as computed for each sample, it is found that there are only 550 accounts greater than $50 and only 280 of less than $50. The sample size required for each sample is larger than each of the two universes!

Sample size formulas adjusted for known size of universes, incorporating the factor $\sqrt{1 - \frac{n}{N}}$ are given in the following sections.

Arithmetic Means—Universe Known

The following formula may be used for computing sample sizes for inferences involving arithmetic means when the size of the universe is known:

$$n = \frac{1}{\left(\dfrac{\overline{X} - \mu}{\sigma z}\right)^2 + \dfrac{1}{N}}$$

where: n = size of the sample

N = known size of the universe

$\overline{X} - \mu$ = estimated deviation of sample mean from population mean; or one-half the estimated confidence interval; or the estimated difference between two sample means; or the estimated deviation of a sample mean from the grand mean in analysis of variance

σ = standard deviation of the population (known or estimated)

z = standard normal deviate (2.576 for 99%; 1.96 for 95% confidence levels)

In the preceding description of the notation $\overline{X} - \mu$ it is apparent that the formula will serve for computing sample sizes under the following circumstances:

1. When a test of significance (a T-test) is to be made between a sample arithmetic mean and a universe or population mean, or between a sample mean and a hypothetical mean (as in quality control).
2. When an arithmetic mean is to be inferred to a universe from the evidence of a sample, with a confidence interval constructed at a given confidence level.
3. When a test of significance (a T-test) is to be made between two sample means, and the size of each sample is needed.
4. When a test of significance (analysis of variance) is to be made among several means simultaneously, and the sample size for each of the samples can be computed by using as $\overline{X} - \mu$ the estimated deviation of just one of the sample means from the grand mean.

An example of the use of the formula is given in the following application.

As part of an analysis of the endowment portfolios of small private colleges in Texas, a comparison of each college portfolio was to be made with the portfolios of mutual income funds. To minimize the massive comparison work involved, it was decided to use a sample of the twenty-four mutual income funds in the United States that had similar characteristics of size, composition, objectives, etc. After the determination of sample size, a table of random numbers would be used to select the sample from the list of twenty-four funds.

The sample size was determined on the element of yield, since the yield comparisons would be the most important element of portfolio comparison. The standard deviation was estimated as one-sixth of the range of yields (assuming a normal distribution of yield deviations). Since the range of yields was from two percent to eight percent, or six, then one-sixth of this range yielded one percent. It was desired that the confidence interval be confined to one-half of one percent on either side of the universe mean at a 95 percent confidence level (1.96 standard deviations).

$$n = \cfrac{1}{\left(\cfrac{\overline{X} - \mu}{\sigma z}\right)^2 + \cfrac{1}{N}} = \cfrac{1}{\left(\cfrac{.5}{1 \times 1.96}\right)^2 + \cfrac{1}{24}} = \cfrac{1}{.255102^2 + .041667}$$

$$= \cfrac{1}{.065077 + .041667} = \cfrac{1}{.106744} = 9.37 \text{ rounded} = 10$$

But, 10 is a small sample, so substitute 2.262 for 1.96 from Student's t-distribution table (Appendix B)—degrees of freedom are $10 - 1 = 9$; then recompute:

$$n = \cfrac{1}{\left(\cfrac{.5}{1 \times 2.262}\right)^2 + \cfrac{1}{24}} = \cfrac{1}{.221043^2 + .041667} = \cfrac{1}{.048860 + .041667}$$

$$= \frac{1}{.090527} = 11.05 \text{ rounded up} = 12$$

But, 12 is a small sample differing from 10, so substitute 2.201 for 2.262 from Appendix B—12 − 1 = 11 degrees of freedom; and recompute:

$$n = \frac{1}{\left(\dfrac{.5}{1 \times 2.201}\right)^2 + \dfrac{1}{24}} = \frac{1}{.227169^2 + .041667} = \frac{1}{.051606 + .041667}$$

$$= \frac{1}{.093273} = 10.72 \text{ rounded} = 11$$

But, 11 is a small sample differing from 12, so substitute 2.228 for 2.201 from Appendix B—11 − 1 = 10 degrees of freedom; and recompute:

$$n = \frac{1}{\left(\dfrac{.5}{1 \times 2.228}\right)^2 + \dfrac{1}{24}} = \frac{1}{.2244165^2 + .041667} = \frac{1}{.050363 + .041667}$$

$$= \frac{1}{.092030} = 10.87 \text{ rounded} = 11$$

Sample size has stabilized at 11, so 11 mutual income funds are to be selected (using a random number table—Appendix E) from the list of 24 funds.

Proportions—Universe Known

The following formula may be used for computing sample sizes for inferences involving proportions when the size of the universe is known:

$$n = \frac{pq}{\left(\dfrac{p - P}{z}\right)^2 + \dfrac{pq}{N}}$$

where: n = size of the sample

N — known size of the universe

$p - P$ = estimated deviation of sample proportion from population proportion; or one-half the estimated confidence interval; or the estimated difference between two sample proportions

p = the sample proportion

$q = 1 - p$

z = standard normal deviate (2.576 for 99%; 1.96 for 95% confidence levels)

In the preceding description of the notation $p - P$, it is apparent that the formula will serve for computing sample sizes under the following circumstances:

1. When a test of significance (a T-test) is to be made between a sample proportion and a universe or population proportion, or between a sample proportion and a hypothetical proportion.
2. When a proportion is to be inferred to a universe from the evidence of a sample, with a confidence interval constructed at a given confidence level.
3. When a test of significance (a T-test) is to be made between two sample proportions.

The application of the formula is given in the following illustration involving the example of the credit manager of a department store wishing to test delinquency rates in the section of this chapter "Two-Sample Proportions." It will be remembered that the sample size computed there was 647.

The credit manager of a department store that requires a credit check only on accounts greater than $50 suspects that the smaller accounts—less than $50— actually have a higher delinquency rate. Samples will be taken to make the comparison, and the computed sample size turns out to be 647. However, there are only 550 accounts greater than $50, and only 280 of less than $50. Using these known universe sizes, the two sample sizes are recomputed, with assumptions of 30 percent delinquency and a test that will show a 5 percent difference at a 95 percent probability.

For accounts greater than $50:

$$n = \frac{pq}{\left(\frac{p - P}{z}\right)^2 + \frac{pq}{N}} = \frac{.30 \times .70}{\left(\frac{.05}{1.96}\right)^2 + \frac{.30 \times .70}{550}} = \frac{.21}{.02551^2 + \frac{.21}{550}}$$

$$= \frac{.21}{.0006508 + .0003818} = \frac{.21}{.0010326} = 203.37 \text{ rounded} = 204$$

For accounts less than $50:

$$n = \frac{pq}{\left(\frac{p - P}{z}\right)^2 + \frac{pq}{N}} = \frac{.30 \times .70}{\left(\frac{.05}{1.96}\right)^2 + \frac{.30 \times .70}{280}} = \frac{.21}{.02551^2 + \frac{.21}{280}}$$

$$= \frac{.21}{.0006508 + .0007500} = \frac{.21}{.0014008} = 149.91 \text{ rounded up} = 150$$

The samples of 204 accounts over $50 and 150 under $50 will be taken (by a random method), and the comparison then made, using techniques presented in chapter 9.

SEQUENTIAL ANALYSIS SAMPLING

Sequential analysis sampling is a data-collection technique that makes it possible during the sampling process to determine when the sample is large enough. This procedure can often reduce the number of cases needed in a sample and result in a saving in time and cost of a survey. It may also be advantageous to be able to tell when a sample is of adequate size during the sampling process so that the results may be estimated before disbanding the field force.

A sample must be large enough so that the data in it, such as averages, are accurate enough to give the researcher data that are usable for his purposes. The larger the sample collected by any given sample-selection technique, the smaller, of course, the experimental error involved in the inference to the universe. Cost and time considerations usually dictate that a sample should not be larger or more accurate than necessary for the particular research project under consideration. Therefore, sequential analysis is often useful in enabling a research project to be halted at the point at which the sample is considered large enough to give the results to the desired level of reliability.

As an example, assume that the manager of a factory producing shoes decided that he would shut down his plant and install new machinery if more than 20 percent of his output was found to fail to meet certain specifications. He may or may not compute the specific size of sample needed by one of the formulas given in preceding paragraphs. However, he could proceed by taking samples from the production line and testing them consecutively until he was satisfied that he had enough data of accurate enough level to end the sampling procedure. His procedure would be somewhat as follows: Finished shoes would be withdrawn in a systematic manner from the end of the production line. Tests on the shoes would start after, say, a batch of 10 pairs of shoes had been selected. The results of the tests on each successive batch of 10 would be reported as soon as they had been completed. As each successive batch was tested, the percentage of failures on all tested pairs would be calculated by adding the test results from each new group to the results for the total number of pairs tested up to that time. The reports might become available every hour after the first few hours of testing had occurred. Assume that out of the first group of 10 pairs of shoes, one pair or 10 percent failed to pass the specifications test. That 10 percent failure figure would be recorded. Next, tests on the second group of 10 pairs showed that two of them were faulty. The proportion of failures, thus, on the first 20 pairs would be seen to be 3 out of 20 or 15 percent.

As successive groups of shoes were tested, perhaps the percentage of all tested pairs which failed to meet the predetermined specifications would begin to fluctuate closely around 17 percent, neither rising above nor falling below that figure by more than 1 percent. Assume that the central tendency figure 17 percent was established after 40 pairs had been tested. Suppose further that the average of the failures stayed within 1 percent of that 17 percent figure when three more groups of 10 had each been tested, or a total of 70 pairs. Under these conditions, it is probably safe to assume that the size of the sample of shoes tested was large enough to establish with a reasonable degree of certainty that not over 20 percent of the shoes being produced during the period covered by the test failed to meet the specifications for which they were tested. Sampling and testing could therefore be stopped.

Another example concerns a survey that was conducted among the retail businesses of a city to determine what kinds of floor covering were used in their buildings. The survey technique was based on observation by field workers. Reports on the stores visited in all parts of the universe, that is, all stores of the city, were tabulated at the end of each two hours after the survey was started. The percentages of different kinds of floor coverings were computed. As successive sets of reports were sent in, the percentage for each type of floor covering began to stabilize. After further reports were found to make no appreciable change in the percentages, the sampling was stopped. The collection of additional observations and reports was no longer needed.

Sequential analysis sampling can be used only if the sample data can be obtained, studied, and analyzed as the sampling is being done. Reports from field workers must be made at relatively short and frequent intervals, such as every few hours or perhaps at least at the end of each day. In some instances, the field worker can be instructed to stop after a stated period of time or after a certain number of cases have been collected in order to tabulate and report his totals to his central office or to a designated research worker.

Another important requirement for satisfactory sequential analysis sampling is that the periodic reports must be obtained from representative cases drawn from all parts of the universe. Care must be exercised to see that the entire universe is being sampled while the survey is continuing. Otherwise, bias would enter the sample, and the averages or other characteristics being studied in the sample would fail to stabilize as successive groups of data were collected.

REPRESENTATIVENESS

The *representativeness* of a sample refers to the degree of similarity between the characteristics of the sample and the characteristics of the universe from which the sample was drawn. Ideally, the characteristics with which the sample study is concerned should be found in the sample in the same proportions as they occur in the universe. If probability sampling is followed, it is presumed that the probability of occurrence of the various characteristics in the universe will appear in the sample. Thus, a probability sample may be expected to be representative of the universe.

The two major reasons for inaccuracy in samples are: (1) the human factor or bias and (2) distortion due to the selection system. The human factor or bias is caused by the tendency of the research worker or field case worker in selecting cases to choose, for example, friends or acquaintances; friendly persons; intelligent-appearing persons; objects or persons who are painted or dressed in pleasing colors; persons who are willing to supply information because they are not busy, or are at home, or are cooperative;

persons or objects found in convenient places, on shady sides of streets, in better or more familiar parts of town; persons who are good looking, of the opposite or same sex; persons or objects available at convenient times of day, week, or year; and so forth. Often the personal biases and preferences that are so damaging to the process of sampling are not fully recognized even by the researcher or field case worker himself. This fact makes it all the more important that a sampling technique be adopted that eliminates the human factor as much as possible.

The inaccuracy due to the selection system itself, called *distortion*, can arise from any conditions which cause a sampling plan to draw too heavily from certain types of cases in the universe. Sometimes the distortion is due to the fact that not all the universe is covered in the sampling either because the universe was not clearly defined and located or because the system of selection did not allow all cases the same probability of being chosen. Suppose that the families in a sample were to be selected by one of the following procedures: from the telephone directory, from names on automobile registration file cards in the county courthouse, from school lists of parents and guardians of school children, or by interviews with persons at home during the afternoons of a certain week. None of these procedures would completely cover all of the families in a city or give every family an equal chance of being selected because some families do not have telephones, registered automobiles, children in school, or some person at home every afternoon.

To avoid biased, distorted samples, the sampling technique must provide for definite, standardized procedures that will insure a probability sample being chosen.

VALIDATION PROCEDURES

The process of determining the representativeness of a sample is sometimes called *validation*. Ordinarily, four or five factors would be a minimum number of validation characteristics to be used in testing a sample for representativeness. The specific factors to be used will depend on the particular survey being conducted. It is desirable to use factors that are considered to have some importance in the problem being studied. Sometimes, however, it is not possible to use the most significant factors because the distribution of these factors in the universe is not known. In such a situation, certain other known factors will have to be used even though they are of lesser importance. The use of *validation questions* in questionnaires has already been discussed. These validation questions are used for the purpose of comparing the proportions of answers in the questionnaires constituting the sample to the proportions known to exist in the universe.

The factors used to determine the representativeness of a sample should be independent of one another. For example, the number of cars per family and the number of income earners in a family are not necessarily independent factors. Number of persons living in a household and brand of coffee used in that household will usually be examples of relatively unrelated or independent factors. The reason that the factors should be independent is that it is desirable to test for representativeness by the use of as many different kinds of factors as is feasible. If these factors are not independent, but instead dependent on one another, the result is that they actually constitute one factor only.

The U.S. Bureau of Census reports, being exceedingly complete and complex reports of all kinds of characteristics of the population, are usually the source of validation data. One of the most important of the possible uses of the various federal censuses is to supply information about the people, businesses, and other characteristics of the nation that can be used in planning surveys and in testing samples for extent of representativeness. Unfortunately, however, the census reports are often not published until a year or more after the census has been taken. Also, the censuses are conducted infrequently so that some of the data are probably out of date at the time a business research project is undertaken. If, however, federal census data are unavailable or inadequate to use as validation data, it is often possible to find some other data about the frequency and distribution of certain characteristics of the universe to be sampled. The data may be in customer records of businesses, in private censuses that have been conducted either by trade associations or by chambers of commerce, in reports or records of associations of the types of persons or businesses that might compose the universe in which the researcher is interested, in city or telephone directories or business or professional directories, in socio-economic data books, and in some special studies in libraries.

In general, the procedure to follow in validation is to compute the proportion of the characteristic being used for validation in the sample and compare that proportion as it exists in the universe from which the sample was drawn based on data from the federal census or other accepted source to represent the universe. When four or five such factors are found to be validated, it may be assumed by the researcher that other factors in the sample will be representative of the universe. This is the basis of the validation procedure.

Exhibit 10-1 illustrates an effective tabular method of presenting a comparison between selected characteristics in a sample and the universe from which the sample was drawn. Such a table can be used to show the degree of conformity between the sample and its universe. The extent of the similarity of the sample and the universe or the degree of representativeness of the sample are shown in the column headed "Difference." The research director or users of the research findings will need to decide whether the differences are small enough to make the sample results acceptable for decision making purposes.

THE PROBLEM OF NONRESPONSE

The problem called *nonresponse* sometimes arises in surveys. It often will be found that, when a survey is conducted, only a small proportion of the contacted respondents will actually respond by returning the questionnaires. In such a case, the question arises as to whether the respondents are representative of the universe which they are purported to represent.

EXHIBIT 10-1
Comparison of Sample with Universe-Degree
of Representativeness

Factor	Sample (Hypothetical)	Universe (Source: 1970 U.S. Census Dallas SMSA)	Difference (Percent)
1. Median family income	$10,631	$10,019	6.1
2. Median number school years completed by persons twenty-five and over	12.4	12.2	1.6
3. Average number persons per occupied housing unit	2.6	2.7	3.7
4. Median age of population	25.6	26.3	2.7

The problem is one of attempting to gauge the nonrespondents' characteristics in the light of the respondents' characteristics. If there happens to be evidence or knowledge on the part of the researcher that the nonrespondents would have the same characteristics as the respondents, then no further action is necessary. However, if such information is not available, and the facts are not known, then a second survey may be necessary, called *follow-up procedures*. Follow-up procedures are conducted in order to get further sampling of the section of the sample that did not respond in the first place. Such follow-up procedures are sometimes conducted by telephone survey methods, sometimes by mail methods, sometimes by personal interview. After a sample is forthcoming from the group of nonrespondents, it is evident that two samples will exist. Sometimes a chi-square test of the two distributions will yield a definitive result as to whether or not the two distributions differ or are alike in respect to the chief characteristics under study. The chi-square test is a powerful tool for such a purpose. Where more than two such samples are drawn, i.e., several successive samples, they are sometimes designated as *replications*. Such replications are successive or duplicate samples independently selected from the same population. Chi-square tests may be conducted among them; sometimes analysis of variance tests are conducted among them to test the significance of the difference among the means of certain characteristics among the replications. If no differences are found among nonrespondents and respondents, the separate samples or replications are added together. When they differ markedly, separate analysis may become necessary, since different populations are involved. In all such cases, the effort is directed toward securing representativeness in the total research study.

SAMPLING TECHNIQUES

Most sampling selection techniques provide that the sample be a probability sample, which has already been defined as one in which each item in the universe has had an equal chance of being chosen and, further, that a given sample selected was selected in such a manner that each such sample that could exist in the universe had an equal chance of being chosen. The term *random sample* and sometimes the term *simple random sample* have been applied to such probability samples. Since randomness in the selection of the sample would insure that pure chance dictated the selection of each item, the sample would be made up according to the laws of probability.

Sometimes very elementary methods of selection are used, such as drawing playing cards from a deck with only certain numbers chosen; or taking numbers from a hat; or choosing among slips of paper of different lengths. Such simple random techniques are usually not used, however, giving way in favor of more sophisticated methods, such as the use of a table of random numbers. The *Table of 105,000 Random Decimal Digits* published by the Interstate Commerce Commission is such a table. The first three pages of this table are reproduced in Appendix E, "5-Digit Random Numbers." Its use requires that the universe be numbered, since a pattern of systematic selection of the random numbers from the table provides that numbered cases be selected from a given universe. Such a table of random numbers is useful when sampling accounting records, purchase orders, sales slips, and all other such accounting or financial data that are ordinarily numbered.

The table may be used by simply selecting each number in sequence, or every fifth number, or every tenth, or taking a pattern from every other column—these examples indicate that the numbers selected from a random number table must be selected by some systematic method. The numbers must not be selected at random from the random number table because such a procedure may contribute to runs of certain digits or regular recurrence of digits, thus damaging the randomness of the table. Where a universe consists of only hundreds of items, the first three digits of the 5-digit numbers may be used, or the middle three, or the last three; and where large universes exist, for instance of 100,000 items or more, columns may simply be combined, using the doubled columns throughout.

Most computer centers will have, as part of their *software*, a *subprogram* (sometimes called a *subroutine*) known as *random number generator*. A random number generator will consist of a few cards which may be inserted in a program; sometimes it will consist of a section of a tape which may be called into a given program when a random number is needed. The random number will be computed and furnished to the program by the subroutine, and then the regular program continued. Such a random number generator may be used to generate a series of random numbers which may then be employed as the numbers of the items to be selected from a universe to go into a sample. In this case, also, a universe consisting of numbered cases is required.

There are other specific techniques for securing probability samples under different conditions and for specific kinds of research studies. These are explained in some detail in the following paragraphs.

AREA SAMPLING

In *area sampling*, the universe is divided into geographic areas, some of which are then chosen on a probability basis for the purpose of establishing areas from which sample members are to be drawn. For example, a transparent sheet with a grid system of lines could be laid over a city map. The grid system would divide the city into, say, 100 areas of equal size. These areas would be numbered. A certain number of the areas would be chosen on a probability basis. The chosen areas, then, would be the ones in which the interviews or observations would occur.

In actual practice, a sound system of choosing the sample areas must (1) give all areas an equal chance of being chosen, and (2) provide that the areas selected compose a representative sample of the universe.

An illustration of area sampling follows, step by step, in the usual order in which the steps would be taken. The sample is assumed to be composed of interviews with the homemakers of a city. The interviews are to occur at the residences of the respondents.

1. Determine how many cases are needed in the sample, usually by one of the mathematical methods explained earlier in this chapter in the section "Adequacy." Suppose that the size of the sample is set at 100.
2. Divide the city into a certain number of areas. To accomplish this, assume that the superimposed grid system plan is followed, and that the city is thereby divided into 100 areas of equal size. Suppose that 23 of these areas are found to be composed of business and other nonresidential districts, leaving 77 areas in the actual universe from which the sample is to be drawn. These 77 areas would then be numbered from 1 to 77.
3. Estimate, as closely as possible, the average number of cases (dwelling units) in each of the 77 individual areas in the universe. Let it be assumed that the average number of dwelling units in each of the 77 areas is estimated to be 85. These estimates can be based on house counts in certain blocks throughout the city, from study of plats in the city engineering office, from tax and real estate data maps, from block statistics shown for the larger cities in federal census reports, and from accurate aerial maps.
4. Determine the number of sample areas to be chosen and the interval between the residences at which interviews are to be obtained. This would be done by considering the number of cases needed in the sample and the average number of cases included in each of the 77 sample areas. The size of the sample was set at 100 interviews, and the average number of residences in each of the 77 areas estimated to be 85. Thus, if 11 areas were selected for the general sample, there would be 11 × 85 or 935 dwelling units in the 11 sample areas. When the number of cases in the 11 areas to be sampled, 935, is divided by the desired sample size of 100, it is seen that the interval between the

residences should be between 9 and 10; or 935 ÷ 100 = 9.35. If the interval between the residences at which interviews are to be obtained is set at 9, the number of interviews in the sample would be approximately 100, or to be more exact, 104 (935 ÷ 9 = 104).

5. The next step would be to select the particular 11 areas to be covered in the general sample. First, the interval between the numbers of the areas to be included in the sample would be established by dividing the number of areas in the universe, 77 here, by the number of areas from which it is desired to draw the sample members, 11 in this illustration. The interval would be found to be 7 (77 ÷ 11 = 7). Then, a number would be randomly selected from slips of paper numbered from 1 to 7 to determine the first area to be chosen for the sample. Suppose that the number selected was 3. Since the number of the first sample area drawn is 3, and the interval is 7, the second area would be number 10, the third 17, and so forth until all 11 areas had been selected.

This systematic-interval method of selecting sample areas is usually superior to other methods because such methods as pulling all of the area numbers from a hat, or throwing dimes on a map, or even using a table of random numbers, can often result in sample areas being clustered in certain parts of the universe. The systematic-interval method assures that all portions of the universe will be included because the sample areas will be well scattered over the universe.

6. Finally, determine the actual residences to be included in the sample. The selection of the individual dwelling units to be visited in the 11 areas chosen in step 5 would follow the pattern established in step 4, that is, every ninth unit in each sample area would be selected for interviewing. The field interviewer would be required to visit every ninth dwelling unit, that is, single houses and living units in multiple unit buildings. The research director could select the addresses and furnish a list and street map to the interviewer. Or, the interviewer could be instructed how to start at a given address and systematically walk through the entire area stopping at each ninth address he comes to after the starting address given him by the research director.

The starting point may be marked on a street map and the route of travel also be drawn through all streets or portions of streets bordering the blocks to be covered. The interviewer may be instructed to find each address on his list and to interview an adult member of the household. If no adult is at home, the interviewer is usually instructed to return one time. If no interview can be obtained on this second attempt, the next dwelling unit in the direction of travel along the interview route will be substituted for the originally selected unit. If no interview is obtained in the substitute dwelling, usually no more attempts will be made to substitute for he originally selected household, even though this practice results in the reduction of the number of households included in the sample. Excessive substitutions can result in an unrepresentative sample with a disproportionate number of households with retired persons, nonworking adults, or other "stay-at-homes."

If it is not possible to supply interviewers with the names and addresses of the households where the interviews are to be obtained, the interviewers can be told to go to an intersection of two streets marked on an interviewer's map. The first house to be visited could be designated as the one nearest the northeast corner of the marked block. Thereafter every ninth (or whatever interval is chosen to obtain the size of sample needed) dwelling unit whether in a single family house or a multiple unit building would be visited. The interviewer would travel around the block counterclockwise. All the marked blocks on the map would be covered in this manner. In apartment houses, the top floors would be visited first and the counting and selection of dwelling units would be made by starting at the apartment with the highest number on the top floor and continuing to the lower floors. Dwelling units in backyards should be included in the counting and interviewing procedures.

SYSTEMATIC SAMPLING

Systematic selection is a term applied to the process of choosing the cases in a sample by a predetermined plan of selection. An example would be selecting every nth card from files covering a universe of 3,000 file cards containing information in which the researcher is interested. The cases in this universe may be numbered or counted off and every 25th case chosen for the sample. The interval between the cases, then, would be 25; and hence if the first case chosen at random was number 17, the second would be 42, the third 67, and so on. The size of the interval will depend on the number of cases in the universe and the size of the sample desired. In a universe of 3,000 cases from which a sample of 120 was to be drawn, the interval would be 25, counted as follows: $3,000 \div 120 = 25$.

As can be seen from this brief description, systematic selection is not an entirely separate and distinct sampling technique. Actually, it is a procedure for choosing individual cases in a sample that can be used in conjunction with various sampling techniques. In fact, true probability sampling will require the use of a plan of systematic selection. The need to get a sample that is free from the bias and personal preferences of field and other research workers will dictate the use of some procedure of systematic selection.

In a broad sense, systematic selection could be applied to various planned procedures for determining the particular cases to be included in a sample, whether the universe is numbered or not. Suppose that a 20 percent sample of gasoline filling stations in a city was to be obtained in a survey. The process of selecting the stations could involve stopping at every fifth station passed as the observer drove along each street in the area. If a list of the addresses of all filling stations was available, every fifth address could be chosen for the sample.

If the population to be interviewed or observed was customers in a department store, the observer would need to have a selection plan to follow. He might stand at various predetermined locations throughout the store for certain periods of time. He could be instructed to select first the person farthest to his right as he faced the front of the store and looked directly ahead. When that interview was completed, he would be expected to return to his former position, and then to select the person on his extreme left. This procedure would be continued in each location for the required periods of time, or perhaps until a given number of interviews had been completed in each location. The exact procedure would depend on the nature of the project and type of sample desired.

When a manufacturer desires to sample his output, or to sample items that he may want to purchase in large quantity, a systematic sampling plan can be of value. He may need to weigh, measure, or test in some manner the items involved. His procedure for selecting the items to be tested must assure him that he will obtain a representative sample. If the items are numbered or arranged in stacks, or are coming along an assembly line, it may be relatively easy to use a systematic selection plan.

The person selecting the sample cases must realize, of course, that the items available to him at any given time may not be representative of all the items in which he is actually interested (the universe). The quality of a series of products moving along an assembly line may vary from time to time. The items to be tested may be stacked in a warehouse in such a way that the newer or better items are placed in front, on top, or at the back. The selection system, therefore, must include whatever procedures are necessary to obtain a sample that is drawn from all parts of the universe and in the correct proportions to reflect accurately the characteristics of the universe. To accomplish this, the cases may have to be chosen at different times and from various locations.

DOUBLE SAMPLING

Double sampling refers to a procedure in which a certain proportion of the cases of a larger sample are again interviewed or observed in a second survey. The purpose of the second survey is to obtain added information from cases with special characteristics of particular significance to the researcher. The main reason for the first, larger sample may be to discover the relative frequency and the location of the cases to be studied in greater detail in the second survey.

The directors of an adult education television program wanted to know what types of persons watched the program and what they thought about it. In order to locate a sample of persons who had seen the program, a telephone inquiry survey was conducted. For three successive weeks, persons were called during the half-hour period that the weekly program was on the air. This first, larger survey provided such information as the percentage of homes with television sets, the percentage of the sets that were in use, the percentage of the television audience watching each program on the air at the time of the call, and the number of persons who were viewing the adult education program. The names and addresses of these viewers were then used to compile a second sample of persons to be visited and personally interviewed in greater detail about their reactions to the program. It was realized that homes with telephones were not representative of all homes in the city, but it was assumed that the television program concerned was of a type that would be viewed almost entirely by persons in the socio-economic group that would be listed in the telephone directory. The persons who were discovered in the telephone inquiry to be viewers of the adult education television program were, therefore, considered to be a representative sample of the persons who watched this program.

MULTIPHASE SAMPLING

Multiphase sampling is a type of sampling in which the added information desired from certain cases is obtained in the first contact instead of being secured in a second survey. Two types of situations may call for a multiphase sample:

1. When it is desired to obtain certain data about all the cases in a large sample, at the same time that more detailed information is required from those cases found to possess a given set of characteristics.
2. When the amount of information desired is so large that it would be too time consuming and costly to ask for all of the data from each respondent. Therefore, only every third or some other proportion of the respondents would be asked certain questions.

The multiphase technique is appropriate only in surveys in which the general sample is large enough that the subsamples in which the added questions are asked will be large enough themselves to constitute a significant number of cases.

Suppose that the main purpose of a survey is to obtain information from users of mechanical household water softeners. One thousand dwelling units are visited and certain questions are asked at each house. In those homes with mechanical water softeners, additional questions are asked about the experiences and opinions of the respondents in regard to these softeners. If 15 percent of the dwelling units in the universe have water softeners, the subsample of users will contain 150 cases itself, which may be quite ample as far as size is concerned.

The major purpose of a survey may be to collect all the information possible without having to spend too much money or time on the project. The questionnaire may contain thirty questions, but only every third respondent will be asked to answer all thirty. The rest of the respondents are not asked the last ten questions. A variation of this approach would be to alternate the questions. The first fifteen questions would be asked every other respondent, and the second fifteen would be asked of the rest of the respondents.

In these illustrations, it should be remembered that the general sample would have to be rather large or else the subsamples would probably be too small to provide a group of sufficient size for analysis. There are some instances, however, even in the cases of smaller business firms, in which the universe may be quite large, and the general sample consequently can be large, also. For instance, suppose that it is desired to observe and test a product that is being produced at the rate of several thousands of units daily. The testing procedure could be based on a multiphase sampling technique that would select perhaps 500 items over a period of time. All

500 items could be put through, say, three simple tests, while only every fifth item, or a total of 100, would be subjected to six additional more expensive and time-consuming tests.

DISPROPORTIONATE SAMPLING

Disproportionate sampling is a technique for selecting cases that intentionally allows certain types of cases to be numerically overrepresented in the sample. For instance, a certain type of case that is known to compose, say, 10 percent of the cases in the universe could be deliberately collected in a disproportionate sample in such a manner that they constitute 20 percent of the sample. Three conditions under which a disproportionate selection pattern may be especially appropriate are:

1. When the universe contains some small but important subgroups.
2. When certain subgroups are quite heterogeneous while others are homogeneous.
3. When it is expected that there will be an appreciable difference in the response rates of the several subgroups in the universe.

When the universe is composed of some subgroups that constitute a very small part of the total, a proportional sample would include too few of the cases in these subsamples to enable significant analysis to be made of the findings for these subgroups. To illustrate, let it be assumed that a survey is being planned to cover four classes of employees in a factory, the smallest class containing only 200 men or 2 percent out of 10,000 men in the plant. A total sample of 500 men is to be obtained. In a proportional sample of 500, the quota for the men in the class with 200 would be only 10 men (2 percent of 500 = 10). This subsample is so small that the probable margin of error inherent in it would be very large. Little accurate information, therefore, could be obtained about this class of 200 employees. Consequently, this small class of 200 men would be sampled disproportionately; that is, their numerical quota would be raised from 10 men to perhaps 30 men. The assumption is that these 30 men would be enough to supply satisfactory information about their subuniverse of the 200 workers in that class.

Disproportionate sampling undertaken for the purpose of increasing the number of cases in small subgroups may be especially useful when the small subgroups are composed of persons or cases of considerable importance. In the example given in the preceding paragraph, the small class of employees which constituted only 2 percent of the total might have been such a key group as foremen, supervisors, or engineers.

When the cases in the universe fall into several different classes that vary in degree of heterogeneity, the more heterogeneous classes may have to be sampled disproportionately. For instance, suppose that it is known that there are four classes of persons who use a certain consumer product. It is also known that the persons in three of these classes compose rather homogeneous groups; that is, all the persons in each of these three classes have about the same level of income, plane of living, and type of occupation. On the other hand, the fourth class of persons to be included in the proposed sample are known to be a quite heterogeneous group, composed of various levels of income, planes of living, and occupations. Under these conditions, it may be necessary to get a larger than proportional quota of this heterogeneous fourth class in the sample in order to give all the different types of persons a chance to be represented in the subsample for this class.

When it is expected that there will be an appreciable difference in the response rates of the several subgroups in the universe, a third type of situation is found which may require disproportionate sampling. For example, in a mail survey, it might be assumed that certain types of respondents, say, manual workers, may be only one-fourth as likely to respond as will the other persons in the universe. The number of questionnaires mailed to manual workers, therefore, would have to be four times as large as the proportion of the universe that is assumed to be composed of manual workers. Or to put it another way, four times as many questionnaires will have to be mailed to manual workers in order to induce one to respond as will be required to obtain a reply from other types of persons in the sample.

If a disproportionate sample has been obtained in a survey, corrections for these overrepresented quotas must be made when averages and totals are being calculated for the whole sample. For instance, in the case of the 10,000 employees in the earlier example, suppose that it is desired to determine the percentage who want a pension plan. If there are three times as many supervisors proportionally in the sample as there are in the plant (the universe), then the answers of these supervisors will have to be weighted downward by the proportionate amount of their overrepresentation. This could be done by counting the answer of each supervisor as one-third of a full answer, or in proportion to whatever the excess was of the quota granted to supervisors in the sample.

Disproportionate sampling ordinarily is inadvisable for universes with unknown proportions of characteristics because correctly sized proportions for the samples cannot be determined. This difficulty may occur in the use of any kind of quota, proportionate, or disproportionate sampling procedure. It must be remembered that disproportionate sampling, when it is appropriate, has as its main purpose the facilitation of the analysis of subsamples. Its use, however, must not be allowed to unbalance the final calculations of averages and totals derived from the whole sample.

SUMMARY

Sampling procedures require that a statistically adequate sample be collected—one that is large enough that inferences will be accurate to a given level of probability. It must also be representative of the universe. To achieve representativeness, most samples are *probability samples*. A probability sample is one in which each item in the universe had an equal chance of being chosen for the sample.

Adequacy refers to such a size of sample that a given level of probability can be attached to the inference. Where a sample mean is to be inferred to a universe, or where a test of significance of the difference between a mean estimated from a sample and a universe mean is to be made, the following formula may be used to compute the sample size:

$$n = \left(\frac{\sigma}{\frac{\overline{X} - u}{z}} \right)^2$$

In the analysis of variance this formula may be applied to one of the samples in respect to the deviation of that one mean to the grand mean of all of the samples. The same sample size can then be used for the other samples.

When it is desired to test the significance of the difference in the means computed from two samples, the following formula is used for sample size:

$$n = \frac{2\sigma^2}{\left(\frac{\overline{X}_1 - \overline{X}_2}{z} \right)^2}$$

Very often the size of sample computed from this formula, or the first formula, will be small ($n < 30$). In this case, the value of z will not be obtained from the areas under the normal curve. Student's t-distribution applies, and therefore the value of z will have to be obtained from Student's t-distribution. The size of sample is recomputed. If the sample size is different, the new z-value is inserted, and a new sample size is computed. The sample size will stabilize at some number below $n = 30$.

For a test of significance between a sample estimate and a universe proportion, or to estimate a universe proportion to a given level of confidence, the following formula will give the size of sample:

$$n = \frac{pq}{\left(\frac{p - P}{z} \right)^2}$$

Where two sample proportion estimates are to be tested for significance of difference, the variation in the formula gives:

$$n = \frac{2pq}{\left(\frac{p_1 - p_2}{z} \right)^2}$$

Proportions have no small sample theory; therefore Student's t-distribution is not used. Sample sizes for proportions are large, numbering in the hundreds and even thousands.

When the size of the universe is known, the standard error may be reduced by considering the ratio of the size of sample to the size of the universe. This will narrow confidence limits and will "tighten up" the test of significance. For arithmetic means, when this adjustment is included, the sample size is computed as follows:

$$n = \frac{1}{\left(\dfrac{\overline{X} - \mu}{\sigma z}\right)^2 + \dfrac{1}{N}}$$

For proportions, the following formula is used when the size of universe is known:

$$n = \frac{pq}{\left(\dfrac{p - P}{z}\right)^2 + \dfrac{pq}{N}}$$

On occasion, a technique called *sequential analysis sampling* may be applied. In this case, sequential samples are taken and the mean or proportion computed; the subsequent sample results are incorporated with the preceding results until the mean or proportion does not change with any further samples. At this point sampling ends because the sampling is sufficient.

The subject of representativeness refers to the degree of similarity between the characteristics in the sample and those same characteristics in the universe. Inaccuracy in samples can result from (1) the human factor, or bias, or (2) distortion due to the selection system. If the sample is truly representative of the universe, these two inaccuracies will be optimally reduced.

To test for representativeness, validation procedures may be used. Specific answers on questionnaires or in interviews may give information so that proportions of certain characteristics in the sample may be compared to known proportions in the universe, for example from U.S. census data. If there is no difference in the characteristic—median income, or age group, for example—the sample may be *validated*.

The problem of nonresponse in surveys—lack of returns for some part or parts of a universe—may be resolved by follow-up sampling. If the same results are obtained when resampling occurs, the new data are simply included in the total, and nonresponse has no effect. If they differ, new studies or surveys may be required, or the study broken into separate parts.

Certain sampling techniques may be listed as follows: (1) area sampling, in which the universe is broken up geographically for sampling; (2) systematic sampling in which cases are chosen by some predetermined plan of selection; (3) double sampling, in which a certain proportion of the cases are observed again in a second survey; (4) multiphase sampling, which involves collecting more information from certain responders than from others; (5) disproportionate sampling, a technique of intentionally selecting larger proportions of data from the smaller segments of a heterogeneous universe so that the smaller segments are adequately represented.

EXERCISES

1. Describe the procedure of probability sampling. What is its effect?
2. Explain each of the following concepts:
   a. representativeness
   b. adequacy
3. The size of sample must be determined for a quality-control procedure to maintain the proper weight of 10-pound packages. The estimate of variation obtained from the supervisor is interpreted as a standard deviation of 1.5 ounces. An error of .5 ounce on either side of the universe mean (10 pounds) is to be permitted at the .05 significance level. What size sample is needed for the quality-control test procedure?
4. In order to estimate the average sale price charged by retailers of his product, a manufacturer adopts a standard deviation of $.50 based on past experience, and a confidence interval of $.15 at the .95 confidence level. What size sample is required? (Use .95 confidence level as 2σ instead of 1.96σ).
5. How may sample size be determined for an analysis of variance experiment?
6. A multiplant firm wishes to test the charge that hourly wage rates of common labor differ in two of its plants in the Eastern region. It is desired to detect a difference of $.06 per hour in the two averages at the .95 confidence level (use $.95 = 2\sigma$). U.S. Department of Labor statistics show a standard deviation of $.12 for previous similar studies. What size sample should be collected from each plant?
7. Cast steel braces for machine-tool installations must have a breaking strength of at least 2,000 pounds. They are purchased from a subcontractor who specializes in such parts. To test for the minimum strength, the firm establishes a 60-pound deviation of the sample mean from the universe mean of 2,000 pounds as satisfactory. A standard deviation of 90 pounds is adopted from historical records. At the .05 level for a one-tailed test, what size sample is required? He needs as small a sample as possible because the braces are destroyed when tested.
8. To estimate the percentage of credit customers that would wish a department store to begin using credit cards, a sample size is needed in order to make a sampling study. Since no information exists concerning the percentage, $p = 50$ percent is adopted. A confidence interval of 5 percent will be permitted, with a 10 percent critical probability. Compute the sample size.
9. Suppose that the department store in exercise 8 had only 1,000 credit customers to survey. They could survey them all, of course; but they would prefer a sample. With this additional information, recompute the sample size.
10. To test the effectiveness of an orientation program for new employees, a firm wishes to compare a control group of employees who have *not* experienced the program to an experimental group who *have* experienced the program. Percentage scores on a test will be compared. It is estimated that 80 percent of employees should pass the test. A difference of 10 percent needs to be detected at the .05 level of significance. What is the number of emloyees to be sampled in each group?
11. In exercise 10, suppose there were several hundred employees available for the control group, but only 100 employees had been through the orientation program. Recompute the sample size.
12. "Sequential analysis sampling is a data-collection technique that makes it possible during the sampling process to determine when the sample is large enough." Explain how this is done.
13. How can inaccuracy in sampling be avoided?
14. Define validation in your own words. Explain how it may be accomplished.

15. How may the problem of nonresponse be handled? Explain explicitly.
16. What effect does randomness in the selection of sample observations have on the sampling procedure?
17. Describe each of the following in a brief, succinct statement:
    a. area sampling
    b. systematic sampling
    c. double sampling
18. What is the usefulness of multiphase sampling? When should it be employed?
19. What is the difficulty in a research project that disproportionate sampling can overcome?

SELECTED REFERENCES

Balsley, Howard L. *Basic Statistics for Business and Economics*. Columbus, Ohio: Grid, 1978.

Balsley, Howard L. *Quantitative Research Methods for Business and Economics*. New York: Random House, 1970.

Mendenhall, William; Ott, Lyman; and Shaeffer, Richard L. *Elementary Survey Sampling*. Belmont, Calif.: Wadsworth, 1971.

Parten, Mildred. *Surveys, Polls, and Samples: Practical Procedures*. New York: Cooper Square, 1966.

Raj, Des. *The Design of Sample Surveys*. New York: McGraw-Hill, 1972.

11

Correlation, Regression, and Trend Analysis

John Stuart Mill, in his work *A System of Logic*, defined what he called *concomitant variation* as a causal relationship between variables which, acting under like circumstances, moved in association with each other in either the same direction or opposite directions. This definition is a definition of *correlation*: measurement of the association of variables. The correlation coefficient measures the degree by which two or more variables move in association with each other, either in the same direction or in opposite directions. The measure is widely used in business research, since it is often desired to test whether two variables or more than two variables, in many cases, are associated. Rising costs may be associated with increasing wage rates; declining profits may be associated with rising wage rates when prices are not increased; number of mistakes in handling products may be associated with speed of handling. When correlation is established between two variables, one variable, if it may be defined as *dependent* on the other which therefore becomes the *independent* variable, may be predicted on the basis of known information about the independent variable. Thus, the effect on profits of an increase in wage rates may be predicted. The number of employees for summer construction may be predicted on the basis of the total value of building permits taken out in the spring for summer construction. In research, therefore, the purpose of correlation often is to enable predictions of a dependent variable from information possessed about an independent variable. The first step is to establish correlation, the second step is to define the *regression* line which describes the relationship between the two variables, and third, the regression line is projected in order to make a prediction.

The fact that a causal relationship among the variables involved in correlation analysis is often assumed when a substantial correlation among variables is discovered does not mean that the correlation study itself can reveal the nature of the causal relationship. It is true that an independent variable such as rain could cause the corn—the dependent variable—to grow, and the reverse could hardly be true. However, the relationship is not so plain for many relationships. The following relationships could exist to explain the causal association of variables:

1. One variable could cause the other to react, thus an independent variable could cause a dependent variable.
2. The two variables, if it is bivariate analysis, could act on each other, each causing the other to react.
3. Outside influences could act on both of the variables causing them to react, and neither would actually cause each other to react.
4. The variables may be found to be associated through sheer chance, in other words, no reason for their association can be discovered.

Thus, while a correlation study can determine the degree of association between two or among more than two variables, it cannot explain the causal relationship existing. Only other knowledge of an economic nature or of a social nature will enable the analyst to come to conclusions concerning the causal nature of the correlation of the variables.

It has already been mentioned that the correlation of two variables could be in the same direction or in opposite directions. When two variables are associated in the same direction, the term *direct* is applied to their association; when they move in opposite directions, their association is termed *inverse correlation*. Other terms are used in correlation. *Linear correlation* refers to the correlation of two variables which is described by a straight line, whereas *nonlinear correlation* refers to the association of two variables whose relationship is described by a curved line when their values are plotted on a scatter diagram. *Simple correlation* refers to correlation between two variables, sometimes called *bivariate analysis*. *Multiple correlation* is concerned with the correlation among three or more variables simultaneously. *Partial correlation* is concerned with the correlation of two variables among three or more while the remaining variables are held constant. In this chapter, the treatment will deal with simple, linear, direct and inverse correlation. Thus, the analysis will be concerned with correlation between only two variables, and this correlation between two variables will be such as will be described by a straight line, either upward sloping or downward sloping on the mathematical grid.

The study of correlation actually deals with three separate kinds of measurements, all making up what might be called *correlation theory*:

1. The first of these is the correlation coefficient r. The correlation coefficient measures the degree of association between the two variables. Its value ranges between zero and plus or minus one. A coefficient of $+1$ would indicate perfect, positive association between two variables, and a -1 would indicate perfect, inverse association between two variables. A zero correlation, which could not be computed since any two variables being subjected to correlation analysis would yield some number other than zero, would indicate a complete lack of correlation. Thus, correlation coefficients approaching one,

plus or minus, indicate a high degree of association; correlation coefficients approaching zero, on the other hand, indicate a smaller and smaller degree of association; and correlation coefficients close to zero indicate practically no association in the variables.

2. The *regression equation* is the line which describes the association of the two variables. Where a straight line describes the association, the regression formula will be the equation for a straight line. The regression equation may be projected for prediction purposes where one variable is to be predicted based on a given value of the other variable.

3. The *standard error of the estimate* is a measure of the reliability of the regression prediction. It is analogous to the *standard error of the mean*, but instead of being a measure of dispersion around a mean, it is a measure of dispersion of observed values away from the regression line. Therefore, when a prediction is made, the standard error of the estimate may be used to estimate the confidence interval around the predicted value.

Each of these three topics will receive attention in the following paragraphs.

Besides correlation and regression, the subject of *trend analysis* will receive detailed attention in this chapter. Trend analysis is concerned with the subject of analyzing long-term trend in the affairs of business whether of a firm, of an industry, or of an economy. Trend analysis is part of time-series analysis, which includes methods of study of seasonal and cyclical aspects of time series. However, attention in this chapter will be focused exclusively on trend analysis, both nonmathematical and mathematical techniques of analyzing trend. Some attention will also be given to *lags* and *leads* for prediction or forecasting purposes in the future, which is the chief purpose of trend analysis.

The mathematical technique of straight-line curve fitting for trend analysis is the least-squares technique. This least-squares technique is the same as is employed for computing the regression equation in correlation analysis. However, whereas in correlation analysis the regression formula describes the relationship of a dependent to an independent variable, in trend analysis the trend equation describes the relationship of a variable to a time series, usually years. The least-squares technique derives its name from the fact that the sum of the squared deviations of the observations from the regression equation or the trend line will be at a minimum. Thus, the same technique can be used for a regression line or for a trend line. Some slight difference in computational method, however, will be involved between the computation of a regression line and the computation of a trend line due to the fact that the years are always equal distances apart since they are, of course, one year apart, and a simplification of the analysis is made possible by this fact.

CORRELATION AND REGRESSION

In exhibit 11-1, a scatter diagram of the relationship of two variables complete with a fitted regression line and a predicted value is presented. The situation pictured is that of the plotting on a mathematical grid of the speed in bags per minute and the percent defectives among these bags for a paper bag-making machine by Consul Paper, Limited. The black dots represent the locations of the intersection points of the variables on the mathematical grid. For example, referring to exhibit 11-2, the first value of the X-variable, "Speed in bags per minute," is 88, and the equivalent value of the Y-variable, "Percent defectives," is 8.2. These two values plotted on the chart yield the left-most black dot on the scatter diagram. The other

EXHIBIT 11-1

**Scatter Diagram and Linear Regression Line Showing
Association of Machine Speed and Percent Defectives**

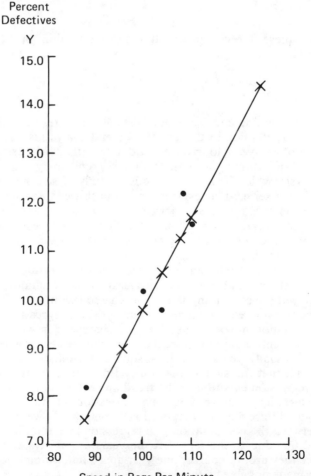

Speed in Bags Per Minute

dots were located accordingly. A scatter diagram is usually plotted in order to enable a visual inspection to take place to judge as to the kind of curve that would best describe the data. It was decided in this case that a straight line would satisfactorily describe the relationship of speed in bags per minute and percent defectives. The regression formula was computed, and the regression line fitted. The X's located on the regression line, it is seen, are vertically opposite their respective dots. The locations of these X's represent the straight line. A prediction has been made of the percent defectives, given that speed in bags per minute was 124. In such a case, it is seen that the percentage defectives to be expected would be 14.4, reading from the chart.

The technique of regression analysis will be discussed at length after attention is given to correlation analysis. The regression line was included in exhibit 11-1 in order to show that the relationship of the two variables may be indeed described by a straight line. At this point, the student should pay attention to the fact that it appears that the straight line does satisfactorily describe the relationship of the two variables, "Speed in bags per minute," and "Percent defectives."

LINEAR CORRELATION

It has already been explained that a rather usual procedure in research is to explore the correlation between two variables and if a satisfactory correlation is discovered, to compute the regression equation and then make the prediction of the value of the dependent variable based upon an estimate of the independent variable, presuming of course that the prediction requirement was the aim of the research. The research may indeed be simply for the purpose of discovering the sheer association of variables—in other words, it may be concerned solely with correlation. Whether or not the research is concerned solely with correlation, or the correlation is studied in order to establish if sufficient correlation exists for predictions to be made, the following formula will be useful for either direct or inverse linear correlation:

$$r = \frac{\Sigma xy}{N \sigma_X \sigma_Y}$$

where: r = Pearsonian coefficient of correlation

xy = products of the deviations of the values of the variables from their arithmetic means ($x = X - \overline{X}$ and $y = Y - \overline{Y}$ for each pair)

N = number of observations

σ_X = standard deviation of the X-variable, $\sqrt{\dfrac{\Sigma x^2}{N}}$

σ_Y = standard deviation of the Y-variable, $\sqrt{\dfrac{\Sigma y^2}{N}}$

The situation described earlier for exhibit 11-1 is explained in more detail in exhibit 11-2. Speed in bags per minute is listed with the equivalent percent defectives for each speed. The normal operating procedure for a paper bag-making machine producing, for example, one-pound or two-pound brown paper bags, is to start a run by turning on the machine and continuing by varying speeds, until heavy amounts of defectives cease to appear. The first bags produced will be, to a large extent, waste. It is only after a given speed has been achieved and the machine has stabilized its speed that the run will begin to become successful. When this condition is achieved, the operator generally tends to leave the machine alone until the entire run is completed. The question here, however, is to experiment with different set speeds for the machine, and having completed these experiments with different set speeds of the machine, different percents of defectives have been discovered. If a positive, that is, direct correlation, is discovered between the speed of the machine and the percent of defectives, then it will be the task of the engineer or supervisor to seek a speed such that the costs will be balanced so that the yield of bags will be maximized in terms of either output or profit, whatever the criterion may be.

EXHIBIT 11-2
Correlation of Speed of Machine and Percent Defectives for Bag-Making Machine, Consul Paper, Ltd.

X Speed in Bags per Minute	Y Percent Defectives	x $(X - \bar{X})$	y $(Y - \bar{Y})$	x^2	y^2	xy
88	8.2	-13	-1.8	169	3.24	$+23.4$
96	8.0	-5	-2.0	25	4.00	$+10.0$
100	10.2	-1	$+.2$	1	.04	$-.2$
104	9.8	$+3$	$-.2$	9	.04	$-.6$
108	12.2	$+7$	$+2.2$	49	4.84	$+15.4$
110	11.6	$+9$	$+1.6$	81	2.56	$+14.4$
$6\lfloor 606$	$6\lfloor 60.0$			334	14.72	$+63.2$
$\bar{X} = 101$	$\bar{Y} = 10$					$-.8$
						62.4

$$r = \frac{\Sigma xy}{N \, \sigma_X \, \sigma_Y} = \frac{62.4}{6 \times 7.46 \times 1.57} = \frac{62.4}{70.2732}$$
$$= .888 \text{ rounded} = .89$$

where: $\sigma_X = \sqrt{\frac{\Sigma x^2}{N}} = \sqrt{\frac{334}{6}} = \sqrt{55.6667} = 7.46$

$\sigma_Y = \sqrt{\frac{\Sigma y^2}{N}} = \sqrt{\frac{14.72}{6}} = \sqrt{2.4533} = 1.57$

In exhibit 11-2, the computation of the correlation coefficient has been completed. The computations are included below the data, and the columns are carried out. The standard deviation of the X-variable was found to be 7.46; the standard deviation of the Y-variable was found to be 1.57. These standard deviations, besides being used in the computation of the correlation coefficient r, will also be used in computing the regression equation later. The correlation coefficient r equals .89 and represents a substantial direct correlation. The anlayst would note, of course, that only six observations are included in this study, and this is certainly a sparse number of observations upon which to base any conclusions. However, given that this is all the data he has, he would conclude that the correlation was probably substantial. An r equal to .89 approaches closely toward 1, which would be perfect correlation. In this situation, the causal relationship could be only one: the changing speed of the machine could account for the percent defectives; the reverse could not possibly be true. Therefore, it is evident that increasing the speed of the machine increases the percent defectives in a given production run. Decisions might subsequently be called for in deciding on the proper speed of the machine, yielding a given percent defectives, in order to maximize output at a given percent defectives considering the number of bags produced per unit of time, the cost of the supervisor's time, the cost of labor, and so forth to arrive at an optimum in some kind of cost mix.

Suppose that by installing improved parts in the machine and overhauling the machine, a new and higher speed could be achieved. It would be expected that a higher percent of defectives would be produced at a new, higher speed. A higher speed could possibly be feasible from the point of view of the considerably greater production per unit of time in spite of the increased percent of defectives that would be yielded and thus might possibly be a wise course of action. The information would be requested, therefore: What percent defectives could be expected at the new speed? The result can be determined by a prediction based upon regression analysis.

The Regression Formula

One of the standard formulas for computing the regression line for a given problem follows:

$$Y_C = a + bx$$

where: Y_C = values of the Y-variable fitted to the X-variable

$$a = \frac{\Sigma Y}{N}$$

$$b = \frac{\Sigma xY}{\Sigma x^2}$$

and: $x = X - \overline{X}$

however: $b = \frac{\sigma_Y}{\sigma_X} \times r_{YX}$

The statement $Y_C = a + bx$ is, of course, the basic formula for a straight line. The constant a is obviously the arithmetic mean of the Y series. The constant b is a computed value representing the slope of the regression line, and this constant is multiplied by x which in turn represents the deviation of the given value of X from the mean of X, that is, $X - \overline{X}$. However, it is noted in the formula that the slope b also can be computed by dividing the standard deviation of the Y series by the standard deviation of the X series and multiplying by the correlation coefficient. Since these values had already been computed in the correlation analysis for the given problem of Consul Paper, Ltd., these values can be substituted into this formula for b, and the regression equation $Y_C = a + bx$ computed directly. The computations for deriving all of the Y_C values follow:

$$a = \frac{\Sigma Y}{N} = \frac{60.0}{6} = 10$$

$$b = \frac{\sigma_Y}{\sigma_X} \times r_{YX} = \frac{1.57}{7.46} \times .888 = \frac{1.394}{7.46} = .1869 \text{ rounded} = .19$$

$$Y_C = a + bx = 10 + .19x$$

where:
$$x = -13 \quad Y_C = 10 + .19(-13) = 10 - 2.47 = \quad 7.5 \text{ rounded}$$
$$x = -5 \quad Y_C = 10 + .19(-5) \; = 10 - \quad .95 = \quad 9.0$$
$$x = -1 \quad Y_C = 10 + .19(-1) \; = 10 - \quad .19 = \quad 9.8$$
$$x = +3 \quad Y_C = 10 + .19(+3) \; = 10 + \quad .57 = 10.6$$
$$x = +7 \quad Y_C = 10 + .19(+7) \; = 10 + 1.33 = 11.3$$
$$x = +9 \quad Y_C = 10 + .19(+9) \; = 10 + 1.71 = 11.7$$

The X-values, the Y-values, and the Y_C-values are listed as follows:

X	Y	Y_C
88	8.2	7.5
96	8.0	9.0
100	10.2	9.8
104	9.8	10.6
108	12.2	11.3
110	11.6	11.7

Referring to exhibit 11-1, the heavy black dots on the grid represent the intersections of the X- and Y-variables, while the X's on the regression line are at the intersections of the X- and Y_C-variables. Thus, the Y_C-values represent the Y-variable fitted to the X-variable. The dotted extension of the regression line in exhibit 11-1, it has already been explained, represents the projection to give a prediction of the percent defectives that would result from a given increase in the speed of the machine. The following example applies to the given prediction.

Assume that the speed of the machine in exhibit 11-1 could be increased to 124 bags per minute by installing improved parts and overhauling the machine. What percent defectives could be expected at the new speed?

$$Y_C = 10 + .19x$$
$$x = X - \overline{X} = 124 - 101 = 23$$
$$Y_C = 10 + (.19 \times 23) = 10 + 4.37 = 14.37 \text{ rounded} = 14.4$$

It is apparent that increasing the speed of the machine to 124 bags per minute will increase the percent defectives to 14.4. Referring to exhibit 11-1, this value can be checked on the grid as the prediction. If it is desired that the predicted value be stated to a given degree of reliability, it is necessary to compute the standard error of the estimate and construct a confidence interval to a given level of probability for the predicted percent defectives at the new, increased speed.

The Standard Error of the Estimate

The formula for the standard error of the estimate requires that the differences between the Y-values and the Y_C-values be squared, then summed, then divided by the number of observations, then the square root extracted. These computations are indicated in the following formula:

$$S_y = \sqrt{\frac{\Sigma(Y - Y_C)^2}{N}}$$

where: S_y = standard error of the estimate

$(Y - Y_C)^2$ = squared deviations of the observed values of Y from the fitted curve

N = number of observations

The problem posed for the Consul Paper, Ltd., in increasing the speed of their machines to 124 bags per minute with a resulting increase in the percent defectives may be considered to be one not only of predicting the per-

EXHIBIT 11-3
**Prediction of Percent Defectives to a Given Confidence
Level for an Increased Bag-Making Machine Speed**

X	Y	Y_C	$Y - Y_C$	$(Y - Y_C)^2$
88	8.2	7.5	+ .7	.49
96	8.0	9.0	-1.0	1.00
100	10.2	9.8	+ .4	.16
104	9.8	10.6	- .8	.64
108	12.2	11.3	+ .9	.81
110	11.6	11.7	- .1	.01
				3.11

$$S_y = \sqrt{\frac{\Sigma(Y - Y_C)^2}{N}} = \sqrt{\frac{3.11}{6}} = \sqrt{.5183} = .72$$

95% confidence level 5 d.f. ($N - 1$) from Student's t-distribution table = 2.571

$2.571 \times .72 = 1.85$

Predicted percent defectives of 14.37 $\pm$ 1.85 yields 12.52 and 16.22 rounded to a confidence interval of 12.5 and 16.2

cent defectives but of predicting that percent of defectives to a given level of confidence. This prediction is shown in exhibit 11-3 along with the computation of the confidence interval employing the standard error of the estimate.

The confidence level computed was 12.5 percent and 16.2 percent defectives. Thus, while the specific prediction in percent defectives for an increase in machine speed to 124 bags per minute was 14.4, this prediction is accomplished to zero degree of probability. There is a probability of 95 percent that the true prediction would lie between 12.5 percent and 16.2 percent. Thus, the analyst is able to make a statement involving a high degree of probability in the reliability of his statement.

RANK CORRELATION

There may be occasions when it is either desirable or necessary to compute the correlation coefficient of two variables, either or both being non-mathematical variables which can be placed in order of rank; such is the case with colors which may be arranged in a spectrum, to be correlated with another variable that is numerical. Another example lies in grades or assessments of performances which are given in letters such as A+, A, A−, B+, B, lending themselves to ranking, which may be correlated to another variable such as intelligence quotients. Often it is desired to correlate a dependent variable with a time series, for example, in years; this practice is fairly common to detect shifts in seasonal patterns when a given month over a period of years is suspected of increasing in importance relative to other months, as regards sales or employment or costs or some other economic factor. In such a case, the numerical variable can be correlated with the years placed in order of succession and therefore in order of rank. A standard procedure to be used in such cases is to employ *Spearman's rank correlation coefficient*. The formula for computing this coefficient of correlation follows:

$$\rho = 1 - \frac{6 \Sigma d^2}{n^3 - n}$$

where: ρ = Spearman's coefficient of rank correlation "rho"

    1 and 6 = constants

      d^2 = squared differences in the X, Y ranks

       n = number of observations

The formula for Spearman's coefficient of rank correlation obviously does not include consideration of the standard deviations and, therefore, does not include consideration of the deviations of the observed values around a regression line. For this reason, it is not considered as accurate an estimate of correlation as is the Pearsonian r computed by fitting a least-squares regression line. Its use is nearly restricted to giving an estimate of the closeness of the directional movement of a dependent variable to an independent variable without including a measurement of the fluctuation of the dependent variable around the independent. Nevertheless, rank correlation is useful when one of the variables does not lend itself to numerical calculations but does lend itself to ranking. Exhibit 11-4 presents the data on labor turnover rates in manufacturing in January for the years 1968–1977 and shows the calculation of Spearman's coefficient of rank correlation.

EXHIBIT 11-4
Labor Turnover Rates in Manufacturing in January, 1968–1977
(per 100 employees)

X Year	Y Rate	X Rank	Y Rank	d Differences in Rank	d^2 Squared Differences
1968	4.2	1	6	−5	25
69	4.6	2	10	−8	64
70	4.0	3	3.5	−.5	.25
71	3.5	4	1	3	9
72	4.1	5	5	0	0
73	4.5	6	7	−1	1
74	4.6	7	8.5	−1.5	2.25
75	4.6	8	8.5	−.5	.25
76	3.8	9	2	7	49
1977*	4.0	10	3.5	6.5	42.25
					193

$$\rho = 1 - \frac{6 \Sigma d^2}{n^3 - n} = 1 - \frac{6(193)}{10^3 - 10} = 1 - \frac{1,158}{990} = 1 - 1.17 = -.17$$

*Estimated

Source: *Monthly Labor Review* (Washington: U.S. Department of Labor), April 1973, p. 104; March 1977, p. 100.

In exhibit 11-4, the problem is to determine whether labor turnover rates in manufacturing have been increasing in the month of January over the period of years 1968–1977. Offhand, one might expect the rates to increase in an expanding economy and, therefore, would expect a coefficient of correlation approaching one. It turns out that this correlation coefficient is −.17, indicating no evidence at all of any degree of correlation. Since the correlation coefficient is so low, the conclusion is that labor turnover rates in January have not been increasing—nor decreasing—over the years in question. In this situation, rank correlation was indicated because the independent variable, the years, represented a ranking rather than numerical values to be correlated with the labor turnover rates. Note that, in converting to ranks, any ties are averaged: the third and fourth ranks of the Y-variable are added together and divided by 2, i.e., $3 + 4 = 7 \div 2 = 3.5$ each; and the eighth and ninth ranks, yielding 8.5 each.

SIMPLE REGRESSION

There may be occasions when a regression equation would need to be computed directly. A correlation may be known to exist already through other studies, perhaps by the trade association of which the firm is a member, or studies may have been made by other firms of which the analyst is aware, in which correlation between the variables under study had already been established. In any situation in which it is not necessary to compute the correlation coefficient first, the regression equation may be computed from the following formula.

$$Y_C = a + bx$$

where: $Y_C =$ values of the Y-variable fitted to the X-variable

$$a = \frac{\Sigma Y}{N}$$

$$b = \frac{\Sigma xY}{\Sigma x^2}$$

$$x = X - \overline{X}$$

The slope b is commonly written as $\frac{\Sigma xy}{\Sigma x^2}$; the computation gives the same result as $\frac{\Sigma xY}{\Sigma x^2}$, since x and y are deviations from their respective means, their sums being zero.

This formula has already been presented in previous paragraphs when it was explained how to derive the slope b from the two standard deviations and the correlation coefficient in order to secure the regression equation. Again, in the formula immediately preceding, the constant a is the simple arithmetic mean of the Y-variable, and the constant b is a computed value while x represents the deviations of each observed value of X from the mean of the X-variable. Exhibit 11-5 illustrates the computations involved in computing the regression equation directly for the speed of machine and percent defectives for the bag-making machine of the Consul Paper, Ltd.

Comparing the resulting regression equation $Y_C = 10 + .19x$ with the regression equation secured in the discussion of correlation where the slope b was computed from the standard deviations and the correlation r, it is found that the regression equations are identical. From the computations in Exhibit 11-5, the Y_C-values may be computed in exactly the same way they were computed in the earlier paragraphs.

EXHIBIT 11-5
Simple Regression Analysis of Speed of Machine and Percent Defectives for Bag-Making Machine, Consul Paper, Ltd.

X Speed in Bags Per Minute	Y Percent Defectives	x $(X - \bar{X})$	x^2	xY
88	8.2	-13	169	-106.6
96	8.0	-5	25	- 40.0
100	10.2	-1	1	- 10.2
104	9.8	+3	9	+ 29.4
108	12.2	+7	49	+ 85.4
110	11.6	+9	81	+104.4
6⌐606	6⌐60.0		334	219.2
				-156.8
$\bar{X} = 101$	$\bar{Y} = 10.0$			62.4

$$Y_C = a + bx = 10 + .19x$$

$$a = \frac{\Sigma Y}{N} = \frac{60.0}{6} = 10.0$$

$$b = \frac{\Sigma xY}{\Sigma x^2} = \frac{62.4}{334} = .1868 \text{ rounded} = .19$$

Where:
$x = -13$	$Y_C = 10 + .19(-13) = 10 - 2.47 =$	7.5 rounded
$x = -5$	$Y_C = 10 + .19(-5) = 10 - .95 =$	9.0
$x = -1$	$Y_C = 10 + .19(-1) = 10 - .19 =$	9.8
$x = +3$	$Y_C = 10 + .19(+3) = 10 + .57 =$	10.6
$x = +7$	$Y_C = 10 + .19(+7) = 10 + 1.33 =$	11.3
$x = +9$	$Y_C = 10 + .19(+9) = 10 + 1.71 =$	11.7

X	Y	Y_C
88	8.2	7.5
96	8.0	9.0
100	10.2	9.8
104	9.8	10.6
108	12.2	11.3
110	11.6	11.7

Comparison of the three columns X, Y, and Y_C with the same columns produced in the earlier analysis in the section on linear correlation reveals that the values are identical.

A prediction of the value of the Y-variable from an estimated or known value of the X-variable may be accomplished in exactly the same way from the regression equation as was explained in the earlier paragraphs in the section on linear correlation. The computation of the standard error of the estimate is likewise identical, including the construction of the confidence interval as desired.

It should be pointed out that the formulas and the techniques explained in the sections on linear correlation and on simple regression in this chapter are not exhaustive. They are standardized techniques which will be useful in most cases in business and economic research. They apply in those generalized situations in which a straight line seems to describe the relationship of two series of data. This situation prevails probably even more often than is suspected. A linear relationship between two variables is common.

TREND ANALYSIS

Trend analysis is considered an aspect of the analysis of time-series data. The analysis of time-series data means the study of historical data in respect to any one of four kinds of time-series influences: trend, seasonal, cyclical, and erratic. The historical records of a firm will reveal information concerning sales, costs, personnel activities, wage rates, salaries, shipping expenses, wrapping and packaging expenses, research costs, and so forth. The recurrence of such costs or other data on a seasonal basis may require study, in which case the *seasonal* influence on the data will be studied. For example, it is well known that the pre-Easter and the pre-Christmas sales are the heaviest in the year for most retailers, particularly retailers of clothing. The influence of weather on purchases by customers of rain gear, winter overcoats, summer playsuits, and such items can play a part in inventory acquirement. Therefore, every firm is interested in the seasonal influences in its business and, therefore, possibly interested in the historical records revealing the patterns of such seasonal influences.

The *cyclical* changes that occur in business affairs are of interest to every businessperson, and, in an attempt to keep up with cyclical changes, he generally turns his attention to the *Wall Street Journal*, *Barron's*, *Newsweek*, *Forbes' Magazine*, and other such national periodicals. He also gets information from his trade association and from his local or national chamber of commerce. Few local businesspersons conduct research studies into the cyclical influence on their own businesses. As for *erratic* influences, they are defined as random influences occurring in very short periods of time such as heavy rain storms, or floods, or such occurrences which may stop sales or radically affect business operations for a matter of a day or a few days. While these are interesting and must receive attention in studying the business records of a firm, they afford no opportunity for studying a pattern and thus, little area for research.

All firms are interested in *trend* analysis, however. Each individual firm is interested in the trend of its own sales, the trend within the industry in respect to the products it handles, the trend in the change of styles or habit patterns of the customers, the trends in employment practices, the trends involved in requirements by federal government or state control agencies, and other trend influences. Therefore, an examination of the historical records of the firm over a period of years, particularly with a view toward prediction for the next year or two into the future, is often of much importance to the individual business firm. It is because of the importance of trend analysis that attention is given to it in this chapter.

The study of trend, whether in production, sales, costs, or another economic factor, involves estimating a curve that will describe the past years' records; this curve may then be projected into the future in an effort to make a prediction for the following year or the following few years. The curves that may be fitted to time-series data in trend analysis may be made by nonmathematical methods, in which case they may be called *approximations to trend*, or by the mathematical technique of least-squares curve fitting. Both of these generalized techniques will receive attention in the following paragraphs.

APPROXIMATIONS TO TREND

Approximating the trend of a variable involves estimating its direction of movement over, usually, a period of years. The period of years may consist of a few years or a great number of years, perhaps twenty or thirty. Few studies will involve as many years as twenty or thirty although rarely one finds a trend study involving decades and even centuries in some cases. Such would hardly be the case for an individual firm. Usually half a dozen years to ten or fifteen years is the case. Probably the two most widely used methods of approximating the direction of a variable over a period of years are (1) graphic and (2) semiaverage methods.

The Graphic Method

The graphic process of approximating the trend requires the plotting of the data on the mathematical arithmetic grid and then drawing in a free-hand trend line that would describe the direction of the data and would closely fit the data themselves. It is expected, of course, that since such a trend line is drawn freehand, it would be an approximation and would not stand a rigorous test for closeness of fit. Professional analysts, however, becom skilled in drawing freehand lines on scatter diagrams to describe the data. Very often their lines closely approximate the curves that would be fitted by mathematical methods. Exhibit 11-8 presents a scatter diagram and least-squares trend of the labor participation rates of wives with children under eighteen years of age over a period of years. Referring to this exhibit, it is noted that the trend line was fitted by a mathematical technique—and therefore a precise fit to the data was secured. However, in a freehand trend line the analyst would have drawn in such a line and it would have undoubtedly been a straight line, since inspecting the black dots appearing on the scatter diagram with the years across the bottom on the X-axis and the labor participation rates listed on the Y-axis, the data appear best described by a straight line. A skilled analyst would have drawn in a straight line very closely approximating the straight line that has been drawn in on exhibit 11-8 by the mathematical technique of least squares.

The data of labor participation rates of wives with children under eighteen years of age for the years 1964–1972 will be used throughout the succeeding discussion of trend analysis in order that the various methods of trend fitting may be compared. In the case of graphic analysis, of course, while the skilled analyst would likely have closely approximated the straight line that was actually fitted in exhibit 11-8 by the least-squares technique, the less skilled business executive may have drawn it in subject to some considerable error. Therefore, where amateurs are making a trend analysis, they would be wise to confine their research to the more mathematical techniques of fitting curves.

The Semiaverage Method

While the semiaverage method of fitting a straight line to data plotted on a scatter diagram is considered an approximation to trend, it is hardly to be considered nonmathematical since it does require the computation of two arithmetic means and the subsequent calculation of trend values. The reason it is called an approximation is that its values may not be the same as those secured by fitting a least-squares curve to the data and, therefore, in a test of best fit would certainly come off second best to the least-squares technique. The following steps are followed in the semiaverage method of computing the trend values:

1. List the data by years, divide the data into halves, and compute the arithmetic mean of each half.
2. Subtract the mean of the first half from the mean of the second half of the data (the result will be a plus or minus, for an increasing or decreasing trend); then, divide the difference by the number of years separating the means to obtain the annual increment (or decrement).
3. Center the arithmetic mean of either half in a new column headed "Trend Values" by one of the following:
   a. If the halves possess odd numbers of data, the mean is placed opposite the middle year of its half.
   b. If the halves possess even numbers of data, place the mean opposite one of the two middle values of the half of data by first deducting from or adding to the mean one-half of an annual increment.
   The result of either (a) or (b) is to locate one trend value opposite a given year in the list of data.
4. Add or subtract consecutively on either side of the trend value located in step 3 the value of the increment or decrement (keeping account of the minus or plus sign indicating a declining or increasing trend), until trend values have been assigned for all years. The result is a straight-line trend (a constant arithmetic change throughout).

The preceding four steps in the computation of the semiaverage trend are illustrated in exhibit 11-6. In this exhibit the labor force participation rates of wives with children under eighteen years of age for the years 1964–1972 are listed. The first year is omitted from the calculations in order to provide equal halves. The mean of each half is computed, and the second mean is centered opposite the second of the two middle values of the second half. This was accomplished by adding one-half an annual

EXHIBIT 11-6
Semiaverage Trend Computations for Labor Force Participation Rates of
Wives With Children Under 18 Years, March 1964–1972*

X Year	Y Rate		Trend Values		Rounded Trend Values†
1964	32.0 (omit)		31.134375		31.13
65	32.2		32.440625		32.44
66	33.2	$\overline{X} = 34.4$	33.746875		33.75
67	35.3		35.053125		35.05
68	36.9		36.359375		36.36
69	38.6		37.665625		37.67
70	39.7	$\overline{X} = 39.625$	38.971875	Centered	38.97
71	39.7		40.278125	← Trend	40.28
1972	40.5		41.584375	Value	41.58

Annual increment: $(39.625 - 34.4)/4 = 5.225/4 = 1.30625$

One-half increment: $1.30625/2 = .653125$

Centered Trend Value: $39.625 + .653125 = 40.278125$

Source: *Monthly Labor Review* (Washington: U.S. Department of Labor), April 1973. p. 34.

*Labor force participation rate as percent of population.

†Trend values rounded to one decimal place more than original observations.

increment to the second mean. Once the centered trend value is located, the other trend values may be obtained by consecutively adding and deducting the amount of the annual increment.

It is noted in the list of steps that if the halves of the data possess odd numbers of data, the mean of each half is automatically opposite the middle year of each half. Therefore, no adjustment backward or forward by half an increment is necessary. The semiaverage method requires that the total number of observations under study be an even number, of course, so that the two halves may be equal. If an odd number of data exists, the first item of data is simply dropped from the analysis determining the increment.

It may be interesting to compare the trend values resulting in exhibit 11-6 from using the seimaverage trend method with the trend values that resulted from the least-squares trend computations of exhibit 11-7. It is noted that there is a difference in the two, part of which, of course, is due to only eight years of data being included in the computations for the semiaverage trend while all nine years of data were included in the computations for the least-squares trend. In all cases, of course, the least-squares trend computations will more accurately describe the data than will the semiaverage trend. In those cases where a relatively quick fit of a straight line to data is required, the semiaverage trend method will give relatively sound results. It is highly useful to the amateur researcher, to the businessperson doing his own study, and to the student requiring a curve fit for either purposes of prediction or purposes of securing the line of fit when absolute accuracy is not required. Further, it must be remembered that predictions into the future whether for one year, two years, or longer periods of time are fraught with uncertainty, and the results are subject to considerable margins of error. Thus, making a prediction from a semiaverage trend is no more subject to error than is making a prediction from a least-squares trend. Both are subject to the same uncertainties; both are subject to the same wide margins of error that can occur in the unknown future.

THE LEAST-SQUARES TREND

The least-squares technique for fitting a curve to data is a technique that gives a curve such that the sum of the squared deviations of the observed values from that curve will be at a minimum. For this reason, it is called a *least-squares* technique. The following formula is used for fitting the curve:

$$Y_C = a + bx$$

where: Y_C = trend values (Y-variable fitted to the time series)

$a = \dfrac{\Sigma Y}{N}$ the trend value at the origin, $x = 0$

$b = \dfrac{\Sigma x Y}{\Sigma x^2}$

x = deviations in time intervals from the origin, $x = 0$

The preceding formula appears to be precisely the same as the formula used in exhibit 11-5 in fitting the simple regression curve to the speed of machine and the percent defectives for the bag-making machine of Consul Paper, Ltd. There is a difference between the regression curve and the trend curve, however, although the elements of the formula appear identical. The x-deviation in the regression formula employed in exhibit 11-5 is the deviation of each value of the X-variable from the mean of X, $(X - \overline{X})$. The x-deviation in the least-squares trend equation, however, represents deviations in time intervals, that is, in years from the origin at the middle of the years—the origin where $x = 0$. The result is that the value of a given as $\Sigma Y/(N)$ is the mean of the Y-variable, but becomes the trend value at the origin where $x = 0$. This mathematical formality is made possible because in trend analysis, the years are the X-variable and are exactly one year apart. Therefore, the computations in the analysis may be shortened by making the x-deviations in terms of years or in the case of an even-numbered series of data, in six-month intervals. These differences, as explained, are clearly shown in exhibit 11-7 which presents least-squares trend computations for labor participation rates of wives with children under eighteen years of age for the years 1964–1972.

Examining the column headed "x", it is apparent that the location of the x-deviations was started at the origin year of 1968. When an odd number of years of data is involved, the middle year of the series will be the origin and at that origin the value of x will be zero. From the point of $x = 0$, the x-values then become -1, -2, -3, -4, and so forth for preceding years

EXHIBIT 11-7
Least-Squares Trend Computations for Labor Force Participation Rates of Wives With Children Under 18 Years, March 1964–1972*

X Year	Y Rate	x	x^2	xY	Y_C Trend Values	Y_C Rounded Trend Values †
1964	32.0	−4	16	−128.0	31.60224	31.60
65	32.2	−3	9	− 96.6	32.81557	32.82
66	33.2	−2	4	− 66.4	34.02890	34.03
67	35.3	−1	1	− 35.3	35.24223	35.24
68	36.9	0	0	0	36.45556	36.46
69	38.6	+1	1	38.6	37.66889	37.67
70	39.7	+2	4	79.4	38.88222	38.88
71	39.7	+3	9	119.1	40.09555	40.10
1972	40.5	+4	16	162.0	41.30888	41.31
	328.1		60	399.1		
				−326.3		
				72.8		

$$Y_C = a + bx = 36.45556 + 1.21333$$

$$a = \frac{\Sigma Y}{N} = \frac{328.1}{9} = 36.45556$$

$$b = \frac{\Sigma xY}{\Sigma x^2} = \frac{72.8}{60} = 1.21333$$

Sample calculations:

1964: 36.45556 + (1.21333 × −4) = 36.45556 − 4.85332
      = 31.60224 rounded = 31.60

1964: 36.45556 + (1.21333 × −3) = 36.45556 − 3.63999
      = 32.81557 rounded = 32.82

1972: 36.45556 + (1.21333 × +4) = 36.45556 + 4.85332
      = 41.30888 rounded = 41.31

Source: *Monthly Labor Review* (Washington: U.S. Department of Labor), April 1973, p. 34.

*Labor force participation rate as percent of population.

†Trend values rounded to one decimal place more than original observations.

and +1, +2, +3, +4, and so forth for succeeding years. Thus, where there is an odd total of items of data, the x-values are one year apart.

For an even-numbered series of data, the value of b will be in a six-month increment. Since a minus one and a plus one must separate the middle two years because a zero would be precisely between them, the resulting x-values must be the value of two removed successively from each other. Thus, the x-values are in six-month intervals rather than in yearly intervals. The values will be -1, -3, -5, etc., and $+1$, $+3$, $+5$, etc. The resulting Y_C-values will be removed from each other consecutively by twice the value of b. The difference in the x-values being either six months apart or one year apart results in a difference in the value of b, that is, the slope of the curve. The constant arithmetic increment will occur throughout the data since the technique is a straight-line technique.

In the discussion of the semiaverage method of fitting a straight line to a series of annual data, it was explained that the Y_C-values in exhibit 11-6 differed from the Y_C-values obtained by the least-squares trend method used in exhibit 11-7. The least-squares method by its definition permits a comparison of the trend values with the trend values secured by other curves fitted to data. Therefore, since the least-squares method is so defined because the sum of the squares of the differences between the observed values and the fitted values is at a minimum, this computation as a testing procedure may be carried forward by taking the difference between each Y-value and each Y_C-value, squaring each difference, and totaling all of these differences by the following formula:

$$\Sigma(Y - Y_C)^2$$

The preceding formula will yield the sum of squared deviations for a given curve fit to a given set of data. It therefore constitutes a test of accuracy of curve fit.

Forecasting

The forecasting of a value of the Y-variable for a future year may be accomplished in one of two ways:

1. The trend line may be extended on the graph and the value of the Y-variable read off at the point of intersection of the given future year.
2. The calculation of the prediction may follow the same procedure as for the calculation using the regression formula as explained in the section on correlation and regression.

Exhibit 11-8 presents the scatter diagram and least-squares trend of labor force participation of wives with children under eighteen years of age for March 1964–1972. The black dots represent the original observations and constitute the intersections of the participation rates with the years in which the rates occurred. The X's on the straight line represent the fitted Y_C-values, the Y-variable fitted to the time series of years. The least-squares trend on this grid could be extended to 1973, and at the point of intersection of the vertical ordinate with the extension of the trend line, the value on the Y-axis could be read off as the forecast participation rate. The second method of forecasting employing the technique explained for prediction using the regression formula is illustrated for the year 1973. In this year, the value of x becomes $+5$ since it is one more interval removed from 1968. The calculations are shown as follows:

1973: $x = +5$

$36.45556 + (1.21333 \times +5) = 36.45556 + 6.06665$
$= 42.52221$ rounded $= 42.52$

The forecast participation rate for 1973 is 42.52. This is precisely the same value that would have been read off the graph had the least-squares trend line been continued and the value read off the Y-axis. Both of these methods give exactly the same answer since the least-squares trend was used in both cases for making the forecast.

EXHIBIT 11-8

Scatter Diagram and Least-Squares Trend of Labor Force Participation Rates of Wives With Children Under 18 Years, March 1964-1972

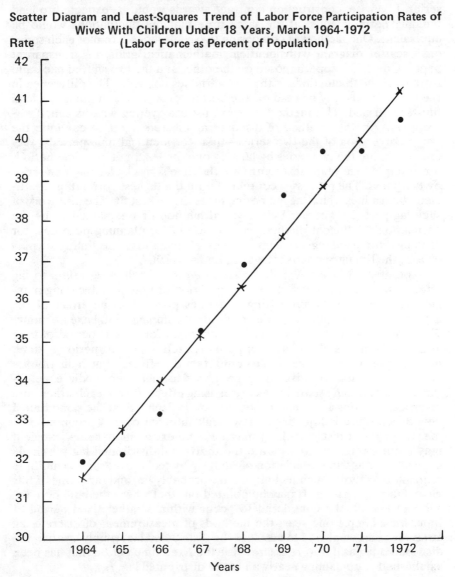

Rate (Labor Force as Percent of Population)

Years

Lags and Leads

Comparison of two variables over time to determine if one leads or lags the other may on occasion be important. It would be expected that inventory procurement for retail sales would lead the sales, and the fluctuations in inventory procurement would be relatively of the same magnitudes as the fluctuations in sales, the difference being that the fluctuations for the inventory procurement series would occur at an earlier period, perhaps a month or several months preceding the equivalent fluctuations in the sales series. Likewise, construction contract awards would be expected to lead building permits issued at the same time that the fluctuations would be equivalent. One method of comparing two such series is to plot each series on a scatter diagram with identical mathematical grids, on transparent paper. One grid is superimposed on the other and the two shifted back and forth until the fluctuations in the two variables coincide. The difference in the time periods may be read off the bottom or X-axis, and the lag or lead thus established. This method is useful for discovering what is called *discrete lag*. Another method of discovering discrete lag is to compute the linear correlation of the two series—first, for identical time periods; second, correlate the two series by lagging one the length of one time period, for example, one year; next, correlate the time series by lagging one series by two years. The process is continued until the highest correlation coefficient determines which lagged period gives the closest fit. The discovery of such lag periods, whether by the visual method first explained or by the correlation coefficient method, can be useful for planning purposes, for example, for planning the acquirement of inventory, the timing of purchases, the timing of contract awards, and so forth.

Another kind of lag is called *distributed lag*. Such a lag refers to lag effects that are distributed over a long period of time in a declining manner. For example, in advertising and sales promotion the effect of the advertising campaign or the sales promotion campaign will have an immediate and large effect. This effect will continue for a short period of time and then dwindle and decline over perhaps a relatively long period of time, for example, a year or longer. To counteract the effects of such distributed lag, it is common for advertising programs to include periodic expenditures for advertising so that peak advertising effects follow each other, and distributed lag for a preceding expenditure is declining at the same time a new expenditure is injecting a new peak into the overall program. The measurement of distributed lag may become exceedingly complicated; it may require attempts to separate the individual distributed lag for single expenditures and the calculation of such lag by techniques such as multiple regression analysis. Such techniques are probably beyond the scope of this elementary discussion. It may be pointed out that where the bulk of a distributed lag may be considered to occur within a rather fixed period of time, for example one year, the methods of measurement of discrete lag are sometimes employed to measure the distributed lag, simply treating the distributed lag as if it were discrete for the fixed time period that has been established as containing nearly all of the distributed lag.

SUMMARY

Correlation refers to the association of variables. The correlation coefficient measures the degree by which two or more variables move together or inversely. The coefficient measures only the degree of association; it does not describe the causal relationship. Two variables may react on each other, one may cause the other, outside influences could act on both, or they could be associated by coincidence. The study of correlation includes three kinds of measurement: (1) the correlation coefficient r; (2) the regression equation; (3) the standard error of the estimate.

Simple linear correlation is computed by the following formula:

$$r = \frac{\Sigma xy}{N \, \sigma_X \, \sigma_Y}$$

The regression formula for simple linear correlation-regression is given as follows:

$$Y_C = a + bx$$

$$\text{where: } a = \frac{\Sigma Y}{n}$$

$$b = \frac{\Sigma xY}{\Sigma x^2}$$

$$\text{however: } b = \frac{\sigma_Y}{\sigma_X} r_{YX}$$

Thus, when the correlation coefficient r has been computed, b can be computed from the ratio of σ_Y to σ_X times r, and a is the mean of the Y-series.

The standard error of the estimate measures the reliability of the association, and may be computed as follows:

$$S_y = \sqrt{\frac{\Sigma(Y - Y_C)^2}{N}}$$

Rank correlation is a technique permitting correlation analysis of non-mathematical variables like colors or ratings. It may be computed as follows:

$$\text{rho} \rightarrow \rho = 1 - \frac{6 \Sigma d^2}{n^3 - n}$$

Trend analysis is a part of time-series analysis, which includes not only trend analysis, but also seasonal influences, cyclical fluctuations, and erratic occurrences. Trend may be approximated by plotting the values of the observations against the time variable on an arithmetic grid, and drawing in a freehand curve representing the association. Another approximation to trend is given by the semiaverage method, in which the observations are divided into halves when arranged in time sequence, the mean of each half computed, and a straight line plotted through the means on an arithmetic grid. With either method, values for given years may be read off the chart, and forecasts for future years made.

The least-squares trend is a mathematical technique that may be applied with the following formula:

$$Y_C = a + bx$$

where: Y_C = trend values (Y fitted to time, X)

$$a = \frac{\Sigma Y}{N}, \text{ the trend value at the origin, } x = 0$$

$$b = \frac{\Sigma xY}{\Sigma x^2}$$

x = deviations in time intervals from the origin, $x = 0$

Whatever method of trend fitting is used, forecasts can be made for future periods. This is the chief reason for trend analysis.

In comparing variables over time, one variable may be causal to the other, and occur earlier. Lags and leads therefore may exist. A lagging variable may be predicted from a leading one.

ADDENDUM: MULTIPLE CORRELATION-REGRESSION

This addendum is provided so that instructors may or may not include the analysis of multiple correlation-regression in their course, depending on the level at which the course is taught and the limitations of time. The fact is, multiple correlation-regression analysis will be run on a computer where one is available; standardized computer programs are available at all computer centers, the programs providing in the print-out as a minimum the multiple regression equation, the standard error of the estimate, and the coefficient of multiple correlation. Many instructors, however, desire their students to study multiple correlation-regression in some depth to gain the most in understanding, and in addition assign problems to be solved by hand methods. The subject matter in this addendum is therefore presented in detail.

The subject of multiple correlation-regression deals with the situation in which a dependent variable is associated with two or more independent variables simultaneously. Where a high degree of association is exhibited as measured by the multiple correlation coefficient R, prediction of a value of the dependent variable may be made based on firm knowledge of the independent variables. Predictability to a given level of significance, for example 95 percent or 99 percent, may be established by employing the standard error of the estimate.

The example used in explaining the techniques of multiple correlation-regression is derived from the example presented in exhibit 11-2, concerning the correlation of speed of a paper bag-making machine, which is the independent variable X, and the percent defectives, which is the dependent variable Y. In the current example, a third variable is added, the machine roller temperature in degrees Fahrenheit. In the new example, the variables are given different designations, standard practice for multiple correlation; the dependent variable, percent defectives, is designated X_1; the first independent variable, speed, is designated X_2; and the second independent variable, temperature, is designated X_3. The presumption is that the percent defectives in a production run is associated with, and thereby may be predicted from the speed of the machine and the roller temperature.

Addendum Exhibit 1 shows the observations taken of the three variables, and includes the basic calculations necessary to arrive at sums needed in the computations for the multiple regression equation, the standard error of the estimate, and the coefficient of multiple correlation.

ADDENDUM EXHIBIT 1
Percent Defectives, Speed in Bags Per Minute, and Machine Roller Temperature in Six Production Runs of Bag-Making Machine, Consul Paper, Ltd.

X_1 Percent Defectives	X_2 Speed in Bags Per Minute	X_3 Machine Roller Temp. °F.	X_1^2	X_2^2	X_3^2	X_1X_2	X_1X_3	X_2X_3
8.2	88	130	67.24	7,744	16,900	721.6	1,066.0	11,440
8.0	96	110	64.00	9,216	12,100	768.0	880.0	10,560
10.2	100	140	104.04	10,000	19,600	1,020.0	1,428.0	14,000
9.8	104	140	96.04	10,816	19,600	1,019.2	1,372.0	14,560
12.2	108	160	148.84	11,664	25,600	1,317.6	1,952.0	17,280
11.6	110	160	134.56	12,100	25,600	1,276.0	1,856.0	17,600
60.0	606	840	614.72	61,540	119,400	6,122.4	8,554.0	85,440

THE MULTIPLE REGRESSION EQUATION

Although a prediction of a value of the dependent variable from firm knowledge of the independent variables through the use of the multiple regression equation would not ordinarily be made until the computation of the multiple correlation coefficient verified the existence of a high degree of association, a standard procedure calls for the following sequence in the computations of the analytical elements: first, the multiple regression equation; second, the standard error of the estimate; third, the coefficient of multiple determination R^2, followed by the multiple correlation coefficient R.

Solving the normal equations simultaneously provides a direct method of computing the multiple regression equation. Where three variables are involved, these are of the following form. (Where more than three variables are involved, other methods may be required; however, with a considerable number of variables the analyst will use the electronic computer—indeed, he will use it whenever it is available! The purpose of the text presentation is to teach the techniques of multiple correlation-regression, not to provide a general solution.)

I. $\quad \Sigma X_1 = Na_{1.23} + b_{12.3} \Sigma X_2 + b_{13.2} \Sigma X_3$

II. $\quad \Sigma X_1 X_2 = a_{1.23} \Sigma X_2 + b_{12.3} \Sigma X_2^2 + b_{13.2} \Sigma X_2 X_3$

III. $\quad \Sigma X_1 X_3 = a_{1.23} \Sigma X_3 + b_{12.3} \Sigma X_2 X_3 + b_{13.2} \Sigma X_3^2$

Substitute the proper values from Addendum Exhibit 1 into the equations:

I. $\quad 60 = 6a_{1.23} + 606b_{12.3} + 840b_{13.2}$

II. $\quad 6{,}122.4 = 606a_{1.23} + 61{,}540b_{12.3} + 85{,}440b_{13.2}$

III. $\quad 8{,}554 = 840a_{1.23} + 85{,}440b_{12.3} + 119{,}400b_{13.2}$

Multiply equation I by 101, which is 606/6, so that modified equation I may be deducted from equation II, to yield equation A:

II. $\quad 6{,}122.4 = 606a_{1.23} + 61{,}540b_{12.3} + 85{,}440b_{13.2}$

I. $\quad \underline{6{,}060.0 = 606a_{1.23} + 61{,}206b_{12.3} + 84{,}840b_{13.2}}$

A. $\quad 62.4 = \phantom{606a_{1.23} +} 334b_{12.3} + 600b_{13.2}$

Multiply equation II by 1.38614, which is 840/606, so that modified equation II may be deducted from equation III, to yield equation B with the same unknowns as equation A:

III. $\quad 8{,}554 = 840a_{1.23} + 85{,}440b_{12.3} + 119{,}400b_{13.2}$

II. $\quad \underline{8{,}486.5 = 840a_{1.23} + 85{,}303b_{12.3} + 118{,}432b_{13.2}}$

B. $\quad 67.5 = \phantom{840a_{1.23} +} 137b_{12.3} + 968b_{13.2}$

Solve equations A and B simultaneously for $b_{13.2}$ as follows:

A. $\quad 62.4 = 334b_{12.3} + 600b_{13.2}$

B. $\quad 67.5 = 137b_{12.3} + 968b_{13.2}$

Multiply equation A by .4102, which is 137/334, so that modified equation A may be deducted from equation B:

B. $\quad 67.5 = 137b_{12.3} + 968b_{13.2}$

A. $\quad \underline{25.6 = 137b_{12.3} + 246.1b_{13.2}}$

$\quad 41.9 = \phantom{137b_{12.3} +} 721.9b_{13.2}$

Solve for $b_{13.2}$:

$$b_{13.2} = \frac{41.9}{721.9} = .05804$$

Substitute $b_{13.2}$ into equation B to solve for $b_{12.3}$:

B.
$$67.5 = 137b_{12.3} + 968(.05804)$$
$$-137b_{12.3} = -67.5 + 56.18$$
$$-137b_{12.3} = -11.32$$
$$+b_{12.3} = +.0826$$

Substitute $b_{12.3}$ and $b_{13.2}$ into original equation I and solve for $a_{1.23}$:

I.
$$60 = 6a_{1.23} + 606(.0826) + 840(.05804)$$
$$-6a_{1.23} = -60 + 50.0556 + 48.7536$$
$$-6a_{1.23} = -60 + 98.8092$$
$$-6a_{1.23} = +38.8092$$
$$+a_{1.23} = -6.4682$$

The multiple regression equation, stated in theoretical form first and in solved form for the preceding problem second, appears as follows:

$$X_{c1.23} = a_{1.23} + b_{12.3}X_2 + b_{13.2}X_3$$
$$X_{c1.23} \doteq -6.4682 + .0826X_2 + .05804X_3$$

The multiple regression equation is also called the *estimating equation* by statisticians, since it is used for estimating or predicting a value for the dependent variable X_1 given firm information of X_2 and X_3. However, it has already been noted that a given level of confidence would be desired in predicting X_1, and that a high R would be desired to establish the association in the first place. Thus, the standard error of the estimate and the coefficients of multiple determination and correlation will be completed before a prediction example is presented.

THE STANDARD ERROR OF THE ESTIMATE

Computing the standard error of the estimate requires solving the regression equation for the original observations in order to secure the *predicted* or *theoretical* values of the solved equation, which represent the associated values from which the original observations will then be considered as deviations.

The standard error of the estimate is given by the following formula:

$$s_{1.23} = \sqrt{\frac{\Sigma(X_1 - X_{c1.23})^2}{N}}$$

The computations follow, using the computed multiple regression formula, $X_{c1.23} = -6.4682 + .0826X_2 + .05804X_3$:

$$X_{c1.23} = -6.4682 + .0826\ (88) + .05804(130)$$
$$= -6.4682 + 7.2688 + 7.5452 = 8.3458$$

$$X_{c1.23} = -6.4682 + .0826\ (96) + .05804(110)$$
$$= -6.4682 + 7.9296 + 6.3844 = 7.8458$$

$$X_{c1.23} = -6.4682 + .0826(100) + .05804(140)$$
$$= -6.4682 + 8.2600 + 8.1256 = 9.9174$$

$$X_{c1.23} = -6.4682 + .0826(104) + .05804(140)$$
$$= -6.4682 + 8.5904 + 8.1256 = 10.2478$$

$$X_{c1.23} = -6.4682 + .0826(108) + .05804(160)$$
$$= -6.4682 + 8.9208 + 9.2864 = 11.7390$$

$$X_{c1.23} = -6.4682 + .0826(110) + .05804(160)$$
$$= -6.4682 + 9.0860 + 9.2864 = 11.9042$$

X_1	$X_{c1.23}$	$X_1 - X_{c1.23}$	$(X_1 - X_{c1.23})^2$
8.2	8.3458	−.1458	.02125764
8.0	7.8458	.1542	.02377764
10.2	9.9174	.2826	.07986276
9.8	10.2478	−.4478	.20052484
12.2	11.7390	.4610	.21252100
11.6	11.9042	−.3042	.09253764
			.63048152

$$s_{1.23} = \sqrt{\frac{\Sigma(X_1 - X_{c1.23})^2}{N}} = \sqrt{\frac{.63048152}{6}} = \sqrt{.1050802533}$$

$$s_{1.23} = .32416$$

THE COEFFICIENTS OF MULTIPLE DETERMINATION AND CORRELATION

Computing the coefficient of multiple determination, which gives the proportion of variance in the dependent variable accounted for by the independent variables, requires computing the variance of the dependent variable to solve the following formula (it is noted that the standard error of the estimate, $s_{1.23}$, has already been computed—thus, its square is the numerator variance required):

$$R^2 = 1 - \frac{s_{1.23}^2}{s_{x_1}^2}$$

The formula deducts the ratio of unexplained variance to total variance of the dependent variable from unity, thus achieving a ratio of explained variance to total variance, that is, the proportion of the total variance in the dependent variable *explained* or *accounted for* by the independent variables.

A formula for computing the variance of the dependent variable, $s_{x_1}^2$, from values already obtained in Addendum Exhibit 1 follows:

$$s_{x_1}^2 = \frac{N \Sigma X^2 - (\Sigma X)^2}{N^2}$$

For the given problem of Addendum Exhibit 1:

$$s_{x_1}^2 = \frac{(6 \times 614.72) - (60)^2}{6^2} = \frac{3,688.32 - 3,600}{36} = \frac{88.32}{36} = 2.45333$$

Substituting $s_{1.23}^2$ and $s_{x_1}^2$ into the formula for R^2:

$$R^2 = 1 - \frac{.32416^2}{2.45333} = 1 - \frac{.10508}{2.45333} = 1 - .042832 = .957168 \text{ rounded} = .96$$

The coefficient of multiple correlation is computed as follows:

$$R = \sqrt{1 - \frac{s_{1.23}^2}{s_{x_1}^2}} = \sqrt{.957168} = .9783 \text{ rounded} = .98$$

INTERPRETATION AND PREDICTION

A coefficient of multiple correlation, R, of .98 is very high, indeed. Comparing it to the coefficient of correlation, r, of .89 obtained in exhibit 11-2 when the dependent variable was correlated with one independent variable, it is seen that the addition of the second pertinent independent variable has improved the association, and thus any prediction made from the multiple regression equation may be made with more assurance than a prediction from the simple linear regression equation computed in conjunction with the two-variable analysis in chapter 11. A comparison of the coefficients of determination yields similar results: The coefficient of multiple determination, R^2, is .96, meaning that 96 percent of the variance in the dependent variable is explained by the two independent variables; but the coefficient of determination, r^2, is .79, indicating that only 79 percent of the variance in the dependent variable is explained or accounted for by the one independent variable in that analysis.

As an example of prediction by multiple correlation-regression, assume that the Consul Paper, Ltd., can increase the speed of the paper bag-making machine to 124 bags per minute by installing improved parts and overhauling the machine. At the same time, it is judged that any increased roller temperatures can be contained within acceptable limits, at about 170°F. With a 5 percent error probability, thus a 95 percent confidence interval, what percent defectives can be expected? Since a small sample is involved—only six observations, which admittedly is very small for making a prediction—Student's t-distribution will provide the confidence level in standard deviations: 95 percent confidence level at five degrees of freedom $(N - 1)$ from Student's t-distribution $= 2.571 = z$.

Required:

X_1 given that $X_2 = 124$ and $X_3 = 170$

Confidence interval given that $s_{1.23} = .32416$ and $z = 2.571$

Compute:

$$X_1 = -6.4682 + .0826(124) + .05804(170)$$
$$= -6.4682 + 10.2424 + 9.8668$$
$$= -6.4682 + 20.1092 = 13.641 \text{ rounded} = 13.6$$
$$s_{1.23}z = .32416 \times 2.571 = .83341536$$

Confidence interval: $13.641 \pm .83341536 = 12.80758464$ and 14.47441536

Prediction: With a speed of 124 bags per minute and a roller temperature of 170°F., 13.6 percent defectives may be expected; however, this is a point estimate to a zero probability; there is a 95 percent probability that the percent defectives will fall between 12.8 and 14.5.

EXERCISES

1. Define correlation in your own words. Then, explain its relation to causal association.
2. What is regression? How is it related to correlation?
3. What is the purpose of trend analysis? How does it differ from regression analysis?
4. A rural bank wishes to know if federal agricultural payments are associated with bank loans. They suspect that a negative association may exist: i.e., that federal payments to farmers reduces the needs of farmers for bank loans. The data are from 6 townships. Compute Pearson's coefficient of correlation r; then explain your findings.

Federal payments to farmers (per capita)	Farm loans ($thousands)
180	210
212	300
110	320
60	104
40	90
100	200

5. A mail-order house wants to investigate the association of labor cost per shipping order with size of order, suspecting that shipping labor cost has no relation to size of order; thus, large orders have a higher profit than small orders in respect to shipping costs. One hour's observation yielded the following preliminary data. Compute Pearson's correlation coefficient r, and analyze your findings.

Labor cost per shipment	Size of order
$.80	$48
.35	20
.90	52
.90	50
.40	40
.55	45
.60	40
.70	65

6. Given the results of exercise 5, derive the regression equation from the values computed in solving the problem. Make a point forecast of size of order from a labor cost of $1. Is this a worthwhile forecast? Explain.

7. How does Spearman's rank correlation coefficient differ from Pearson's r? How is it useful?

8. Compare and contrast the graphic method and the semiaverage method of approximations to trend. How are they alike, and how do they differ?

9. What is meant by *least squares*? How does it apply in trend analysis?

10. State government debt in the United States has grown as follows, in billions of dollars: 1970, 42; 1971, 48; 1972, 54; 1973, 59; 1974, 65; 1975, 71.
    a. Plot a scatter diagram and draw in a freehand trend line.
    b. Plot the semiaverage trend on the diagram.
    c. Compare the two trends.
    d. Do they fit the data well?

11. A food broker insists that his trade is chiefly for high-grade canned goods, even though he also handles some lower qualities. Do a rank correlation of the following classification of one month's shipments, and explain your results.

Grade	Cases shipped
Hotel	870
Superior	650
Choice	300
Standard	400
Special	80

12. Sales of home trash compactors are highly correlated with per capita income according to existing research. Ten metropolitan precincts yielded the following observations. Using regression analysis, forecast the sales for a standard precinct with a per capita income of $4,000, employing the .95 confidence level.

Average precinct per capita income	Average unit sales
1,300	10
2,300	15
1,900	15
2,700	18
4,100	29
3,800	40
2,900	30
3,200	71
3,500	70
4,300	82
30,000	380

13. Fit a linear trend to the following data by least squares; then, forecast sales for 1979.

Year	Sales	
1972	$ 7.0	millions
73	8.4	
74	9.6	
75	11.0	
76	12.1	
77	13.7	
1978	15.2	

14. Define discrete lag in your own words. How does it differ from distributed lag?

SELECTED REFERENCES

Balsley, Howard L. *Basic Statistics for Business and Economics*. Columbus, Ohio: Grid, 1978.

Chou, Ya-Lun. *Statistical Analysis*. 2d ed. New York: Holt, Rinehart and Winston, 1975.

12

Tables, Charts, and Graphs

Formal statistical reports nearly always include some tables presenting information in the most precise and complete form. Many statistical reports also include charts or graphs of various kinds. Charts, however, while excellent media for giving general comparisons of items or for emphasizing points of analysis, are inferior to tables in exactitude and in comprehensiveness. Tables may include the exact numerical values of all of the items concerned; whereas charts, for example a bar chart or a line chart, present only the general magnitudes of the items. If a reader wishes to know the exact magnitude involved in a chart, he turns to a supporting table. For these reasons, tables are probably far more widely used than charts. Tables are used when raw data are to be presented in an organized form, and they are also used to show the statistical analysis that has been followed during a statistical study.

TABULAR PRINCIPLES

Tabular principles involve defining the kinds of tables and enumerating the various classifications of tables. Tables may be classified according to the function or purpose of the data. They may be further classified as to the nature of the data; whether the data are geographical in nature, or in a time series, or if the data consist of different kinds of items or of the same items broken down into varying degrees of magnitude. Following a discussion of these tabular principles, the principles of acceptable table construction will be examined.

THE KINDS OF TABLES

The two terms—repository tables and analytical tables—distinguish tables as to function, that is, the use to which the data are to be put.

Repository Tables

Many federal government tables are repository tables containing original collections of information printed in complete and precise form for the
general use of the public. The purpose of the repository table is a general
one: to make as much data available to as many people as may need it.
Repository tables usually contain primary data. Original collections of statistical information, whether by government or by business units or by private institutions other than business firms, will usually be printed in a form
suitable for general usage. From such general purpose tables the statistician will secure information that he wishes to analyze further and present
in special reports. Exhibit 12-1 is an example of a repository table—a U.S.
Census data presentation.

EXHIBIT 12-1
A Repository Table of the Population of the
Corn Belt States by Race, 1970 Census

	White	Negro	Indian	Japanese	Chinese	Filipino	All Others
Ohio	9,646,997	970,477	6,654	5,555	5,305	3,400	13,539
Indiana	4,820,324	357,464	3,887	2,279	2,115	1,365	6,235
Illinois	9,600,381	1,425,674	11,413	17,299	14,474	12,654	32,081
Iowa	2,782,762	32,596	2,992	1,009	993	614	3,410

Source: U. S. Bureau of the Census, *Statistical Abstract of the United States: 1972*. Tables
30, 32, pp. 28-29.

Analytical Tables

In an analysis of statistical data, only the desired information will be
given, and it will be given in a form that emphasizes the point to be made
or the comparisons to be drawn. Such tables are for special purposes.
While general or repository tables contain the exact magnitudes of all data
involved to the final degree possible, analytical tables sometimes use
abbreviated approximations of such data. For example, referring to exhibit
12-1, which is a repository table, the data presented therein are exact in
every detail. An analytical table using that information might present the
items in thousands, or in tens of thousands, using decimal points, and thus
make all of the data in each column approximate.

Analytical tables often show the statistical analysis that has been followed in a study. Exhibit 12-2 is an example of an analytical table that
shows the steps in analysis that have resulted in the desired information
listed in the last column. It is apparent that the "Average Hourly Earnings"
figures equal the "Average Weekly Earnings" divided by the "Average
Weekly Hours" (rounded from the original calculations).

EXHIBIT 12-2
An Analytical Table of Average Hourly Earnings of Manufacturing Production Workers in the Corn Belt States, 1975

	Average Weekly Earnings	Average Weekly Hours	Average Hourly Earnings
Ohio	$224	40.3	$ 5.55
Indiana	219	39.8	5.49
Illinois	215	39.7	5.40
Iowa	214	39.7	5.40
Totals	$872	159.5	$21.84
Averages	$218	39.9	$ 5.46

Source: U.S. Bureau of the Census, *Statistical Abstract of the United States: 1976*, table 611, p. 380.

TABLE CLASSIFICATION

The preceding discussion of the two kinds of tables—repository and analytical—in effect considered tables according to the function or purpose of the tables. A second kind of approach would distinguish the kinds of tables according to the nature of the data. Four kinds of tables distinguished in this way are qualitative, quantitative, geographical, and time series tables. It will become evident that these four kinds of tables, based on the nature of the data, are mutually exclusive in use only in respect to the *primary* classification of the table, that is, the first or most important classification of the table. One table may contain data of all four classifications; but the single classification being emphasized would appear in the *stub*—the listing in the farthest left column.

Qualitative Classifications

A qualitative classification of data lists items which are different kinds of things; such classifications are based on *differences of kind*. Exhibit 12-3 shows two kinds of items, average age and average efficiency ratings of employees of a company.

EXHIBIT 12-3
Average Age and Average Efficiency Rating of All Employees,
The L. A. Durham Co., Ltd.

Average Age*	42 Yrs.
Average Efficiency Rating†	89%

Source: Personnel Dept., Dec. 31, 1977.

*Average age to nearest birthday.
†Efficiency rating maximum = 100.

Quantitative Classifications

When the same quality—the same *kind of thing*—is listed in a table, but broken down into various degrees or values of that quality, the classification is based on *differences in degree of the same characteristic*. Probably the most common of single characteristics to be classified in different groups is money, whether in the form of income, sales, expense, or otherwise. This kind of classification is also called a *frequency distribution*, since it shows the frequency of occurrence of the cases occurring in the subgroups.

Quantitative classifications may be presented in qualitative terms, and thus appear at first glance to be qualitative classifications. Workers may be classified by age groups, but these age groups may be presented as young, middle-aged, and old—which results in a quantitative classification presented in qualitative form. Exhibit 12-4 shows the difference in forms of presentation. Both tables in the exhibit contain the same information. With the ages of workers classified in a frequency distribution of age groups, there is no doubt about the quantitative nature of the data. When the data, however, are classified as young, middle-aged, and old, the classification appears to be qualitative, since youth is a different quality than middle age, and both of those are different qualities than old age. Nevertheless, the information is basically quantitative rather than qualitative.

EXHIBIT 12-4
Tables Showing a Quantitative Classification

(Figure A, presented in quantitative terms; figure B, presented in qualitative terms.)

Ages of All Employees The L. A. Durham Co., Ltd.		Ages of All Employees The L. A. Durham Co., Ltd.	
Age Group	Number of Employees	Age Group	Number of Employees
21 – 35	270	Young	270
36 – 50	433	Middle-Aged	433
51 – 65	187	Old	187

Source: Personnel Dept., Dec. 31, 1977.   Source: Personnel Dept., Dec. 31, 1977.

Figure A   Figure B

Geographical Classifications

Geographical information may be listed by political division, for example, by city or by state; or by economic region, by soil-type region, by climatic-type region, or by any one of a number of other kinds of geographical organizations of information. Exhibit 12-5 shows a geographical classification of efficiency ratings of employees.

EXHIBIT 12-5
Average Efficiency Ratings of Employees
in the Cincinnati, Denver, and Houston Plants,
The L. A. Durham Co., Ltd.

(Efficiency rating maximum = 100)

Plant	Average Efficiency Rating
Cincinnati	86
Denver	86
Houston	85

Source: Personnel Dept., Dec. 31, 1977.

Time Series Classifications

Time series are data organized on the basis of time intervals and may be by years, by months, by weeks, by days, or indeed by seasons and sometimes by five-year intervals and by decades. Exhibit 12-6 is an example of the efficiency ratings of employees listed in a time series.

It is not to be thought that every table may be precisely identified as a certain kind of classification excluding all other classifications. Most tables, while primarily one classification, may contain the elements of several of the four basic classifications of tables.

EXHIBIT 12-6
Average Efficiency Ratings of All Employees, for 1975, 1976, and 1977,
The L. A. Durham Co., Ltd.

(Efficiency rating maximum = 100)

Year	Average Efficiency Rating
1975	84
1976	84
1977	85

Source: Personnel Dept., Dec. 31, 1977.

Exhibit 12-7 presents a table which combines the information presented in the preceding exhibits of The L.A. Durham Co., Ltd., and contains elements of all of the four classifications. Efficiency ratings of employees are the basic information, and these data are presented primarily according to age groups, which is a frequency distribution, of course, and therefore a quantitative classification. However, there are also elements of the time series classification, and elements of the geographical classification; further, different kinds of things are listed: ages and efficiency ratings, which are qualitative elements.

288

EXHIBIT 12-7

Average Efficiency Ratings of Employees, Classified by Age Group, in the Cincinnati, Denver, and Houston Plants, for 1975, 1976, and 1977, The L. A. Durham Co., Ltd.

(Efficiency rating maximum = 100)

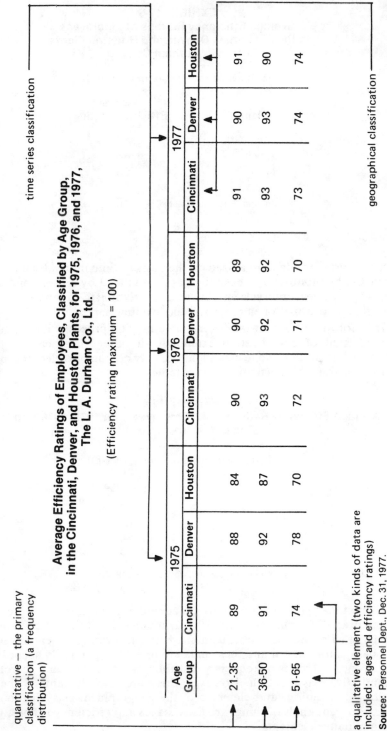

time series classification

geographical classification

Age Group	1975			1976			1977		
	Cincinnati	Denver	Houston	Cincinnati	Denver	Houston	Cincinnati	Denver	Houston
21-35	89	88	84	90	90	89	91	90	91
36-50	91	92	87	93	92	92	93	93	90
51-65	74	78	70	72	71	70	73	74	74

quantitative — the primary classification (a frequency distribution)

a qualitative element (two kinds of data are included: ages and efficiency ratings)

Source: Personnel Dept., Dec. 31, 1977.

TABLE CONSTRUCTION

There are certain principles of table construction which promote clear, concise, and well-organized tabular presentations. These principles of good table construction are described in considerable detail in this section,

EXHIBIT 12-8

Table 6. Age of All Persons and of Citizens by Sex, for the United States, Urban and Rural.

(Age classification based on completed years)

Area and Age	All Persons			Citizens[1]		
	Total	Male	Female	Total	Male	Female
TOTAL U. S.						
All ages				769		
Under 5 years				26		
5 to 14 years				115		
15 to 24 years				139		
25 to 34 years				178		
35 to 44 years				205		
45 and over				106		
URBAN						
All ages				453		
Under 5 years				15		
5 to 14 years				73		
15 to 24 years				86		
25 to 34 years				104		
35 to 44 years				116		
45 and over				59		
RURAL						
All ages				316		
Under 5 years				11		
5 to 14 years				42		
15 to 24 years				53		
25 to 34 years				74		
35 to 44 years				89		
45 and over				47		

[1] Includes both native and naturalized.

Source: Derived from U. S. Bureau of the Census, *Bureau of the Census Manual of Tabular Presentation,* by Bruce L. Jenkinson (U. S. Government Printing Office, Washington, D. C., 1949), pp. 10-11.

EXHIBIT 12-9

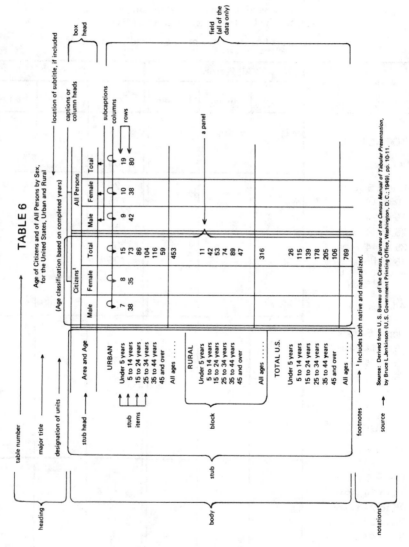

TABLE 6

Age of Citizens and of All Persons by Sex,
for the United States, Urban and Rural

(Age classification based on completed years)

Area and Age	Citizens¹			All Persons		
	Male	Female	Total	Male	Female	Total
URBAN						
Under 5 years	7	8	15	9	10	19
5 to 14 years	38	35	73	42	38	80
15 to 24 years			86			
25 to 34 years			104			
35 to 44 years			116			
45 and over			59			
All ages			453			
RURAL						
Under 5 years			11			
5 to 14 years			42			
15 to 24 years			53			
25 to 34 years			74			
35 to 44 years			89			
45 and over			47			
All ages			316			
TOTAL U.S.						
Under 5 years			26			
5 to 14 years			115			
15 to 24 years			139			
25 to 34 years			178			
35 to 44 years			205			
45 and over			106			
All ages			769			

¹ Includes both native and naturalized.

Source: Derived from U. S. Bureau of the Census, *Bureau of the Census Manual of Tabular Presentation,*
by Bruce L. Jenkinson (U.S. Government Printing Office, Washington, D. C.; 1949), pp. 10-11.

Labels:
table number
major title
designation of units
location of subtitle, if included
captions or column heads
box head
field (all of the data only)
subcaptions
columns
rows
a panel
stub head
stub items
block
footnotes
source
heading
body
notations
stub

but it should be understood that variations from these principles occur in actual practice. The main point to be kept in mind in constructing a table is that the table, whether a repository table or an analytical table, should be made up so that it achieves the purpose for which it is designed in the clearest and most efficient manner possible.

THE PARTS OF A TABLE

Governmental presentations of statistical data often depart from the principles normally adopted for business use. Specifically, governmental tables, whether federal or state or local presentations, usually follow a pattern in which the totals of columns appear at the top rather than at the bottom, and in which the totals of rows appear at the left instead of at the right. These practices are common and are accepted because data in governmental repository tables are for the general use of the public, and it may be assumed that the public is more interested in totals than in details. Therefore, the totals are placed in preferred positions, where they will catch the eye.

With commercial, economic, and industrial data, the opposite practice is usually followed. Exhibit 12-8, a table secured from a U.S. government publication, is an excellent example of a clear, concise complex table containing some elements of analysis and containing all of the basic elements that go to make up a governmental tabular presentation.

The data in exhibit 12-8, as presented by a business firm, or for business purposes by a statistical agency, would probably have been organized so that the totals of columns appeared at the bottom and the totals of rows appeared at the right. Exhibit 12-9 presents the same information as exhibit 12-8 reorganized in the form which is usually adopted for business and economic data. Exhibit 12-9 points out all of the various parts of a table. In some cases, different names might be applied to these various parts, but the names listed have the advantage of general usage.

The various parts of the table are classified as follows:

A. Heading
   1. Table number
   2. Major title
     a. Subtitle, if any
     b. Designation of units
B. Body
   1. Stub
     a. Stub head
     b. Block
       (1) Block heading
       (2) Stub items
   2. Box head
     a. Captions
       (1) Subcaptions or column headings
   3. Panel
   4. Field

       a. Rows
       b. Columns
  C. Notations
     1. Footnotes
     2. Source

THE ARRANGEMENT OF ITEMS

A number of principles govern the arrangement of the data appearing in the field. While sometimes it will be found that these principles seemingly conflict, they will serve as guides in organizing the data for presentation that will result in clear, well-organized, and effective tables.

Size

In the organization of the table, usually a larger number of items will be listed vertically than horizontally. This means simply that usually a table is made up most effectively if the table is longer than it is wide. While this rule is not invariably followed, for example see exhibit 12-7 in this chapter, it is a general practice well worth following. Sometimes the application of this principle will be obvious, for example, in a geographical distribution listing average per capita income by states. In this case, the fifty states would be listed vertically with the average per capita income for each state opposite. There would be two columns and fifty rows of data. One would certainly not organize the data so there would be two rows and fifty columns.

Comparisons

When data are to be compared, whether they consist of information in two columns to be compared, or information in rows that are to be compared, they should be placed next to one another if at all possible. For example, if in a table comparative data are given in raw numerical form and also as percentages of the totals, and it is the percentages that are to be compared and therefore emphasized, the percentage columns should be placed next to one another to facilitate comparison. This same principle should be followed in rows of data which are to be compared. Of course, with highly complex and detailed tables where several comparisons are to be drawn from the data presented, it may not be possible to place all of the data in adjacent columns or rows for each comparison.

Totals

The totals of columns are normally placed at the bottom of the columns and the totals of rows at the extreme right of the rows. It has already been pointed out that the repository tables published by government agencies practice the opposite and place the totals of columns at the beginning and the totals of rows at the extreme left. Both practices are correct, and both practices are widely followed. In general, however, private business firms and private organizations place the totals last, whether in columns or rows.

Miscellaneous

Occasionally a "Miscellaneous" classification will have to be included in a table. When, in a listing of data organized by some basic classification or criteria, several groupings of data at the end have very small numbers of items of data included in each grouping, it is wise to combine all such groups together into a "Miscellaneous" category. Sometimes a category designated "Others" is included for this purpose. Occasionally, an *open-end* classification is included in a frequency distribution; for example, "Under 21" and "Over 65" groupings may be the first and last frequency intervals of a distribution of employees' ages. Such *open-end* groupings are essentially *miscellaneous* groupings, since they include in one grouping several categories of data in which very few items of data occur.

Bases of Arrangement

The data in a table may have their arrangement based essentially on one or a combination of a number of different bases of arrangement. These bases for arranging items are eight in number, as follows:

(1) **Alphabetical.** Many repository tables have the data arranged alphabetically. This practice is common when states are listed in a geographical table—they begin with Alabama and end with Wyoming. The practice may be followed with the names of workers or the names of customers, and is the logical basis for such listings.

(2) **Chronological.** Normally, all historical data are listed in chronological order, i.e., from oldest to most recent; thus, in a time series of years, normally the latest year will be last on the list, and the earliest year included will be first and, of course, they are listed in succeeding order. Monthly data are always listed chronologically, of course, by January, February, March, etc., and never alphabetically or in any other order.

(3) **Geographical.** Data of a geographical nature, as already indicated, are sometimes listed alphabetically; however, geographical data are often listed by nations of the world in order of importance, or by city in order of size, or by region according to some customary order. In any of these cases, the data are, of course, basically geographical.

(4) **In order of size.** Data are often arranged in order of size. It has already been mentioned that geographical data might be listed in order of size of nation. The income groupings of people might be listed in order of size from smallest to largest. On the other hand, the order of size may be from largest to smallest, for example, in grain-crop production in the United States—the most important grain would appear first and the least important grain would appear last. Both orders of size arrangement are widely used.

(5) **In order of causal relationship.** Analytical tables will often present the data arranged in some kind of order of statistical analysis. For example, in the presentation of the analysis of a trend series, the columns would consist of the various steps followed in the computation of the trend, per-

haps with directions appearing in each column caption explaining how that particular column was derived from the data in the other columns. Naturally, such an organization would follow the logical steps or procedure followed in the statistical analysis. Each column can be construed as *causing* the next columns, since it has served as a basis for computing the next column of figures. Exhibit 12-2 in this chapter is an example of such an analytical table.

(6) **In order of interest.** Data may be arranged in columns or in rows according to the interest that the reader is expected to have in the data. This order of arrangement is similar to the *order of size* arrangement, since the largest item is often the one that will attract the most interest. In such a case, the largest item would be listed first, as in our example of the production of grains, and the least important listed last. If data comparing several or all of the states of the United States are presented, these states would normally be listed in alphabetical order; but for a study within a particular state and of chief interest only to the residents of that state, that particular state may be listed first and placed in bold-face type, while the remainder of the states would be listed alphabetically. This practice makes comparisons easier, and places the most *interesting* item first.

(7) **According to custom.** The items of data may be arranged according to some kind of customary listing. An example is in the geographical classification of data by regions of the United States. These regions are the New England States, Middle Atlantic States, East North Central States, etc. The arrangement of items is according to custom, moving from the East Coast to the West Coast but not in exact order of westward progression. Another example is in the presentation of data concerning men, women, and children; the order given is invariably followed.

(8) **According to desired emphasis.** Many analytical tables may have the items of data arranged in some kind of order that emphasizes certain relationships. The example of *order of interest*, in which the given state which is most *interesting* is listed first and in bold-face type, is also *according to desired emphasis*, since it was desired by the statistician to have that state's production or other quality emphasized. A particular business firm may desire to emphasize its position in comparison to other business firms out of a group listed; in this case, the data would be arranged so that the particular information which it was desired to bring to the attention of the reader forcefully was in a position making the emphasis plain.

STATISTICAL CHARTS: LINE CHARTS

The purpose of graphic presentation is to show the general magnitudes of data in an effective, visual manner. Graphs are effective in catching interest because of the pictorial manner in which they are presented, and they serve particularly to give instant comparisons of data. Graphs are not to be considered substitutes for tables, since tables are used to show the specific values of the magnitudes involved. On a graph, it is unusual to state the exact value of an item of data, but the approximate value can be

EXHIBIT 12-10

Total Labor Force in the United States, 1960 to 1980*
(in millions of persons 16 years of age and over)

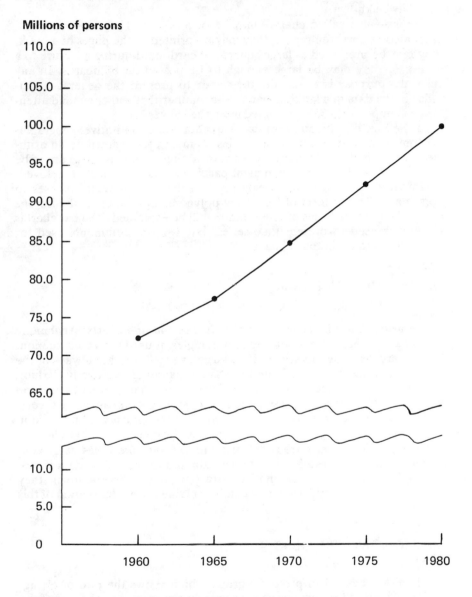

Millions of persons

Source: Adapted from data in U.S. Bureau of the Census, *Statistical Abstract of the United States: 1976*, table 569, p. 355.

*Projection of 1980 based on trends in labor force participation rates between 1947 and 1964.

shown as a line or as a bar or as a picture. Thus, graphic presentation has its own purpose, separate and distinct from the purpose of a table. Sometimes reports contain both tables and graphs of the same data, the graph giving a picture which the eye perceives instantly and with facility, and the table serving as a source of reference for the exact values if it is desired that they be known.

Graphs—also called charts—may be of any size. They may be small, embodied in a written report; they may be printed in the pages of a book; they may be presented as large squares of cardboard during a lecture to a group; or they may be large enough to be posted on billboards. In any case, the purpose is essentially the same: to present the general magnitudes of the data in a striking manner—a manner that will command attention and impress the fact presented upon the viewer.

Of the four classifications of data—qualitative, quantitative, geographical, time series—the latter, time series, is most often shown on an arithmetic or geometric line chart. When several time series variables are to be shown on one chart, the component parts line chart is usually employed. Quantitative classifications (frequency distributions) lend themselves to presentation in the form of frequency polygons, ogives, or by the Lorenz curve. All of these forms of presentation will be explained. The bar chart is sometimes used to present time series, but is more commonly used for qualitative and geographical data.

THE ARITHMETIC LINE CHART

The arithmetic line chart is the simplest of the line charts. Arithmetic graph paper, consisting of squares or rectangles, is used in its construction. The squares may be of various sizes, large or small, but are always of the same magnitude horizontally and the same magnitude vertically. Exhibit 12-10 shows a complete and formal arithmetic line chart. Such charts—and this is true of all graphic presentations—must be accompanied by a complete title and a source, as well as descriptions on the axes, with any footnotes necessary being placed at the bottom of the chart.

Arithmetic line charts are widely used to present time series data, as in exhibit 12-10. Their use for qualitative data and geographical data is limited. When applied to quantitative data (frequency distributions), they result in the frequency polygon, which is explained in a later section of this chapter.

THE GEOMETRIC LINE CHART

When it is desired to present a graph which shows the rate of change from one item to the next—usually to present percentages, index numbers, and ratios—the geometric line chart is used. This chart is drawn on *semilogarithmic* graph paper. Such graph paper is paper on which the X-axis possesses an arithmetic progression of lines but the Y-axis possesses a geometric progression of lines. This paper is constructed by the use of log-

EXHIBIT 12-11

Total Labor Force in the United States, 1960 to 1980*
(in millions of persons 16 years of age and over)

Millions of persons

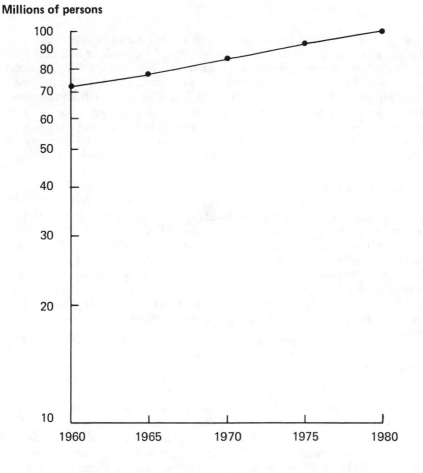

Source: Adapted from data in U.S. Bureau of the Census, *Statistical Abstract of the United States: 1976*, table 569, p. 355.

*Projection of 1980 based on trends in labor force participation rates between 1947 and 1964.

arithms, but is not normally constructed by the statistician, since it is commercially printed and sold in all bookstores. Such logarithmic paper may contain only one *phase* or *cycle*; or it may contain two or three or more such phases or cycles.

The same data plotted in exhibit 12-10 are plotted on logarithmic single-phase paper in exhibit 12-11. The difference in the results of these two exhibits is revealed in that exhibit 12-11 presents a line that describes visually the *rate of change* from one item of data to the next, whereas on the arithmetic line chart in exhibit 12-10, the difference from one item of data to the next is the exact arithmetic value of that difference.

Advantages

A geometric line chart has an advantage in that a constant percentage rate of change will appear on it as a straight line. This straight line may be steep or shallow; the steeper the slope of the straight line, the higher the constant rate. This quality makes possible estimating quickly whether the relationship of the items is one of a constant rate or not. Such knowledge may be valuable when the item being investigated is, for example, an increase in sales over a period of time or an increase in production over time, an increase in price over time, etc. Another advantage of the geometric line chart is that changes in rates appear as a curved line, either increasing or decreasing.

One of the chief reasons for making such estimates of rates of change is that they allow estimates concerning the future to be made. Analysts suggest that progressions as to future trends of such factors as production, prices, sales, etc., are usually more accurate when predicted on rates of change that have occurred in the immediate past than when predicted in arithmetic amounts of change.

Another advantage of the geometric chart is that the growth or decline in several factors may be compared on the same chart, even though the factors may be of widely varying general magnitudes. Multiphase ratio paper may be used for such comparisons. Exhibit 12-12 presents an illustration.

Disadvantages

The geometric line chart has a number of disadvantages. In the first place, it does not give a visual idea of the absolute magnitudes involved. Since the difference from one point to the next on the vertical scale represents a geometric progression, the actual arithmetic increase cannot readily be estimated from the chart; only the rate of change may be estimated.

A second disadvantage is that the distance above the base line does not indicate an arithmetic value visually. Of course, one can read the arithmetic value from the scale at the edge of the chart, but the line itself gives no indication of the exact arithmetic magnitude. Furthermore, a geometric progression must begin from a value other than zero. It cannot begin from zero since a geometric progression of zero would result in zero on to infinity.

Since such a chart cannot show zero values and cannot, therefore, show negative values, its use is again restricted. A percentage or ratio can decline infinitely down toward zero—never actually reaching it—and can never go below zero; there may be no negative percentages.

EXHIBIT 12-12

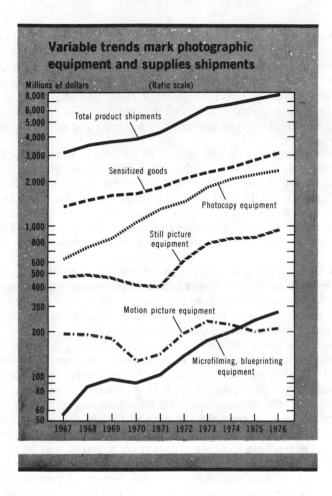

Variable trends mark photographic
equipment and supplies shipments

Millions of dollars   (Ratio scale)

Total product shipments

Sensitized goods

Photocopy equipment

Still picture
equipment

Motion picture equipment

Microfilming, blueprinting
equipment

1967 1968 1969 1970 1971 1972 1973 1974 1975 1976

Source: U.S. Department of Commerce, *U.S. Industrial Outlook: 1976*, p. 269.

Another disadvantage of the geometric line chart is that it is not widely understood, and so should not be used for general purposes, but only for relatively complicated analyses for persons who will understand its use. This considerable limitation upon the use of the geometric line chart is an important one. A final disadvantage of the geometric line chart is that it is sometimes mistakenly used to plot two or three series of data of widely varying magnitudes on one chart when it is actually the differences in magnitudes that the chart designer wishes to compare, rather than the differences in the rates of change within each series. This could be a serious error in a statistical analysis.

THE COMPONENT PARTS LINE CHART

The component parts line chart presents in one picture two or more components, or parts, of a total series. The component parts line chart is commonly used for time series data. There are actually three kinds of component parts charts: the component parts line chart, which is explained in the following paragraphs; the component parts bar chart, which is discussed in the section on bar charts; and the circle, or pie, chart, which presents the component parts as segments of a circle, and which is explained in later paragraphs.

The components for each time period to be shown on the line chart are added successively to the total of the preceding components, that is, they are *stacked* on top of one another. A study of exhibit 12-13 will make this stacking clear. Exhibit 12-13 shows the original data from which the chart was prepared, as well as the chart itself. It is clear that a number of *belts* or *bands* of information result from data presented on such a chart. The component parts line chart is often named a *belt chart*, or *band chart*, or *strata chart*.

A practice commonly followed in constructing such charts is to place the largest, or most important, or least variable component at the bottom, with smaller, or less important, or more variable components being placed successively higher in position. If one component has a very great variability, it is often placed at the top to catch immediate interest.

The component parts line chart is useful in indicating how the "shares" going to the various components change over the years. Exhibit 12-13 shows that "Conventional" mortgages have grown over the years 1972–1975 slightly more rapidly than "F.H.A.-insured" and "V.A.-guaranteed" mortgages. The cost components of a business unit—labor, materials, overhead—may be presented in such a chart to show how these relative shares of total operating costs have changed over a period of time. The production of several plants of a multiplant corporation may be presented thus, showing how the relative production of each plant has changed over a number of years. The shares going to the factors of production of an industry or a business unit—rent, interest, wages, profits—may be shown on this kind of chart, usually with profits as the top band because it is considered the "residual" share, and often shows the greatest variability.

THE FREQUENCY POLYGON

The line chart called a *frequency polygon* is often defined as a *many-sided, closed figure*. This concise definition is an accurate one. The charted line begins at the base line and ends at the base line, making the figure described a *closed* one. The figure is *many-sided* in that, since it originates at the base line and ends at the base line and consists of a series of points plotted and connected, it must possess *many sides*. The frequency polygon results from plotting the frequencies of a continuous fre-

EXHIBIT 12-13

Mutual Savings Bank Holdings of Residential Mortgages in the United States by Type of Loan, 1972–1975 (in billions of dollars)

Year	Conventional	V.A. Guaranteed	F.H.A. Insured	Total
1972	$28.5	$12.6	$16.0	$57.1
1973	32.6	12.9	15.5	61.0
1974	34.4	12.7	14.8	61.9
1975	36.1	12.7	14.9	63.7

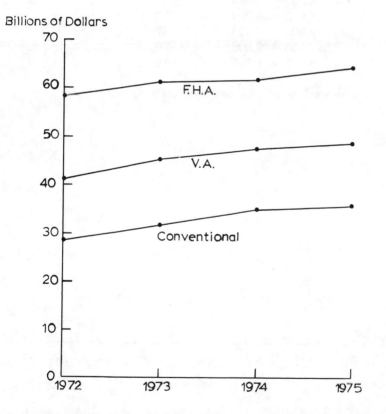

Source: Adapted from data in U.S. Bureau of the Census, *Statistical Abstract of the United States: 1976*, table 785, p. 489.

302

quency distribution. The class intervals of the continuous frequency distribution always appear on the X-axis of the graph and the number of frequencies on the Y-axis. Exhibit 12-14 is an example of a frequency polygon plotted from the continuous frequency distribution that accompanies it.

EXHIBIT 12-14
Manufacturing Employees Owning Capital Stock
in the Exaco Corporation, Organized by Income Group
June 30, 1977

Income Group	Number of Employees
$1,000 – $1,999	4
2,000 – 2,999	8
3,000 – 3,999	11
4,000 – 4,999	14
5,000 – 5,999	22
6,000 – 6,999	12
7,000 – 7,999	6
8,000 – 8,999	5

Source: Company Employee Survey, June 30, 1977.

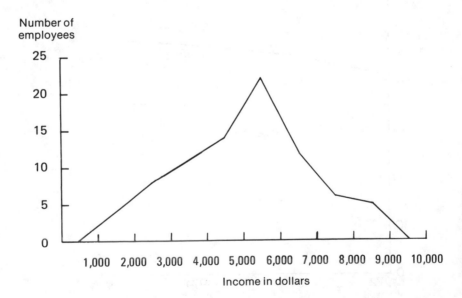

A point to be noted concerns the method by which the ends of the frequency distribution are *closed*. The first and last points plotted above the base line on a graph obviously are the values of the frequencies in the first and last class intervals. These points are connected to the base line by plotting a point one full class interval to the left directly on the X-axis, and the point at the right is connected with the base line the distance of one full class interval to the right of the last class interval. The closing of the many-sided figure has no important significance; it is more or less a convention long used and still continued by statisticians. The frequency polygon may be drawn with either straight lines connecting the points, or a curved line may be used to approximate the points; in the latter case, the chart is referred to as a *frequency curve*.

The frequency polygon gives an instant, comprehensive picture of a frequency distribution, allowing observations to be made as to the *normality* of the distribution. For example, the *hump* or *peak* of the frequencies may occur in the middle, indicating a relatively *normal* distribution, or it may occur towards one end or the other, resulting in *skewness*. These terms and their significance are treated in detail in other sections of this textbook. At this point, it is necessary to observe only the usefulness of the frequency polygon in presenting a comprehensive picture of the statistical distribution.

THE OGIVE

The ogive is a line chart plotted on arithmetic graph paper from a cumulative frequency distribution. Such distributions may, of course, be cumulated downward or upward. The terms "less than" and "more than," which are used to describe the kind of cumulative frequency distribution computed, are also used with the ogive, resulting in "less than" ogives and "more than" ogives, respectively. Exhibit 12-15 presents a cumulative frequency distribution with "less than" and "more than" cumulations, with the resulting ogives presented respectively in figure A and figure B.

While the ogive cannot be considered a widely used form of line chart, it has been found particularly useful in plotting population, per capita income, per capita earnings, etc., when frequency distributions are made up in an attempt to learn the characteristics of such data. They indicate the pattern of increase—whether the increase is a rapid one or a slow one, or whether the changes in the frequencies from class interval to class interval are abrupt or gradual—and they allow analytical observations to be made as to the proportions "less than" or "more than" given amounts.

Two or more distributions may be compared by converting the data of the distributions to percentages of the total, then cumulating the percentages and plotting the ogives on the same grid. The differences in steepness and shape of the ogives facilitate comparative observations.

THE LORENZ CURVE

The Lorenz curve is a line chart used to compare the proportionality in two quantitative variables. It reveals the departure from *symmetry*, or the degree of *skewness*, in the distribution of one of the variables in terms of the other. A common use of this line chart is to show the degree by which the distribution of income per family departs from the distribution of the number of families; it shows that a disparate proportion of the income goes to a few families.

EXHIBIT 12-15

Manufacturing Employees Owning Capital Stock in the Exaco Corporation, Organized by Income Group, June 30, 1977

Income Group	Number of Employees	"Less Than" Cumulation	"More Than" Cumulation
$1,000 – $1,999	4	4	82
2,000 – 2,999	8	12	78
3,000 – 3,999	11	23	70
4,000 – 4,999	14	37	59
5,000 – 5,999	22	59	45
6,000 – 6,999	12	71	23
7,000 – 7,999	6	77	11
8,000 – 8,999	5	82	5
Total	82		

Source: Company Employee Survey, June 30, 1977.

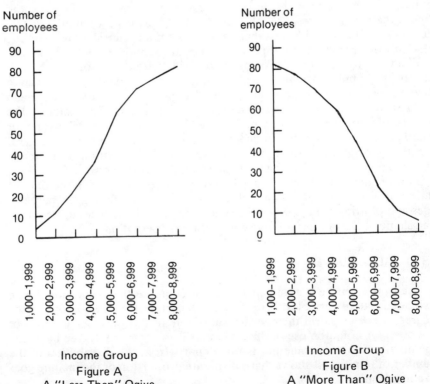

Income Group
Figure A
A "Less Than" Ogive

Income Group
Figure B
A "More Than" Ogive

The curve is plotted from cumulative percentages of the total of each of the variables. A study of exhibit 12-16 will serve to explain the procedure. The midpoints of the class intervals represent the income groups; they are multiplied by their respective frequencies to yield the total income distribution. This distribution (column D) is then converted to percentages of the total (column F), and the percentages accumulated (column H). These cumulated percentages of total income are plotted on the Y-axis of the grid, constituting the *dependent* variable. The percentages of the total number of employees are then computed (column E), and the percentages accumulated (column G). These cumulated percentages of total number of employees are plotted on the X-axis of the grid, constituting the *independent* variable.

The "Line of equal distribution" is a line which would have been obtained if the two distributions had been *proportional*. The line designated "Actual distribution" reveals that, of the manufacturing employees owning stock in the Exaco Corporation, the distribution of income is unequal compared to the distribution of the number of employees. Thus, 5 percent of the employees receive only 2 percent of the income, and 15 percent of the employees receive only 7 percent of the income. Looking at the chart from the upper income end, 90 percent of the income is received by 94 percent of the employees, which means that the top 6 percent of workers receive 10 percent of the total income.

In the Lorenz curve, the more the "actual distribution" line departs from the "line of equal distribution," the more unequal is the Y-variable in terms of the X-variable, and the more disproportionate is the relationship. This line chart is not restricted in use to income analysis; it may be used in the analysis of any kind of data organized in a frequency distribution.

BAR CHARTS

Bar charts, consisting of either vertical or horizontal bars to represent variables, are probably the most effective pictorial medium for comparing data. The eye can perceive instantly the differences in the values to be compared. Generally, the bars in a bar chart are wider than the spaces between the bars; this practice lends emphasis to the bars themselves. Occasionally, the actual numerical values of the bars are placed either inside the bars or on the chart at the immediate ends of the bars. This practice is not a common one, but it is effective when not only the picture is to be presented but the actual numerical values involved must be shown.

VERTICAL BAR CHARTS

Vertical bar charts are simply bar charts with the values of the bars on the Y-axis. Exhibit 12-17 illustrates a typical vertical bar chart. This chart presents a time series, with, therefore, the time unit—years—being placed on the X-axis since time is always an independent variable.

EXHIBIT 12-16
Manufacturing Employees Owning Capital Stock in the Exaco Corporation, Organized by Income Group, June 30, 1977

Col. A Income Group	Col. B Number of Employees	Col. C Midpoints of Income Group	Col. D Total Income Distribution (Col. B x Col. C)	Col. E Percentage of Total Employees (From Col. B)	Col. F Percentage of Total Income (From Col. D)	Col. G Cumulated Percentage of Total Employees	Col. H Cumulated Percentage of Total Income
$1,000 – $1,999	4	$1,500	6,000	5	2	5	2
2,000 – 2,999	8	2,500	20,000	10	5	15	7
3,000 – 3,999	11	3,500	38,500	13	9	28	16
4,000 – 4,999	14	4,500	63,000	17	15	45	31
5,000 – 5,999	22	5,500	121,000	27	29	72	60
6,000 – 6,999	12	6,500	78,000	15	19	87	79
7,000 – 7,999	6	7,500	45,000	7	11	94	90
8,000 – 8,999	5	8,500	42,500	6	10	100	100
	82		414,000	100	100		

Percentage of Total Income

100 90 80 70 60 50 40 30 20 10 0

Line of Equal Distribution

Actual Distribution

10 20 30 40 50 60 70 80 90 100

Percentage of Total Employees

Source: Company Employee Survey, June 30, 1977.

The vertical bar chart is commonly used for presenting time series data. Qualitative distributions and geographical distributions are very rarely presented in a vertical bar chart; normally, they are presented in horizontal bar charts. The quantitative distribution, i.e., the frequency distribution, is also presented in vertical bar charts but generally in the form of the *histogram*, a discussion of which immediately follows.

EXHIBIT 12-17

U.S. Social Security Expenditures, 1960 to 1975

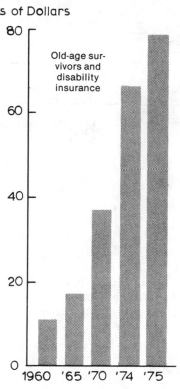

Source: U.S. Bureau of the Census, *Statistical Abstract of the U.S.: 1976*, p. 292.

HISTOGRAMS

The histogram is a vertical bar chart of a frequency distribution. Exhibit 12-18 presents a histogram constructed from the data of exhibit 12-14. The class intervals of the frequency distribution appear on the X-axis, and the number of employees in each classification is recorded on the Y-axis.

The bars in the histogram are adjacent to one another, no space being left between them because the class intervals of the distribution are considered to be continuous. In some histograms, the lines designating the bars

308

EXHIBIT 12-18

**Histogram of Manufacturing Employees Owning Capital Stock
in the Exaco Corporation, Organized by Income Group,
June 30, 1977**

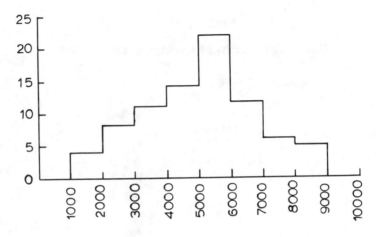

Source: Company Employee Survey, June 30, 1977.

may be left in the chart. In exhibit 12-18, these lines have been eradicated. This histogram, thus, has the appearance of a *stepped* line chart. The histogram is used solely for presenting such quantitative distributions in chart form.

HORIZONTAL BAR CHARTS

The horizontal bar chart is illustrated in exhibit 12-19. This particular exhibit presents a geographical distribution. The differences in immigration of the various nations listed are graphically shown. The X-axis variable is placed across the top of such a chart simply by mere convention. In a normal mathematical grid, these values would be placed at the bottom. Statisticians have, however, adopted the practice, which is now practically uniform, of placing these values at the top where they are seen more quickly. The geographical classification appears on the Y-axis.

Horizontal bar charts are commonly used for qualitative distributions as well as for geographical distributions. They are also often used for quantitative distributions which are discrete instead of continuous.

EXHIBIT 12-19
U.S. Immigrants by Selected Country of Birth, 1975

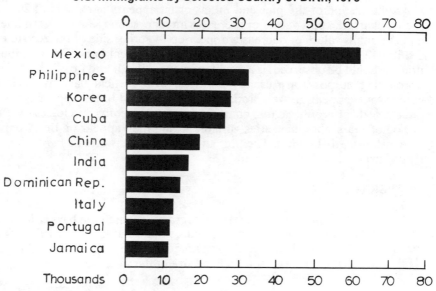

Source: U.S. Bureau of the Census, *Statistical Abstract of the U.S.: 1976*, p. 101.

EXHIBIT 12-20

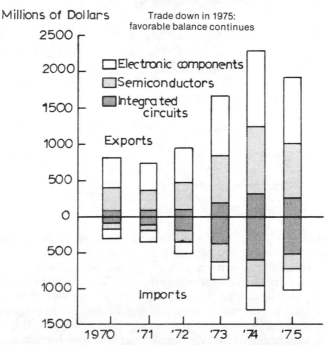

Source: U.S. Department of Commerce, *U.S. Industrial Outlook: 1976*, p. 283.

PLUS AND MINUS CHARTS

An illustration of the plus and minus chart appears in exhibit 12-20. In such a chart, the plus values or increases appear on one side of a zero line; and the minus values or decreases appear on the other side of the zero line. Exhibit 12-20 shows the values in the form of vertical bars. The distribution, it should be observed, is a qualitative one. "Profit and Loss" charts for accounting purposes are usually arranged with vertical bars. In such a case, profits appear above a horizontal zero line and losses appear below. Such a vertical profit and loss chart may show the profits and losses over a period of years; the time series variable would then appear on the X-axis, where it properly belongs. The plus and minus chart is often a *percentage-type* chart.

PICTOGRAMS

A variation of the bar chart is the pictogram, in which the bars consist of pictures of the item or characteristic under study. Exhibit 12-21 presents a pictogram. Attention is directed to the fact that the symbols are all identical, so that each one represents a fixed size of the variable.

EXHIBIT 12-21
Decline in Farms in the United States, 1940 to 1975

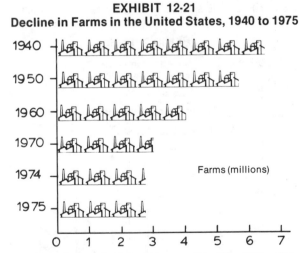

Source: U.S. Bureau of the Census, *Statistical Abstract of the U.S.: 1976*, p. 628.

Although exhibit 12-21 is of the horizontal bar type, such pictograms may be presented in the form of vertical bars as well. Whether the data are presented in a vertical bar pattern or a horizontal bar pattern, however, the principle of the fixed size unit is invariably followed. Such charts are truly bar charts and are extremely useful in attracting attention and in giving an immediate comparative picture of the differences in magnitudes. The pictogram is usually restricted to qualitative distributions. It is sometimes used for geographical distributions, however, and for quantitative and time series distributions.

COMPONENT PARTS BAR CHARTS

The component parts bar chart is employed to show comparisons involving two or more variables on a single chart. Thus, in exhibit 12-22, two variables—durable goods and nondurable goods—are included. This chart reveals clearly that nondurable goods sales are increasing faster than durable goods sales.

EXHIBIT 12-22

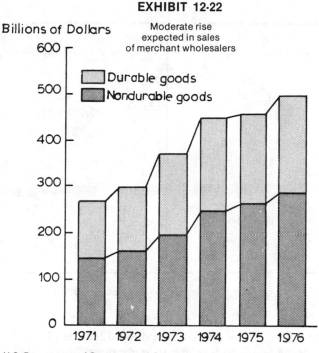

Source: U.S. Department of Commerce, *U.S. Industrial Outlook: 1976*, p. 163.

Such component parts bar charts are highly versatile in use, i.e., the analyst has choice in organizing his data to present more than one idea. Sometimes the bars themselves may be placed in groups: Each bar in such a case consists actually of three or four bars, instead of each bar including three or four segments.

Component parts bar charts may consist of horizontal bars as well as vertical bars. In presenting a time series, vertical bars are usually used; but, in presenting segments of a qualitative distribution, horizontal bars may properly be used.

CIRCLE OR PIE CHARTS

The circle or pie chart is a component parts chart. The component parts form the segments of the circle. Exhibit 12-23 is an illustration of such a chart. The circle chart is usually, but not always a percentage chart, the percentages being placed around the circumference of the circle. The data are converted to percentages of the total; and the proportional segments, therefore, give a clear picture of the relationship among the component parts.

EXHIBIT 12-23

Land Owned by the U.S. Government, 1975

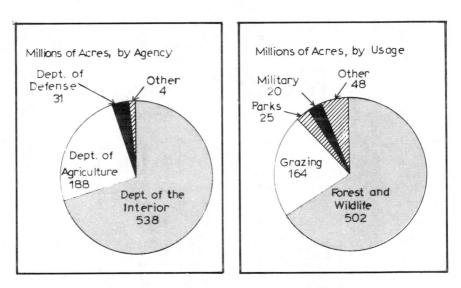

Source: U.S. Bureau of the Census, *Statistical Abstract of the U.S.: 1976*, p. 204.

Very often the legend, as shown in exhibit 12-23, is placed inside the chart itself, the name of each segment being placed inside its own area. The exact percentage or the exact arithmetic amount of each part may also be placed within the segment itself. When the legends are to appear inside the parts of the circle, a segment may be found to be too small to contain the legend. In such a case, an arrow may be drawn to the segment and the legend placed outside, in a horizontal position.

Sometimes the circle is divided into degrees. After converting the arithmetic amounts to percentages of the total, each of the percentages is then multiplied by the constant 3.6 so that the total, instead of equaling 100 percent, will equal 360°. The ordinates in degrees would be placed around the circumference of the circle as in the case of percentages. Circle charts presented in degrees, however, are far less common than circle charts presented in percentages.

National income in the United States is often shown by distributive shares. The component parts—wages, profits, interest, and rent—are commonly presented in such a chart also for individual firm analyses and for individual industry analyses. The cost structure of a firm may be presented in this form of chart; sometimes such charts appear in annual statements of condition of the firm.

STATISTICAL MAPS

Statistical data are often presented in the form of a statistical map when such data are distributed geographically. These maps are sometimes called *cartograms*. They are highly effective in giving an immediate and comprehensive picture of the geographical distribution. They may consist of maps of countries or of states or of regions of one kind or another; economic, climatic, etc. Such maps are of two basic kinds: the dot map and the crosshatch map.

THE DOT MAP

Exhibit 12-24 illustrates a dot map, showing states with most employees on nonagricultural payrolls in the United States, with each dot representing 1,000,000 employees. The concentration of such employment in the eastern half of the United States and along the Pacific Coast is apparent in this map. In exhibit 12-24, large dots are used.

The dots on such a map may be large or small, with the dot size being fixed for any given map. In exhibit 12-25, small dots are used. Each dot represents a smaller unit; the concentration of a large number of dots then gives the effect of degrees of shading. With a heavy concentration on a small-dot map, the coloring is nearly black; with lesser concentrations the dots present a grayish appearance. Thus, the shading of the map gives an immediate impression of the degree of concentration.

A prime rule in the preparation of dot maps is that the dots must be of uniform size on the map. Many times economic maps are prepared in which a single dot will be used to represent a given concentration; and the dots, therefore, will be of varying sizes on the map. The question arises: Is the area of each dot being compared or is the diameter or radius of each dot being compared? It is apparent that bias may appear in such a presentation. One dot twice the size of another in respect to diameter looks many times larger to the human eye, while a dot twice the size of another in respect to area does not look twice as large. In order to avoid such bias in map presentation, therefore, the rule is adopted that the dots, whether they be large or small, must be of uniform size. Each dot in such a case represents a given unit.

THE CROSSHATCH MAP

The crosshatch map, sometimes called a *shaded* map, is most useful for presenting frequency distributions which are distributed geographically. Exhibit 12-26 presents a crosshatch map of a frequency distribution of cash receipts from farm marketings in the United States distributed by individual states. The frequency distribution classification is presented in the legend, and each state is classified into one of the three categories. The method of crosshatching or shading may be as shown in exhibit 12-26, but often colors are substituted for the crosshatching. In other cases, different shades of gray are employed. Whatever the method of distinguishing the classifications, the effect is identical: to contrast the various geographical segments.

314

EXHIBIT 12-24
States with Most Employees on Nonagricultural Payrolls in the United States
by State, 1975

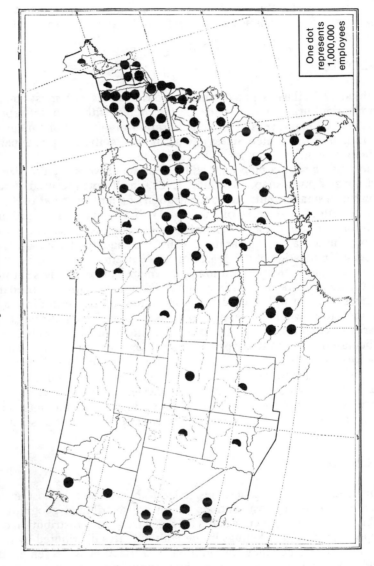

One dot
represents
1,000,000
employees

Source: U.S. Bureau of the Census, *Statistical Abstract of the U.S.: 1976,* p. 367.

EXHIBIT 12-25
Unemployment Rates of Arkansas Counties, Spring 1977

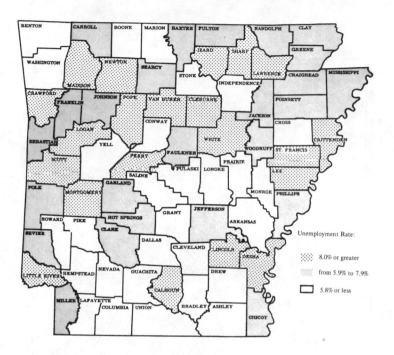

Source: *Arkansas Business and Economic Review*, Spring 1977, p. 28.

THE TRACT SURVEY MAP

If it is desired to know the geographical distribution or location of certain conditions or facts, a tract survey map containing such information may be constructed. For example, one of the purposes of a research project could be to determine which tract areas in a city have the highest average levels of family income and the largest number of employed persons. Exhibit 12-27 presents a tract map of Lubbock, Texas, based on the 1970 Census, with five classifications of data shown in each tract area. To allow the placement of the maximum amount of data in each relatively small tract area, the titles with the statistical items can be listed in a given order on some blank space on the map and then in each area the numerical data only can be listed in the same order. This practice was followed in exhibit 12-27.

BIAS IN GRAPHIC PRESENTATION

The possibility of bias occurring in charts has been mentioned in two respects: the pictures in a pictogram and the dots in a statistical map. In both cases, the rule that the pictures or dots must be of uniform size on a

EXHIBIT 12-26

Cash Receipts from Farm Marketings in the United States by State, 1975

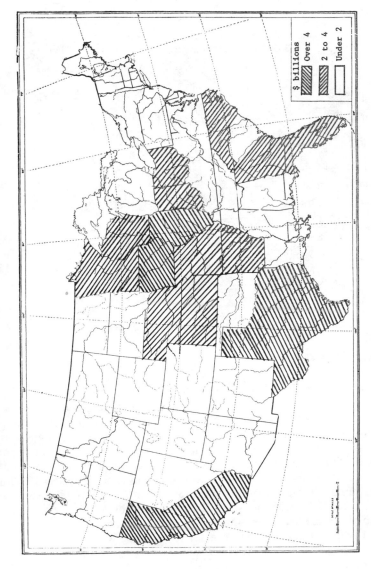

Source: U.S. Bureau of the Census, *Statistical Abstract of the U.S.: 1976*, p. 648.

EXHIBIT 12-27

Income, Education, Housing, and Labor Status of Lubbock, Texas (1970 Census Data)

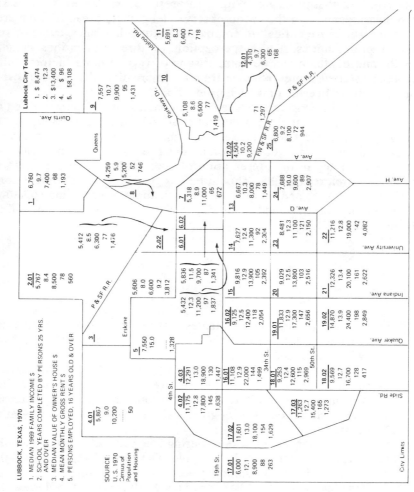

LUBBOCK, TEXAS, 1970

1. MEDIAN 1969 FAMILY INCOME $
2. SCHOOL YEARS COMPLETED BY PERSONS 25 YRS. AND OVER
3. MEDIAN VALUE OF OWNER'S HOUSE $
4. MEAN MONTHLY GROSS RENT $
5. PERSONS EMPLOYED, 16 YEARS OLD & OVER

SOURCE:
U.S. 1970
Census of
Population
and Housing

Lubbock City Totals

1. $ 8,474
2.   12.3
3. $13,400
4. $ 96
5. 58,108

given chart was explained. The reason for this rule lies in the fact that the human eye is easily deceived by proportions. This deception was explained in respect to the dot map: When one dot is twice as large as another dot in respect to diameter, it actually appears much larger; when one dot is twice as large as another in respect to area, it does not appear that large to the eye.

With linear comparison in which the lengths of two lines—or two bars—are compared, the eye is not deceived, for there is only one relationship to observe, i.e., that of length. With area presentation, however, there are two measurements for the eye to observe: length and breadth. Such area representations are difficult to compare. On the other hand, cubic or volume representations require perception of three dimensions: length, width, and depth. Accurate comparisons of two or more factors which appear as volume representations are much more difficult. The eye is very easily confused in estimating such proportions.

The preceding considerations lead to a conclusion: For comparing two or more items, the bar chart is without peer. Whether the bar is vertical or horizontal, whether it appears as a histogram or a pictogram, the comparison is similar: A simple observation of linear relationships is provided. To achieve accuracy in the presentation of statistical data by any pictorial method, therefore, the chart should be designed so that only linear comparisons are made; and, at all times, for example in preparing statistical maps, the use of areas and volumes for comparison purposes should be avoided.

SUMMARY

There are two general kinds of tables: (1) repository tables, which are original collections of data containing complete information; (2) analytical tables, in which some kind of analysis is presented.

Four methods of classification of the tables are: (1) qualitative classifications, in which different kinds of things are listed; (2) quantitative classifications, which present different values of one variable, and therefore are frequency distributions; (3) geographical classifications; (4) time-series classifications.

Table construction involves considering the parts of a table and the methods of arranging the items in the table. The parts of a table are (1) the heading, including table number and title; (2) the body, which contains the stub, heading, panels, and fields; (3) end materials including footnotes and source.

The items may be arranged in a table as follows: (1) in order of size; (2) for comparison purposes; (3) in order of totals; (4) sometimes a miscellaneous classification is included. While these are general arrangements, the bases for such arrangements may be listed as follows: (1) alphabetical; (2) chronological; (3) geographical; (4) in order of size; (5) in order of causal relationship; (6) in order of interest; (7) according to custom; (8) according to desired emphasis.

Charts may be line charts: (1) arithmetic line charts; (2) geometric line charts; (3) component parts line charts; (4) frequency polygons; (5) ogives; (6) Lorenz curves.

Bar charts are classified as: (1) vertical bar charts; (2) horizontal bar charts; (3) the histogram; (4) plus and minus charts, either horizontal or vertical; (5) pictograms; (6) component parts bar charts.

Circle, or pie, charts are in wide use. Statistical maps are also often presented; these may be: (1) large-dot maps; (2) small-dot maps; (3) cross-hatch maps.

The matter of bias in graphic presentation may be largely avoided by using bar charts, which provide that only a linear comparison need be made.

EXERCISES

1. Compare and contrast analytical tables and repository tables.
2. Describe the characteristics of each of the following classifications of tables: qualitative, quantitative, geographic, time series. Present an example of each.
3. Write a two-page paper describing the arranging of items in a table.
4. Describe the facts—trends, comparisons, etc.—revealed by the following table:

Soybean Statistics for Arkansas

Year	Harvested (thousand acres)	Yield (bushels per acre)	Average price (per bushel)
1971	4,300	21.5	$3.00
1972	4,050	20.0	4.13
1973	4,650	25.0	5.66
1974	4,300	19.0	6.96
1975	4,700	24.0	4.50

Source: *Arkansas Business and Economic Review* (Spring 1977), p. 9.

5. Use the data in exercise 4 to construct an arithmetic line chart showing the trend in value of yield per acre 1971 to 1975.
6. Why would a geometric line chart not be suitable for presenting the trend of the prices of soybeans per acre from exercise 4?
7. When is a geometric line chart suitable for presenting trends? What are the peculiarities of such a chart?
8. Write a one-page paper interpreting the facts shown in exhibit 12-13 of the text.
9. Construct a frequency polygon from the following frequency distribution:

Age groups	Number of males
21–30	27
31–40	56
41–50	32
51–60	18
61–70	12

10. Construct a "less than" cumulation and an ogive from the frequency distribution presented in exercise 9.
11. Using the frequency polygon constructed in exercise 9, construct a histogram.
12. Construct a bar graph of the value of yield per acre for 1971 to 1975 from data in exercise 4.
13. Explain how the pictogram and the bar graph are alike. How do they differ from the plus and minus chart?
14. What is the usefulness of circle charts?
15. How is bias eliminated in making dot maps. In making pictograms?

SELECTED REFERENCES

Balsley, Howard L. *Basic Statistics for Business and Economics*. Columbus, Ohio: Grid, 1978.

Enrick, Norbert Lloyd. *Effective Graphic Communication*. New York: Petrocelli, 1972.

U.S. Bureau of the Census. *Bureau of the Census Manual of Tabular Presentation*, by Bruce L. Jenkinson. U.S. Government Printing Office, Washington, D.C., 1949.

13

Preparing Business Reports

Reports of business and economic research projects are often classified as technical reports—those reports containing technical matters as contrasted to, for example, conference reports, annual meeting reports, and progress reports.* Different types of reports have their own unique, generalized formats, and these formats are customarily followed. The discussion in this chapter is limited to technical reports within the subject area of business and economic research.

THE PURPOSES AND FORMS OF REPORTS

The central purpose of any report, and specifically of the research report in business and economics, is to communicate results of the study. In writing his report, the researcher should always keep in mind the basic necessity of communicating with the person who is to receive the report. Reports to governmental units will normally follow an established procedure set up by the particular governmental unit. Usually, if not always, reports of research conducted within governmental units will begin with a summary of the conclusions of the report; there is some evidence of a

---

*Much of the material in this chapter first appeared as a monograph, *An Essay on the Writing of Business Reports*, by Howard L. Balsley (Lubbock, Texas: College of Business Administration, Texas Tech University).

trend for all reports—nongovernmental as well as governmental—to follow this pattern. Placing the summary at the beginning of the report makes more feasible a quick survey of the results on the part of supervisors, legislators, and executives.

Reports within business establishments will often follow an established procedure, particularly if the business unit is a large corporation. It is common practice in petroleum refining, for example, for both basic and applied research studies to be presented in a standardized form prescribed in a book of procedures that is published by the corporation.

Research conducted within universities is normally reported by an established procedure, which sometimes is absolutely fixed. For example, each university will have specific requirements for the master's thesis and the doctor's dissertation. The requirements will be contained in a brochure published by the university in which the detailed requirements are set forth; these requirements will even specify the quality and weight of paper that must be used. Sometimes they specify the brand name of the paper required. Matters of margins, indentations, spacing, etc., will be stated specifically and in detail.

Research conducted by faculty members will often be reported in a format dictated by the sponsor of the program. For example, foundations or business units contracting research with university professors will require the results to be submitted in a specific format which may be furnished by way of a brochure or a printed statement to the professor. Research conducted by individuals, of course, may be for private publication in a professional journal. In such a case, the format requirements of the professional journal must be followed. These vary with the subject area the journal is devoted to, the standard practices in the subject area, and the level of the audience at which the publication is aimed.

The basic forms in which research reports may be submitted are *oral* and *written*. Brief oral reports may be given over the telephone. Such reports, when needed very quickly, may be given in such a way, then followed by a written report. Sometimes reports are delivered orally person to person, in which case the researcher reports directly to his supervisor, or to an executive. Such reports are normally brief and give the results of a research project with little elaboration. However, when reports are delivered orally in a conference meeting, or to a board of directors, or to a group of cooperating scientists, the oral report will take on a much more formal nature. As much care may be given to preparing such a report as is given to producing a formal written report. Alternatively, these reports sometimes are made from a series of notes; the researcher, being entirely familiar with all the details and aspects of the research study, may be able to make an oral report to a group by simply relying on his notes.

Written reports may go to a superior within the business organization, to a board of directors, or to a directing group within an organization; the written reports may go to an employer, for example, in the case of a faculty member in a university doing research under a contract for a business firm. The written report, of course, may be for publication in a professional journal. In all cases, the report should be given great care in its organization, in its style of presentation, and in the accuracy of the typing and in many other detailed aspects.

THE ELEMENTS OF A RESEARCH REPORT

It is understood that the written report and the formal oral report will always contain certain amounts of beginning material, a body consisting of the details of the study itself, and some elements of ending material. Exhibit 13-1 is a breakdown of the elements of a report that lists the specific items under each grouping.

EXHIBIT 13-1

Front matter

    Title page
    Notices
    Foreword
    Abstract
    Contents
    List of illustrations
    List of tables

Main body

    Technical discussion

        Summary

            Research processes;
            Procedures; equipment
            Final solutions
            Recommendation
            References

Terminal matter

    References
    Bibliographies
    Appendixes
    Exhibits
    Addenda

Source: Alison R. Stafford and Billie Jean Culpepper, *The Science-Engineering Secretary*, © 1963, p. 298. Reprinted by permission of Prentice-Hall, Inc., Englewood Cliffs, New Jersey.

FRONT MATTER

The *title page* will contain the title of the study, the name of the author, and usually his position; and, possibly, a reference to the sponsor of the program at the bottom of the title page. The title itself should be explanatory, so that upon publication the classification of the research report may be readily made by professional librarians. A title should, of course, be as brief as possible. Nevertheless, it should contain a succinct statement of the subject matter of the research report. Not only do librarians need to classify research reports, but the reader will need to judge whether he will be interested in the report. The title should be as specific as possible; a title, for example of "Research Report of Test Marketing" is more general and less desirable than a specific title such as "Bayesian Decision Theory Applied to Test Market Situations."

There may or may not be *notices* or a *foreword* in a given report. A notice may consist of a paragraph naming the sponsor of a program, or a statement concerning a patent or copyright restriction, or a notification that the current project is part of a larger project. If such notices are very brief, they may be placed at the bottom of the title page. A foreword is sometimes used when introductory remarks need to be made concerning the reasons for making the study, or concerning the study's connection with other studies, or concerning the sponsorship of the program, or concerning acknowledgments to contributors to the project. Normally, a foreword is presented on a separate page or pages.

An *abstract* may or may not be required. It is common practice for universities to require abstracts of doctoral dissertations. Some require abstracts also of master's theses. Many scientific associations and editorial boards require abstracts of scientific research reports. An abstract is a succinct statement of the findings of the research project, furnished so that the results of the research are made available at the beginning of the report in a brief form. The reader can then decide whether he wishes to read the entire report. Sometimes abstracts are published separately. For example, the *Journal of Economic Literature* publishes abstracts of articles appearing in leading professional journals. A number of universities publish brochures of abstracts annually, containing abstracts of all of the theses and dissertations completed at the institution during that year.

The *contents* is usually a page or two, listing each chapter title. Sometimes the subsections within each chapter are included under the chapter headings. Page numbers are given opposite the list. Besides the contents, a list of exhibits or illustrations or tables or charts may be included. Each of these lists the pertinent items with the page numbers at the right. Each would be a separate listing with a separate heading, for example, "List of Exhibits."

MAIN BODY OF THE REPORT

The body of the report contains the introduction to the problem and the orientation to the problem area. It includes the presentation of the evidence and the conclusions drawn from the evidence. Therefore, the main body may be further subdivided into *introduction*, *presentation of the evidence*, and *conclusions*. The breakdown in exhibit 13-1, as presented by Stafford and Culpepper, indicates that the main body of the paper should contain a technical discussion, then a summary of the research, the processes or procedures, a description of the equipment, followed by the final solutions and recommendations, and including references to substantiate the material presented. The following paragraphs discuss the subsections of the main body of the report.

The *introduction* will always include a statement of the problem. The origin or reasons for the problem may be given. Previous research, that is, library investigation, may be presented which will show the orientation of the specific problem covered to the general research which has already been accomplished. The specific hypothesis, if one has been posed, will be stated, and the methods or procedures used in attempting to test the hypothesis will be delineated. The design of the experiment may be explained in this introductory section.

The *presentation of the evidence* consists of a discussion and interpretation of the evidence. Here the step-by-step procedure in uncovering the evidence, in analyzing the evidence, and in appraising the evidence is given. The techniques of analysis are applied, which may be scientific, including statistical, in attempting to arrive at conclusions.

The *conclusions* and *findings* are the final part of the main body of the report. Sometimes conclusions or findings are listed numerically. Sometimes they consist of a generalized discussion, including inferences as to the impact or usefulness of applications of the results. Sometimes *recommendations* are made; very often, of course, executive groups in business corporations desire to make recommendations themselves and to implement these recommendations by making decisions. Therefore, they may desire that no recommendations be made but simply that the evidence be presented with conclusions.

Distinguishing the differences between conclusions and findings often puzzles the beginning researcher; stating them and listing them therefore is difficult. The *findings* may be defined as the specific facts learned from each part of the study. Sometimes the specific facts—findings—are listed for each question on the summary questionnaire that contains the counts collected in a survey. The *conclusions*, however, are the generalized statements—the generalizations—arrived at for the original hypotheses through considered judgment of the specific findings. Thus, findings are facts; conclusions are inferences, and relate to hypotheses.

Exhibit 13-2 is an example of a moving expense survey completed in 1977. The survey was a "Committee of 500 Survey" conducted by the Administrative Management Society. The Committee of 500 is a survey panel comprised of members throughout the United States and Canada. Both the body of the report and the questionnaire used are presented.

EXHIBIT 13-2

Company Policies in Reimbursement of Moving Expenses*

Movement or transfer of employees may be necessary for a firm operating in various cities and/or states. The move may be a good opportunity for the employee, but it may be expensive, especially during an inflationary period. This survey shows companies recognize the need to assist employees with the economics of moving which, in some cases, will offset some of the psychological effects.

This survey does not attempt to specifically analyze all of the details involved with various programs companies have to reimburse for moving expenses. It does reflect general areas of concern and should be examined accordingly.

Source: "Committee of 500 Survey," Administrative Management Society. Reprinted with permission from the Administrative Management Society, Willow Grove, Pa.

Question 1—The large percentage of positive responses (77%) indicates the general feelings for a need to reimburse employees.

Question 2—A 78% majority said "yes" which coincides with Question 1. Not only is the need to reimburse employees recognized, but also a specific program to enhance understanding and equality of application.

Question 3—In most cases, it was felt expenses should be reimbursed only if the company initiated the move as 90% indicated this as part of their program.

Question 4—A majority of 63% cover both new employees and transferees. Only 12% cover new employees only and 25% cover just transferees. There were also comments to the effect that only new employees hired to fill a critical skill were covered.

Question 5—Considering 44% indicated "Company only" and 35% said "Employee from approved list," it is apparent the company controls the selection of the carrier.

Question 6—The most popular method of payment for the movement of household goods is for the company to pay all expenses, as 90% of responses indicated this as part of their program.

Question 7—People have items in addition to their household goods, and some programs provide for reimbursement. The survey indicated:

 4% Aircraft
34% Autos
16% Boats
 5% Campers
 5% Fireplace wood
15% Frozen foods
13% Live plants
 5% Greenhouses
 1% Playhouses
 2% Swimming pools

For these special items, limitations were indicated, such as a set mileage cost limit and/or a limit as to the number. Some respondents indicated they give a convenience allowance to cover these items and some said such items are reviewed individually.

Question 8—Packing and unpacking lead the list of supplementary services paid for with 93% and 84% respectively. Storage is next with 64% followed by 12% for cleaning and 13% for loss or damage insurance.

Question 9—The survey indicated 35% of the firms reporting give no assistance in real estate transactions for the former home. The 65% who do give assistance outlined their assistance as follows:

24% Reimbursement of all sales expense
13% Reimbursement of some sales expense
23% Guarantee of sales price
 8% Dual payment
 4% Set allowance
28% Cost of breaking lease

Additional comments were given as follows:
• No assistance to new employees
• Two firms said assistance includes mortgage financing
• One firm gives assistance up to $500; another said $2,500
• One firm pays house payment until home is sold
• One firm purchases former home
• One firm pays duplicate rent up to $300

Question 10—For assistance in real estate transactions for the new home, 64% of the companies, with formal programs, assist as follows:

25% Loan for purchase
27% Closing costs
 3% Cleaning of home
19% Set allowance
17% Installation of appliances
 5% Cleaning carpets & drapes
 4% Purchase of new items (Drapes, carpets, etc.)

Again, there were specific comments, such as: No assistance to new employees, assistance with mortgage financing, set allowance is up to $300, four firms said set allowance is up to $1,000.

Question 11—An overwhelming majority of companies having a formal program pay for personal trips as follows:

a) To seek housing (89%):
  13% 1 trip
  11% 2+ trips
  22% Wife's expenses paid
  22% Transportation
  22% Lodging and subsistence
  10% Child care baby sitting
b) Enroute to new location (92%):
  51% Lodging and subsistence
  47% Transportation
   2% Set allowance
c) Awaiting arrival of furniture or delay of new quarters (90%):
   9% Under one week
  35% One to two weeks
  21% Over two weeks
  35% Other

The "other" comments were: Thirteen companies indicated one month, one firm said they pay for three months up to $600, another paid employees' expenses for three months & family limit of one month, one company pays up to $775 maximum, another pays lodging and subsistence for eight weeks, another paid after one week— company pays up to $80 per week up to eight months. Others said "reasonable amount" depending on circumstances.

Company Policies in Reimbursement of
Moving Expenses Questionnaire

Do not fill in this questionnaire. It is presented only for your use in reviewing the survey results on pages one and two.

1. Does your company reimburse employees for relocation to another city?

   ____ Yes   ____ No

   (If Yes, please complete balance of this survey, if No, return survey)

2. Does the company have a formalized moving policy?

   ____ Yes   ____ No

3. What types of moves are covered?

   ____ Company initiated only
   ____ Company or employee initiated

4. What types of employees are covered?

____ New employees (hired at a different location than job)
____ Transferees
____ Both

5. Who selects the carrier?

____ Company only
____ Employee only
____ Employee from approved list

6. Who pays for the movement of household goods?

____ Company pays all expense
____ Company pays to a set limit (Either dollars or pounds)

7. Does the company pay for any of the following items?

____ Aircraft
____ Autos
____ Boats, campers
____ Fireplace wood
____ Frozen foods
____ Live plants
____ Greenhouses, playhouses, swimming pools

8. What supplementary services are paid for by the company?

____ Packing
____ Storage
____ Loss or damage insurance over movers minimum
____ Unpacking
____ Cleaning

9. What type of assistance does company give in real estate transactions for former home?

____ No assistance
Assistance including:
____ Reimbursement of all sales expense
____ Reimbursement of some sales expense
____ Guarantee of sales price (Based on appraised, or market value)
____ Dual payment
____ Set allowance
____ Cost of breaking lease

10. What type of assistance does company give in real estate transaction for new home?

____ No assistance
Assistance including:
____ Loan for purchase
____ Closing costs
____ Cleaning of home
____ Installation of appliances
____ Cleaning carpets and drapes
____ Purchase of new items—drapes, carpets, etc.
____ Set allowance

11. What types of personal trips are paid for by the company?

a. To seek housing
___ None
___ 1 trip
___ 2 + trips
___ Wife's expenses paid
___ Transportation
___ Lodging and subsistence
___ Child care baby sitting
b. Enroute to new location
___ None
___ Lodging and subsistence
___ Transportation
___ Set allowance
c. Awaiting arrival of furniture or delay in obtaining new quarters
___ None
___ Lodging and subsistence
Length of subsistence
___ Under 1 week
___ 1 to 2 weeks
___ Over 2 weeks
___ Other

What are the conclusions, and what are the findings of the report illustrated in exhibit 13-2? The first two paragraphs of the report explaining the results are conclusions, since they are inferences relating to the hypothesis that business firms reimburse employees for moving expenses. They are not titled "Conclusions" and this is often the case. Sometimes such conclusions are titled and sometimes they are not.

The remaining paragraphs of the report refer to specific findings of the specific questions on the questionnaire. The findings are numbered with the question numbers from the questionnaire. The findings are listed in the greatest detail.

Conclusions and findings are both necessary to an understanding of the results of a research project. Neither is complete by itself. Sometimes the conclusions and findings are woven together in the statements of the results; this often is done with very brief reports of surveys and studies that are small and highly limited in scope.

THE TERMINAL MATTER

The ending material will normally include the *bibliography* of the reference works used in both the investigation of previous research and also in substantiating the analysis and findings of the study. Sometimes these bibliographies are in the form of *annotated bibliographies*, in which case each reference is described and appraised as to the subject matter it contains, its application, and its usefulness as related to the research study.

Appendixes may be included at the end of a research report when there is supplementary material to be presented. Sometimes exhibits in the form of tables or charts, where they are very long and detailed, are included in an appendix rather than in the text of the body of the material. Sometimes the appendix is a table of computed values to be used for reference purposes. An appendix may also contain standardized procedures, for example, mathematical equations or derivations which are not included in the text material.

Glossaries of terms are given to insure that definitions used by the analyst are understood by the reader. New terms may need to be introduced in a manuscript; in this case a glossary should be included, explaining the new terms. Finally, any *addenda* that are required, pointing out possibilities of further research, possibilities for other steps in the given research program, and criticisms that might have been made by colleagues, can be presented.

PRACTICES IN RESEARCH REPORT WRITING

Certain practices when followed diligently, will result in a readable, accurate, and useful research report. Some attention should, therefore, be given to the subject of sound practice in writing the report.

STYLE

The matter of style in writing is a very personal one to the novelist or poet. To the research report writer, however, the matter of style can be reduced to an attempt to attain certain characteristics in the text material that will make it more useful in communicating the information and ideas to others. Probably the first requirement in the matter of style is that of *accuracy*. It is obvious that a research report must be accurate if it is to be useful. Some specific points need mention, however. To be accurate, a report should delegate more space to important matters and lesser space to unimportant matters. The main theme throughout the report should receive emphasis and not be subordinated to material of lesser value. There should be an absence of exaggeration. Superlatives, such as *very*, should normally be avoided. Since the report is necessarily factual in nature, it should present the facts as objectively as possible. Thus, to achieve accuracy, the report writer should attempt to give the proper emphasis as among concepts, avoid the use of superlatives, and attempt to give an objective presentation.

In the attempt to achieve accuracy, *clarity* may be forthcoming as a matter of course. Clarity should receive attention, however, since statements that are unclear, or the presentation of concepts that are unclear, will damage the effort to communicate to others. The terminology should be standard, and good English usage should be practiced. Abnormally long sentences should be avoided, although sometimes long sentences are necessary in order to modify and explain correctly. Where unusual terms are included, they should be defined explicitly in the text or in a footnote; they may also become part of a glossary at the end of the manuscript. The sentences should flow together in order to advance the reading of the report. The sentences, therefore, should be connected in a sequence that results in the presentation of a single concept, idea, or consequence. Each such idea or consequence will constitute a paragraph, and each paragraph should therefore be a relatively complete entity in itself.

Conciseness in a report refers to the absence of waste wordage. Usually the attempt to achieve clarity will result in succinct statements, statements of precision, and thus, a certain degree of economy of expression will be attained. However, each manuscript should be examined for economy of expression. Useless words, superlatives, and words that have no real meaning may be eliminated. Details of the data may be eliminated when they are unnecessary in furthering communication. Sometimes pertinent data really needed by the reader in order to follow the reasoning of the report may be left out. Such an omission is a mistake, for all of the pertinent data needed should be included. If great masses of data are required, they should appear in the appendix to the report.

Every research report should be as *readable* as it can be made. It is understood that many research reports are so highly technical that only experts in the field will be able to digest their meaning. This does not mean that they are not readable; it simply means that they are beyond average comprehension. Even such highly technical works should be readable, however, to further the understanding of the reader. Thus, if the report is accurate, if the statements are clear and unambiguous, if economy has been practiced in the careful choice of words, then readability may be expected to follow. If clichés and excess wordage have been eliminated, readability will be furthered. A few suggestions may help to achieve readability:

1. Use active verbs rather than passive verbs; this keeps interest alive.
2. Be precise; this means using correct and exact names, references, data, and figures, yet avoiding unnecessary masses of details.
3. Use familiar terms and common words when they serve the purpose and are really indicated as the ones that are desired; this means avoiding long and obscure words when there is no real reason for using them.
4. Vary the lengths of sentences so that a succession of short sentences or a succession of long sentences is avoided.

The matter of *unity* refers to the need for the report writer to keep the central problem of his research project in mind throughout all phases of writing the report. In keeping in mind the problem to be solved, the hypothesis to be tested, the evidence to be presented, and the conclusions to be drawn, the report writer will achieve unity because he will have left out extraneous materials. Paragraphs or sentences that do not further the thought of the research report should be eliminated. Each sentence, each concept, should advance the report one step further. Thus, if all that is pertinent is included and all that is extraneous is excluded, unity will be achieved.

GRAMMAR AND USAGE

It is fundamental that correct grammar and good English usage be practiced in writing a research report. To this end, proofreading the manuscript should be done with the aim of correcting all errors in spelling and all errors in sentence structure, remembering that each sentence must consist of at least a subject and a verb. The paragraph construction should receive final attention in the proofreading. The elements of grammar cannot be presented in this space, of course; the research report writer who feels on shaky ground should have his manuscript read by an expert, and corrections made. There is really no excuse for a misspelled word or an ungrammatical sentence.

Standard usage in paragraphing, and in heading topics and subtopics, has been followed in this book. The student may, therefore, refer to the breakdowns into subtopics as followed throughout this book as a standard method. The general grouping is from "major centered headings" to "marginal headings" to "paragraph headings," then to individual paragraphs. The illustration in exhibit 13-3 shows these relationships.

EXHIBIT 13-3

MAJOR, CENTERED HEADING

The major centered heading is placed in the center of the page and is usually in solid capitals. It is sometimes placed in capitals and small letters and underlined. It is separated from other textual material by three or four lines of space.

Marginal Heading

The marginal heading is used as a major subdivision. It seldom follows the statement of the major centered heading directly, since almost always an introductory paragraph will intervene. The introductory paragraph introduces the material to be discussed under the major centered heading, of which marginal headings and the succeeding paragraph headings are component parts.

Paragraph Heading. The paragraph heading is used to begin a paragraph of an important nature following or to be included within subject matter discussed under a marginal heading.

Every paragraph does not necessarily have a paragraph heading. Under a given paragraph heading there may be included several paragraphs, each consisting of a unified topic or idea relatively completely explained within that paragraph.

A chapter may contain two or three or several major centered headings; under each centered heading there will be at least two and perhaps more marginal headings. Under each marginal heading there will be at least two and perhaps more paragraph headings.

ILLUSTRATIONS

Many, if not all, research reports will contain illustrations of one kind or another. Such illustrations are usually titled *exhibits*. Books and articles and research reports may separate illustrations into *tables*, in which case each table will have a separate number. Sometimes *photographs* are included and are often given the label of *plates* and are numbered. Further, *equations* are sometimes given; and, when they are, they are normally placed in the center of the page so that the space around them causes them to stand out. Equations are sometimes derived from basic assumptions in the body of the report; when this is done, the basic assumption should be stated and the step-by-step procedure in deriving the final equation should be explained. Where the steps are elementary or understood, it is not necessary to state them, but enough of the intervening reasoning should be shown in the derivation to insure that the reader of the paper can understand what has been done.

In employing tabular and graphic presentations for illustrative purposes, the exhibit must be both discussed and interpreted. The discussion consists of a description of the material being presented. This description is not enough, however; the exhibit should be interpreted, its parts analyzed, its meaning shown clearly. Sometimes several pages are written around one exhibit. Where photographs are included, they normally require much less in the way of description or interpretation than do tables and charts. Photographs, however, should be used sparingly because it is usually quite difficult to get in a photograph the exact material that needs to be presented. Photographs of research equipment are useful in showing the setup employed; in such a case they can make unnecessary the lengthy descriptions of sequences in experimentation that might otherwise be required.

PROCEDURES IN WRITING RESEARCH REPORTS

The procedures to be followed in writing the research report can vary. Sometimes an outline is written before the study begins. Sometimes the outline is developed section by section as the study proceeds. Sometimes the study is completed without written outlines because its nature and the steps involved are clear to the researcher, and pen is not put to paper until the research itself has been accomplished.

THE USE OF OUTLINES

An outline for the report is sometimes prepared in topical form, in which case the outline may be relatively detailed as to topics and subtopics, but only the names of the topics are given. An example of such an outline is shown in exhibit 13-4.

The outline may be in sentence form, in which case under each subtopic would be a sentence consisting of a statement, possibly of some descriptive matter listing the steps to be taken, or things to be done in the research process, or noting items to be included in the report.

The outline may, of course, be inclusive of all the research procedures to be followed, or it may be an outline of only the report to be written. There may be, therefore, two sets of outlines to be drawn up. There are firm advocates of outlining as a procedure in developing a research project, and in writing a report. Other authorities disagree on the importance of the outline and feel that the outline should proceed and develop along with the research, particularly when a required experimental design more or less establishes the plans or procedures. There is no doubt, however, that an outline does lend cohesiveness and direction and helps delineate the steps to be taken in producing a final manuscript. However, outlines, even when drawn up in relatively complete detail before a report is started should not be considered as iron-bound procedures to be followed. They

EXHIBIT 13-4

I. Title: Performance Evaluation of Barrel-Filling Machines

II. Background and objectives
    A. History of use
    B. Need for evaluation

III. Evaluation methods
    A. Qualitative
        1. Effects on personnel
        2. Effects on routines
        3. Effects on production
    B. Quantitative
        1. Comparisons
            a. Percentages
            b. Chi-square tests
            c. Analysis of variance

IV. Data requirements
    A. Time period
    B. Production
    C. Cost

V. Conclusions

VI. Recommendations

VII. Cost Analysis

should be flexible, and the researcher should always keep in mind that elements of the outline can be discarded or new ones added or the emphasis changed.

Experienced researchers are so knowledgeable and familiar usually with the requirements of the study and/or the report that they often work from rough notes not in outline form. Often their outlines are understood and not put down on paper. Sometimes, when a research proposal is designed to be submitted for funding, the organization to provide the funds will have a required format for proposals; in such an event, the researcher follows an outline. Exhibit 13-5 is an example of an outline for writing a proposal.

EXHIBIT 13-5

THE PERFORMANCE OF PUBLIC HOUSING IN SMALL CITIES: BENEFITS AND COSTS

(A research proposal submitted to the Assistant Secretary for Policy Development and Research, United States Department of Housing and Urban Development, by Dr. Jack E. Adams, Associate Professor of Economics at Southeastern Louisiana University.)

OUTLINE OF PROPOSAL

INTRODUCTION

Statement about low-rent public housing: legal basis, characteristics, limitations.

Source: Reprinted by permission of Dr. Jack E. Adams, currently Associate Professor of Economics at the University of Arkansas at Little Rock.

PROBLEM

Need for information on benefits and costs of low-rent housing in small cities.

STUDY OBJECTIVES

To measure performance of public housing in small cities: federal expenditures; public vs. private; benefits and costs.

STUDY DESIGN

State methodology, assumptions, definitions, conditions of research.

Measurement of Net Tenant Benefits
Concept of consumers' surplus as measure; Cobb-Douglas utility function to generate benefits measure; cash needs.

Measurement of External Benefits
Spillover effects on property values; benefits of fire, police, medical costs from public housing.

Measurement of Direct Costs to the Federal Government
Social opportunity rate of return on capital, plus rate of instantaneous depreciation on stock of low-rent public housing, times capital cost of low-rent public housing during initial period.

Measurement of Indirect Costs
Detrimental welfare effects on citizens in area of public housing project, monetized value of effects; psychological costs.

EMPIRICAL STUDY

To collect socio-economic characteristics of public housing tenants, rental characteristics of rental units, net tenant benefits, program costs, externalities.

Public Housing Projects Included in the Empirical Study
Stratified random sample of public housing projects, for benefits and costs from small cities.

CONCLUSIONS OF THE STUDY

Study to provide framework for answering questions about public housing in small cities: efficiency of federal expenditures; distribution of benefits; public vs. private housing; external benefits and costs; proportion of income for housing; effects of inflationary pressures and alternatives for reducing effects.

BUDGET

Detailed account of costs of research project and funds needed.

THE USE OF EXHIBITS

When exhibits are to be included in a report, it is often useful to produce the exhibit first, before writing the text material the exhibit is to illustrate. If the exhibit is a table or a chart, it will furnish the foundation around which the explanation or interpretation can be written. When a report consists of a series of exhibits, then, the description and interpretation of each of the exhibits form the body of the material. In such a case, an outline might not be required. In other cases, an outline can be made up following the description and interpretation of the series of exhibits. Such an outline would possibly be of help in pointing the direction of the remainder of the report. Some reports will consist chiefly of the description and interpretation of a single example or a series of examples. When the analyst has studied the example thoroughly and has explained the example and derived his measurements and formed his conclusions, the paper may, indeed, almost write itself.

REWRITING THE PARAGRAPH

One of the most difficult steps in producing the final report is the difficulty of getting words on paper at the very beginning. If the researcher keeps in mind that rewriting is going to be necessary anyway, and a good deal of revision is going to be done, he will be less averse to starting the actual writing of the report. Often the neophyte researcher will feel that his report should be perfect from the beginning; and therefore, he sets down each word with great care and consequently writes only laboriously if at all. The important consideration is to get the research report on paper in some kind of form that is reasonably acceptable. If the researcher realizes that the first attempt is a "rough" draft rather than finished material, he may write rapidly, and indeed express himself rather well since he is writing informally and with the expectation of correction and rewriting.

Rewriting may be a heavy chore, indeed. Few papers are well written in the first draft form. Further, as criticisms and suggestions are received from colleagues, rewriting will normally be expected to improve the manuscript. During the rewriting process, of course, careful proofreading for grammar, misspelled words, poor sentence structure, can also be done. Manuscripts are sometimes rewritten a good many times. Again, for the neophyte, rewriting is difficult. He feels that each of his words is precious and must not be destroyed. However, as he grows more experienced, he will become ruthless in striking out unnecessary words and in insisting upon absolute precision in his expression.

PROOFREADING

After a rewritten and revised copy—perhaps one that has been rewritten and revised several times—has been produced, the final preparation of the manuscript is in order. The manuscript should be typed correctly according to the required format for the paper, whether it be for a periodical or for professional publication, or as a thesis to be submitted for graduate credit, or as a formal report to be submitted to an employer or a supervisor. Proofreading of the final manuscript is always necessary. Too often, the researcher assumes that the final typewritten manuscript is perfect. The proofreading should consist of a word-by-word search for misspellings, mispunctuations, and typing errors. Pages with noticeable erasures should be retyped. The final manuscript should be neat and clean and inviting to the eye.

EVALUATION

There is no universally accepted set of standards for evaluating a research report. Satisfactory reports have taken many different forms. The following checklist is offered as one that can be helpful as a summary and general guide to estimating the probable effectiveness of a research report.

1. Does the report have the arrangement of subject matter and the devices of presentation such as adequate graphs or charts that are most appropriate for the persons who will read and use the report?
2. Does it have headings and subheadings that facilitate the reading and understanding of the report?
3. Are the findings and their interpretations clearly stated and adequately substantiated by evidence cited in the report?
4. Are the conclusions logical? Are they based on evidence supplied in the report? Could any alternative or perhaps contrary conclusions have been reached? If so, have adequate explanations been given as to why they were not?
5. Are the recommendations practical? Are they feasible in view of the financial and other conditions of the organization concerned? Have the recommendations taken into consideration the persons making the decisions?
6. Have the research methods and sources of information used been described in sufficient detail to enable the reader of the report to evaluate their soundness?
7. Has the report been written in an impersonal, unbiased, unemotional and logical manner?
8. Are the physical characteristics of the report appropriate in view of the persons who will read it, and the uses to which it will be put, including filing and other handling requirements? (Physical characteristics include: cover, binding, size, form of reproduction, paper used, etc.)
9. In general, is the report satisfactorily complete, concise, clear, consistent, and correct?

A COMPREHENSIVE EXAMPLE

An actual business report is reproduced in the following pages. It is an economic impact study of *Fairfield Bay Investment: Its Impact on an Area of Rural Arkansas*, a research project undertaken by Fairfield Communities Land Company. The two consultants were professors at the University of Arkansas at Little Rock. The report contains a cover map, a title page, a page of acknowledgments, an executive summary, an introduction, a history of Fairfield Bay investment, the Fairfield Bay economic impact on the counties, a conclusion, and an appendix. This format of the report was devised by the consultants.

Following the report as reproduced on succeeding pages is a considerable discussion, broken down into the following parts:

1. consideration of the problem, hypothesis, and the sources of data
2. discussion of the conclusions, findings, and possible recommendations
3. an outlin of the report
4. the eleven steps of scientific research procedure as delineated in chapter 2 of this book applied to the research project.

The report is reproduced by permission of the Fairfield Communities Land Company of Little Rock and the consultants.

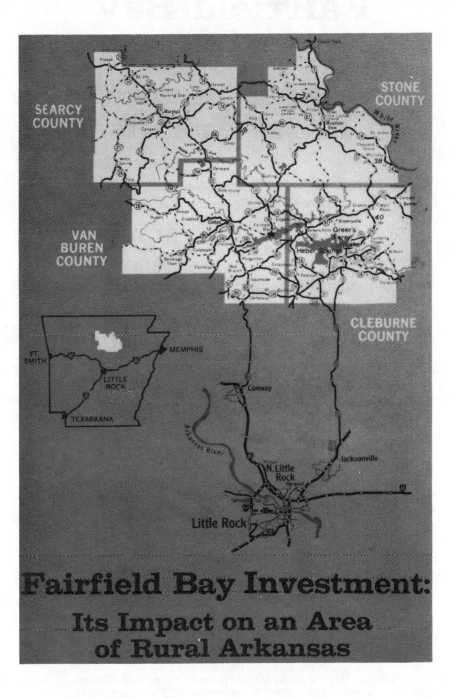

Fairfield Bay Investment:
Its Impact on an Area of Rural Arkansas

Fairfield Bay Investment:
Its Impact on an Area of Rural Arkansas

July 5, 1975

The Fairfield Communities Land Company is an Arkansas-based corporation with headquarters in Little Rock, Arkansas. The long-term objective of the company is to plan and develop large scale retirement/recreational communities at a profit.

Three comprehensive retirement/recreational communities are currently being developed:

1. Fairfield Bay, Arkansas
2. Fairfield Glade, Tennessee (12,000 acres in a mountain setting 70 miles west of Knoxville)
3. Fairfield Green Valley, Arizona (4,700 acres 19 miles south of Tucson)

This report is about FAIRFIELD BAY and the impact it has had on the Ozark region of Arkansas.

Prepared for

Fairfield Communities Land Company

1207 Rebsamen Park Road, Little Rock, Arkansas 72202

By Business Consultants:

Allan Glubok,

B.S.B.A., Washington University;
M.S., St. Louis University;
D.B.A., Washington University.

Academic Experience: Assistant Professor of Finance, Colorado State University; Associate Professor of Finance, Louisiana Tech University; Associate Professor of Finance, University of Arkansas, at Little Rock.

Wayne Ferguson,

B.B.A., M.B.A., University of Texas;
Ph.D., North Texas State University.

Academic experience: Assistant Professor, School of Business Administration, University of Texas at Arlington; Associate Professor, Business and Economics School, and Director, Center for Business Training and Economic Research, Weber State College; Associate Professor of Marketing, University of Arkansas at Little Rock.

Executive Summary

Fairfield Bay, a 12,000-acre retirement/recreational community located on the shores of scenic Greers Ferry Lake, is being developed by the Fairfield Communities Land Company in keeping with the organization's operating objectives. These objectives are:

1. To purchase large tracts of unimproved real estate;
2. To develop the tracts into comprehensive recreational and retirement communities;
3. To sell the surrounding lots to persons desiring vacation and retirement homes.

The comprehensive development of Fairfield Bay, in the Ozark region approximately 80 miles north of Little Rock, is proof that these operating objectives are being successfully accomplished.

As a result of the development of the Fairfield Bay retirement/recreational community, there has been a very favorable stimulation of the economy in the area and an improvement in the standard of living for local citizens. Fairfield Bay has invested approximately $33 million in permanent improvements since 1966. Considering the rural nature of the area in which Fairfield Bay is located, this amount represents a significant investment by a private corporation. This large investment signifies to homesite purchasers that Fairfield Communities Land Company has a long-term commitment to excellence at Fairfield Bay.

The $33 million investment made during the past nine years can be divided into several major categories: First, approximately $4.2 million has been invested in 12,000 acres of underdeveloped land.

Second, $6 million has been spent for community-support facilities.

Third, more than $14.3 million has gone into the construction of homes and condominiums — a total of 691 housing units. The typical lot and house at Fairfield Bay cost approximately $30,000.

Additional amounts were spent for taxes and real estate commissions. The gross payroll for local employees was over $1.7 million in 1974. In general terms, the $33 million represents the expenditure for land, labor and resources in the local area. The resulting economic stimulation has been beneficial to the entire region.

A broader perspective of Fairfield Bay's contribution to the economic expansion in the region can be gained by examining employment, income, population and bank deposit data of Van Buren County. (Van Buren County is highlighted because Fairfield Bay investment is concentrated there.) The following table indicates that Van Buren County's economy has made substantial strides since 1966 when Fairfield Bay began investing in the region.

VAN BUREN COUNTY:

Economic Indicators	Annual Percentage Growth Rates	
	6 Years Before Fairfield Bay 1960-1965	8 Years After Fairfield Bay 1966-1973
Non-agriculture Employment	1.5%	8.2%
Total Personal Income	7.4	13.3
Effective Buying Income per Household	—0.5	9.0
Population	—0.1	3.4

Source: See tables in this report for original sources.

The total covered payroll for 1960 in Van Buren County was $916,000; by 1973 it had risen to $8,738,000. Bank deposits jumped to $14,480,000 in 1973 from $2,487,000 in 1960.

Other indications of Fairfield Bay's impact on the economy of the region can be gained by some additional analysis. Fairfield Bay's estimated 600 permanent residents represent 25 percent of the County's population increase since 1965. About 20 percent of all non-agriculture employment and 20 percent of the covered payroll of the county is generated in Fairfield Bay. Approximately 80 percent of all new housing units built in Van Buren County since 1965 were built in Fairfield Bay. Perhaps 20 percent of all retail sales in the county can be attributed to tourists and permanent residents of Fairfield Bay. Additional retail purchases are made by Fairfield Bay employees.

In the opinion of the authors, Fairfield Communities Land Company has made well-balanced investment in the Fairfield Bay development. The development has been and should continue to be a positive catalyst in Van Buren County. Assuming a continuation of past trends, Fairfield Bay will continue to be an exemplary model for other retirement/recreational communities.

Introduction

Fairfield Bay, a 12,000-acre retirement/recreational community, is located on the shores of scenic Greers Ferry Lake, 80 miles north of Little Rock. Since 1966, Fairfield Bay has invested approximately $33 million in housing, a golf course, a tennis complex, a marina, roads and utilities.

The rustic beauty of the Ozarks creates a desirable location for a retirement/recreational community. Greers Ferry Lake, which covers 40,000 acres, was created in the early 1960's by the construction of

Greers Ferry Dam on the Little Red River. Although the primary purposes of the Dam are flood control and generation of electric power, the Lake also offers superb boating and fishing. Wild game abounds in the area and offers hunting activities in the prescribed seasons. The rolling, tree-covered hills enhance the enjoyment of leisure-time activities throughout the year. Capitalizing on the natural beauty and resources of the Ozark region, Fairfield Bay has committed its energies to the development of its recreational/retirement community.

Fairfield Bay Investment

By the end of 1975, Fairfield Bay will have invested more than $33 million in permanent improvements of its planned community development. The initial investment at Fairfield Bay was for the purchase of rural acreage in Van Buren and Cleburne counties. For clarification, it should be noted that virtually all of the property purchased was underdeveloped and was making little economic contribution to the region. By the close of 1974, the company had purchased about 12,000 acres for a total expenditure of more than $4.2 million.

After acquisition of the land, the developers began the process of making "social overhead" types of investments. They have spent approximately $6 million for community-supporting facilities such as roads, a marina, golf course, tennis complex and two swimming pools. A Town Center was constructed for community services — such as a post office, a bank, restaurants, a doctor's office, a beauty parlor, a grocery store and a children's play area. Fairfield Bay management has donated land for three churches.

A significant part of the $6 million expenditure was for an independent water and sewerage plant. Both of the facilities exceed the requirements of the Environmental Protection Agency. No government funds were used in this construction. Based on the design and planning incorporated into all the social overhead investments, Fairfield Bay management can be characterized as being aware of ecological and aesthetic needs.

Since Fairfield Bay is a retirement/recreational development, it is not surprising that the investment in housing — both single-family homes and condominiums — represents the largest single aggregate expenditure. Since 1967, more than $9.8 million has been spent for home construction at Fairfield Bay. The construction cost of condominiums totals over $4.5 million. On a combined basis, housing represents a total investment of $14.3 million. Additional funds were spent for taxes and real estate selling commissions.

To amplify the importance of Fairfield Bay housing

development in the Van Buren and Cleburne counties, other indicators should be kept in perspective. For example, at the conclusion of 1974 there were 451 permanent homes completed and occupied. The average price of a house and lot was approximately $30,000. In addition to the homes, 240 condominiums had been completed and sold. These 691 housing units represent a significant net addition to housing available in the region. It is reasonable to anticipate that most of the building supplies were purchased from local suppliers. Wages paid to construction workers on their housing projects flowed into the local economy. In addition to some local financing, a majority of the funds for this housing was provided by financial institutions from outside Van Buren County adding to the spendable funds in the local communities.

Other measures of the impact of investments at Fairfield Bay are the number of employees and the payroll. Due to the seasonal nature of activities at the development, the number of employees fluctuates; however, in 1974 the average number of employees was 350. Virtually all full-time employees are drawn from the local labor force and live in the surrounding communities. The annual gross payroll in 1974 totaled over $1.7 million.

Fairfield Bay's investment goes beyond the $33 million spent to date. Although Fairfield Bay's marketing effort is primarily aimed at selling its own development, a major by-product is the creation of a more favorable image for the State of Arkansas and the Ozark region. In general terms, the Ozarks have been characterized as being rural, inaccessible and lacking in attractive tourist accommodations. The 70,500 families who have visited the very modern, comfortable facilities at Fairfield Bay since 1969 could not help but come away with favorable impressions of the region. A large majority of these visitors were from outside of the region. They spent an average of 3.5 days in the area. In 1974, Fairfield Bay spent $1.1 million marketing Fairfield Bay, the Ozark region and the State of Arkansas.

Fairfield Bay Impact on
Van Buren and Cleburne Counties

To have a broader perspective of Fairfield Bay's contribution to the economic expansion of the region, a number of economic indicators will be examined. Employment, population, income and bank deposit data will be presented in the following pages. Economic data will be presented for four contiguous counties which are similar in topography and, until recently, were similar in economic development. They are Van Buren, Cleburne, Stone and Searcy.

Fairfield Bay incorporates land in both Van Buren and Cleburne counties; however, the bulk of the investment is in Van Buren County. The development of Greers Ferry Lake in the mid-1960's has opened Van Buren and Cleburne to recreation-related industries. Blanchard Springs Caverns and the Ozark Folk Center

have made Stone County attractive to tourists. But nothing has changed Searcy County's essentially rural economy. Fairfield Bay's greater impact has been on Van Buren County and, to a lesser extent, on Cleburne.

In 1965, there were 1,300 people in Van Buren County employed in non-agriculture jobs. By 1973 the total had grown to 2,450. Prior to the Fairfield Bay development, this type of employment grew at a meager 1.5 percent per year in Van Buren County which ranked near the bottom of the four-county region. Since the advent of Fairfield Bay, Van Buren County's non-agricultural employment has had the most rapid growth rate in the region, a brisk 8.2 percent annually. Table 1 shows the annual growth rates for each county before and after Fairfield Bay.

TABLE 1   Non-Agriculture Employment: Annual Percentage Growth Rates

	County			
	Van Buren	Cleburne	Stone	Searcy
Before Fairfield Bay — 1961-1965	1.5%	1.2%	5.9%	10.9%
After Fairfield Bay — 1966-1973	8.2	5.1	7.6	1.3

Source: Arkansas Department of Labor, Employment Security Division. (See Appendix Table 1 for detailed data.)

As employment grew in Van Buren County, payrolls shot up dramatically. Although the figures for payrolls covered under the Arkansas Law in 1960 and 1973 are not directly comparable due to changes in the law, an indication of the relative growth of payrolls in the

region can be seen by examining Figure 1. In 1973 Van Buren reported nearly $9 million, the largest of the four counties, although in 1960 only $916,000 had been reported, well below the leading county.

FIGURE 1   Total Covered Payroll: 1960 and 1973

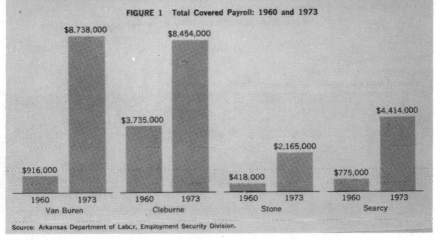

$8,738,000	$8,454,000		$4,414,000
$3,735,000		$2,165,000	
$916,000	$418,000	$775,000	
1960 1973	1960 1973	1960 1973	1960 1973
Van Buren	Cleburne	Stone	Searcy

Source: Arkansas Department of Labor, Employment Security Division.

Until recent years, Arkansas' population showed little or no growth. This is reflected in population statistics for the four counties. Prior to 1965, Cleburne was the only county of the four showing any growth and it was less than one-half of one percent per year.

Since 1965 only Searcy County, which does not have the benefit of tourism or recreation, has continued to lose population. Table 2 shows that the population of Van Buren, Cleburne and Stone are all growing between 3 and 4 percent per year.

TABLE 2 POPULATION CHANGES: Annual Percentage Growth Rates

	County			
	Van Buren	Cleburne	Stone	Searcy
Before Fairfield Bay — 1960-1965	—0.1%	0.4%	—1.4%	0.0%
After Fairfield Bay — 1966-1973	3.4	4.0	3.3	—0.2

Source: State and County Economic Data for Arkansas, Industrial Research Center, University of Arkansas. (See Appendix Table 2 for detailed data.)

Along with the rapid growth in employment, Van Buren County's total personal income is expanding far more rapidly than it is in the other three counties. The annual growth rate in total personal income has nearly doubled in Van Buren since Fairfield Bay located in the county.

Table 3 shows that prior to 1965 personal income in Van Buren and Stone were growing at approximately the same rate. Since 1965, Van Buren County's 13.3 percent growth rate has substantially exceeded the growth rate of personal income of the other three counties.

TABLE 3 TOTAL PERSONAL INCOME: Annual Percentage Growth Rate

	County			
	Van Buren	Cleburne	Stone	Searcy
Before Fairfield Bay — 1960-1965	7.4%	5.4%	7.5%	6.2%
After Fairfield Bay — 1966-1972	13.3	11.5	11.7	9.5

Source: State and County Economic Data for Arkansas, Industrial Research and Extension Center, University of Arkansas. (See Appendix Table 3 for detailed data.)

Another measure of income is the effective buying income per household published by *Sales Management Magazine.* From 1960 to 1965 the effective buying income per household actually decreased in Van Buren County, the only county to perform that poorly. Since

Fairfield Bay, Van Buren has shown the largest growth in effective buying income — 9.0 percent — followed by Cleburne's 8.0 percent. Table 4 shows that the other two counties lag well behind.

TABLE 4 EFFECTIVE BUYING INCOME PER HOUSEHOLD: Annual Percentage Growth Rates

	County			
	Van Buren	Cleburne	Stone	Searcy
Before Fairfield Bay — 1960-1965	—0.5%	1.5%	0.0%	2.3%
After Fairfield Bay — 1966-1973	9.0	8.0	5.8	6.4

Source: Sales Management Magazine. (See Appendix Table 4 for detailed data.)

Bank deposits in all four counties have grown substantially since 1960. Cleburne continues to lead the others with nearly $30 million followed by Van Buren with over $14 million. Table 5 shows the details for each county during selected years.

TABLE 5 Bank Deposit Data

	County			
	Van Buren ($000)	Cleburne ($000)	Stone ($000)	Searcy ($000)
1960	$ 2,487	$ 4,737	$1,067	$ 2,832
1970	8,314	15,281	3,789	7,204
1973	14,430	29,952	8,313	11,274

Source: State and County Economic Data for Arkansas, Industrial Research and Extension Center, University of Arkansas.

Conclusions

The preceding data indicate that the economy of Van Buren County has developed at a far more rapid rate since Fairfield Bay located in the region. Not all the growth can be attributed to Fairfield Bay, but the following facts show the substantial impact of Fairfield Bay's development on Van Buren County.

• The estimated 600 permanent residents of Fairfield Bay represent 25 percent of the increase in Van Buren County's population since 1965.

• Approximately 20 percent of all non-agriculture employment in Van Buren worked at Fairfield Bay in 1973 thereby generating nearly 20 percent of the covered payroll in the county.

• The 691 housing units built in Fairfield Bay represent approximately 80 percent of all new units built in the county since 1965.

• It has been estimated that nearly 20 percent of all retail sales made in Van Buren County since 1965 can be attributed to tourists and permanent residents of Fairfield Bay. This figure does not include purchases by Fairfield Bay employees in Van Buren County.

In summary, the data emphasize that Fairfield Bay is a major contributor to the economic growth of Van Buren County.

Appendix

TABLE 1 NON-AGRICULTURE EMPLOYMENT Source: Arkansas Department of Labor, Employment Security Division.	Year	Van Buren	County Cleburne	Stone	Searcy
	1961	1,225	2,025	775	1,025
	1965	1,300	2,125	975	1,550
	1973	2,450	3,175	1,750	1,725

TABLE 2 TOTAL RESIDENT POPULATION: ACTUAL 1960; ESTIMATED 1965 AND 1973 Source: State and County Economic Data for Arkansas, Industrial Research and Extension Center, University of Arkansas.	Year	Van Buren	County Cleburne	Stone	Searcy
	1960	7,228	9,059	6,294	8,124
	1965	7,201	9,226	5,861	8,112
	1973	9,400	12,600	7,600	8,000

TABLE 3 TOTAL PERSONAL INCOME Source: State and County Economic Data for Arkansas, Industrial Research and Extension Center, University of Arkansas.	Year	Van Buren	County Cleburne	Stone	Searcy
	1960	$ 6,669,000	$10,569,000	$ 4,939,000	$ 7,006,000
	1965	9,551,000	13,718,000	7,103,000	9,496,000
	1972	22,878,000	29,352,000	15,427,000	17,871,000

TABLE 4 EFFECTIVE BUYING INCOME ESTIMATES PER HOUSEHOLD Source: Sales Management Magazine.	Year	Van Buren	County Cleburne	Stone	Searcy
	1960	$3,784	$3,566	$3,262	$3,743
	1965	3,690	3,837	3,655	3,737
	1973	7,364	7,110	6,004	5,868

346

PROBLEM, HYPOTHESIS, DATA

The Fairfield Communities Land Company faced a problem that was essentially one of public relations. Promotion of the Fairfield Bay development was accomplished by the usual methods of advertising, showing prospective buyers the properties, establishing lines of communication between buyers and lending agencies, and other aspects of promotional sales. These activities, of course, had taken place during the original development phase of the project that occurred during the years 1965 and following. At the point of decision to undertake an economic impact study, the Fairfield Bay development had been progressing for several years. The date of this study was 1975. Examining the data in the report, it is seen that a comparison was made before Fairfield Bay, 1960–61 to 1965, with after Fairfield Bay, 1966 to 1972–73.

A public relations project showing the economic impact of the Fairfield Bay development on the counties it has affected, if favorable, could be used for promoting public good will. Not only was public good will desired, but, if such a report existed, it could influence bankers to be willing to lend to prospective purchasers, it could impress building contractors, it could improve political relations with the governments of the counties and towns affected, it could impress other possible investors not yet investing in the development. In 1974 and 1975 some "land fraud" schemes received wide publicity, and were investigated by governmental agencies. Possible legislation unfavorable to legitimate land development was feared. An economic impact study, if it showed a favorable impact, would be an answer to critics and would make governmental action less damaging to useful projects.

It was decided, therefore, that the problem was one of public relations; establishing good relations with bankers, with building contractors, with government, with investors.

Having defined the problem, the hypothesis for the project was apparent: the economic impact of the Fairfield Bay development was favorable, and substantially so, on the county in which it was located. This hypothesis could be tested by employing independent outside consultants to conduct the economic impact study. Such independent consultants could be expected to make an objective, unbiased appraisal, and to test the hypothesis posed.

The data to be gathered depended on the consultants' decision as to what was needed to determine whether the hypothesis would be substantiated or rejected. The consultants decided to study four counties, the county containing the development, and the three counties adjacent. If it could be shown that the county Van Buren, in which Fairfield Bay was located, had been growing economically more rapidly than the other three counties during the years after the inception of Fairfield Bay, as contrasted with their records of growth during the years before Fairfield Bay, a favorable economic impact could be demonstrated; the hypothesis could then be substantiated.

Six areas of inquiry were to be covered:

1. growth of nonagricultural employment
2. total payroll in the counties
3. growth in population
4. growth in total personal income
5. growth in effective buying income per household
6. bank deposit increases

The data for these variables were available from already published sources. These data were, therefore, secondary data. The sources were:

1. State of Arkansas Department of Labor, Employment Security Division
2. *State and County Economic Data for Arkansas*, obtained from the Industrial Research and Extension Center of the University of Arkansas
3. *Sales Management* magazine.

CONCLUSIONS, FINDINGS, RECOMMENDATIONS

The conclusions of the study are stated on the last page of the reproduced report. These consist of four general statements related to the hypothesis. These are inferences which substantiate the hypothesis, these inferences having been drawn from the findings which are presented in the four tables and the chart in figure 1. Thus, in this study, the relation between conclusions and findings is relatively precise. The findings are the specific facts presented in the tables and graph. The conclusions on the last page of the report are inferred from the findings and are related to the hypothesis of a favorable, substantial economic impact due to the Fairfield Bay development.

The four conclusions concern the:

1. favorable increase in population
2. contribution to nonagricultural employment
3. the large number of housing units built
4. contribution to retail sales of the area

The final statement of conclusion is quoted here: "In summary, the data emphasize that Fairfield Bay is a major contributor to the economic growth of Van Buren County." Thus, the hypothesis of a favorable, substantial economic impact was considered to be substantiated.

No recommendations were given by the consultants on this project. They were not asked to make recommendations, and were, indeed, not employed to make recommendations. The economic impact study did not contemplate that any recommendations would be forthcoming; it contemplated only the testing of an hypothesis of a favorable, substantial economic impact of Fairfield Bay on Van Buren County and the surrounding counties.

OUTLINE OF THE REPORT

The experience of the two consultants for the Fairfield Bay study was such that detailed outlines of their procedures and the writing of the final report were not necessary. The beginning researcher, however, needs to set down on paper the specific, individual steps to be taken during a study and in setting up the form for a report. This will insure that nothing pertinent is omitted, and that nothing nonpertinent is included. As researchers become more experienced, the grasp of the requirements for a viable research study, whether survey, observation, or experimental techniques are used, is inherent to them. They contain the outlines in their heads, not needing to set them down on paper. For the Fairfield Bay economic impact study no written outlines were made; however, an outline of the report may be made after the fact (exhibit 13-6) to illustrate how the report might have been outlined.

EXHIBIT 13-6

    I. *Executive Summary.* A one-page executive summary to be presented to give a quick look at the results for executives.
        A. Objectives of Fairfield Bay investment
            1. Land purchase
            2. Land development
            3. Sales
        B. Resulting economic impact
            1. Payroll
            2. Population
            3. Investment made
            4. Examine economic indicators
                a. Employment
                b. Income
                c. Population
                d. Bank deposits
        C. Table showing economic indicators for Van Buren County

   II. *Introduction.* A brief introduction about the development.
        A. What it is
        B. Where it is
        C. Nature of the physical area

  III. *Fairfield Bay Investment.* A description of the development.
        A. Investment
        B. Acquisition of land
        C. Development of utility facilities
        D. Investment in housing

  IV. *Fairfield Bay Impact on Van Buren and Cleburne Counties.* Body of the report, to include the following:
        A. Comparison before Fairfield Bay 1960–61 to 1965 to after Fairfield Bay 1966 to 1972–73
        B. Four counties studied
            1. Van Buren
            2. Cleburne
            3. Stone
            4. Searcy
        C. Payroll comparisons of the four counties for 1960 and 1973

D. Population changes for the four counties before-after
E. Total personal income changes for the four counties before-after
F. Effective buying income per household changes for the four counties before-after
G. Bank deposit data for the four counties
  1. 1960
  2. 1970
  3. 1973

V. *Conclusions.* To contain inferences drawn from findings of preceding section, and relating to the hypothesis of a favorable economic impact.
  A. Population
  B. Nonagricultural employment
  C. Housing units built
  D. Retail sales
  E. Summary statement

VI. *Appendix.* Tables presenting data of the four counties for the years 1960–61, 1965, 1972–73.
  A. Nonagricultural employment
  B. Resident population
  C. Total personal income
  D. Effective buying income per household

THE ELEVEN STEPS IN SCIENTIFIC RESEARCH

In chapter 2 of this book, the eleven steps in the procedures of scientific research were listed and described. These eleven steps are applied to the Fairfield Bay economic impact study in the following discussion.

Step 1: Become aware that a problem exists. The Fairfield Communities Land Company had developed the Fairfield Bay area over a period of years since 1965. While the project had been successful to date, the company was also engaged in developing Fairfield Glade, Tennessee, and Fairfield Green Valley, Arizona. An improvement in public relations was possible in the face of the restrictive governmental actions that might result from the bad publicity of "land fraud" schemes in 1974 and 1975, governmental action that might damage legitimate community economic development. It was felt that improvement in public relations was possible, improved relations with the communities, with federal, state, and local governments, with bankers and other financial institutions, with building contractors, with future investors, and with the public that might be expected to be home buyers.

Step 2: Define the problem and purposes of the research. To solve the problem of improving public relations, it was decided that an economic impact study was a feasible method of solving the problem. Thus, the problem could be defined as one of an economic impact study to find out the actual impact of Fairfield Bay on the immediately surrounding territory. The purpose of the research was to establish the extent of the economic impact, and whether it was good, bad, or indifferent.

Step 3: Set forth the hypotheses as to causes and/or solutions of the problem. The hypothesis to be posed for the impact study was that the economic impact of Fairfield Bay was favorable, and substantially so, on Van Buren County.

Step 4: Determine what information will be required. It was determined that economic data for the four counties would be needed, these being Van Buren, Cleburne, Stone, and Searcy. The data would concern nonagricultural employment, population changes, income changes, effective buying income per household, and bank deposit data. The years involved would be the period before Fairfield Bay, 1960–61 to 1965, and the period after Fairfield Bay, 1966 to 1972–73.

Step 5: Decide which methods to use in collecting information. Three sources, it was found, would provide the data for the study for the counties and for the years desired: (1) Arkansas Department of Labor, Employment Security Division; (2) Industrial Research and Extension Center, University of Arkansas; and (3) *Sales Management* magazine.

Step 6: Collect information or evidence. Since the data were secondary in nature, it was only necessary to contact the sources to obtain the information from them. *Sales Management* magazine contained some of the data. Personal visits were made by the consultants to the Arkansas Department of Labor and the Industrial Research and Extension Center, both located in Little Rock.

Step 7: Compile the findings in systematic form. The data secured was to be used in a format, and tables set up for this format, as follows: A before-after study was indicated, before Fairfield Bay 1960–61 to 1965, and after Fairfield Bay 1966 to 1972–73. The percentage changes for four counties were to be computed and listed: Van Buren, Cleburne, Stone, and Searcy. The following economic variables were to be studied before-after for the four counties: nonagricultural employment, payroll, population, total personal income, effective buying income per household, and bank deposits for the years 1960, 1970, and 1973.

Step 8: Analyze findings to determine if they substantiate or eliminate hypotheses. The findings were listed in tables 1, 2, 3, and 4, constituting the percentages compiled in showing growth, and the actual bank deposits shown in table 5, of the report. In the appendix, tables 1, 2, 3, and 4 present the actual counts and dollar amounts. The findings concern employment, payroll, population, personal income, and effective buying income per household.

Step 9: Write final research report to bring out full significance of findings and any indicated conclusions. The complete research report is reproduced verbatim in the earlier pages of this discussion. The report consisted of the following: (1) executive summary; (2) introduction; (3) Fairfield Bay investment; (4) Fairfield Bay impact on Van Buren and Cleburne counties; (5) conclusions; (6) appendix.

Step 10: Make specific recommendations as to feasible actions. In this research project no recommendations were required of the two consultants who made the study. Only the economic impact study, with its findings and conclusions, was desired. Therefore, the final report contains no recommendations.

Step 11: Follow-up. No follow-up was conducted for this particular research. It could be considered in the future, however. A few years hence, a new impact study of Fairfield Bay could be feasible. Whether this is done in the future is a matter for decision at such future time. A similar economic impact study of Fairfield Glade, Tennessee, was completed in 1975.

SUMMARY

Of the various kinds of reports, reports for business research are classified as technical reports. They may be oral or written. If written, the reports will generally contain the following kinds of material: (1) front matter, including title page, foreword, and contents; (2) main body, containing the technical discussion and possible summary and/or descriptions of procedure; they may contain findings, conclusions, and recommendations; (3) terminal matter, consisting of references, bibliographies, appendixes.

In the writing of reports, the matter of style requires that the following characteristics prevail: (1) accuracy; (2) clarity; (3) conciseness; (4) unity. Further, grammar and usage should be correct.

The report may be divided into sections such as: (1) major, centered headings; (2) marginal headings; (3) paragraph headings. Discussions may thus be connected and given their order of importance.

The use of outlines is often recommended in devising the procedure and in writing the report; these outlines may be topical or descriptive. Exhibits are often required. Paragraphs often must be rewritten. Proofreading, as well as revision, should always be practiced in order to correct and improve spelling, punctuation, and grammar. The evaluation of a report may be necessary.

A comprehensive example of business research is given by "Fairfield Bay Investment." The problem, hypothesis, data are considered, as well as the findings and conclusions. An outline is presented. Finally, the eleven steps in scientific research procedure are related to the example.

EXERCISES

1. What is the essential purpose of business reports? In what ways may this be effected?
2. Describe each of the three main elements of a research report.
3. Compare and contrast the findings and the conclusions of a research report.
4. Describe the desirable characteristics of *style* in writing reports.
5. Devise a research problem in production, in finance, in accounting, in administration, or in marketing. Make up an outline of the research procedure.
6. Write a two-page paper explaining how to evaluate a research report.

7. Find a report of a research study in business or economics. (Professional periodicals like *Accounting Review*, *Journal of Marketing*, *Journal of Business* will provide sources.) Criticize the study relative to the problem, the hypotheses, and the data.
8. Evaluate the research study selected in exercise 7 from the point of view of good evaluative procedures.

SELECTED REFERENCES

Berenson, Conrad. *Research and Report Writing*. New York: Random House, 1971.

Parten, Mildred. *Surveys, Polls, and Samples: Practical Procedures*. New York: Cooper Square, 1966.

Turabian, Kate L. *A Manual for Writers of Term Papers, Theses, and Dissertations*. Chicago: The University of Chicago Press, 1967.

APPENDIX A

TABLE OF AREAS OF THE NORMAL CURVE*

APPENDIX A
TABLE OF AREAS OF THE NORMAL CURVE*

$\frac{x}{\sigma}$	Area Between Maximum Ordinate And Ordinate at $\frac{x}{\sigma}$	$\frac{x}{\sigma}$	Area Between Maximum Ordinate And Ordinate at $\frac{x}{\sigma}$	$\frac{x}{\sigma}$	Area Between Maximum Ordinate And Ordinate at $\frac{x}{\sigma}$
.00	.00000				
.01	.00399	.51	.19497	1.01	.34375
.02	.00798	.52	.19847	1.02	.34614
.03	.01197	.53	.20194	1.03	.34849
.04	.01595	.54	.20540	1.04	.35083
.05	.01994	.55	.20884	1.05	.35314
.06	.02392	.56	.21226	1.06	.35543
.07	.02790	.57	.21566	1.07	.35769
.08	.03188	.58	.21904	1.08	.35993
.09	.03586	.59	.22240	1.09	.36214
.10	.03983	.60	.22575	1.10	.36433
.11	.04380	.61	.22907	1.11	.36650
.12	.04776	.62	.23237	1.12	.36864
.13	.05172	.63	.23565	1.13	.37076
.14	.05567	.64	.23891	1.14	.37286
.15	.05962	.65	.24215	1.15	.37493
.16	.06356	.66	.24537	1.16	.37698
.17	.06749	.67	.24857	1.17	.37900
.18	.07142	.68	.25175	1.18	.38100
.19	.07535	.69	.25490	1.19	.38298
.20	.07926	.70	.25804	1.20	.38493
.21	.08317	.71	.26115	1.21	.38686
.22	.08706	.72	.26424	1.22	.38877
.23	.09095	.73	.26730	1.23	.39065
.24	.09483	.74	.27035	1.24	.39251
.25	.09871	.75	.27337	1.25	.39435
.26	.10257	.76	.27637	1.26	.39617
.27	.10642	.77	.27935	1.27	.39796
.28	.11026	.78	.28230	1.28	.39973
.29	.11409	.79	.28524	1.29	.40147
.30	.11791	.80	.28814	1.30	.40320
.31	.12172	.81	.29103	1.31	.40490
.32	.12552	.82	.29389	1.32	.40658
.33	.12930	.83	.29673	1.33	.40824
.34	.13307	.84	.29955	1.34	.40988
.35	.13683	.85	.30234	1.35	.41149
.36	.14058	.86	.30511	1.36	.41309
.37	.14431	.87	.30785	1.37	.41466
.38	.14803	.88	.31057	1.38	.41621
.39	.15173	.89	.31327	1.39	.41774
.40	.15542	.90	.31594	1.40	.41924
.41	.15910	.91	.31859	1.41	.42073
.42	.16276	.92	.32121	1.42	.42220
.43	.16640	.93	.32381	1.43	.42364
.44	.17003	.94	.32639	1.44	.42507
.45	.17364	.95	.32894	1.45	.42647
.46	.17724	.96	.33147	1.46	.42785
.47	.18082	.97	.33398	1.47	.42922
.48	.18439	.98	.33646	1.48	.43056
.49	.18793	.99	.33891	1.49	.43189
.50	.19146	1.00	.34134	1.50	.43319

* This table is condensed, and derived, from *Tables of Normal Probability Functions*, National Bureau of Standards, Applied Mathematics Series 23 (Washington, D. C.: U. S. Government Printing Office; 1953).

	Area Between Maximum Ordinate And Ordinate		Area Between Maximum Ordinate And Ordinate		Area Between Maximum Ordinate And Ordinate
$\frac{x}{\sigma}$	at $\frac{x}{\sigma}$	$\frac{x}{\sigma}$	at $\frac{x}{\sigma}$	$\frac{x}{\sigma}$	at $\frac{x}{\sigma}$
1.51	.43448	2.11	.48257	2.71	.49664
1.52	.43574	2.12	.48300	2.72	.49674
1.53	.43699	2.13	.48341	2.73	.49683
1.54	.43822	2.14	.48382	2.74	.49693
1.55	.43943	2.15	.48422	2.75	.49702
1.56	.44062	2.16	.48461	2.76	.49711
1.57	.44179	2.17	.48500	2.77	.49720
1.58	.44295	2.18	.48537	2.78	.49728
1.59	.44408	2.19	.48574	2.79	.49736
1.60	.44520	2.20	.48610	2.80	.49744
1.61	.44630	2.21	.48645	2.81	.49752
1.62	.44738	2.22	.48679	2.82	.49760
1.63	.44845	2.23	.48713	2.83	.49767
1.64	.44950	2.24	.48745	2.84	.49774
1.65	.45053	2.25	.48778	2.85	.49781
1.66	.45154	2.26	.48809	2.86	.49788
1.67	.45254	2.27	.48840	2.87	.49795
1.68	.45352	2.28	.48870	2.88	.49801
1.69	.45449	2.29	.48899	2.89	.49807
1.70	.45543	2.30	.48928	2.90	.49813
1.71	.45637	2.31	.48956	2.91	.49819
1.72	.45728	2.32	.48983	2.92	.49825
1.73	.45818	2.33	.49010	2.93	.49831
1.74	.45907	2.34	.49036	2.94	.49836
1.75	.45994	2.35	.49061	2.95	.49841
1.76	.46080	2.36	.49086	2.96	.49846
1.77	.46164	2.37	.49111	2.97	.49851
1.78	.46246	2.38	.49134	2.98	.49856
1.79	.46327	2.39	.49158	2.99	.49861
1.80	.46407	2.40	.49180	3.00	.49865
1.81	.46485	2.41	.49202	3.01	.49869
1.82	.46562	2.42	.49224	3.02	.49874
1.83	.46638	2.43	.49245	3.03	.49878
1.84	.46712	2.44	.49266	3.04	.49882
1.85	.46784	2.45	.49286	3.05	.49886
1.86	.46856	2.46	.49305	3.06	.49889
1.87	.46926	2.47	.49324	3.07	.49893
1.88	.46995	2.48	.49343	3.08	.49896
1.89	.47062	2.49	.49361	3.09	.49900
1.90	.47128	2.50	.49379	3.10	.49903
1.91	.47193	2.51	.49396	3.11	.49906
1.92	.47257	2.52	.49413	3.12	.49910
1.93	.47320	2.53	.49430	3.13	.49913
1.94	.47381	2.54	.49446	3.14	.49916
1.95	.47441	2.55	.49461	3.15	.49918
1.96	.47500	2.56	.49477	3.16	.49921
1.97	.47558	2.57	.49492	3.17	.49924
1.98	.47615	2.58	.49506	3.18	.49926
1.99	.47670	2.59	.49520	3.19	.49929
2.00	.47725	2.60	.49534	3.20	.49931
2.01	.47778	2.61	.49547	3.21	.49934
2.02	.47831	2.62	.49560	3.22	.49936
2.03	.47882	2.63	.49573	3.23	.49938
2.04	.47932	2.64	.49585	3.24	.49940
2.05	.47982	2.65	.49598	3.25	.49942
2.06	.48030	2.66	.49609	3.26	.49944
2.07	.48077	2.67	.49621	3.27	.49946
2.08	.48124	2.68	.49632	3.28	.49948
2.09	.48169	2.69	.49643	3.29	.49950
2.10	.48214	2.70	.49653	3.30	.49952

$\frac{x}{\sigma}$	Area Between Maximum Ordinate And Ordinate at $\frac{x}{\sigma}$	$\frac{x}{\sigma}$	Area Between Maximum Ordinate And Ordinate at $\frac{x}{\sigma}$	$\frac{x}{\sigma}$	Area Between Maximum Ordinate And Ordinate at $\frac{x}{\sigma}$
3.31	.49953	3.56	.49981	3.81	.49993
3.32	.49955	3.57	.49982	3.82	.49993
3.33	.49957	3.58	.49983	3.83	.49994
3.34	.49958	3.59	.49983	3.84	.49994
3.35	.49960	3.60	.49984	3.85	.49994
3.36	.49961	3.61	.49985	3.86	.49994
3.37	.49962	3.62	.49985	3.87	.49995
3.38	.49964	3.63	.49986	3.88	.49995
3.39	.49965	3.64	.49986	3.89	.49995
3.40	.49966	3.65	.49987	3.90	.49995
3.41	.49968	3.66	.49987	3.91	.49995
3.42	.49969	3.67	.49988	3.92	.49996
3.43	.49970	3.68	.49988	3.93	.49996
3.44	.49971	3.69	.49989	3.94	.49996
3.45	.49972	3.70	.49989	3.95	.49996
3.46	.49973	3.71	.49990	3.96	.49996
3.47	.49974	3.72	.49990	3.97	.49996
3.48	.49975	3.73	.49990	3.98	.49997
3.49	.49976	3.74	.49991	3.99	.49997
3.50	.49977	3.75	.49991		
3.51	.49978	3.76	.49992		
3.52	.49978	3.77	.49992		
3.53	.49979	3.78	.49992		
3.54	.49980	3.79	.49992		
3.55	.49981	3.80	.49993		

APPENDIX B

TABLE OF STUDENT'S t-DISTRIBUTION
FOR SMALL SAMPLES (N = 30 OR LESS)

APPENDIX B
STUDENT'S *t*-DISTRIBUTION TABLE
FOR SMALL SAMPLES (*N* = 30 OR LESS)

Critical Probability
(Upper row for two-tailed test; lower row for one-tailed test)

Degrees of Freedom	.20 / .10	.10 / .05	.05 / .025	.02 / .01	.01 / .005	.001 / .0005
1	3.078	6.314	12.706	31.821	63.657	636.619
2	1.886	2.920	4.303	6.965	9.925	31.598
3	1.638	2.353	3.182	4.541	5.841	12.924
4	1.533	2.132	2.776	3.747	4.604	8.610
5	1.476	2.015	2.571	3.365	4.032	6.869
6	1.440	1.943	2.447	3.143	3.707	5.959
7	1.415	1.895	2.365	2.998	3.499	5.408
8	1.397	1.860	2.306	2.896	3.355	5.041
9	1.383	1.833	2.262	2.821	3.250	4.781
10	1.372	1.812	2.228	2.764	3.169	4.587
11	1.363	1.796	2.201	2.718	3.106	4.437
12	1.356	1.782	2.179	2.681	3.055	4.318
13	1.350	1.771	2.160	2.650	3.012	4.221
14	1.345	1.761	2.145	2.624	2.977	4.140
15	1.341	1.753	2.131	2.602	2.947	4.073
16	1.337	1.746	2.120	2.583	2.921	4.015
17	1.333	1.740	2.110	2.567	2.898	3.965
18	1.330	1.734	2.101	2.552	2.878	3.922
19	1.328	1.729	2.093	2.539	2.861	3.883
20	1.325	1.725	2.086	2.528	2.845	3.850
21	1.323	1.721	2.080	2.518	2.831	3.819
22	1.321	1.717	2.074	2.508	2.819	3.792
23	1.319	1.714	2.069	2.500	2.807	3.767
24	1.318	1.711	2.064	2.492	2.797	3.745
25	1.316	1.708	2.060	2.485	2.787	3.725
26	1.315	1.706	2.056	2.479	2.779	3.707
27	1.314	1.703	2.052	2.473	2.771	3.690
28	1.313	1.701	2.048	2.467	2.763	3.674
29	1.311	1.699	2.045	2.462	2.756	3.659
30	1.310	1.697	2.042	2.457	2.750	3.646

Source: This table is taken from Table III of Fisher and Yates: *Statistical Tables for Biological, Agricultural and Medical Research*, published by Longman Group Ltd., London. (previously published by Oliver & Boyd, Edinburgh), and by permission of the authors and publishers.

APPENDIX C

VALUES OF THE χ^2 DISTRIBUTION

APPENDIX C
VALUES OF THE χ^2 DISTRIBUTION

Degrees of Freedom	Critical probability			
	10%	5%	1%	0.1%
1	2.706	3.841	6.635	10.827
2	4.605	5.991	9.210	13.815
3	6.251	7.815	11.345	16.266
4	7.779	9.488	13.277	18.467
5	9.236	11.070	15.086	20.515
6	10.645	12.592	16.812	22.457
7	12.017	14.067	18.475	24.322
8	13.362	15.507	20.090	26.125
9	14.684	16.919	21.666	27.877
10	15.987	18.307	23.209	29.588
11	17.275	19.675	24.725	31.264
12	18.549	21.026	26.217	32.909
13	19.812	22.362	27.688	34.528
14	21.064	23.685	29.141	36.123
15	22.307	24.996	30.578	37.697
16	23.542	26.296	32.000	39.252
17	24.769	27.587	33.409	40.790
18	25.989	28.869	34.805	42.312
19	27.204	30.144	36.191	43.820
20	28.412	31.410	37.566	45.315
21	29.615	32.671	38.932	46.797
22	30.813	33.924	40.289	48.268
23	32.007	35.172	41.638	49.728
24	33.196	36.415	42.980	51.179
25	34.382	37.652	44.314	52.620
26	35.563	38.885	45.642	54.052
27	36.741	40.113	46.963	55.476
28	37.916	41.337	48.278	56.893
29	39.087	42.557	49.588	58.302
30	40.256	43.773	50.892	59.703

For larger values of n, the expression $\sqrt{2\chi^2} - \sqrt{2n-1}$ may be used as a normal deviate with unit standard error, interpreting the deviate as in a one-tailed test.

Source: This table is taken from Table IV of Fisher and Yates: *Statistical Tables for Biological, Agricultural and Medical Research*, published by Longman Group Ltd., London. (previously published by Oliver & Boyd, Edinburgh), and by permission of the authors and publishers.

APPENDIX D

VALUES OF THE F-DISTRIBUTION*
(95th percentile in upper row; 99th percentile in lower row)

APPENDIX D

VALUES OF THE "F" DISTRIBUTION*

(95th percentile in upper row: 99th percentile in lower row)

n_1 = degrees of freedom for numerator

n_2	1	2	3	4	5	6	7	8	9	10	11	12	14	16	20	24	30	40	50	75	100	200	500	∞
1	161 4,052	200 4,999	216 5,403	225 5,625	230 5,764	234 5,859	237 5,928	239 5,981	241 6,022	242 6,056	243 6,082	244 6,106	245 6,142	246 6,169	248 6,208	249 6,234	250 6,258	251 6,286	252 6,302	253 6,323	253 6,334	254 6,352	254 6,361	254 6,366
2	18.51 98.49	19.00 99.00	19.16 99.17	19.25 99.25	19.30 99.30	19.33 99.33	19.36 99.34	19.37 99.36	19.38 99.38	19.39 99.40	19.40 99.41	19.41 99.42	19.42 99.43	19.43 99.44	19.44 99.45	19.45 99.46	19.46 99.47	19.47 99.48	19.47 99.48	19.48 99.49	19.49 99.49	19.49 99.49	19.50 99.50	19.50 99.50
3	10.13 34.12	9.55 30.82	9.28 29.46	9.12 28.71	9.01 28.24	8.94 27.91	8.88 27.67	8.84 27.49	8.81 27.34	8.78 27.23	8.76 27.13	8.74 27.05	8.71 26.92	8.69 26.83	8.66 26.69	8.64 26.60	8.62 26.50	8.60 26.41	8.58 26.35	8.57 26.27	8.56 26.23	8.54 26.18	8.54 26.14	8.53 26.12
4	7.71 21.20	6.94 18.00	6.59 16.69	6.39 15.98	6.26 15.52	6.16 15.21	6.09 14.98	6.04 14.80	6.00 14.66	5.96 14.54	5.93 14.45	5.91 14.37	5.87 14.24	5.84 14.15	5.80 14.02	5.77 13.93	5.74 13.83	5.71 13.74	5.70 13.69	5.68 13.61	5.66 13.57	5.65 13.52	5.64 13.48	5.63 13.46
5	6.61 16.26	5.79 13.27	5.41 12.06	5.19 11.39	5.05 10.97	4.95 10.67	4.88 10.45	4.82 10.27	4.78 10.15	4.74 10.05	4.70 9.96	4.68 9.89	4.64 9.77	4.60 9.68	4.56 9.55	4.53 9.47	4.50 9.38	4.46 9.29	4.44 9.24	4.42 9.17	4.40 9.13	4.38 9.07	4.37 9.04	4.36 9.02
6	5.99 13.74	5.14 10.92	4.76 9.78	4.53 9.15	4.39 8.75	4.28 8.47	4.21 8.26	4.15 8.10	4.10 7.98	4.06 7.87	4.03 7.79	4.00 7.72	3.96 7.60	3.92 7.52	3.87 7.39	3.84 7.31	3.81 7.23	3.77 7.14	3.75 7.09	3.72 7.02	3.71 6.99	3.69 6.94	3.68 6.90	3.67 6.88
7	5.59 12.25	4.74 9.55	4.35 8.45	4.12 7.85	3.97 7.46	3.87 7.19	3.79 7.00	3.73 6.84	3.68 6.71	3.63 6.62	3.60 6.54	3.57 6.47	3.52 6.35	3.49 6.27	3.44 6.15	3.41 6.07	3.38 5.98	3.34 5.90	3.32 5.85	3.29 5.78	3.28 5.75	3.25 5.70	3.24 5.67	3.23 5.65
8	5.32 11.26	4.46 8.65	4.07 7.59	3.84 7.01	3.69 6.63	3.58 6.37	3.50 6.19	3.44 6.03	3.39 5.91	3.34 5.82	3.31 5.74	3.28 5.67	3.23 5.56	3.20 5.48	3.15 5.36	3.12 5.28	3.08 5.20	3.05 5.11	3.03 5.06	3.00 5.00	2.98 4.96	2.96 4.91	2.94 4.88	2.93 4.86
9	5.12 10.56	4.26 8.02	3.86 6.99	3.63 6.42	3.48 6.06	3.37 5.80	3.29 5.62	3.23 5.47	3.18 5.35	3.13 5.26	3.10 5.18	3.07 5.11	3.02 5.00	2.98 4.92	2.93 4.80	2.90 4.73	2.86 4.64	2.82 4.56	2.80 4.51	2.77 4.45	2.76 4.41	2.73 4.36	2.72 4.33	2.71 4.31
10	4.96 10.04	4.10 7.56	3.71 6.55	3.48 5.99	3.33 5.64	3.22 5.39	3.14 5.21	3.07 5.06	3.02 4.95	2.97 4.85	2.94 4.78	2.91 4.71	2.86 4.60	2.82 4.52	2.77 4.41	2.74 4.33	2.70 4.25	2.67 4.17	2.64 4.12	2.61 4.05	2.59 4.01	2.56 3.96	2.55 3.93	2.54 3.91
11	4.84 9.65	3.98 7.20	3.59 6.22	3.36 5.67	3.20 5.32	3.09 5.07	3.01 4.88	2.95 4.74	2.90 4.63	2.86 4.54	2.82 4.46	2.79 4.40	2.74 4.29	2.70 4.21	2.65 4.10	2.61 4.02	2.57 3.94	2.53 3.86	2.50 3.80	2.47 3.74	2.45 3.70	2.42 3.66	2.41 3.62	2.40 3.60

* Reprinted by permission of the Iowa State University Press, Ames, Iowa, from STATISTICAL METHODS, 5th edition, by George W. Snedecor ©1956.

∞	500	200	100	75	50	40	30	24	20	16	14	12	11	10	9	8	7	6	5	4	3	2	1	n_2
2.30 3.36	2.31 3.38	2.32 3.41	2.35 3.46	2.36 3.49	2.40 3.56	2.42 3.61	2.46 3.70	2.50 3.78	2.54 3.86	2.60 3.98	2.64 4.05	2.69 4.16	2.72 4.22	2.76 4.30	2.80 4.39	2.85 4.50	2.92 4.65	3.00 4.82	3.11 5.06	3.26 5.41	3.49 5.95	3.88 6.93	4.75 9.33	12
2.21 3.16	2.22 3.18	2.24 3.21	2.26 3.27	2.28 3.30	2.32 3.37	2.34 3.42	2.38 3.51	2.42 3.59	2.46 3.67	2.51 3.78	2.55 3.85	2.60 3.96	2.63 4.02	2.67 4.10	2.72 4.19	2.77 4.30	2.84 4.44	2.92 4.62	3.02 4.86	3.18 5.20	3.41 5.74	3.80 6.70	4.67 9.07	13
2.13 3.00	2.14 3.02	2.16 3.06	2.19 3.11	2.21 3.14	2.24 3.21	2.27 3.26	2.31 3.34	2.35 3.43	2.39 3.51	2.44 3.62	2.48 3.70	2.53 3.80	2.56 3.86	2.60 3.94	2.65 4.03	2.70 4.14	2.77 4.28	2.85 4.46	2.96 4.69	3.11 5.03	3.34 5.56	3.74 6.51	4.60 8.86	14
2.07 2.87	2.08 2.89	2.10 2.92	2.12 2.97	2.15 3.00	2.18 3.07	2.21 3.12	2.25 3.20	2.29 3.29	2.33 3.36	2.39 3.48	2.43 3.56	2.48 3.67	2.51 3.73	2.55 3.80	2.59 3.89	2.64 4.00	2.70 4.14	2.79 4.32	2.90 4.56	3.06 4.89	3.29 5.42	3.68 6.36	4.54 8.68	15
2.01 2.75	2.02 2.77	2.04 2.80	2.07 2.86	2.09 2.89	2.13 2.96	2.16 3.01	2.20 3.10	2.24 3.18	2.28 3.25	2.33 3.37	2.37 3.45	2.42 3.55	2.45 3.61	2.49 3.69	2.54 3.78	2.59 3.89	2.66 4.03	2.74 4.20	2.85 4.44	3.01 4.77	3.24 5.29	3.63 6.23	4.49 8.53	16
1.96 2.65	1.97 2.67	1.99 2.70	2.02 2.76	2.04 2.79	2.08 2.86	2.11 2.92	2.15 3.00	2.19 3.08	2.23 3.16	2.29 3.27	2.33 3.35	2.38 3.45	2.41 3.52	2.45 3.59	2.50 3.68	2.55 3.79	2.62 3.93	2.70 4.10	2.81 4.34	2.96 4.67	3.20 5.18	3.59 6.11	4.45 8.40	17
1.92 2.57	1.93 2.59	1.95 2.62	1.98 2.68	2.00 2.71	2.04 2.78	2.07 2.83	2.11 2.91	2.15 3.00	2.19 3.07	2.25 3.19	2.29 3.27	2.34 3.37	2.37 3.44	2.41 3.51	2.46 3.60	2.51 3.71	2.58 3.85	2.66 4.01	2.77 4.25	2.93 4.53	3.16 5.09	3.55 6.01	4.41 8.28	18
1.88 2.49	1.90 2.51	1.91 2.54	1.94 2.60	1.96 2.63	2.00 2.70	2.02 2.76	2.07 2.84	2.11 2.92	2.15 3.00	2.21 3.12	2.26 3.19	2.31 3.30	2.34 3.36	2.38 3.43	2.43 3.52	2.48 3.63	2.55 3.77	2.63 3.94	2.74 4.17	2.90 4.50	3.13 5.01	3.52 5.93	4.38 8.18	19
1.84 2.42	1.85 2.44	1.87 2.47	1.90 2.53	1.92 2.56	1.96 2.63	1.99 2.69	2.04 2.77	2.08 2.86	2.12 2.94	2.18 3.05	2.23 3.13	2.28 3.23	2.31 3.30	2.35 3.37	2.40 3.45	2.45 3.56	2.52 3.71	2.60 3.87	2.71 4.10	2.87 4.43	3.10 4.94	3.49 5.85	4.35 8.10	20
1.81 2.36	1.82 2.38	1.84 2.42	1.87 2.47	1.89 2.51	1.93 2.58	1.96 2.63	2.00 2.72	2.05 2.80	2.09 2.88	2.15 2.99	2.20 3.07	2.25 3.17	2.28 3.24	2.32 3.31	2.37 3.40	2.42 3.51	2.49 3.65	2.57 3.81	2.68 4.04	2.84 4.37	3.07 4.87	3.47 5.78	4.32 8.02	21
1.78 2.31	1.80 2.33	1.81 2.37	1.84 2.42	1.87 2.46	1.91 2.53	1.93 2.58	1.98 2.67	2.03 2.75	2.07 2.83	2.13 2.94	2.18 3.02	2.23 3.12	2.26 3.18	2.30 3.26	2.35 3.35	2.40 3.45	2.47 3.59	2.55 3.76	2.66 3.99	2.82 4.31	3.05 4.82	3.44 5.72	4.30 7.94	22
1.76 2.26	1.77 2.28	1.79 2.32	1.82 2.37	1.84 2.41	1.88 2.48	1.91 2.53	1.96 2.62	2.00 2.70	2.04 2.78	2.10 2.89	2.14 2.97	2.20 3.07	2.24 3.14	2.28 3.21	2.32 3.30	2.38 3.41	2.45 3.54	2.53 3.71	2.64 3.94	2.80 4.26	3.03 4.76	3.42 5.66	4.28 7.88	23
1.73 2.21	1.74 2.23	1.76 2.27	1.80 2.33	1.82 2.36	1.86 2.44	1.89 2.49	1.94 2.58	1.98 2.66	2.02 2.74	2.09 2.85	2.13 2.93	2.18 3.03	2.22 3.09	2.26 3.17	2.30 3.25	2.36 3.36	2.43 3.50	2.51 3.67	2.62 3.90	2.78 4.22	3.01 4.72	3.40 5.61	4.26 7.82	24
1.71 2.17	1.72 2.19	1.74 2.23	1.77 2.29	1.80 2.32	1.84 2.40	1.87 2.45	1.92 2.54	1.96 2.62	2.00 2.70	2.06 2.81	2.11 2.89	2.16 2.99	2.20 3.05	2.24 3.13	2.28 3.21	2.34 3.32	2.41 3.46	2.49 3.63	2.60 3.86	2.76 4.18	2.99 4.68	3.38 5.57	4.24 7.77	25

n_2	1	2	3	4	5	6	7	8	9	10	11	12	14	16	20	24	30	40	50	75	100	200	500	∞
26	4.22 7.72	3.37 5.53	2.98 4.64	2.74 4.14	2.59 3.82	2.47 3.59	2.39 3.42	2.32 3.29	2.27 3.17	2.22 3.09	2.18 3.02	2.15 2.96	2.10 2.86	2.05 2.77	1.99 2.66	1.95 2.58	1.90 2.50	1.85 2.41	1.82 2.36	1.78 2.28	1.76 2.25	1.72 2.19	1.70 2.15	1.69 2.13
27	4.21 7.68	3.35 5.49	2.96 4.60	2.73 4.11	2.57 3.79	2.46 3.56	2.37 3.39	2.30 3.26	2.25 3.14	2.20 3.06	2.16 2.98	2.13 2.93	2.08 2.83	2.03 2.74	1.97 2.63	1.93 2.55	1.88 2.47	1.84 2.38	1.80 2.33	1.76 2.25	1.74 2.21	1.71 2.16	1.68 2.12	1.67 2.10
28	4.20 7.64	3.34 5.45	2.95 4.57	2.71 4.07	2.56 3.76	2.44 3.53	2.36 3.36	2.29 3.23	2.24 3.11	2.19 3.03	2.15 2.95	2.12 2.90	2.06 2.80	2.02 2.71	1.96 2.60	1.91 2.52	1.87 2.44	1.81 2.35	1.78 2.30	1.75 2.22	1.72 2.18	1.69 2.13	1.67 2.09	1.65 2.06
29	4.18 7.60	3.33 5.42	2.93 4.54	2.70 4.04	2.54 3.73	2.43 3.50	2.35 3.33	2.28 3.20	2.22 3.08	2.18 3.00	2.14 2.92	2.10 2.87	2.05 2.77	2.00 2.68	1.94 2.57	1.90 2.49	1.85 2.41	1.80 2.32	1.77 2.27	1.73 2.19	1.71 2.15	1.68 2.10	1.65 2.06	1.64 2.03
30	4.17 7.56	3.32 5.39	2.92 4.51	2.69 4.02	2.53 3.70	2.42 3.47	2.34 3.30	2.27 3.17	2.21 3.06	2.16 2.98	2.12 2.90	2.09 2.84	2.04 2.74	1.99 2.66	1.93 2.55	1.89 2.47	1.84 2.38	1.79 2.29	1.76 2.24	1.72 2.16	1.69 2.13	1.66 2.07	1.64 2.03	1.62 2.01
32	4.15 7.50	3.30 5.34	2.90 4.46	2.67 3.97	2.51 3.66	2.40 3.42	2.32 3.25	2.25 3.12	2.19 3.01	2.14 2.94	2.10 2.86	2.07 2.80	2.02 2.70	1.97 2.62	1.91 2.51	1.86 2.42	1.82 2.34	1.76 2.25	1.74 2.20	1.69 2.12	1.67 2.08	1.64 2.02	1.61 1.98	1.59 1.96
34	4.13 7.44	3.28 5.29	2.88 4.42	2.65 3.93	2.49 3.61	2.38 3.38	2.30 3.21	2.23 3.08	2.17 2.97	2.12 2.89	2.08 2.82	2.05 2.76	2.00 2.66	1.95 2.58	1.89 2.47	1.84 2.38	1.80 2.30	1.74 2.21	1.71 2.15	1.67 2.08	1.64 2.04	1.61 1.98	1.59 1.94	1.57 1.91
36	4.11 7.39	3.26 5.25	2.86 4.38	2.63 3.89	2.48 3.58	2.36 3.35	2.28 3.18	2.21 3.04	2.15 2.94	2.10 2.86	2.06 2.78	2.03 2.72	1.98 2.62	1.93 2.54	1.87 2.43	1.82 2.35	1.78 2.26	1.72 2.17	1.69 2.12	1.65 2.04	1.62 2.00	1.59 1.94	1.56 1.90	1.55 1.87
38	4.10 7.35	3.25 5.21	2.85 4.34	2.62 3.86	2.46 3.54	2.35 3.32	2.26 3.15	2.19 3.02	2.14 2.91	2.09 2.82	2.05 2.75	2.02 2.69	1.96 2.59	1.92 2.51	1.85 2.40	1.80 2.32	1.76 2.22	1.71 2.14	1.67 2.08	1.63 2.00	1.60 1.97	1.57 1.90	1.54 1.86	1.53 1.84
40	4.08 7.31	3.23 5.18	2.84 4.31	2.61 3.83	2.45 3.51	2.34 3.29	2.25 3.12	2.18 2.99	2.12 2.88	2.07 2.80	2.04 2.73	2.00 2.66	1.95 2.56	1.90 2.49	1.84 2.37	1.79 2.29	1.74 2.20	1.69 2.11	1.66 2.05	1.61 1.97	1.59 1.94	1.55 1.88	1.53 1.84	1.51 1.81
42	4.07 7.27	3.22 5.15	2.83 4.29	2.59 3.80	2.44 3.49	2.32 3.26	2.24 3.10	2.17 2.96	2.11 2.86	2.06 2.77	2.02 2.70	1.99 2.64	1.94 2.54	1.89 2.46	1.82 2.35	1.78 2.26	1.73 2.17	1.68 2.08	1.64 2.02	1.60 1.94	1.57 1.91	1.54 1.85	1.51 1.80	1.49 1.78
44	4.06 7.24	3.21 5.12	2.82 4.26	2.58 3.78	2.43 3.46	2.31 3.24	2.23 3.07	2.16 2.94	2.10 2.84	2.05 2.75	2.01 2.68	1.98 2.62	1.92 2.52	1.88 2.44	1.81 2.32	1.76 2.24	1.72 2.15	1.66 2.06	1.63 2.00	1.58 1.92	1.56 1.88	1.52 1.82	1.50 1.78	1.48 1.75
46	4.05 7.21	3.20 5.10	2.81 4.24	2.57 3.76	2.42 3.44	2.30 3.22	2.22 3.05	2.14 2.92	2.09 2.82	2.04 2.73	2.00 2.66	1.97 2.60	1.91 2.50	1.87 2.42	1.80 2.30	1.75 2.22	1.71 2.13	1.65 2.04	1.62 1.96	1.57 1.90	1.54 1.86	1.51 1.80	1.48 1.76	1.46 1.72
48	4.04 7.19	3.19 5.08	2.80 4.22	2.56 3.74	2.41 3.42	2.30 3.20	2.21 3.04	2.14 2.90	2.08 2.80	2.03 2.71	1.99 2.64	1.96 2.58	1.90 2.48	1.86 2.40	1.79 2.28	1.74 2.20	1.70 2.11	1.64 2.02	1.61 1.96	1.56 1.88	1.53 1.84	1.50 1.78	1.47 1.73	1.45 1.70

n_2	1	2	3	4	5	6	7	8	9	10	11	12	14	16	20	24	30	40	50	75	100	200	500	∞
50	4.03 / 7.17	3.18 / 5.06	2.79 / 4.20	2.56 / 3.72	2.40 / 3.41	2.29 / 3.18	2.20 / 3.02	2.13 / 2.88	2.07 / 2.78	2.02 / 2.70	1.98 / 2.62	1.95 / 2.56	1.90 / 2.46	1.85 / 2.39	1.78 / 2.26	1.74 / 2.18	1.69 / 2.10	1.63 / 2.00	1.60 / 1.94	1.55 / 1.86	1.52 / 1.82	1.48 / 1.76	1.46 / 1.71	1.44 / 1.68
55	4.02 / 7.12	3.17 / 5.01	2.78 / 4.16	2.54 / 3.68	2.38 / 3.37	2.27 / 3.15	2.18 / 2.98	2.11 / 2.85	2.05 / 2.75	2.00 / 2.66	1.97 / 2.59	1.93 / 2.53	1.88 / 2.43	1.83 / 2.35	1.76 / 2.23	1.72 / 2.15	1.67 / 2.06	1.61 / 1.96	1.58 / 1.90	1.52 / 1.82	1.50 / 1.78	1.46 / 1.71	1.43 / 1.66	1.41 / 1.64
60	4.00 / 7.08	3.15 / 4.98	2.76 / 4.13	2.52 / 3.65	2.37 / 3.34	2.25 / 3.12	2.17 / 2.95	2.10 / 2.82	2.04 / 2.72	1.99 / 2.63	1.95 / 2.56	1.92 / 2.50	1.86 / 2.40	1.81 / 2.32	1.75 / 2.20	1.70 / 2.12	1.65 / 2.03	1.59 / 1.93	1.56 / 1.87	1.50 / 1.79	1.48 / 1.74	1.44 / 1.68	1.41 / 1.63	1.39 / 1.60
65	3.99 / 7.04	3.14 / 4.95	2.75 / 4.10	2.51 / 3.62	2.36 / 3.31	2.24 / 3.09	2.15 / 2.93	2.08 / 2.79	2.02 / 2.70	1.98 / 2.61	1.94 / 2.54	1.90 / 2.47	1.85 / 2.37	1.80 / 2.30	1.73 / 2.18	1.68 / 2.09	1.63 / 2.00	1.57 / 1.90	1.54 / 1.84	1.49 / 1.76	1.46 / 1.71	1.42 / 1.64	1.39 / 1.60	1.37 / 1.56
70	3.98 / 7.01	3.13 / 4.92	2.74 / 4.08	2.50 / 3.60	2.35 / 3.29	2.23 / 3.07	2.14 / 2.91	2.07 / 2.77	2.01 / 2.67	1.97 / 2.59	1.93 / 2.51	1.89 / 2.45	1.84 / 2.35	1.79 / 2.28	1.72 / 2.15	1.67 / 2.07	1.62 / 1.96	1.56 / 1.88	1.53 / 1.82	1.47 / 1.74	1.45 / 1.69	1.40 / 1.62	1.37 / 1.56	1.35 / 1.53
80	3.96 / 6.96	3.11 / 4.83	2.72 / 4.04	2.48 / 3.56	2.33 / 3.25	2.21 / 3.04	2.12 / 2.87	2.05 / 2.74	1.99 / 2.64	1.95 / 2.55	1.91 / 2.48	1.88 / 2.41	1.82 / 2.32	1.77 / 2.24	1.70 / 2.11	1.65 / 2.03	1.60 / 1.94	1.54 / 1.84	1.51 / 1.78	1.45 / 1.70	1.42 / 1.65	1.38 / 1.57	1.35 / 1.52	1.32 / 1.49
100	3.94 / 6.90	3.09 / 4.82	2.70 / 3.98	2.46 / 3.51	2.30 / 3.20	2.19 / 2.99	2.10 / 2.82	2.03 / 2.69	1.97 / 2.59	1.92 / 2.51	1.88 / 2.43	1.85 / 2.36	1.79 / 2.26	1.75 / 2.19	1.68 / 2.06	1.63 / 1.98	1.57 / 1.89	1.51 / 1.79	1.48 / 1.73	1.42 / 1.64	1.39 / 1.59	1.34 / 1.51	1.30 / 1.46	1.28 / 1.43
125	3.92 / 6.84	3.07 / 4.78	2.68 / 3.94	2.44 / 3.47	2.29 / 3.17	2.17 / 2.95	2.08 / 2.79	2.01 / 2.65	1.95 / 2.56	1.90 / 2.47	1.86 / 2.40	1.83 / 2.33	1.77 / 2.23	1.72 / 2.15	1.65 / 2.03	1.60 / 1.94	1.55 / 1.85	1.49 / 1.75	1.45 / 1.68	1.39 / 1.59	1.36 / 1.54	1.31 / 1.46	1.27 / 1.40	1.25 / 1.37
150	3.91 / 6.81	3.06 / 4.75	2.67 / 3.91	2.43 / 3.44	2.27 / 3.14	2.16 / 2.92	2.07 / 2.76	2.00 / 2.62	1.94 / 2.53	1.89 / 2.44	1.85 / 2.37	1.82 / 2.30	1.76 / 2.20	1.71 / 2.12	1.64 / 2.00	1.59 / 1.91	1.54 / 1.83	1.47 / 1.72	1.44 / 1.66	1.37 / 1.56	1.34 / 1.51	1.29 / 1.43	1.25 / 1.37	1.22 / 1.33
200	3.89 / 6.76	3.04 / 4.71	2.65 / 3.88	2.41 / 3.41	2.26 / 3.11	2.14 / 2.90	2.05 / 2.73	1.98 / 2.60	1.92 / 2.50	1.87 / 2.41	1.83 / 2.34	1.80 / 2.28	1.74 / 2.17	1.69 / 2.09	1.62 / 1.97	1.57 / 1.88	1.52 / 1.79	1.45 / 1.69	1.42 / 1.62	1.35 / 1.53	1.32 / 1.48	1.26 / 1.39	1.22 / 1.33	1.19 / 1.28
400	3.86 / 6.70	3.02 / 4.66	2.62 / 3.83	2.39 / 3.36	2.23 / 3.06	2.12 / 2.85	2.03 / 2.69	1.96 / 2.55	1.90 / 2.46	1.85 / 2.37	1.81 / 2.29	1.78 / 2.23	1.72 / 2.12	1.67 / 2.04	1.60 / 1.92	1.54 / 1.84	1.49 / 1.74	1.42 / 1.64	1.38 / 1.57	1.32 / 1.47	1.28 / 1.42	1.22 / 1.32	1.16 / 1.24	1.13 / 1.19
1000	3.85 / 6.66	3.00 / 4.62	2.61 / 3.80	2.38 / 3.34	2.22 / 3.04	2.10 / 2.82	2.02 / 2.66	1.95 / 2.53	1.89 / 2.43	1.84 / 2.34	1.80 / 2.26	1.76 / 2.20	1.70 / 2.09	1.65 / 2.01	1.58 / 1.89	1.53 / 1.81	1.47 / 1.71	1.41 / 1.61	1.36 / 1.54	1.30 / 1.44	1.26 / 1.38	1.19 / 1.28	1.13 / 1.19	1.08 / 1.11
∞	3.84 / 6.64	2.99 / 4.60	2.60 / 3.78	2.37 / 3.32	2.21 / 3.02	2.09 / 2.80	2.01 / 2.64	1.94 / 2.51	1.88 / 2.41	1.83 / 2.32	1.79 / 2.24	1.75 / 2.18	1.69 / 2.07	1.64 / 1.99	1.57 / 1.87	1.52 / 1.79	1.46 / 1.69	1.40 / 1.59	1.35 / 1.52	1.28 / 1.41	1.24 / 1.36	1.17 / 1.25	1.11 / 1.15	1.00 / 1.00

APPENDIX E

5-DIGIT RANDOM NUMBERS*

APPENDIX E
5-DIGIT RANDOM NUMBERS*

Line Col.	(1)	(2)	(3)	(4)	(5)	(6)	(7)	(8)	(9)	(10)	(11)	(12)	(13)	(14)
1	10480	15011	01536	02011	81647	91646	69179	14194	62590	36207	20969	99570	91291	90700
2	22368	46573	25595	85393	30995	89198	27982	53402	93965	34095	52666	19174	39615	99505
3	24130	48360	22527	97265	76393	64809	15179	24830	49340	32081	30680	19655	63348	58629
4	42167	93093	06243	61680	07856	16376	39440	53537	71341	57004	00849	74917	97758	16379
5	37570	39975	81837	16656	06121	91782	60468	81305	49684	60672	14110	06927	01263	54613
6	77921	06907	11008	42751	27756	53498	18602	70659	90655	15053	21916	81825	44394	42880
7	99562	72905	56420	69994	98872	31016	71194	18738	44013	48840	63213	21069	10634	12952
8	96301	91977	05463	07972	18876	20922	94595	56869	69014	60045	18425	84903	42508	32307
9	89579	14342	63661	10281	17453	18103	57740	84378	25331	12566	58678	44947	05585	56941
10	85475	36857	53342	53988	53060	59533	38867	62300	08158	17983	16439	11458	18593	64952
11	28918	69578	88231	33276	70997	79936	56865	05859	90106	31595	01547	85590	91610	78188
12	63553	40961	48235	03427	49626	69445	18663	72695	52180	20847	12234	90511	33703	90322
13	09429	93969	52636	92737	88974	33488	36320	17617	30015	08272	84115	27156	30613	74952
14	10365	61129	87529	85689	48237	52267	67689	93394	01511	26358	85104	20285	29975	89868
15	07119	97336	71048	08178	77233	13916	47564	81056	97735	85977	29372	74461	28551	90707
16	51085	12765	51821	51259	77452	16308	60756	92144	49442	53900	70960	63990	75601	40719
17	02368	21382	52404	60268	89368	19885	55322	44819	01188	65255	64835	44919	05944	55157
18	01011	54092	33362	94904	31273	04146	18594	29852	71585	85030	51132	01915	92747	64951
19	52162	53916	46369	58586	23216	14513	83149	98736	23495	64350	94738	17752	35156	35749
20	07056	97628	33787	09998	42698	06691	76988	13602	51851	46104	88916	19509	25625	58104
21	48663	91245	85828	14346	09172	30168	90229	04734	59193	22178	30421	61666	99904	32812
22	54164	58492	22421	74103	47070	25306	76468	26384	58151	06646	21524	15227	96909	44592
23	32639	32363	05597	24200	13363	38005	94342	28728	35806	06912	17012	64161	18296	22851
24	29334	27001	87637	87308	58731	00256	45834	15398	46557	41135	10367	07684	36188	18510
25	02488	33062	28834	07351	19731	92420	60952	61280	50001	67658	32586	86679	50720	94953

* Includes first three pages of *Table of 105,000 Random Decimal Digits*, Bureau of Transport Economics and Statistics, Statement No. 4914 (Washington, D. C.: U. S. Interstate Commerce Commission, 1949).

Line	Col. (1)	(2)	(3)	(4)	(5)	(6)	(7)	(8)	(9)	(10)	(11)	(12)	(13)	(14)
26	81525	72295	04839	96423	24878	82651	66566	14778	76797	14780	13300	87074	79666	95725
27	29676	20591	68086	26432	46901	20849	89768	81536	86645	12659	92259	57102	80428	25280
28	00742	57392	39064	66432	84673	40027	32832	61362	98947	96067	64760	64584	96096	98253
29	05366	04213	25669	26422	44407	44048	37937	63904	45766	66134	75470	66520	34693	90449
30	91921	26418	64117	94305	26766	25940	39972	22209	71500	64568	91402	42416	07844	69618
31	00582	04711	87917	77341	42206	35126	74087	99547	81817	42607	43808	76655	62028	76630
32	00725	69884	62797	56170	86324	88072	76222	36086	84637	93161	76038	65855	77919	88006
33	69011	65795	95876	55293	18988	27354	26575	08625	40801	59920	29841	80150	12777	48501
34	25976	57948	29888	88604	67917	48708	18912	82271	65424	69774	33611	54262	85963	03547
35	09763	83473	73577	12908	30883	18317	28290	35797	05998	41688	34952	37888	38917	88050
36	91567	42595	27958	30134	04024	86385	29880	99730	55536	84855	29080	09250	79656	73211
37	17955	56349	90999	49127	20044	59931	06115	20542	18059	02008	73708	83517	36103	42791
38	46503	18584	18845	49618	02304	51038	20655	58727	28168	15475	56942	53389	20562	87338
39	92157	89634	94824	78171	84610	82834	09922	25417	44137	48413	25555	21246	35509	20468
40	14577	62765	35605	81263	39667	47358	56873	56307	61607	49518	89656	20130	77490	18062
41	98427	07523	33362	64270	01638	92477	66969	98420	04880	45585	46565	04102	46880	45709
42	34914	63976	88720	82765	34476	17032	87589	40836	32427	70002	70663	88863	77775	69348
43	70060	28277	39475	46473	23219	53416	94970	25832	69975	94884	19661	72828	00102	66794
44	53976	54914	06990	67245	68350	82948	11398	42878	80287	88267	47363	46634	06541	97809
45	76072	29515	40980	07391	58745	25774	22987	80059	39911	96189	41151	14222	60697	59583
46	90725	52210	83974	29992	65831	38857	50490	83765	55657	14361	31720	57375	56228	41546
47	64364	67412	33339	31926	14883	24413	59744	92351	97473	89286	35931	04110	23726	51900
48	08962	00358	31662	25388	61642	34072	81249	35648	56891	69352	48373	45578	78547	81788
49	95012	68379	93526	70765	10592	04542	76463	54328	02349	17247	28865	14777	62730	92277
50	15664	10493	20492	38391	91132	21999	59516	81652	27195	48223	46751	22923	32261	85653

Line	Col. (1)	(2)	(3)	(4)	(5)	(6)	(7)	(8)	(9)	(10)	(11)	(12)	(13)	(14)
51	16408	81899	04153	53381	79401	21438	83035	92350	36693	31238	59649	91754	72772	02338
52	18629	81953	05520	91962	04739	13092	97662	24822	94730	06496	35090	04822	86774	98289
53	73115	35101	47498	87637	99016	71060	88824	71013	18735	20286	23153	72924	35165	43040
54	57491	16703	23167	49323	45021	33132	12544	41035	80780	45393	44812	12515	98931	91202
55	30405	83946	23792	14422	15059	45799	22716	19792	09983	74353	68668	30429	70735	25499
56	16631	35006	85900	98275	32388	52390	16815	69298	82732	38480	73817	32523	41961	44437
57	96773	20206	42559	78985	05300	22164	24369	54224	35083	19687	11052	91491	60383	19746
58	38935	64202	14349	82674	66523	44133	00697	35552	35970	19124	63318	29686	03387	59846
59	31624	76384	17403	53363	44167	64486	64758	75366	76554	31601	12614	33072	60332	92325
60	78919	19474	23632	27889	47914	02584	37680	20801	72152	39339	34806	08930	85001	87820
61	03931	33309	57047	74211	63445	17361	62825	39908	05607	91284	68833	25570	38818	46920
62	74426	33278	43972	10119	89917	15665	52872	73823	73144	88662	88970	74492	51805	99378
63	09066	00903	20795	95452	92648	45454	09552	88815	16553	51125	79375	97596	16296	66092
64	42238	12426	87025	14267	20979	04508	64535	31355	86064	29472	47689	05974	52468	16834
65	16153	08002	26504	41744	81959	65642	74240	56302	00033	67107	77510	70625	28725	34191
66	21457	40742	29820	96783	29400	21840	15035	34537	33310	06116	95240	15957	16572	06004
67	21581	57802	02050	89728	17937	37621	47075	42080	97403	48626	68995	43805	33386	21597
68	55612	78095	83197	33732	05810	24813	86902	60397	16489	03264	88525	42786	05269	92532
69	44657	66999	99324	51281	84463	60563	79312	93454	68876	25471	93911	25650	12682	73572
70	91340	84979	46949	81973	37949	61023	43997	15263	80644	43942	89203	71795	99533	50501
71	91227	21199	31935	27022	84067	05462	35216	14486	29891	68607	41867	14951	91696	85065
72	50001	38140	66321	19924	72163	09538	12151	06878	91903	18749	34405	56087	82790	70925
73	65390	05224	72958	28609	81406	39147	25549	48542	42627	45233	57202	94617	23772	07896
74	27504	96131	83944	41575	10573	08619	64482	73923	36152	05184	94142	25299	84387	34925
75	37169	94851	39117	89632	00959	16487	65536	49071	39782	17095	02330	74301	00275	48280

Line	Col. (1)	(2)	(3)	(4)	(5)	(6)	(7)	(8)	(9)	(10)	(11)	(12)	(13)	(14)
76	11508	70225	51111	38351	19444	66499	71945	05422	13442	78675	84081	66938	93654	59894
77	37449	30362	06694	54690	04052	53115	62757	95348	78662	11163	81651	50245	34971	52924
78	46515	70331	85922	38329	57015	15765	97161	17869	45349	61796	66345	81073	49106	79860
79	30986	81223	42416	58353	21532	30502	32305	86482	05174	07901	54339	58861	74818	46942
80	63798	64995	46583	09785	44160	78128	83991	42865	92520	83531	80377	35909	81250	54238
81	82486	84846	99254	67632	43218	50076	21361	64816	51202	88124	41870	52689	51275	83556
82	21885	32906	92431	09060	64297	51674	64126	62570	26123	05155	59194	52799	28225	85762
83	60336	98782	07408	53458	13564	59089	26445	29789	85205	41001	12535	12133	14645	23541
84	43937	46891	24010	25560	86355	33941	25786	54990	71899	15475	95434	98227	21824	19585
85	97656	63175	89303	16275	07100	92063	21942	18611	47348	20203	18534	03862	78095	50136
86	03299	01221	05418	38982	55758	92237	26759	86367	21216	98442	08303	56613	91511	75928
87	79626	06486	03574	17668	07785	76020	79924	25651	83325	88428	85076	72811	22717	50585
88	85636	68335	47539	03129	65651	11977	02510	26113	99447	68645	34327	15152	55230	93448
89	18039	14367	61337	06177	12143	46609	32989	74014	64708	00533	35398	58408	13261	47908
90	08362	15656	60627	36478	65648	16764	53412	09013	07832	41574	17639	82163	60859	75567
91	79556	29068	04142	16268	15387	12856	66227	38358	22478	73373	88732	09443	82558	05250
92	92608	82674	27072	32534	17075	27698	98204	63863	11951	34648	88022	56148	34925	57031
93	23982	25835	40055	67006	12293	02753	14827	23235	35071	99704	37543	11601	35503	85171
94	09915	96306	05908	97901	28395	14186	00821	80703	70426	75647	76310	88717	37890	40129
95	59037	33300	26695	62247	69927	76123	50842	43834	86654	70959	79725	93872	28117	19233
96	42488	78077	69882	61657	34136	79180	97526	43092	04098	73571	80799	76536	71255	64239
97	46764	86273	63003	93017	31204	36692	40202	35275	57306	55543	53203	18098	47625	88684
98	03237	45430	55417	63282	90816	17349	88298	90183	36600	78406	06216	95787	42579	90730
99	86591	81482	52667	61582	14972	90053	89534	76036	49199	43716	97548	04379	46370	28672
100	38534	01715	94964	87288	65680	43772	39560	12918	86537	62738	19636	51132	25739	56947

Line	Col. (1)	(2)	(3)	(4)	(5)	(6)	(7)	(8)	(9)	(10)	(11)	(12)	(13)	(14)
101	13284	16834	74151	92027	24670	36665	00770	22878	02179	51602	07270	76517	97275	45960
102	21224	00370	30420	03883	94648	89428	41583	17564	27395	63904	41548	49197	82277	24120
103	99052	47887	81085	64933	66279	80432	65793	83287	34142	13241	30590	97760	35848	91983
104	00199	50993	98603	38452	87890	94624	69721	57484	67501	77638	44331	11257	71131	11059
105	60578	06483	28733	37867	07936	98710	98539	27186	31237	80612	44488	97819	70401	95419
106	91240	18312	17441	01929	18163	69201	31211	54288	39296	37318	65724	90401	79017	62077
107	97458	14229	12063	59611	32249	90466	33216	19358	02591	54263	88449	01912	07436	50813
108	35249	38646	34475	72417	60514	69257	12489	51924	86871	92446	36607	11458	30440	52639
109	38980	46600	11759	11900	46743	27860	77940	39298	97838	95145	32378	68038	89351	37005
110	10750	52745	38749	87365	58959	53731	89295	59062	39404	13198	59960	70408	29812	83126
111	36247	27850	73958	20673	37800	63835	71051	84724	52492	22342	78071	17456	96104	18327
112	70994	66986	99744	72438	01174	42159	11392	20724	54322	36923	70009	23233	65438	59685
113	99638	94702	11463	18148	81386	80431	90628	52506	02016	85151	88598	47821	00265	82525
114	72055	15774	43857	99805	10419	76939	25993	03544	21560	83471	43989	90770	22965	44247
115	24038	65541	85788	55835	38835	59399	13790	35112	01324	39520	76210	22467	83275	32286
116	74976	14631	35908	28221	39470	91548	12854	30166	09073	75887	36782	00268	97121	57676
117	35553	71628	70189	26436	63407	91178	90348	55359	80392	41012	36270	77786	89578	21059
118	35676	12797	51434	82976	42010	26344	92920	92155	58807	54644	58581	95331	78629	73344
119	74815	67523	72985	23183	02446	63594	98924	20633	58842	85961	07648	70164	34994	67662
120	45246	88048	65173	50989	91060	89894	36036	32819	68559	99221	49475	50558	34698	71800
121	76509	47069	86378	41797	11910	49672	88575	97966	32466	10083	54728	81972	58975	30761
122	19689	90332	04315	21358	97248	11188	39062	63312	52496	07349	79178	33692	57352	27862
123	42751	35318	97513	61537	54955	08159	00337	80778	27507	95478	21252	12746	37554	97775
124	11946	22681	45045	13964	57517	59419	58045	44067	58716	58840	45557	96345	33271	53464
125	96518	48688	20996	11090	48396	57177	83867	86464	14342	21545	46717	72364	86954	55580

380

Line	Col. (1)	(2)	(3)	(4)	(5)	(6)	(7)	(8)	(9)	(10)	(11)	(12)	(13)	(14)
126	35726	58643	76869	84622	39098	36083	72505	92265	23107	60278	05822	46760	44294	07672
127	39737	42750	48968	70536	84864	64952	38404	94317	65402	13589	01055	79044	19308	83623
128	97025	66492	56177	04049	80312	48028	26408	43591	75528	65341	49044	95495	81256	53214
129	62814	08075	09788	56350	76787	51591	54509	49295	85830	59860	30883	89660	96142	18354
130	25578	22950	15227	83291	41737	79599	96191	71845	86899	70694	24290	01551	80092	82118
131	68763	69576	88991	49662	46704	63362	56625	00481	73323	91427	15264	06969	57048	54149
132	17900	00813	64361	60725	88974	61005	99709	30666	26451	11528	44323	34778	60342	60388
133	71944	60227	63551	71109	05624	43836	58254	26160	32116	63403	35404	57146	10909	07346
134	54684	93691	85132	64399	29182	44324	14491	55226	78793	34107	30374	48429	51376	09559
135	25946	27623	11258	65204	52832	50880	22273	05554	99521	73791	85744	29276	70326	60251
136	01353	39318	44961	44972	91766	90262	56073	06606	51826	18893	83448	31915	97764	75091
137	99083	88191	27662	99113	57174	35571	99884	13951	71057	53961	61448	74909	07322	80960
138	52021	45406	37945	75234	24327	86978	22644	87779	23753	99926	63898	54886	18051	96314
139	78755	47744	43776	83098	03225	14281	83637	55984	13300	52212	58781	14905	46502	04472
140	25282	69106	59180	16257	22810	43609	12224	25643	89884	31149	85423	32581	34374	70873
141	11959	94202	02743	86847	79725	51811	12998	76844	05320	54236	53891	70226	38632	84776
142	11644	13792	98190	01424	30078	28197	55583	05197	47714	68440	22016	79204	06862	94451
143	06307	97912	68110	59812	95448	43244	31262	88880	13040	16458	43813	89416	42482	33939
144	76285	75714	89585	99296	52640	46518	55486	90754	88932	19937	57119	23251	55619	23679
145	55322	07598	39600	60866	63007	20007	66819	84164	61131	81429	60676	42807	78286	29015
146	78017	90928	90220	92503	83375	26986	74399	30885	88567	29169	72816	53357	15428	86932
147	44768	43342	20696	26331	43140	69744	82928	24988	94237	46138	77426	39039	55596	12655
148	25100	19336	14605	86603	51680	97678	24261	02464	86563	74812	60069	71674	15478	47642
149	83612	46623	62876	85197	07824	91392	58317	37726	84628	42221	10268	20692	15699	29167
150	41347	81666	82961	60413	71020	83658	02415	33322	66036	98712	46795	16308	28413	05417

Index